A PATHWAY INTO
THE HOLY SCRIPTURE

A Pathway
into the
Holy Scripture

Edited by

P. E. SATTERTHWAITE
and
D. F. WRIGHT

WILLIAM B. EERDMANS PUBLISHING COMPANY
GRAND RAPIDS, MICHIGAN

© 1994 Wm. B. Eerdmans Publishing Company
255 Jefferson Ave. S.E., Grand Rapids, Michigan 49503

Printed in the United States of America

00 99 98 97 96 95 94   7 6 5 4 3 2 1

ISBN 0-8028-4078-7

Contents

PREFACE

Between 4th and 7th July 1994 the Tyndale Fellowship held its jubilee conference at the Hayes Conference Centre, Swanwick. The chapters in this volume are revised versions of papers given at that conference. The editors would like to thank the contributors for their participation in the project, and for their promptness in revising their papers for publication. Indeed, we are grateful to all those who attended the conference and contributed to the (at times) vigorous discussion. It was encouraging, on the occasion of this conference, attended by over one hundred and sixty people, to reflect on how the Tyndale Fellowship has grown from its small beginnings, so that now the whole range of theological disciplines is represented among its members.

The editors are grateful to the Tyndale House Council for making available the desk-top publishing facilities of Tyndale House, without which it would not have been possible to prepare this volume for publication in two months. Thanks are also due to Bruce Winter, Warden of Tyndale House, and Andrew Clarke, Librarian of Tyndale House, for help and advice, and especially to Eileen Poh, Ph.D. student at King's College, London, for her work in producing the indexes.

Lastly, we would like to thank Bill Eerdmans Jr., President of Wm. Eerdmans Publishing Company, for his willingness to accept this volume for publication and for his generous encouragement.

Philip E. Satterthwaite,
David F. Wright,

7th September 1994.

INTRODUCTION

William Tyndale and the Tyndale Fellowship for Biblical and Theological Research

David F. Wright

For a body of Christians which owns no one denominational or confessional allegiance, there are obvious diplomatic advantages in bearing the name of a Reformer who belonged to the still undivided church in England—one might almost say, to the Catholic church in England, although by the time of William Tyndale's death in 1536 it was no longer the *Roman* Catholic church. But other loftier reasons than these induced the founding fathers of the Tyndale Fellowship for Biblical Research ('Theological' was added in 1980) and of Tyndale House in Cambridge to identify them with the pioneer translator of the Hebrew and Greek Scriptures into English.[1] (The Wycliffite versions of more than a century before Tyndale had been made solely from the Latin of the Vulgate.)

Tyndale studied at both Oxford and Cambridge.[2] He deployed an impressive knowledge of languages—some seven or so in all. That so much of his translation of the New Testament survived not only into

1

the King James ('Authorized') Version of 1611—some 90 per cent—but
also into the more testing Revised Version of 1881—some 75 per cent—
attests not simply his felicity in English but more fundamentally his
expertise in the original languages.[3] Such careful textual and linguistic
understanding of the Hebrew and Greek Bible lies close to the *raison d'*
être of the Fellowship and House named after him.

The future Reformer may well have first conceived an interest in
translating the Bible into the vernacular at a surprisingly early age (see
Carl Trueman's essay in this volume). Several years later, around 1522,
in the course of a dispute with an unnamed blinkered scholar of the
papal allegiance, Tyndale uttered his famous vow: 'If God spare my
life, ere many years I will cause a boy that driveth the plough shall
know more of the scripture than thou dost.'[4] It carried an unmistakable
allusion to Erasmus's preface to his new Latin translation of the New
Testament with justifying Greek text (1516), from which so many in the
sixteenth century rediscovered the gospel.

To fulfil his own pledge, as more than one essay in this collection
points out, Tyndale had to provide more—but certainly not less—than
an English version of Scripture. His quest for a Bible accessible to all
who could read his native tongue did not dispense with preaching or
teaching—the church's staple magisterial ministry—or with an essentially doctrinal grasp of the gospel. His was no simplistic appeal to
'Scripture alone' or to the celebrated common Reformation conviction
of Scripture's *perspicuitas* or *claritas* (which is more often invoked or
brandished than itself elucidated).

---

[1]The name was first publicly used of the Tyndale Lectures in New Testament and
Old Testament. The very first, in New Testament, was delivered by the late F.F.
Bruce in December 1942 on 'The Speeches in the Acts of the Apostles'. Published
by the Tyndale Press, London, in 1944, it was revisited by the lecturer in 1974, in
'The Speeches in Acts—Thirty Years After', in Robert Banks (ed.), *Reconciliation*
and Hope. New Testament Essays on Atonement and Eschatology presented to Leon
Morris on his 60th Birthday (Exeter: Paternoster, 1974) 53-68. Tom Noble is writing
a brief history of the Tyndale Fellowship and Tyndale House. For the early years
see Bruce, 'The Tyndale Fellowship for Biblical Research', *EQ* 19 (1947) 52-61.
[2]For some uncertainty about his Cambridge residence, see D.D. Smeeton, *Lollard*
Themes in the Reformation Theology of William Tyndale (Sixteenth Century Essays and
Studies VI; Kirksville, MO: Sixteenth Century Journal Publishers, 1986) 46-50.
[3]On Tyndale's aptitude in Hebrew, see G. Lloyd Jones, *The Discovery of Hebrew in*
Tudor England: A Third Language (Manchester: Manchester UP, 1983) 115-23, noting
J.R. Slater's opinion of Tyndale as 'the father of Hebrew scholarship among Eng-
lishmen' (120).
[4]John Foxe, *Acts and Monuments* (ed. S. Cattley; London, 1841) Vol. V, 117.

And so Tyndale wrote his little treatise *A Pathway into the Holy Scripture*.[5] It was in fact an expansion, published c.1530-32, of the prologue to his first aborted printing of his English New Testament, at Cologne in 1525 (of which only the so-called Cologne fragment survives).[6] It served the same purpose as his other prologues to the biblical books he translated—not the setting forth of historical prolegomena but rather the doctrinal mapping of the salient features of the Reformation gospel as the keys for unlocking the whole of Scripture. What better title than *A Pathway into the Holy Scripture* could be devised for a volume of papers on Scripture delivered at the jubilee conference of the Tyndale Fellowship, held at The Hayes, Swanwick, Derbyshire, July 4-7, 1994—in the very year that marked the quincentenary of Tyndale's birth?

Tyndale's mix of skills and commitments suitably challenges a Fellowship which bears his name and declares its aim to be

> to advance the Christian faith by promoting biblical and theological studies and research and disseminating the useful results of such study and research for the public benefit in a spirit of loyalty to the Christian faith as enshrined in the consensus of the Historic Creeds, the Confessions of the Reformation and the Doctrinal Basis of the Fellowship.

During the jubilee conference, members received more than one pointed reminder of the Fellowship's pledge to disseminate the useful results of its work (are some of them useless?) for the good of the Christian community in particular. This is one mark of the Fellowship that differentiates it from most other societies of biblical and theological scholars. As one arm of the wider Universities and Colleges Christian Fellowship (formerly the Inter-Varsity Fellowship), the Tyndale Fellowship acknowledges that it belongs to the church of Jesus Christ and is called to a special service within it. This distinctiveness is also reflected in our naming ourselves a Fellowship, rather than a society or an association. In our shared Christian and evangelical convictions, we

---

[5]Tyndale, *Doctrinal Treatises and Introductions to Different Portions of the Holy Scriptures* (ed. H. Walter; Parker Society; Cambridge: CUP, 1848) 1-28; henceforth cited as *PS* I. Also in *The Work of William Tyndale*, ed. G.E. Duffield (Courtenay Library of Reformation Classics 1; Appleford, Berks.: Sutton Courtenay Press, 1964) 2-24; hereafter *Work*.

[6]Smeeton, *Lollard Themes*, 58-9; but his n.147 here confuses the prologue to the frustrated 1525 New Testament with the prologue to Tyndale's 1526 exposition of Romans (*PS* I, 483-510; *Work*, 119-46).

recognise as members of this Fellowship that we belong to one another in the Spirit, who both inspired the writing of the Scriptures and enables all who seek faithfully to understand and expound them.

Yet if a like faith unites the Tyndale Fellowship with William Tyndale across the centuries, the scholarly study of the Bible has advanced so enormously since his age that continuity in this respect is much less evident. Tyndale's prologues to the Pastoral Epistles betray no suspicion that Paul's authorship was in doubt, nor does the one to Matthew's Gospel raise its relation to the other Gospels, nor his exposition of Matthew's Sermon on the Mount connect it in any way with Luke's Sermon on the Plain. His translation of the Pentateuch (1530) assumes Mosaic authorship throughout, and of Jonah (1531) that the book is historical record.[7]

These examples are chosen not because the Tyndale Fellowship as such has an agreed mind on any of them; indeed, as a Fellowship it has no one formulated position on any question of critical, *i.e.*, historical, study of the Bible. The papers comprising this volume give sufficient evidence of the range of scholarly conviction that the Fellowship encompasses—on the assumption of *ex animo* allegiance to its aims and Doctrinal Basis. But the examples given in the last paragraph are representative of issues to which answers are commonly given by members of the Fellowship which would have baffled not only William Tyndale but even evangelical scholars of a few decades ago. By comparison Tyndale belonged to an age of innocence, although his repeated plea for the plain literal sense in interpreting Scripture sounds a robustly relevant note amid the tinkling cymbals of fanciful literary theories and the grating cacophony of the deconstructionists.

Yet the level of sophistication (others might describe it less respectfully) displayed by evangelical biblical and theological scholarship, for example in the pages of the *Tyndale Bulletin*, does not mean that the Tyndale Fellowship has abandoned its earlier stance. The founders of the House and the Fellowship saw no incompatibility between commitment to the historic Christian faith and the freedom intrinsic to research. A key report in 1944 setting out the principles which the Fellowship and the House should follow put it thus:

> Academic activity of any kind must be FREE if it is to be effective. In all other branches of learning this is generally recognised, and it is equally true of Biblical and historical research. Freedom of teaching and learning, thoroughness of research and investigation with a fear-

---

[7] All of Tyndale's prologues are in *PS* I, 392-531 and in *Work*, 25-167.

less and unequivocal statement of the resultant findings, must therefore be explicitly and unambiguously safeguarded in the inauguration and prosecution of such an enterprise as we envisage... Evangelical scholars have not found the result of their unfettered studies and research to be inimical to the historic Christian faith... Those who, in dependence upon God Whose Word is Truth, set out to discover fresh Truth therefrom, are well assured that Truth can never be self-contradictory, but must invariably promote the glory of Him who says, 'I am the Truth'.[8]

In reality, Tyndale's confidence was not totally dissimilar. It is difficult for westerners in the late twentieth century, on the brink of an epochal transition from a print-dominated culture to one carried by electronic media, to recapture the horror that his first printed English New Testament evoked. Bishop Cuthbert Tunstall of London and later Durham found two thousand pestilential errors in it[9]—and he a friend of the new humanist learning and commended therefore by Erasmus! 'And our great pillars of holy church...bark, and say the scripture maketh heretics, and it is not possible for them to understand it in the English, because they themselves do not in the Latin.'[10] Defying, ultimately unto death, the massy authorities of the venerable Roman Church, which dreaded the unpredictable and hence uncontrollable effects of a free-range vernacular Scripture—like a noxious Pandora's box scattering poisons to the four winds—Tyndale staked his all on the untrammelled availability of the Bible. To be sure, it would sow confusion and breed disorder, but in God's hands it would lead many into all truth.

Tyndale came to the task of translation already convinced of what Scripture taught about salvation and other controverted heads of doctrine. His theological beliefs inevitably coloured his translated text—as they indubitably did its marginalia! All translation is of course interpretation, and it would remain for later generations of translators to purge Tyndale's English of the bright hues of his early Protestantism.

But in broaching his work of translation with his mind and heart already plighted to the new gospel, Tyndale was no different from other scholars before and since. The members of the Tyndale Fellow-

---

[8]Cited by courtesy of Tom Noble from a draft of his forthcoming history (see n.1 above). The report was compiled by F.F. Bruce, Dr. Douglas Johnson, the (first) General Secretary of the I.V.F., and (later Canon) Leo E.H. Stephens-Hodge.
[9]From Tyndale's preface to the Pentateuch (1530), *PS* I, 393, *Work*, 31
[10]*Pathway*, *PS* I, 28, *Work*, 24.

ship are not distinguished from their non-evangelical colleagues in coming to their research already committed to certain basic convictions. The particular convictions they hold—broadly, the fundamentals of the historic faith of the Christian church—may well mark them out as distinctive, but not the fact that they hold them. It is a strange myopia or arrogance that exalts scholars of other stripes as objective, open-minded, unprejudiced—so long as, one assumes, they are not Catholics or Marxists or atheists or Jews or liberal secularists or establishment Anglicans or post-modernists or what you will (to cite only selected possibilities of only one of the numerous variables that make us the persons we are).[11] It is the distinctive badge of the Tyndale Fellowship to pursue biblical and theological research without ecclesiastical or dogmatic restrictions, believing that 'the results of their unfettered studies [will not] be inimical to the historic Christian faith'. Given the subject-matter of our disciplines, it is at the very least no less appropriate a badge than the varied ones our non-evangelical colleagues wear.

This badge of evangelical identity—commitment to the historic Christian faith, including those doctrines itemised in our Doctrinal Basis—has from the outset not been regarded by the generality of the Fellowship as inimical in principle to what one of our essayists calls the historical-critical project. Foremost among our objections to the workings and 'assured results' of liberal biblical criticism has been the personal beliefs—often dismissive or sceptical of credal orthodoxy—that have prejudiced the procedures and conclusions of so many of its practitioners. The Fellowship has probably never been free of some tension on such issues between the more systematically minded and the biblical experts. But such is the commitment of most in the Fellowship to the proper historical study of the Scriptures that they would caution against the more novel literary styles of biblical interpretation precisely because they represent a flight from the *terra firma* of history. Our founders' combined allegiance to both evangelical orthodoxy and the freedom of historical-critical research still seems just about right.

---

[11]*Cf.* Jon D. Levenson, 'The Bible: Unexamined Commitments of Criticism', *First Things* 30 (Feb. 1993) 24-33; 'the secularity of historical criticism represents not the suppression of commitment, but its relocation' (33).

One Bible, One Theology

Although Tyndale was unable to complete his translation of the Old Testament, we must not miss his instinct to bind the two Testaments together. If he can describe the Old as containing God's law and the New God's promises,[12] yet he was aware, as anyone would be who had an inkling of Luther's teaching, that

> In the Old Testament are many promises, which are nothing else but the Evangelion or gospel, to save those that believed them from the vengeance of the law. And in the New Testament is oft made mention of the law, to condemn them which believe not the promises. Moreover, the law and the gospel may never be separate.[13]

Hence Deuteronomy was 'a very pure gospel, that is to wit, a preaching of faith and love: deducing the love to God out of faith, and the love to a man's neighbour out of the love of God'.[14]

Tyndale had a rudimentary covenant theology,[15] and used other traditional frameworks, such as law and promise, to hold the Testaments together.

> All the law and prophets seek, all that Christ did or can yet do, is to bring us to believe in him, and in God the Father through him, for the remission of sins; and to bring us unto that which immediately followeth out of that belief, to love our neighbours for his sake as he loved us.[16]

But if Tyndale's theology of the one Bible evinces obvious limitations, the academy at the end of the second Christian millennium struggles to keep the two Testaments together at all. Nevertheless, in the face of widespread critical dissolution of the unity of the Bible, and of each Testament on its own, and even of the corpus of a single writer, the Tyndale Fellowship's Doctrinal Basis affirms the wholeness of the Scriptures as God-given and authoritative for faith and life. The Fellowship's members are thereby committed, to some extent co-

---

[12]*Pathway, PS* I, 8, *Work,* 4.

[13]*Pathway, PS* I, 11, *Work,* 7.

[14]From his prologue, *PS* I, 441, *Work,* 79.

[15]'Seek therefore in the scripture..., chiefly and above all, the covenants made between God and us'; from the prologue to Genesis, *PS* I, 403, *Work,* 41. *Cf.* Smeeton, *Lollard Themes,* 20-24, 150-57.

[16]Tyndale, *A Fruitful and Godly Treatise...* (on baptism and the Lord's supper), *PS* I, 345-85 at 373, cited by Smeeton, *Lollard Themes,* 99.

operatively but for the most part individually, to contributing by their researches and publications to what is variously described today as 'the return to Scripture' or 'the recovery of Scripture' in both church and academy.[17]

This mission must not be viewed as a threat to the specialisation of disciplines embodied in the Tyndale Fellowship's different Study Groups. It is rather a continual summons to set specialist investigations in, and into, broader perspectives and frameworks. The scholar to whom more than to any other individual the original vision for Tyndale House and Tyndale Fellowship must be credited, W.J. Martin of Liverpool University and Regent College, Vancouver, had no hesitation whatsoever in insisting on the highest standards of technical erudition. The ideal preparation would be an Arts degree and a German doctorate, followed by years of training at specialist institutes in centres like Rome, Cairo and Jerusalem![18] If on the other hand, another pioneer of the House and the Fellowship, Dr. Martyn Lloyd-Jones, warned about the dangers of the technician's expertise—'so easily...master rather than servant of the Gospel'—it was to safeguard the role of 'the Biblical theologian who must be equally careful to maintain a Biblical perspective and to see things whole, when employing the findings of a scholar'.[19]

Such a differentiation between the biblical theologian and the scholar is not wholly satisfactory, for the evangelical scholar is never exempt from the obligation to think biblical-theologically, any more than biblical theologians can afford to be less than scholarly, but the point is well made and taken. It is ironic that, in an age when on biblical grounds the wholistic (or is it holistic?) is very much in favour, whether it be in salvation, ecology, anthropology or spirituality, the Bible itself is explicitly excluded from being treated as a whole. There is, no doubt, an inescapable tension that the evangelical biblical and theological scholar will never outlive—between the most detailed intricacies of technical research (a heavy monograph on a single Greek word, for example) and the exposition of the biblical message for all to receive by the Spirit.

Reformers like William Tyndale were no strangers to the suffocating sophistry of the schoolmen which did nothing to open up the

---

[17]Cf. Peter Ochs (ed.), *The Return to Scripture in Judaism and Christianity* (Mahwah, NJ: Paulist, 1993); Dan Beeby, 'Scripture: from Rumour to Recovery?', *Gospel and Culture* 17 (Summer 1993) 1-6.
[18]From Tom Noble's draft history.
[19]*Ibid.*

Scriptures for the plough-boy. To a man the Reformers resisted the
sundry devices of the Old Church to immure the Bible within the safe
bounds of scholastic theology or the universities or the synod of *periti*.
'Nay, say they, the scripture is so hard, that thou couldst never understand it but by the doctors.'[20] For 'doctors' read 'biblical critics'? God
forbid that the learning that has come to characterise the work of the
Tyndale Fellowship may serve in any way to make the Bible a less
accessible book for today's plough-boy. In the next fifty years may it
prove instead to be for many truly 'a pathway into the Holy Scripture'.

> Then go to and read the stories of the bible for thy learning and com-
> fort, and see everything practised before thine eyes; for according to
> those ensamples shall it go with thee and all men until the world's
> end: so that into whatsoever case or state a man may be brought,
> according to whatsoever ensample of the bible it be, his end shall be
> according as he there seeth and readeth... As there was among them
> but a few true-hearted to God, so shall it be among us; and as their
> idolatry was, so shall ours be, until the end of the world. All mercy
> that is shewed there is a promise unto thee, if thou turn to God. And
> all vengeance and wrath shewed there is threatened to thee, if thou be
> stubborn and resist. And this learning and comfort shalt thou ever-
> more find in the plain text and literal sense.[21]

---

[20]Tyndale, *The Obedience of a Christian Man*, PS I, 127-344 at 153.
[21]Tyndale's prologue to Genesis, PS I, 404-5, *Work*, 42-3.

CHAPTER 1

Pathway to Reformation: William Tyndale and the Importance of the Scriptures

Carl R. Trueman

Summary

For William Tyndale, there was an unbreakable link between the vernacular Scriptures and the reformation of the church. His doctrine of Scripture is similar to that of Luther in several ways: his confidence in its basic perspicuity; his belief that theology must be firmly rooted in, and arise out of, good exegesis; and his positing of law and gospel as fundamental categories of interpretation. Nevertheless, close examination of Tyndale's writings reveals that it is not the radical opposition of law and gospel, in the strict Lutheran sense, which shapes his theology, but that of nature and grace.

I. Introduction

Like that of John Wyclif, the name of William Tyndale is synonymous with Bible translation.[1] Unlike Wyclif, however, Tyndale lived at a time when scholarly skills and technical resources were available to ensure that his work as translator was accurate and easily accessible. That much of his Bible was incorporated into the King James Version means that this fugitive who died in his mid-forties exerted an influence over the English language rivalled only by that of Shakespeare.

The importance of the vernacular Scriptures for Tyndale is obvious and never seriously questioned. A more interesting question which is not often addressed in detail asks why the Scriptures were so important to him. What made them so significant that Tyndale was led to declare that, if Henry VIII allowed a translation, he would himself write no more theological works? The answer, at its most basic level, is that Tyndale perceived the unbreakable link between the Bible and the Reformation both of the church as a whole and of its individual members. Because of this link, the existence of the Scriptures in the vernacular was the *sine qua non* of Reformation. This belief was the basic motivating force behind Tyndale's life and his writings. Indeed, if Luther regarded justification as the article by which the church stands or falls, there is a very real sense in which Tyndale regarded the vernacular Scriptures as the beating heart of a healthy church. As the search for a gracious God drove Luther along the road from Rome, it was Tyndale's pursuit of Scripture translation which formed his pathway to reformation.

The few facts we know of Tyndale's life are eloquent testimony to this. While his writings on the whole betray very little about his background, he does make on passing reference to his childhood, a reference, significantly, to the matter of Bible translation:

> Except my memory fail me, and that I have forgotten what I read when I was a boy, thou shalt find in the English chronicle, how that king Adelstone caused the holy scripture to be translated into the tongue that then was in England, and how the prelates exhorted him thereunto.[2]

---

[1] For varying assessments of Tyndale's life and theology, see the following: W.A. Clebsch, *England's Earliest Protestants 1520-35* (Yale: Yale UP, 1964); J.F. Mozley, *William Tyndale* (London: S.P.R.K., 1937); C.R. Trueman, *Luther's Legacy: Salvation and English Reformers, 1525-1556* (Oxford: OUP, 1994); C.H. Williams, *William Tyndale* (London: Thomas Nelson, 1969).

While Tyndale's memory did fail him, in that it was Alfred the Great and not Athelstan who commissioned the translation, it is interesting to see that the idea of vernacular Scriptures was possibly planted in his mind at a very early stage in his life. Of course, such a fleeting reference scarcely provides more than a glimpse of his youth but it is nevertheless a tantalising hint concerning his intellectual development. However, childhood memories of the English chronicle can scarcely compare with the impact which Erasmus of Rotterdam was to have on Tyndale's life and thought.

II. Tyndale and Erasmus

By the time Tyndale went to Cambridge, sometime between 1516 and 1519, Erasmus had already left his mark there and departed. We have no way of telling exactly what influence his legacy at Cambridge had on Tyndale, but we do know that in the years immediately following Erasmus' time there, his concern for biblical scholarship and a Christian life characterised by practical piety were to become key elements of Tyndale's own approach to reforming the church.

Two events in particular substantiate this claim, the first of which occurred when Tyndale was a tutor in Gloucestershire, the second during his attempts to find a sponsor for a translation of the Scriptures. Having left Cambridge, Tyndale became tutor to the children of a Master Walsh in his native Gloucestershire. Foxe tells us that he soon became known as one who baited the clergy and spoke out against abuses of clerical power. When asked by Mistress Walsh to clarify his views, Tyndale responded by translating into English Erasmus' *Handbook of the Christian Soldier*. Such a choice is an unequivocal indication that the kind of Christianity which Tyndale was advocating was much closer to that of an Erasmus than that of a Luther.[3]

That Tyndale's theology did not at this stage require him to break with the established hierarchy is confirmed by the fact that, upon leaving the Walshes' household, he travelled to London to secure the sponsorship of Bishop Cuthbert Tunstall for his translation project. As I have argued elsewhere, this choice, influenced by Tunstall's reputa-

---

[2]*Doctrinal Treatises and Introductions to Different Portions of the Holy Scriptures*, ed. H. Walter (Cambridge: Parker Society, 1848), 149. Hereafter cited as *Works* 1.
[3]See *Luther's Legacy*, 46. For the account of this incident, see Foxe, *Acts and Monuments*, ed. G. Townsend (8 vols.; London: Seeley, Burnside & Seeley, 1843-9), Vol. 5, 115.

tion as a leading Greek scholar and Erasmian, is significant for
understanding Tyndale's own intellectual sympathies at this time.[4]
But it is important not just for that: it also confirms the point made earlier about the relationship which Tyndale understood as existing
between reform and Scripture. If it is reasonable to assume that Tyndale was not happy with the current state of the church, and such a
supposition seems likely when we remember his experiences of the
Gloucestershire clergy, then it is also reasonable to assume that he did
not regard the church as beyond reform. Had he done so, the choice of
a bishop as potential patron would appear to have been most peculiar.
It is clear that whatever faults existed in the church, Tyndale felt that
the first stage to curing them was the production of a vernacular Scripture. In other words, Scripture translation had to form the foundation
of any reformation. This is why it was only when Tunstall refused to
act as sponsor, thus convincing Tyndale that the church was irreform-
able, that he moved both intellectually and physically in the direction
of Wittenberg and effectively separated himself from the institutional
church.

III. On to Wittenberg

We know little of Tyndale's life after his move to Wittenberg, but what
can be pieced together of the years before his matriculation there in
1524 clearly reveals two important facts about his attitude to the Scriptures. First, his overriding ambition was to make the Bible
comprehensible and available to all. It was his search for a vernacular
Scripture, not for a gracious God, which drove him on, and it was only
when he realised that the English church would not grant him this that
he turned to Lutheranism for help. Secondly, it is also clear that this
desire was rooted in Tyndale's belief that reformation of ecclesiastical
abuses was possible only on the basis of the vernacular Scriptures.
Without them, there was no hope. It is to a more detailed examination
of why Tyndale believed this that we now turn.

Tyndale was led along the road to Reformation by his desire to
see the vernacular Scriptures available to all and sundry, and this
desire was itself rooted in his understanding of the relationship
between God, the Scriptures, and the individual. Thus, in asking why
the Scriptures were so important, we are in fact asking about Tyndale's

---

[4]See *Luther's Legacy*, 46-47.

theological beliefs at their deepest level. To understand Tyndale's view of the Scriptures is to understand Tyndale himself.

There are many ways in which the relationship between Tyndale and the Scriptures could be approached. For example, one could look at the principles that underlay his translation work, or at his understanding of Scripture and tradition. However, this paper will focus on a number of key elements of his thinking which both illuminate his approach to scriptural interpretation and highlight emphases that distinguished him from his esteemed mentor, Martin Luther. Tyndale's theological writings may ultimately have been as insignificant for the English mind as his translation was influential, but they nevertheless give us key insights into the way Luther's thinking was translated and transformed into the English context.

The first point to notice is Tyndale's stress on the basic clarity and perspicuity of the Scriptures, which is probably due to the combined influence of Erasmus and Luther. This emphasis must be understood in terms of the positions against which he was reacting, foremost amongst which was the notion that the meaning of Scripture was either difficult to establish or the preserve only of an intellectual elite. Tyndale sees this belief expressed in essence in medieval four-fold exegesis which he regards as indulging in excessive allegorisation of the biblical text. For Tyndale, there is no need to be schooled in philosophy before one can interpret the Scriptures correctly. Instead, he has a basic confidence in the clarity of the scriptural text which should make it comprehensible to all. There should be no need to look for hidden or arcane senses in the biblical text: the meaning should be plain to every believer, even the proverbial plough-boy. Standing in the mainstream of Reformation thinking on this issue, he argues that, where one passage may appear obscure, any difficulty in interpretation can be easily cleared up through comparison with other, plainer texts. In the light of this, obscuring the Scripture's message appears not simply as inept scholarship but as an act of deliberate and wilful wickedness. It is for this reason that Tyndale ranks bad biblical interpretation alongside transubstantiation as one of the medieval church's principal theological crimes.[5]

Tyndale's confidence in the perspicuity of Scripture is nowhere more graphically displayed than in a conversation recorded by Henry Vaughan in 1531. Vaughan had been despatched by Henry VIII to persuade Tyndale to return from the continent, and claimed that the Reformer offered the following response to his overtures:

I assure you... if it would stand with the king's most gracious pleasure to grant only a bare text of the scripture to be put forth among his people... I shall immediately make faithful promise never to write more, nor abide two days in these parts after the same; but immediately to repair into his realm, and there most humbly submit myself at the feet of his royal majesty, offering my body to suffer what pain or torture, yea, what death his grace will, so this be obtained.[6]

If this report is true (and there is nothing in it which contradicts what we do know of Tyndale's convictions), then it is a graphic example of the importance which the vernacular Scriptures held for Tyndale: not only were they the *sine qua non* of Reformation, but they were worth more on their own than all his other theological endeavours put together. They were sufficient for ensuring that the truth would prevail. This is clear confirmation of what was earlier inferred from his request that Tunstall act as his patron.

This position points towards Tyndale's own understanding of the nature of theology. Like Luther, he regards theology as something which arises out of the Bible and for which the Bible is normative. Doctrinal stability is guaranteed not by the imposition of a creedal structure by the church but through the godly study of the Scriptures through faith. This of course leads us towards the ecclesiological dimension of Tyndale's polemic with the Catholic church: neither church authority nor tradition is the arbiter of what is and is not true doctrine.

IV. Norms for Interpreting Scripture

There is, however, a second, and perhaps almost contradictory, strand to Tyndale's doctrine of Scripture: the need to establish interpretative norms in order that bad and incorrect exegesis may be avoided. This is why Tyndale produced in 1531 the important essay, *A Pathway into the Holy Scriptures*. The tract itself had started life as a much shorter work

---

[5]See Tyndale's extensive evaluation of medieval interpretative method in *Works* 1, 303-31. Tyndale himself emphasises the literal sense as being the only true sense of scripture, although his admission that there may be more than one such sense in a single text makes his position virtually indistinguishable from that of Thomas Aquinas: see *Summa Theologiae* 1a.1.10. Tyndale's dislike of Aristotle in this context is also probably misplaced as Aristotelian empirical epistemology was not at all inimical to so-called literal exegesis: see Tyndale's comments, *Works* 1, 154-55.
[6]Quoted in Mozley, *William Tyndale*, 198.

which had formed the prologue to Tyndale's ill-fated 1525 translation of the New Testament, of which only a part, the so-called 'Cologne fragment', remains. That work was a modified translation of Luther's preface to his own 1522 translation of the New Testament. In 1531, Tyndale retained much of his 1525 text, but the expanded work now fell into three main parts: a series of definitions which clarify the meaning of concepts which Tyndale sees as crucial to understanding the Bible; an outline of salvation history, which sets these concepts in the context of the Bible and the experience of the individual believer; and a final important section on the nature and function of works which has no counterpart in the Lutheran original and which indicates that, while working with Lutheran originals and within a theological vocabulary determined to a large extent by Lutheran theology, Tyndale's thought carried with it his own distinctive emphases.

Tyndale starts the work with a statement of why he feels it necessary to write such a treatise:

> Seeing that it hath pleased God to send unto our Englishmen... the scripture in their mother tongue, considering that there by in every place false teachers and blind leaders; that ye should be deceived of no man, I supposed it very necessary to prepare this Pathway into the scripture for you, that ye might walk surely, and ever know the true from the false.[7]

In the light of what has been said so far concerning Tyndale's supreme confidence in the perspicuity of the Scriptures, it is perhaps surprising that he feels it necessary to preface his translation of the New Testament with an exposition of how to interpret Scripture correctly. However, he was not hopelessly naive and would obviously have been aware that other nations, such as Germany, had enjoyed the vernacular Scriptures for many years, but that this had not been sufficient in and of itself to produce reform and abolish abuses. Possession of the Scriptures in the vernacular was not enough. One had also to understand them correctly.

In making this point at the start of his work, Tyndale touches on the obvious dilemma that lies at the very heart of Protestantism and which has never been conclusively resolved: the balance between individual freedom to possess and interpret the Scriptures without the coercion of a fallible, and thus potentially corrupt, church, and the need to maintain some kind of stable doctrinal core in order to give

---

[7]*Works* 1, 7-8.

notions of truth *etc.* some kind of meaningful content. On the one hand, as we have seen, Tyndale can imply that bare possession of the vernacular Scriptures is sufficient to guarantee the formulation and preservation of true doctrine. On the other hand, his realism means that he knows it is necessary to employ the right exegetical tools in order to obtain the correct theological results. For this reason, Tyndale sets out in *A Pathway* to define a number of terms which need to be understood if the Bible is to be used correctly: Old Testament and New Testament; law and gospel; Moses and Christ; nature and grace; working and believing; deeds and faith. Of course, the most obvious point to make about this list is its clearly Lutheran structure. The dialectical opposition of law and gospel, Moses and Christ, works and belief indicates that Tyndale has moved a long way since offering Mistress Walsh Erasmus as a guide to Christianity. The years in Wittenberg introduced him to a new conceptual vocabulary and a new way of interpreting the Scriptures.

However, before engaging in detailed examination of Tyndale's debt to Luther, there is a second point to be made about this list: these concepts are proposed not as the end, but as the beginning of theology. One is not to read the Bible in order to find proof-texts for these propositions. They are not brought forward as a series of fundamental doctrines which one must believe in order to be saved but as a set of interpretative tools which express the basic structures of the Bible and are to be used in order to understand its message. In other words, Tyndale, like other Reformers, is again pointing towards a Protestantism whose doctrinal stability does not depend upon imposition of dogma or, perhaps worse still, upon a proof-text approach to theology, where the Bible is, in practical terms, functionally subordinate to Protestant tradition. Instead, he is confident that the necessary stability can be achieved through correct biblical exegesis. The Scriptures possess a basic external clarity which means that anyone, given the right tools and guidelines, will be able to find the truth.

V. Law and Gospel

Nevertheless, Tyndale's approach does present us with something of a chicken-and-egg scenario. The concepts which he puts forward as unlocking the Scriptures are themselves thoroughly doctrinal and arguably presuppose a particular interpretation of the Scriptures. Law and gospel are apparently proposed as the basic biblical categories by which Scripture is to be understood, indicating that Tyndale's own theological position has been subject to significant Lutheran influence. Thus, while he proposes a fundamentally biblical-exegetical orientation for theology, there is nevertheless a (perhaps unavoidable) *a priori* doctrinal structure within which exegesis is to take place. Seen in this light, the approach of the early Reformers, as exemplified here by Tyndale, does not seem as much opposed to the approach of later Protestant thinkers who engaged in the rescholasticising of theology in the late sixteenth and seventeenth centuries as is sometimes argued. It is true that these scholastics argued formally for so-called *articuli fundamentales*, or fundamental articles, which constituted the bare minimum amount of doctrinal assent needed to be a true Christian and which operated as doctrinal norms and boundaries for interpretation.[8] But the fact that Tyndale does not engage in formal discussion of fundamental articles should not obscure the fact that the exegetical tools he proposes do themselves contain fundamental doctrinal assumptions. That his fundamental articles are not worked out in the elaborate detail of later scholastic systems is to a large extent due to the fact that polemical pressure is felt almost exclusively from one direction: the alleged tendency of the Catholic church both to control and to obscure the meaning of Scripture, in particular in arguing for justification by works. Thus, the interpretative tools which he proposes address these issues and these issues alone. It is scarcely surprising that, as Tyndale's successors were faced with a multiplicity of heresies from all directions, the criteria for biblical interpretation became more numerous and more elaborate.

Having seen that Tyndale recognises the need for more than a simple, uninformed reading of the Bible if it is to fulfil its function, we must now examine in more detail the precise content of the interpretative principles which he proposes. That these reveal Lutheran influence upon him is obvious. As with Luther, he apparently see the Bible as being structured around the opposition of law and gospel, which terms do not refer to any canonical division between the two Testaments: gospel is found in the Old Testament as law is found in the

---

[8]See 'articuli fundamentales' in R.A. Muller, *A Dictionary of Latin and Greek Theological Terms Drawn Principally from Protestant Scholastic Theology* (Grand Rapids: Baker, 1985). See also his discussion in *Post Reformation Reformed Dogmatics 1: Prolegomena to Theology* (Grand Rapids: Baker, 1987), 277-311. A classic example of Reformed discussion of fundamental articles is to be found in F. Turretin, *Institutio Theologiae Elencticae*, Topic 1, qu. 14.

New.[9] Instead, they refer to the two ways in which humanity can relate to God and thus indicate that the Scriptures have a basically existential and salvific function. To a large extent, Tyndale's understanding of the law-gospel dialectic mirrors that of Luther, as is clear from his definition of the two terms:

> The law condemneth us and all our deeds; and is called of Paul (in 2 Cor. 3) the ministration of death. For it killeth our consciences, and driveth us to desperation; inasmuch as it requireth of us that which is unpossible for our nature to do. It requireth of us the deeds of an whole man. It requireth perfect love, from the low bottom and ground of the heart, as well in all things which we suffer, as in the things which we do... when the law hath passed upon us, and condemned us to death (which is his nature to do), then we have in Christ grace, that is to say, favour, promises of life, of mercy of pardon, freely, by the merits of Christ; and in Christ have we verity and truth, in that God [for his sake] fulfilleth all his promises to them that believe. Therefore is the gospel the ministration of life... In the gospel, when we believe the promises, we receive the spirit of life; and are justified, in the blood of Christ, from all things whereof the law condemned us.[10]

The contrast is clear: the law is death, the gospel is life. Basic to this is the notion that, in the state of post-Fall nature, humans are impotent to do what the law commands. As with Luther, Tyndale regards the law as pointing not to ability but simply to responsibility. The language is unequivocal: the law kills, drives to despair, demands that which we cannot give. In the context of Luther's clash with Erasmus over the nature of the will, it is clear that Tyndale comes down heavily on the side of the Reformer as regards post-Fall humanity's capacity for initiating salvation. It is essential that this basic fact is grasped or else what Tyndale says later about the role of the law is liable to misconstruction. Indeed, failure to grasp this has led to Tyndale being regarded by some as fundamentally Erasmian, with his teaching on the will dismissed as inconsistent with his basic anthropology.[11] There is simply no warrant in Tyndale's writings for such selective use of his theology.

It is also evident from the above passage that the gospel is conceived of in strongly Christological terms. God's promises are made on

---

[9]See *Works* 1, 11.
[10]*Works* 1 11-12.
[11]See the study of J.K. Yost, 'The Christian Humanism of the English Reformers, 1525-1555' (unpublished Ph.D. thesis: Duke University, Durham, NC, 1965).

the basis of Christ. Tyndale is notoriously vague about how exactly the promises relate to Christology, for the whole thrust of his theology is towards the believer's experience of salvation rather than the objective foundations of that salvation in Christ.[12] Nevertheless, there is an obvious echo here of Luther's Christocentricity even though it is not worked out in the same detail, particularly in terms of Luther's theology of the cross. Indeed, the *theologia crucis* plays no real part at all in Tyndale's theology and seems to be an aspect of Luther's thought which had no significant impact upon him, as is the case with others, such as Bucer, upon whom Luther had an otherwise important influence.

VI. Differences from Luther

Tyndale's Christological definition of the gospel shows clear signs of Luther's influence, and has a clear parallel in his negative assessment of the law. In the case of the law, however, Tyndale also shows signs of deviation from Luther's strictly negative approach, a fact which we will find to mirror important differences in theological emphases. Indeed, for Tyndale, law and gospel, while antithetical to each other from the point of view of unbelievers, are actually complementary to each other when set within the context of faith. Hints of this are given by Tyndale's language concerning law which, while sometimes exhibiting the violent negativity of Luther, more often sets the law in a moderately positive light. For example:

> They that have this right faith, consent to the law, that it is righteous and good; and justify God which made the law; and have delectation in the law (notwithstanding that they cannot fulfil it as they would, for their weakness); and they abhor whatsoever the law forbiddeth, though they cannot always avoid it.[13]

There are two highly important aspects of this passage. First, as has been mentioned, the language used to describe the law and the believer's attitude to the law is remarkably positive: believers are said to take a positive delight in the law of God. There is no sign here of the

---

[12]On Tyndale's vagueness concerning the work of Christ, see D.B. Knox, *The Doctrine of Faith in the Reign of Henry VIII* (London: James Clarke, 1961), 5-6; also Trueman, *Luther's Legacy*, 84-88.
[13]*Works* 1, 13.

fundamental tension involved in Luther's *totus homo* anthropology which colours all of his statements about the relationship between the law and the believer. On the contrary, the passage points towards the law taking on a much more positive function once the individual has come to faith.

Secondly, and more importantly, the references to the believer's inability to fulfil the law are qualified by statements which clearly imply that, while complete fulfilment of the law by the believer is out of the question, partial fulfilment is indeed a possibility. This is a crucial element of Tyndale's thinking because it sheds important light upon the function of the law which, as has been seen, he proposes as one of the controlling categories of biblical interpretation, and which, as such, links the objective content of the Scriptures to the individual believer's relationship with God.

Why is it that Tyndale is apparently deviating from Luther's line on the law? One reason is almost certainly his Erasmian background which left him with a lasting concern for the practical, moral outworking of Christianity. This may well have been reinforced through contact with theologians who inclined to a more Reformed stance on the nature of the Christian life, although lack of hard documentary evidence means that such claims are, at best informed speculation.

A second reason, and one which can be demonstrated from texts, is the fact that Tyndale, perhaps unconsciously and whatever a superficial reading of his words might suggest, does not actually see the law-gospel dialectic propounded by Luther as the key to understanding the Bible. This becomes clear as we continue with his argument in *A Pathway*.

That the believer can indeed start to enjoy partially fulfilling the law is clear both from Tyndale's discussion of the relationship between law and gospel and also from his definition of the state of grace. In the first, he makes the following observation:

> the gospel, when we believe the promises, we receive the spirit of life; and are justified, in the blood of Christ, from all things whereof the law condemned us. And we receive love unto the law, and power to fulfil it, and grow therein daily.[14]

Here we see how law and gospel are complementary: the law condemns us and leads us to despair; we then turn and believe the gospel promises; we receive the spirit of life; we thus start to love the law and

---

[14]*Works* 1, 11.

to fulfil it in what Tyndale hints will be an increasingly perfect manner. Thus, the law-gospel antithesis is resolved through the believer's possession of the Spirit. In other words, the relation between law and gospel is determined by the status of the individual.

VII. Nature and Grace

This pattern is both paralleled and elaborated in Tyndale's definitions of nature and of grace.

> By nature, through the fall of Adam, are we the children of wrath, heirs of the vengeance of God by birth, yea, and from our conception... because that of nature we are evil, therefore we both think and do evil, and are under vengeance under the law, convict to eternal damnation by the law, and are contrary to the will of God in all our will, and in all things consent to the will of the fiend. By grace... we are plucked out of Adam, the ground of evil, and grafted in Christ, the root of all goodness... and, when the gospel is preached to us, [God] openeth our hearts, and giveth us grace to believe, and putteth the Spirit of Christ in us; and we know him as our Father most merciful, and consent to the law, and love it inwardly in our heart, and desire to fulfil it, and sorrow because we cannot: which will (sin we of frailty never so much) is sufficient, till more strength be given us; the blood of Christ hath made satisfaction for the rest; the blood of Christ hath obtained all things for us of God.[15]

This paragraph is probably the most important statement Tyndale ever made about salvation, containing as it does all of the essential strands of his thought. When these views on nature and grace are compared to his earlier statements on the law and gospel, an interesting pattern emerges. In the state of nature (*i.e.* fallen nature) men and women are bound over to sin. In this context, the law demands obedience and condemns us because our inherent sinfulness guarantees our moral failure. It thus stands over against the gospel, which demands faith and promises salvation. Then, by believing the gospel and being united with Christ, the Christian is transposed into the realm of grace. Here, the functions of law and gospel are modified: the believer now loves the law and strives to fulfil it; this it is impossible to do perfectly, and so faith retains its significance because it effects the union with

---

[15]*Works* 1, 14-15.

Christ whose blood makes up for whatever is lacking. In other words, salvation for Tyndale combines both an objective basis in Christology and a subjective basis in regeneration and proleptic righteousness. It is hard to imagine Luther writing something with such a strong works-orientation.

What lies at the heart of Tyndale's deviation from Luther is his different understanding of the fundamental categories which control his understanding of the Scriptures. For Luther, it was law and gospel. These two were totally opposed to each other and, when linked with his *totus homo* anthropology, remained so even for the believer. For Tyndale, however, this is not the case, and his use of Lutheran terminology and the priority he gives to the language of law and gospel should not be allowed to mislead us on this issue. The relationship between law and gospel, and thus between the individuals and their relationship to scriptural teaching, is determined by whether they are in the state of nature or the state of grace. Thus, it is not in fact law and gospel but nature and grace, or, more precisely, fallen nature and grace which stand as the basic categories of the Bible and human existence.

The implications of Tyndale's reworking of Luther's theology within this different conceptual framework are significant for his understanding of how the believer is to draw upon scriptural teaching. He understands salvation as the transference of the individual from the state of nature to the state of grace. While this is accomplished in one sense by means of the believer's union with Christ through faith, the basic distinction Tyndale makes between the two states is that, in the former, the unbeliever hates the law and has no power to fulfil it, while in the latter, the believer does love the law and has some power to obey its precept. In other words, the change is primarily a matter of regeneration, a matter of whether one possesses the Holy Spirit or not. As a result, Tyndale's theology exhibits two distinctive characteristics: an emphasis upon works, and the practical, moral dimension of scriptural teaching; and a parallel concern for the work of the Holy Spirit. Both of these elements are closely related to his understanding of the Scriptures.

VIII. Emphasis on the Holy Spirit

To take the latter first, Tyndale's pneumatology is what guarantees that the Scriptures will succeed in achieving the salvation which is

their fundamental goal. Indeed, it is probably more accurate to say that
the Scriptures are themselves the channel through the which the Holy
Spirit operates for salvation, as is clear from the following passage:

> For when the evangelion is preached, the Spirit of God entereth into
> them which God hath ordained and appointed unto eternal life; and
> openeth their inward eyes, and worketh such belief in them.[16]

Thus, as the gospel, the content of the Scriptures, is preached, the Holy
Spirit acts to free individuals from bondage to sin. The perspicuity of
the Scriptures is not enough to cause salvation *ex opere operato*; it has to
be joined with the regenerating work of the Holy Spirit. At times, Tyndale can even make election itself the work of the Holy Spirit in time,
so great is the pneumatological thrust of his thinking.[17] The activity of
the Spirit also underlines the anti-Pelagian credentials of Tyndale's
theology: the sovereign action of the Spirit is what brings an individual
to faith and obedience, not that person's own autonomous decision.

Furthermore, if confirmation were needed that Tyndale's
emphases do not faithfully reflect those of Luther, it is a fact that many
of these passages on the Holy Spirit in both *A Pathway* and its earlier
counterpart, *The Cologne Fragment*, have no textual basis in the
Lutheran original and thus represent the work of Tyndale's own mind.
This difference between Luther's preface of 1522 and Tyndale's works
of 1525 and 1531 points to the distinctive orientations of their theologies and, at the level of scriptural interpretation, to Tyndale's
apparently unconscious modification of Luther's law-gospel model to
that of fallen nature-grace, which allows for a more positive role for
good works in the Christian life.

The second distinctive strand to Tyndale's theology is the way
that his concern for regeneration and actual righteousness is evident
throughout his approach to scriptural interpretation which lays great
stress upon the moral obligations of the believer. This, of course, is no
more than we should expect if what has been said about his views so
far is correct. One obvious example of this is his Christology which
again points to emphases not so apparent in Luther's law-gospel
model. Christ, says Tyndale,

---

[16]*Works* 1, 19.

[17]See *Expositions and Notes on Sundry Portions of the Holy Scriptures together with The
Practice of Prelates*, ed. H. Walter (Cambridge: Parker Society, 1849), 181. Tyndale's
stress on the Holy Spirit has been identified by one recent scholar as the most original aspect of his theology: see D.D. Smeeton, 'The Pneumatology of William
Tyndale', *Pneuma* 3 (1981), 22-30.

standeth us in double stead... First he is our Redeemer, Deliverer, Reconciler, Mediator, Intercessor, Advocate, Attorney, Solicitor, our Hope, Comfort, Shield, Protection, Defender, Strength, Health, Satisfaction and Salvation... Secondarily, after that we be overcome with love and kindness, and now seek to do the will of God (which is a Christian man's nature), then have we Christ an example to counterfeit.[18]

Here we have words that would fit more easily into the mouth of an Erasmus than a Luther: Christ is for the believer a sound moral example to be emulated. In other words, Tyndale's Christology combines the same objective-subjective elements that we noted in his doctrine of justification: Christ as redeemer has objectively achieved salvation and his blood forms the ground of justification; Christ as example gives the believer a pattern of righteousness upon which to model those good works which, though imperfect, point towards a proleptic justification. Thus, we see that Tyndale's interpretation of scriptural teaching about Christ mirrors his understanding of the nature of the Christian's salvation as embodying both objective and subjective elements.

This is again clear in Tyndale's approach to another aspect of the Bible which also indicates his difference from Luther: the use of the law. In the final paragraphs of *A Pathway*, he engages in discussion of the law which he refers to as 'natural right and equity' before dealing separately with each of the commandments.[19] Tyndale's emphasis is not on legal observance of the letter of the law, but on the obligation of love to God and to neighbour on which the commandments are based and which true obedience requires. In this regard, it is arguable that his position is not too dissimilar to that of Luther himself. However, his emphasis on regeneration and the proleptic dimension of justification means that the righteousness engendered by following the law's precepts takes on a much more positive role in salvation than would have been allowed by Luther. As he declares at the end of this passage:

> And thus, as the Spirit and doctrine on God's part, and repentance and faith on our part, beget us anew in Christ, even so they make us grow, and wax perfect, and save us unto the end; and never leave us until all sin be put off, and we be clean purified, and full formed, and fashioned after the similitude and likeness of the perfectness of our Saviour Jesus, whose gift all is.[20]

---

[18]*Works* 1, 20.
[19]See *Works* 1, 24-27.
[20]*Works* 1, 27.

In the context of this, it is not surprising to find that, some twelve months earlier, in his tract *The Practice of Prelates*, Tyndale had already argued for a threefold division of the law into ceremonial and judicial categories were specific to the Jews and were abrogated at Christ's coming, the natural law, embodied in love to God and to neighbour and elaborated in the Decalogue, remained permanently binding.[21] Once again, we see that the fundamental principle underlying Tyndale's biblical interpretation is not that radical opposition of law and gospel which we find in Luther, but rather an understanding that the function of law and gospel in the life of the individual is determined by whether the person concerned is in the state of nature or grace. In the former, the Lutheran opposition holds good; in the latter, there is a considerable degree of mutuality, even to the point where Tyndale argues for what Melanchthon held to be the third use of the law.

It is clear, then, that Tyndale's understanding of the basic theological structure of the Bible is, at the very least, a significant modification of the Lutheran model, and that this closely parallels his views of justification and the Christian life. The question to be asked, therefore, concerns the chicken-and-egg dilemma to which we referred earlier: is Tyndale's theology shaped by his reading of the Bible, or is his reading of the Bible shaped by his theological roots?

In fact, the close parallels between Tyndale's understanding of the nature of the Bible and the nature of personal Christianity are such that the question is virtually impossible to answer with any degree of certainty. I suspect that Tyndale himself would have regarded such a conclusion as a compliment, pointing as it does to his attempts to develop a theology which both made Scripture comprehensible to all and articulated the promises and imperatives of the Christian life. This quest was ultimately to bear fruit in the notion of covenant, which Tyndale described in the following terms in his 1534 preface to the New Testament:

> The right way, yea, and the only way to understand the scripture unto salvation, is that we earnestly and above all things search for the profession of our baptism, or covenants between us and God.[22]

Here we see the mature fruit of Tyndale's theology: the personal covenant between God and the believer, embracing as it does God's promise in Christ and the need for the believer to be obedient, pro-

---

[21]See *Works* 1, 423.
[22]*Works* 1, 469.

posed as the basic hermeneutical key whereby the Scriptures can be unlocked. Here we see the two principal concerns of Tyndale's life, the desire to make the Bible comprehensible and the desire to promote godly living, united in the one biblical concept of covenant. It is at this point, where the two streams flow together, that his thinking stops developing.

IX. Tyndale for Today

How then are we to assess Tyndale the theologian on the five-hundredth anniversary of his birth? This is not the place to draw out pious applications from Tyndale's life for us today; however, there are two basic points which can be made. First, Tyndale must be understood as a biblical theologian. Making the Bible comprehensible to all, both in terms of translation and basic guidelines in interpretation, was the central concern of Tyndale's life. Furthermore, it is the Bible which stands at the centre of his thinking and which underlies all of his theological concerns. The language and categories which he uses are all biblical in origin, and are all focused on making the Bible understandable to all. As such, he stands as a first-class model for those whose task it is to study the Bible. Tyndale understood as well as anyone ever has done that scholarly tools are absolutely essential to good exegesis, but must never be allowed to take on an existence all of their own: it is only as they are related to the Bible, and as they are employed in the task of making the Bible's teaching comprehensible to the church at large, that such tools come to possess any real value.

Finally, Tyndale must be understood as a creative theologian. He was not a great theologian, as were Luther and Calvin, and he was very much a man of his time, working within the agenda set by greater continental contemporaries. But it is quite clear that we must not attempt to categorise him as a mere echo of Martin Luther. Even this brief examination of one aspect of his understanding of biblical interpretation is enough to show that we are dealing with one who reworks Lutheran themes and categories to give them a meaning closer to the Augustinian-Reformed tradition than would have been acceptable in Wittenberg. Further exploration of his thinking from this particular angle will no doubt confirm this more fully. The fact is that Tyndale worked creatively with the concepts available to him, using them to express his own understanding of the Bible's emphases. This faithfulness to what he considered to be scriptural teaching rather than the theology of any particular contemporary was basic to Tyndale, basic to the Reformation, and should be basic to all true Christian scholarship. Indeed, if one had to sum up Tyndale's whole life's work, one could perhaps do no better than to describe him as having been theologically creative through his fidelity to the Bible. This is perhaps something to which all Christian scholars should still aspire.

CHAPTER 2

Faith and Method in Old Testament Study: Story Exegesis

by Carl E. Armerding

Summary

It is the author's conviction that the major problem facing those who study and teach the Old Testament relates to whether anyone is listening. This situation is analysed, both as to its causes and as to its effects. In response, the essay proposes shifting the focus of Old Testament exegesis to telling the story, in its whole and in its parts. Story exegesis makes full use of all existing branches of Old Testament critical study, but always toward the end of helping both critic and reader to hear again the story itself as normative, and as it has been heard and heeded in a variety of responding communities.

I. Introduction

First, let me express my delight at being asked to bring an address on the occasion of the Tyndale Fellowship's golden anniversary. As one whose own spiritual and academic formation was deeply influenced by some of the early pioneers of our Fellowship, I continue to thank God for those whose vision saw beyond the immediate post-World War II years to a time when evangelical scholars might take a more prominent place in the work of the British university and church. Little did they realise how widely their influence would be felt, and as a charter member of the North American Institute for Biblical Research, I want to extend my congratulations to the Fellowship in Britain, together with our combined thanks for the inspiration and model.

Secondly, I am most honoured by the association, through these lectures, with the project to remember the work of our great predecessor, William Tyndale, and to contribute in some small way to a volume bearing the title of his little introduction.

The following essay is offered as a methodological response to my observation that the most critical issues concerning the Old Testament have to do in one way or another with whether it is being taken seriously, by whom, and for what. Looking around us, whether in the university or amongst the wider public, we see the Bible generally, and the Old Testament specifically, rarely thought of as even a repository of wisdom for life, much less an infallible authority through whose secrets life itself may be discovered. In Europe we must evangelise and teach an essentially secular generation, where biblical illiteracy can be taken for granted. Even in America, that most religious of modern societies, Martin Marty claims that the Bible functions almost entirely as an icon, like 'an object in the national shrine, whether read or not, whether observed or not: it is seen as being basic to national and religious communities' existence. They hold it in awe and give *latreia* to it'; but few read it and fewer yet follow its guidance.[1]

In such a climate, the burden of proof lies on those of us who claim the Bible has a continuing relevance to contemporary existence. And although most of us gathered to celebrate the anniversary of the Tyndale Fellowship earn our living from interpreting the Bible, that alone is insufficient ground for us to assume that anyone out there is listening to what we say. Even in the most churchly circles, a popular

---

[1]M. Marty, 'America's Iconic Book' in G.M. Tucker and D.A. Knight (eds.), *Humanizing America's Iconic Book* (Chico, CA: Scholars Press, 1982) 22.

seminar on Christian weight control (the Americans have one called 'Firm Believer') will inevitably out-draw a lecture by a leading biblical scholar. Does it ever occur to us to ask why? If our task, as biblical scholars, includes guiding pilgrims on their 'pathway into Holy Scripture', it behooves us to ask why so few seem to take the journey. Does the world not know, or care, as Paul affirmed in Romans 15:4 and 1 Corinthians 9:9-10, that all these things were 'written for us'?[2]

II. The Enlightenment and Evangelical Scholarship

Further reflection on our culture, both East and West, leads to another observation that may come closer to the methodological questions we face. Studies of contemporary culture consistently demonstrate an erosion of confidence in our basic scholarly method, inherited from the Enlightenment. For two hundred years it has been fashionable to exalt 'pure reason', affirming a scientific method of research and logic that could, with reasonable expectation, produce the right answers. At its philosophical worst, empiricism so penetrated the university, including the theological faculties, that Christians sometimes despaired of finding ground to stand.

But, at its best, there were always things we liked about our Enlightenment heritage. As scholars, I suspect, we find the critical principle of scientific method most reassuring, though as Christians we may share the church's historic ambivalence about it.[3] On the one hand, most of us have no stomach for the days when critical questions, whether in science, social customs or biblical interpretation, were decided by dogmatic rather than reasonable means. Today, on the other hand, we now frequently find ourselves with our backs to the wall, facing the onslaught of a post-modernism that has moved from the philosophical and literary faculties squarely into the realm of biblical interpretation, and we may long for the good old days when empirical method set the rules. Some have even suggested that evangelical scholars have become very good at playing the game by Enlightenment rules, though it was never really our game. Are we, as evangelical scholars, merely 'inconsistent rationalists' or 'part-time

---

[2]See the chapter by B. Rosner under this title.
[3]The effects of Enlightenment thinking and its fruits are succinctly applied to theological education in Edward Farley, *The Fragility of Knowledge* (Philadelphia: Fortress, 1988).

fideists', as James Barr seemed to suggest in his book *Fundamentalism*?[4] The time may have come for a better answer to Barr's question.

I mention this area for two reasons, both of which are critical to Old Testament studies. First, whatever our earlier problems with empirical method, we all now struggle with the general decline of confidence in purely rational solutions. Our historic ambivalence as Christians toward empirical method leaves us wondering just how to react to the new trends, some of which seem, at least on the surface, to share our critique of empiricism as a scholarly method.

The second reason is more apologetic and pastoral. On a popular level as well, rational answers no longer appear convincing, whether inside or outside of the church. Hans Küng, in a centennial address to the Society of Biblical Literature, eloquently summarised the way this loss has eroded ethical norms, and I quote a few of his lines:

> For our grandparents, religion—Christianity—was still a matter of personal conviction. For our parents it remained a least a matter of tradition and good manners. For their emancipated sons and daughters, however, it is becoming increasingly a matter of the past that is no longer binding—*passé et depassé*, passed away and obsolete. Moreover, there are parents today who observe with perplexity that morality has vanished together with religion, as Nietzsche predicted. For, as is becoming increasingly clear, it is not so easy to justify ethics purely rationally, by reason alone, as Sigmund Freud and others wanted to do; we cannot explain why freedom under any circumstances is supposed to be better than oppression, justice better than avarice, nonviolence better than violence, love better than hate, peace better than war. Or more brutally: why, if it is to our advantage or contributes to our personal happiness, we may not lie, steal, commit adultery, or murder; or even why we should simply be 'fair'.[5]

Küng, with many others, blames much of the situation on the Enlightenment's erosion of absolute norms. Surely, as we think of how to do Old Testament studies in general, and ethics in particular, we must face the challenge of the decline of a reasonable society.

But it is not only in social and personal ethics that we feel the loss, and not only in secular circles. A whole series of radical shifts in consciousness are in process throughout the Western world, and they affect very much how people read texts. I have already alluded to the

---

[4]James Barr, *Fundamentalism* (London: SCM, 1977; rev. ed., 1981).
[5]Hans Küng, in the Society of Biblical Literature centennial address entitled, 'To What Can We Still Cling?', in Tucker and Knight (eds.), *op. cit.*, 40.

fact that entire new sections are emerging within biblical societies, especially in Old Testament, made up of people who recite poetry of the New Age far more enthusiastically than the songs of Zion. Some of the papers they read would certainly never have got on the programme in the days of traditional enlightened scholarship, but today such trends are often seen as on the cutting edge, and I hasten to add, not only in America.

While we may argue that the above represents only a small ripple on the calm waters of our well-tended academic pond, I am not sure the argument is convincing. Are we ignoring the implications, or the magnitude, of the shift in how people see reality, and by extension, read texts?

Think for a moment about the church, particularly our old familiar circles within British and American evangelical religion. Only a few years ago John Stott and Jim Packer lamented on the pages of *Christianity Today* that few in Britain had much stomach for good theology any more. Scott Peck, an author celebrated in New Age circles, is probably read more widely by evangelical Christians than either Stott or Packer.

Even in the church, then, there is a hunger for the spiritual side of things, which in many ways our rational Christianity has failed to satisfy. Whether that hunger is fully legitimate begs the question. My concern, as an Old Testament scholar and teacher, is how to respond. Do our Old Testament studies, and the scholarship we produce, address the spiritual side of the people with whom we work, whether in the church or the New Age? According to a recent *U.S. News and World Report* article,[6] current American best-sellers included a book on a near-death experience called *Embraced by the Light*, a 'course in miracles' under the title *A Return to Love*, and yet another book on angels. With regret, I think we can assume that a good percentage of the sales were to folks who sit in evangelical pews. Does this have anything to do with how we read our texts, and what we publish in our journals?

---

[6]This information was taken from *Current Thoughts and Trends*, published by the Navigators, Vol. 10, #7 (July 1994), p. 8, and is a digest of an article carried in the April 25, 1994 edition of *U.S. News and World Report*.

III. Evangelical Faith and Scholarly Method

A few further comments on method follow, which may have implications for how we answer the above questions, from within our faith
setting. We, in the Tyndale Fellowship, are part of a specific, historically definable community, that confesses Christ as Lord, and labours
under the conviction that God has revealed himself in a body of Scriptures, which we confess to be 'inspired'. Specifically with regard to the
foundations of our faith, we have always held to a conviction that God
was free to work in his world, and that freedom was reflected in the
historical process. In other words, we live in a world not bound by the
constraints laid on it by modern philosophical scepticism. Although
this community shares its faith with many in other Christian circles, it
holds a conviction that the gospel is most faithfully proclaimed in the
specific heritage of its own evangelical tradition.

   A major question, then, is the way in which, and the degree to
which, such a confessional commitment influences either method or
conclusions. Does a believing scholar really do anything more, or less,
than his or her secular counterpart? Does the search for truth in the
context of its source in a transcendent God and its application to the
church in the world change the way we discover the semantic range of
a Hebrew expression, *e.g.*, the nominal clauses in Amos 7:14?[7] Perhaps
not, but going beyond the merely technical, and reaching for questions
of truth, the distinctives become more evident. In a day when educa-
tors strive for 'values-neutral' education, believing scholars of all kinds
will reject the spirit of the age, whatever that may mean for our scholarly work. But whether, and how completely, the spirit of the age has
influenced critical method in Old Testament scholarship is a question
that is still a matter of vigorous debate.[8]

   One obvious feature of evangelical belief is the conviction that
the Word studied must also be the Word obeyed and preached. Surely
every evangelical scholar has personally heard God's word to Ezekiel
(Ezk. 3:1-3), and instinctively knows that the exegetical task is complete only when we have 'eaten the scroll', and, with the Word as part

---

[7]Much conservative scholarship might be adduced to illustrate the point. The
above reference is to the 1994 Tyndale Old Testament lecture, given by A. Viberg,
entitled 'Amos 7:14: A Case of Subtle Irony', to be published in *Tyndale Bulletin*. In
the lecture, which proposes a fresh solution for the vexing question of verb tense
in Am. 7:14, conclusions regarding the text and the theology of Amos are suitably
conservative, but nothing in his method reflects special pleading, or the exclusive
concerns of evangelical religion.

of our own being, can 'go, and speak to the house of Israel'. We are not only scholars, but in some sense must be 'watchmen to the house of Israel'.

Less obvious are the ways in which questions of belief, and the life in Christ, influence method. I recall an embarrassing moment some years ago at a regional meeting of the Society of Biblical Literature, when an earnest young Roman Catholic, who had delivered an impressive piece of fresh research on the parables, was asked for the key to his method. After a few moments of silence, he replied quietly, 'Prayer. Yes, I think prayer.' After an awkward moment or two, a slightly embarrassed ripple of laughter was all the assembled group of scholars (most themselves churchmen) could muster. I suspect that Evangelicals shared fully in the embarrassment, though perhaps we could be forgiven, as those who come from a tradition which often misused such claims to affirm a patently false conclusion.

Prayer is, of course, only the human side of the equation. Does the Holy Spirit, in response to prayer, 'make intercession for us' (Rom. 8:26) as scholars, seeking in our infirmities to know the mind of the Spirit through the texts before us? Does the 'mind of the Spirit' (Rom. 8:27) ever include some pregnant insight, or quickened imagination, into what the Lord may be saying to His church in the passage? The Spirit is, after all, the Spirit of life! To what extent might Paul apply his own words about the Spirit revealing 'deep things' to us (1 Cor. 2:10) to the task of exegesis? Is it merely, as many of us have been taught, a matter of appreciation or, at most, application?[9] What, by contrast, does the 'natural man', who cannot 'receive the things of the Spirit' (1 Cor. 2:14) lack, to which we, as spiritual exegetes, have access? Do the spiritual 'insight gifts' (wisdom, revelation, knowledge) of 1 Corinthians 12:8 and Ephesians 1:17 have any relevance to the interpreter of the Old Testament?

---

[8] An example of one approach may be found in Gerhard Maier's *Das Ende der Historisch-Kritischen Methode* (Wuppertal: Brockhaus, 1974); ET, *The End of the Historical-Critical Method* (St. Louis: Concordia, 1977). The title is ambiguous in both languages, but Maier, reacting largely to New Testament Bultmannian scholarship, claims that standard critical method leads inevitably to *das Ende*, a heterodox view of Christ. A less polemical approach is found in Carl E. Armerding, *The Old Testament and Criticism* (Grand Rapids: Eerdmans, 1983, now reprinted by Regent College, Vancouver, Canada). The history of these debates is chronicled by Mark A. Noll, *Between Faith & Criticism: Evangelicals, Scholarship, and the Bible in America* (San Francisco: Harper & Row, 1986).

[9] Paul's modest claim to have made a spiritual judgment regarding the widow (1 Cor. 7:40) might fall into the latter category.

Who are those, in both Testaments, who have 'ears to hear' and 'eyes to see' (Dt. 29:4; Is. 6:10; Mt. 11:15, *etc.*)? Is it possible that, like Elisha and his servant, we stand in the shadow of a mountain filled with horses and chariots of fire (2 Ki. 5:17), but are missing the vision because we fail to ask God's help when we open our Hebrew Bibles?

In this discussion, I am certainly not pleading prayer as a short-cut to careful exegetical work, nor am I suggesting a mystical or cabbalistic substitute for good biblical critical method. But if, as I hope to demonstrate later, the imagination is one of the neglected faculties in exegesis, and the appeal to the spiritual side of the human personality is a major lacuna in our presentation, then surely prayer, and the work of God's Spirit to quicken and renew our minds, have some relevance to the task of evangelical exegesis.

Some evangelical distinctives, then, may deeply influence the questions before us. This essay will dwell on points neither of continuity nor of discontinuity, but will attempt to find a meaningful Old Testament hermeneutic in the context of our own confessional life-setting, although I think much of what I have to say also applies in the wider context. In order to accomplish this, the work of evangelical scholars will be the focus, together with some methodological questions faced by all of us in a specific confessional community.

IV. A Possible Way Forward

I have pondered much the question of where some answers may be found. The good news is that we are already on the way, given the depth of solid work now being done by scholars in the Tyndale Fellowship and its sister societies in other countries. Excellent commentaries have come from Tyndale Fellowship members in recent years, while monograph and dissertation research continues to flourish, much of the latter encouraged by Tyndale House grants. In North America and on the Continent, the situation is equally encouraging, though each setting has its own strengths.[10] Lively, godly, scholarship is being done, and I believe provides an excellent point of departure for the next stage in our scholarly response to what John Stott has called 'double listening' (listening to both the Word and the world).

But the question remains: is there any fresh concept, or method, that might enable us better to relate all of our Old Testament exegesis to the struggle for meaning we find in the world around us? A companion essay already alluded to notes two areas of Old Testament teaching, *i.e.*, our 'hope in Christ' and instructions for ethics, cited in Pauline passages (Rom. 5:4; 1 Cor. 9:9-10), as having been 'written for us' or 'for our instruction'.[11] Is it not striking that these two concerns precisely mirror contemporary failure of the Old Testament to speak to the world? Might the recovery of an Old Testament story of salvation, and a true Old Testament ethic provide a good starting point for the place of the Old Testament in the 're-evangelisation of our culture'?[12]

Again, we have an excellent start made in both areas, but rather than survey the works of scholars like Christopher Wright in ethics,[13] or Leland Ryken, Tremper Longman III and others in areas of story.[14] I want to proceed by taking up a specific point about story from John Goldingay's very useful little book, *Approaches to Old Testament Interpretation*.[15] Goldingay's chapter entitled 'the Old Testament as the Story of Salvation', together with his supplementary 1989 note sug-

---

[10]Evangelical biblical studies in the United States and Canada are well represented by a growing body of widely respected scholars, a number of whom occupy posts in universities and main-line church faculties, as well as in evangelical colleges and seminaries. In Germany and throughout Europe, evangelical scholars have for various reasons had less access to university posts, which are dominated by *Landeskirche* (state church) concerns. There is, nevertheless, a vigorous and developing evangelical scholarship. See Robert W. Yarbrough, 'Evangelical Theology in Germany', *EQ* 65 (1993) 329-53.

[11]Rosner, *op. cit.* Rom. 15:3 quotes Ps. 69, while 1 Cor. 9:9-10 cites a rather everyday kind of societal regulation about oxen, taken from Dt. 25:4. What concerns us here is not Paul's use of the Old Testament as method, but his conclusion that, in the Old Testament scriptures, we can find hope for the future and a basis for behaviour in the present.

[12]This term was used by the Polish journalist, Stefan Wilkanowicz, whose concern was the failure of either politics or the church to provide a credible alternative in the vacuum of values left by the collapse of communism ('The Problem and Tasks Confronting the Church in Central and Eastern Europe Today', in the Keston College journal *Religion in Communist Lands*, 19 [1991], 33).

[13]Christopher J.H. Wright, *Living as the People of God: the Relevance of Old Testament Ethics* (Leicester: IVP, 1983).

[14]Longman's book, *Literary Approaches to Biblical Interpretation* (Grand Rapids: Zondervan Academie, 1987), provides a useful survey of the methods of scholars working on the Bible and literature. Ryken, who teaches English at an American college, has contributed widely to the subject, including an important article, 'Literary Criticism of the Bible: Some Fallacies', in K.R.R. Gros Louis (ed.), *Literary Interpretations of Biblical Narratives* (Nashville: Abingdon, 1974). There is, of course, a wide ranging discussion about the concept of story in Old Testament scholarly circles, to which a note like this could never do justice.

[15]Leicester and Downers Grove: IVP, 1981; rev. ed., 1990.

gesting additional areas of research, seems a fruitful point of departure.

V. Story Exegesis: a Proposal

Taking up that point, I would like to suggest that, in 'story' we may find a comprehensive, unifying concept, that will better allow the Word of God, particularly in its Old Testament form, to be heard again in our day, with potential both to give people hope in Christ, and to effect the re-evangelisation of culture, without which I have little confidence in our ability to survive.

I call this proposal 'Exegesis as Telling Story', or simply 'Story Exegesis'. It will be immediately apparent to my colleagues that there is little especially new in the pieces I have assembled, but making story telling the primary goal of our exegetical and hermeneutic task may help us break through the cultural impasse which has led in our own day, even more than in his, to what James Smart called 'the strange silence of the Bible in the church'.[16]

1. Why Story?

At heart, the reply is deceptively simple, 'Because it *is* story'! Goldingay's summary of the influential work of Hans Frei[17] is worth quoting here:

> Frei argued that we are the heirs or victims of a change in ways of reading Scripture which began to come about in the eighteenth century. Before then, as the writings of the Fathers and the Reformers reveal, people assumed that the narrative they were reading corresponded to events that we would have been able to witness if we had been present, and that the history through which we ourselves live is one with that history. Beginning two hundred years ago, scholars began to look for the actual events behind the narrated events, to see our world as essentially discontinuous from that world, and to incline to judge the narrative's presentation of its world by ours rather than the other way around. Frei's study pointed scholars once more toward the actual text of the OT, the story Israel told, as the proper

---

[16]In his book by that name, (London/Philadelphia: SCM/Westminster, 1970).
[17]In *The Eclipse of Biblical Narrative* (New Haven: Yale UP, 1974). See also the Hans Frei Festschrift, *Scriptural Authority and Narrative Interpretation*, edited by G. Green (Philadelphia: Fortress, 1987).

subject for interpretation, rather than the events which lay behind the story. It is the story which is life-giving.[18]

Pondering Frei's basic point, I have become increasingly convinced that the entire Bible, but especially the Old Testament, is best understood as story, and that story, Israel's 'story of salvation', is fundamental to all other categories of interpretation.

Leland Ryken gives two generally agreed criteria for a work to be called 'literature': firstly, it must present human experience, not primarily abstract thought; secondly, it is artistic in form, i.e, the critic may discern in it a story that is carefully unified around one or more controlling literary principles such as tragedy, comedy, satire or heroism, a plot that has structural unity and pattern, and a story that makes use of narrative forms.[19]

Looking at the Old Testament as a work of literature,[20] Ryken's categories may be fruitfully applied both to the whole and its parts. There is not much purely abstract thought in the Old Testament, and what there may be finds its place in the larger story of God's redemptive work with Israel. Whether we discuss regulations for offering the first-fruits, as in Deuteronomy 26, or the suffering lament of the survivors of Jerusalem, as in the book of Lamentations, there is always a narrative context, whether spoken or implied. The narrative context may be found within any given unit, as in Judges 1, but in the final analysis it is the larger story, *i.e.*, the book of Judges, or even the entire Deuteronomic History, that makes sense of the narrative, or provides a setting for non-narrative materials. Much exegesis, by removing the part from the whole, has in my view become barren and unfruitful precisely because the story-line is lost.[21] Even the most mundane 'legal' concepts, like the muzzling of oxen, are set in the story, rather than forming an abstract code of legal precedents. Equally, the Proverbs, by

---

[18]Goldingay, *op. cit.*, 191f.

[19]Ryken, 'Literary Criticism of the Bible', 25f.

[20]I have purposely chosen literary rather than theological rubrics for this study. In a theological sense, the Old Testament as story of salvation has been thoroughly worked through in the *Heilsgeschichte* theologies popularised by G. von Rad's magisterial work *Old Testament Theology* (ET Edinburgh/New York: Oliver & Boyd/Harper, 1962/1965); G.E. Wright's *God Who Acts: Biblical Theology as Recital* (Chicago: Regnery, 1952) and many others. See my further comments below.

[21]My forthcoming commentary on *Judges* (Word Biblical Commentary) will seek to show how these guidelines make better exegetical sense of a chapter like Judges 1, usually considered secondary. The same points have been developed in fruitful ways by Barry G. Webb, *The Book of Judges: An Integrated Reading* (Sheffield: JSOT Press, 1987) and others (see Webb's bibliography).

association with Solomon and Hezekiah, and the Psalms, reflecting varied life-settings, may be grouped together as part of the larger 'story'.

An aside, from a cross-cultural perspective, may be helpful to those of us in Western cultural circles. When the concept of story has been proposed to students either from Africa or the Middle East, all have consistently affirmed the method. A particularly fascinating aspect of that affirmation has been their enthusiasm for including both proverbial and genealogical material under the rubric. One hears again and again, 'In my country, we only relate proverbs, or give genealogies, as part of story, because they are part of story.' It is not unusual to find one of these students doing research in the West, frustrated because scholarly expectations seem to demand removal of the genre from its story context.

But not only is the Old Testament story, but it was *first heard* as story. We have mentioned Deuteronomy 26:5-16, which involves a constant retelling, in the first person plural, of the story, as one goes about one's daily and yearly cycle. Or listen to the Book of Judges, as an Israelite bard might have told it, whether in the exile or much earlier. As attractive as are the stories of individual heroes, it is again only the larger framework that makes sense of the parts. The entire book has a plot, with structural unity and pattern as K.R.R. Gros Louis recognises in a helpful analysis of the literary qualities of Judges.[22]

The point is no less pregnant when one considers how the original reader, very like our African or Arab student, heard most legal, or genealogical, sections. Compare, for instance, the covenant laws of Exodus 20-24, and the muzzling of the ox in Deuteronomy 25. Typically, both are set within a larger 'story' framework, and neither was, as far as we know, abstracted into a legal code used in Israelite jurisprudence. Remove either from the story, and there is little reason why any ancient Israelite would have cared. But hear them in the context of the story, and the text comes to life. The covenant laws and the muzzling of oxen express the values of the original storytellers, whose history was heard throughout the years as Israel's own.

Or consider the genealogy of Moses and Aaron (Ex. 6:14-27), which is often said to interrupt the narrative of Exodus 6. The genealogy, as Exodus 6:26-27 twice notes, reminded everyone who heard the

---

[22]'The Book of Judges', in Gros Louis, *Literary Interpretations of Biblical Narratives*, especially pp. 141ff. *Cf.* also David Gooding's masterful study of the structure of Judges, 'The Composition of the Book of Judges', in *Eretz Israel* 16 (1982) 70-79.

story, 'It is *this* Moses and *this* Aaron, the ones born to Amram and Jochebed, who went in to challenge Pharaoh.'

A third point about story. Not only did the original hearers listen to it as story, but the Old Testament is *still best heard* as story. Here Frei's point about continuity is particularly poignant. Deuteronomy 26 makes it plain that the Israelites put themselves back into the events of the bondage and the exodus, and if Frei is right, so did Christians at least until the time of the Reformation. 'The Egyptians mistreated *us*, afflicted *us*, and laid hard bondage on *us*. Then *we* cried out to Yahweh, God of our Fathers, and Yahweh heard *our voice*....' Why has American black church exegesis been able naturally to hear such a text, while many of us nurtured on more scholarly exegesis have missed it? Can we, as exegetes, begin to bridge the unnatural gap between hermeneutics and homiletics that still divides the faculties of most theological colleges? Hearing the text as story may be the place to begin.

In our own day, as we weep over Bosnia and Rwanda, do we still feel the pain of the Egyptian foreman's lash? Do we again cry out to Yahweh, the God of our Fathers...the God who hears us, and for three thousand years has always heard us? Do we, as mothers watching the bodies of black children wash down the Rwandan river, weep like Rachel in Jerusalem for her children? As we watch Sarajevo's destruction, or ponder nuclear holocaust as the brink is reached on the Korean peninsula, do we sit again with our Lord on the Mount of Olives, weeping for the destruction that he could see coming? And do we hear that note of hope, in the larger story, that looks to a day when final judgment will make sense of all this mess, when 'God will wipe away every tear from their eyes; there shall be no more death, nor sorrow, nor crying...for the former things have passed away' (Rev. 21:4)? Does this give the believer a basis for 'hope in Christ' through the patience and comfort of the Scriptures (Rom. 15:3-4) of which we spoke earlier?

Here too is a basis for contemporary ethics, the second of our two central concerns. C.J.H. Wright constructs the case for an Old Testament ethic directly from the story of Abraham and his family, taking it as a paradigm for an Old Testament ethic.[23] In Genesis 18:19 the mysterious visitor, whom the text calls 'Yahweh', says to himself[24] regarding Abraham, 'I have known him, in order that he may command his children and his household after him, that they keep the way

---

[23]*Op. cit.*, especially 40ff.
[24]Christian iconography has, for hundreds of years, pictured the three visitors as the members of the Trinity.

of Yahweh, to do righteousness and justice, that Yahweh may bring to Abraham what He has spoken to him.' This, for Wright, is the foundation for both an Old Testament missionary vision and an Israelite concern for ethics. Both points come directly from the story. If our generation again began to hear the story, and in some way again the story became, as it did with an earlier generation, our story, might the basis for mission and ethics take root as part of the story?

2. Story and historical reality

A comment must be added regarding the term 'story' itself. For some it carries overtones of fictional literature, though there is nothing inherent in the term which demands such an interpretation. Jesus told many stories, some of which, *e.g.*, the tower of Siloam in Luke 13:4 were clearly factual. Others, like most parables, do not depend on a specific relationship to an actual occurrence for their meaning. In the Old Testament, Jotham's story (Judg. 9) is clearly a fable, and as such fictional. By contrast, the story of Balaam's talking donkey (Nu. 22), is presented with all the marks of an historical event.[25] With regard to other Old Testament stories, *e.g.*, Jonah's travels, different scholars, using the criteria of internal evidence, have come to varying conclusions. In each case, the category of 'story' remains.

On the level of literary and theological criticism, two further notes must be added. Hans Frei, whose comments have been quoted, together with many literary critics, expresses indifference as to whether 'story' has a historical basis or not. For evangelical Old Testament story exegesis, this question is of utmost importance, for the story claims to relate 'acts of God', like the exodus from Egypt, which are foundational to faith, both for Israel and the church.

A second note must address the difference between story exegesis and traditional *Heilsgeschichte*, or 'salvation history' approaches to Old Testament theology. The most eloquent advocate of this approach, Gerhard von Rad, in my view captures well the sense of Israel's traditions as fundamentally 'story', but from a theological starting point expresses scepticism about the relationship between the related event (what Israel remembers) and what actually happened.[26]

---

[25]Commentators working with genre questions have sometimes called the Balaam account an 'animal fable', but in animal fables, as in Jotham's tree fable, the whole point is that animals and trees do *not* speak. The point of the Balaam story is that, at least according to the narrator, this particular donkey *did* speak. The critical mistake betrays the commentator's bias rather than saying anything about the literature.

Both Frei and von Rad, in their assertions, seem at times to ignore what most children know about story telling, *i.e.*, that almost any story carries within itself a certain amount of internal evidence by which the story's relationship to a particular real sequence of events is to be judged. If, for example, when a child asks for a story, and it begins with 'Once upon a time there were three bears...', the child is left with no ambiguity about whether it is sober history or not. If, on the other hand, Daddy begins, 'Let me tell you about how you learned to swim...', there is equally convincing internal evidence by which to resolve any ambiguity.

The above examples were chosen to illustrate a point, and not every story will contain such clear internal evidence. Sometimes obviously fictional story-form, *e.g.*, historical novel, may mix categories, but convey more truthfully what actually happened than a reporter's notes taken on the scene.[27] Poetic forms, like Deborah's song (Judg. 5) or many of the Psalms, will obviously mediate historical fact in other ways. In any case, the question of the intended meaning must always first be decided by internal evidence. Scepticism regarding the story's self-understanding (presumably related in some way to what the author intended) is warranted only when the story is clearly far-fetched, or the reader knows some obvious fact which falsifies the storyteller's view of reality, but that is going beyond our immediate subject.

3. Story and the challenge of contemporary scholarship.

If, as I have suggested, the greatest single challenge to Old Testament studies is the question whether anyone is listening, story exegesis would seem to have great potential to address the problem. If the story

---

[26]*Op. cit.* For the beginner, Goldingay's chapter (*op. cit.*) provides a sympathetic description and critique of the *Heilsgeschichte* movement in theology. My own indebtedness to this approach will be obvious to other scholars, though in story exegesis I propose to move beyond the 1960s debate. For a more detailed critique of the biblical theology movement, see James Barr, 'Story and History in Biblical Theology' in *The Scope and Authority of the Bible* (Explorations in Theology 7; London: SCM, 1980). See also E.W. Nicholson, 'Story and History in the Old Testament' in S.E. Balentine and J. Barton (eds.), *Language, Theology & the Bible* (Oxford: OUP, 1994).

[27]The hermeneutical bases for this discussion are extensively developed by A.C. Thiselton in several monographs, including *The Two Horizons: New Testament Hermeneutics and Philosophical Description* (Grand Rapids: Eerdmans, 1980) and *New Horizons in Hermeneutics* (London: Marshall Pickering, 1992). See also Thiselton's chapter, 'Authority and Interpretation', in this volume.

began again to be heard, we could only imagine the potential for a flowering of Old Testament scholarship, to say nothing of a reversal of some of the trends about which we have spoken. The re-evangelisation of culture, called for by Stefan Wilkanowicz in post-communist Poland,[28] might take root also in the West.[29]

But what about the concerns, both scholarly and societal, with which we began this paper? Does story exegesis address those concerns, and if so, how? I will finish this essay with six points in response.

(i)   Story exegesis as a scholarly method benefits from the insights of traditional exegetical method (grammatical-historical) as well as the insights of the newer (at least for biblical studies) literary criticism, though it need not be tied to any specific method of either. Story exegesis, as both an historical and a literary discipline, will need to draw upon the best of proven methods like form criticism and grammatical analysis, while reaping the benefits of newer rhetorical and literary studies.

Specifically, story exegesis will employ the following tools, most of which are amply illustrated in contemporary Old Testament exegetical handbooks: grammatical-historical analysis of text, analysis of structural or literary patterns, and literary and theological integration into the larger concerns of the biblical story of God's work from creation to final judgment. The overriding concern of the exegete must be the story, in part and in whole. The critic will at every point wish also to be a reader, or listener, seeking within the story itself the guidelines for its exegesis.

For a believing critic, this process will undoubtedly include prayer, and a desire to hear in the story the voice of him whose voice once 'shook the earth' (Heb. 12:26) and who later came to his people as the Word Incarnate. Surely, whether one is a believer or a seeker, the process of becoming a listener will provoke a response from this One, whose Spirit gives life and lightens the dark places of the mind.

(ii)   Story exegesis honours the integrity of the text. The normal response to a story is to listen to it, not to dissect it. Here the critic must become a reader again, as well as a critic.[30] Of course, the critic must

---

[28]*Op. cit.*

[29]The recently published *A Dictionary of the Biblical Tradition in English Literature* (Grand Rapids: Eerdmans, 1992), edited by David L. Jeffrey, reminds us of the extent to which 'the story' has penetrated our English literary tradition. Culturally, some societies need to hear 'the story' from a much different starting point.

look at the flow of discourse, the markers in the text, and resolutions of various kinds,[31] but none of this important critical work leaves the text fragmented or unreadable. This principle must be held in the light of our earlier comments about story and historical reality, together with comments below dealing with the supernatural.

(iii)   Story exegesis leaves open the question of the supernatural. My book *The Old Testament and Criticism*[32] argued for a criticism, generally along lines scholars follow, which left room for the supernatural. The late Peter Craigie, in the opening section of his 1976 commentary on Deuteronomy, argued eloquently for the same thing.[33] Story exegesis has no problem with this. Stories are quite used to a supernatural presence, and supernatural causes, and the average reader has less problem understanding this element than those of us whose philosophical framework is prejudiced against such. The renewed general interest in the supernatural, or the spiritual, about which we have spoken, may not be simply a resurgence of gullibility but a genuine reawakening of hunger for a reality which Enlightenment thinking has quenched but could not eliminate.

(iv)   Story exegesis addresses the spiritual hunger of our day. Because story concerns not only admit the supernatural, but centre on human experience (see Ryken's definition earlier), there is no separation between the intellectual, or cognitive, and the affective. Human emotions arise in response to story, even as human intellect perceives its content.

(v)   Story exegesis is thoroughly cross-cultural, both in its basic method and its appeal. One thinks of the valuable insight given by the African and Arab students mentioned above, whose world-view is

---

[30]The critic self-consciously employs formal methods and applies accepted criteria to a work of literature, whereas the reader's response is natural and lacks the element of formal analysis. The reader 'hears' the story, while the critic 'analyses' the story. *Cf.* R.M. Fowler, 'Who is "The Reader" in Reader Response Criticism?', in P.R. House (ed.), *Beyond Form Criticism* (Winona Lake: Eisenbrauns, 1992), 376.

[31]A sample of this kind of work, on one book of the Bible, Judges, is to be found in Lillian R. Klein, *The Triumph of Irony in the Book of Judges* (Sheffield: Almond, 1988); Barry G. Webb, *The Book of Judges; an Integrated Reading*; and an unpublished 1989 Manchester dissertation by P.E. Satterthwaite entitled 'Narrative Artistry and the Composition of Judges 17-21'.

[32]*Op. cit.*

[33]*The Book of Deuteronomy* (NICOT; Grand Rapids: Eerdmans, 1976) 76.

probably much closer to the Hebrew than our own. Such insights can only enrich our exegesis. And, as we have all experienced, telling story is one of the most effective means of bridging the cultural gap. People in all places and at all times relate to story, a fact demonstrated in the widespread appeal of the gospel throughout most divergent cultures. One wonders if story exegesis might not be the key to help yet others hear, who at this point seem resistant to Christian faith.[34]

(vi) Story exegesis invites the reader(s)[35] to participate in the story. We return again to Hans Frei's point. The great need in our day is somehow to overcome the discontinuity between the biblical story and ours. As long as contemporary discontinuity remains, and grows in a so-called secular culture, there is probably little chance of the Bible becoming less foreign. But as Jeffrey's dictionary demonstrates, the English literary tradition has never lost the story, though today's reading generation may find its own sources increasingly foreign. One might say the same about art. Does our generation identify with David and Saul, through Rembrandt's visual telling of the story? And what of music? Music lovers for over a hundred years have heard and identified with the Elijah story, in the form of Mendelssohn's magnificent oratorio. And for even longer, music lovers throughout the world have heard the messianic story through Handel's great work.

Although our primary illustrations have been presented from within an English-language cultural world, one thinks immediately of the same ubiquitous and powerful symbols of the biblical story expressed wherever European culture and the preaching of the gospel have been heard, including all the countries of the recently collapsed world of European communism. A different observer will need to chronicle the various ways in which the biblical story has been expressed in non-Western cultural forms, but the Watanabe paintings hanging on my wall remind me that not only in Japan, but throughout the world, various cultures have understood the story and begun to participate in the biblical story, as their own story unfolds culturally and spiritually.

---

[34]One thinks of Muslim-Christian encounter, where much of the debate centres on abstract theological concepts. However, most of the countries where Islam is dominant are story cultures.

[35]As Western readers, we tend to come to a text as individuals, but as exegetes we must keep in mind that the texts with which we work were originally read by, and even now throughout the world are heard by, cultures that are much more corporate or communal than ours.

With such a heritage, work on the forms of both stories, theirs and ours, and the relationship between the two, is a major challenge that could unite Old and New Testament scholars, students of hermeneutics, and those whose job is communicating in contemporary culture.

A final point about 'reader participation' must note an important distinction between story exegesis and some radical forms of reader-response criticism. The point has to do with whose story is normative, and why. Modern criticism, as expressed in both literary and political theory, has at times moved to the notion that it is really the reader who constructs, or re-constructs, the story for him- or herself. Similarly, in the praxis model on which some liberation theology is based, the reader community's story becomes so normative that the original story may be obscured.

In story exegesis, as I am proposing it, the stories come together, but the divine story remains the normative story. Granted that as I present this, it is a theological point, arising from a confessional perspective, but it is also good reading, given the nature of the story. If indeed God moved redemptively in and through the story told in the Old Testament, and if he was present in Jesus Christ both to effect and anticipate the culmination of the story at the last day, that story is one that demands our response. The universality of the gospel means that we can find our own story within its story, but if we turn it around and attempt to make God's story into the image of ours, we will have fallen again into idolatry. It is not without reason that the hymn writer penned the lines, 'Tell me the old, old story, of unseen things above; of Jesus and his glory, of Jesus and his love'. It is only this story, and here I speak both confessionally and experientially, that gives life. It is only this story which can teach us, reprove us, correct us, and instruct us in righteousness. This is the story which was 'written for us'.

CHAPTER 3

Critical Issues in New Testament Studies for Evangelicals Today

Craig L. Blomberg

Summary

Evangelicals need to devote concerted attention to (1) the third quest of the historical Jesus and its mutations, (2) a synthesis of old and new looks on Paul and the law, (3) a reasoned eclecticism in critical methodology, and (4) the globalisation of hermeneutics. Profitable results also await further study and application of (5) Greek verbal aspect, (6) the use of the Old Testament in the New, (7) key themes in New Testament theology, (8) recent work on Acts, (9) institution and charisma in Corinth, (10) theories of epistolary pseudonymity, (11) the Jewish background of Hebrews, and (12) the genre and interpretation of Revelation.

I. Introduction

To survey an entire scholarly discipline in one short essay is an impossible task. All that I can hope for are a few soundings in certain waters which have recently been stirred. My choice of topics is necessarily influenced by my social location; it will be clear that I am not only an Evangelical but a North American, working in the context of theological education, focusing primarily on English-language material, and constrained by the competing demands of a busy life. In other words, I have not read everything I should have to prepare for this task, and my choice of reading is skewed by access to resources and the priorities of my ministry. Doubtless I will miss out entire fields of study which some find absolutely critical. Nevertheless, I hope that my comments may reflect a certain breadth of coverage and may stimulate others to do the in-depth research to which this paper can merely point. I have organised my reflections under four major headings and eight minor ones.

II. Major Needs in New Testament Research

1. Jesus, the Gospels and Judaism

Debates about the historical Jesus continue to rage. What Tom Wright dubbed the 'third quest' has made significant strides in reversing the scepticism of both the Bultmannian 'no quest' and post-Bultmannian 'new quest' eras.[1] Indeed, two of the most significant and prolific contributors to the third quest, E.P. Sanders and J.H. Charlesworth, agree that 'the dominant view today seems to be that we can know pretty well what Jesus was out to accomplish, that we can know a lot about what he said, and that those two things make sense within the world of first-century Judaism.'[2] What we can know still does not often include fully satisfying treatments of Jesus' miracles or his resurrection,[3] but we are grateful for the progress that has been made. But whether or not Charlesworth's quotation of Sanders in 1988 was true as an accurate generalisation then, it is doubtful that it can be sustained

---

[1]Stephen Neill and Tom Wright, *The Interpretation of the New Testament 1861-1986* (Oxford: OUP, 1988) 379-403.

[2]E.P. Sanders, *Jesus and Judaism* (London: SCM, 1985) 2; James H. Charlesworth, *Jesus within Judaism* (New York: Doubleday, 1988) 205.

[3]*Cf.* Craig A. Evans ('Life-of-Jesus Research and the Eclipse of Mythology', *TS* 54 [1993] 3-36), who tries to point in the direction of rectifying this situation.

today. Rapidly on the rise is the approach of the Jesus Seminar, whose four-colour-coded edition of the sayings of Jesus in the *five* Gospels[4] has received immense publicity and no little endorsement by professors of religious studies, at least in North American universities. So, too, have the various monographs of J.D. Crossan and M.J. Borg on the historical Jesus and of B.L. Mack on the origins of Mark and Q.[5]

Common to this stream of scholarship are the affirmations that Jesus is to be read against more of a Greco-Roman background than the third questers usually allow, that less than twenty percent of the traditions of Jesus' words even roughly approximate what he may have actually said, that the Gospel of Thomas regularly (and other apocryphal literature occasionally) preserves material which is at least as reliable as many of the traditions found in our canonical Gospels, that Jesus was an Oriental sage, akin to certain itinerant Cynics, who spoke almost exclusively in pithy aphorisms and subversive parables, and that apocalyptic is a later addition to the more original sapiential stratum of the Jesus tradition. Given that the Jesus Seminar is now continuing their work by turning to the deeds attributed to Jesus, and given their explicitly stated agenda of publicising biblical scholarship more than it usually is, precisely in order to combat the stranglehold they believe televangelists hold on the media (a curious perception indeed),[6] this issue is not likely to disappear in the foreseeable future.

Now many of the assumptions with which the Jesus Seminar and their friends operate have adequately been disputed, though these researchers exhibit the annoying habit of only rarely interacting with dissenting scholarship.[7] In this category, one thinks, for example, of their presuppositions concerning the unreliability and piecemeal nature of the oral tradition of Jesus-sayings, against which the ongoing work of R. Riesner in detail and K.E. Bailey more briefly provide more conservative and more plausible models.[8] Here, too, belong their 'revolutionary' rather than 'evolutionary' models, that assume a grand

---

[4]Robert W. Funk and Roy W. Hoover, (eds.), *The Five Gospels: What Did Jesus Really Say?* (New York: Macmillan, 1993).

[5]John D. Crossan, *The Historical Jesus* (San Francisco: HarperCollins, 1991); Marcus J. Borg, *Jesus: A New Vision* (San Francisco: Harper & Row, 1987); Burton L. Mack, *A Myth of Innocence* (Philadelphia: Fortress, 1988); *idem, The Lost Gospel: The Book of Q and Christian Origins* (San Francisco: HarperCollins, 1993).

[6]Robert W. Funk with Mahlon H. Smith, *The Gospel of Mark: Red Letter Edition* (Sonoma, CA: Polebridge, 1991) xvi-xvii.

[7]*Cf.* the unusually skewed and selective bibliography in Funk and Hoover, *Five Gospels*, 538-41; also Crossan's remarks: 'In quoting *secondary* literature I spend no time citing other scholars to show how wrong they are' (*Historical Jesus*, xxxiv)!

disjunction between oral and written stages of the tradition.[9] But plenty of room remains for Evangelicals to integrate the studies that posit a more conservative oral tradition with a more standard source criticism, that is, without recourse to the more implausible and more wholesale rejection of major tenets of Markan priority and the Q-hypothesis.[10]

Other proposals of Crossan, Mack, et al., require more detailed scrutiny because they reflect more recent paradigm shifts. Turning Jesus into a sage who utters only aphorisms, positing a two-stage Q with wisdom preceding apocalyptic, and relying heavily on Nag Hammadi writings for pre-canonical gospel traditions all require detailed response. J.P. Meier's first volume holds out the promise of doing some of that from a moderate Roman Catholic perspective and N.T. Wright may be helping us along from a reasonably conservative Protestant position,[11] but given the incomplete nature of both of their projects it is too soon to be sure. And each will in any event need to be bolstered with additional detailed work on the fine points of the arguments. Not least at stake are the appropriate balances between Jewish and Greco-Roman influences in Jesus' life and between spiritual and socio-political dimensions of his ministry.

In the area of Gospel introduction, an encouraging sign among certain conservative authors is a renewed willingness to take seriously the early external evidence for authorship, setting, and composition. R.H. Gundry has now given us relatively compelling defences of the traditional authorship of Matthew and Mark, and dated both of those Gospels to a period before A.D. 70.[12] C.J. Hemer has done the same in even greater detail for Luke.[13] Other studies are more speculative but

---

[8]Rainer Riesner, Jesus als Lehrer (WUNT 2.7; Tübingen: Mohr, 1981); idem, 'Jesus as Preacher and Teacher', in Henry Wansbrough (ed.), Jesus and the Oral Gospel Tradition (JSNTS 64; Sheffield: JSOT Press, 1991) 185-210; Kenneth E. Bailey, 'Informal Controlled Oral Tradition and the Synoptic Gospels', AJT 5 (1991) 34-54.

[9]In addition to Mack, Myth, see especially Werner H. Kelber, The Oral and the Written Gospel (Philadelphia: Fortress, 1983); against which see Larry W. Hurtado, 'The Gospel of Mark: Evolutionary or Revolutionary Document?', JSNT 40 (1990) 15-32; and Paul J. Achtemeier, 'Omne Verbum Sonat: The New Testament and the Oral Environment of Late Western Antiquity', JBL 109 (1990) 3-27.

[10]As, e.g., in the recent proposals of John Wenham, Redating Matthew, Mark and Luke (London: Hodder & Stoughton, 1991); and Eta Linnemann, Is There a Synoptic Problem? (Grand Rapids: Baker, 1992).

[11]John P. Meier, A Marginal Jew: Rethinking the Historical Jesus, 2 vols. (New York: Doubleday, 1991-); N.T. Wright, Jesus and the Victory of God (London: SPCK, forthcoming)—Vol. 2 in what is projected to be a five-volume series on Christian Origins and the Question of God.

still suggestive: the possibility that Matthew himself produced Q (and that that is what Papias describes)[14] and attributions of John's Gospel to someone (if not the son of Zebedee than at least the putative John the elder) in a position to report with some accuracy on the events of Jesus' life.[15] These require further investigation.

There is still much room, too, for further evangelical study of the Fourth Gospel. It is ironic that, with the one Gospel for which traditio-critical dissection is on shakiest grounds,[16] theories proliferate which postulate far more stages of that tradition history than ever are found in Synoptic studies. Perhaps most ambitious of all is J. Ashton's recent isolation of eight such stages: (1) a signs source, (2) a passion source and other Synoptic tradition; (3) these combined and received positively in the synagogue; (4) but subsequently rejected there; (5) Jewish-Christian preachers and prophets constructing an *apologia* in response; (6) the expulsion of the Johannine group; (7) a second edition incorporating material reflecting this tension; and (8) a final third edition involving thoroughgoing redaction to make the story intelligible to Gentile readers.[17]

The 'new look on John,' placing it squarely within first-century Judaism, is, like the third quest, to be preferred to its predecessors, but at times it discloses curious inconsistencies. A.T. Hanson, for example,

---

[12]Robert H. Gundry, *Matthew: A Commentary on His Literary and Theological Art* (Grand Rapids: Eerdmans, 1982) 599-622; *idem*, *Mark: A Commentary on His Apology for the Cross* (Grand Rapids: Eerdmans, 1993) 1026-45.

[13]Colin J. Hemer, *The Book of Acts in the Setting of Hellenistic History* (WUNT 49; Tübingen: Mohr, 1989) 308-410.

[14]*Cf.* Matthew Black, 'The Use of Rhetorical Terminology in Papias on Mark and Matthew', *JSNT* 37 (1989) 31-41; Donald A. Hagner, *Matthew 1-13* (WBC 33A; Dallas: Word, 1993) xliii-xlvi.

[15]On John the apostle as author, see especially Domingo León, 'Es el apóstol Juan el discípulo amado?', *EstBib* 45 (1987) 403-92. On John the elder, *cf.* Richard Bauckham, 'Papias and Polycrates on the Origin of the Fourth Gospel', *JTS* 44 (1993) 24-69; with Martin Hengel, *The Johannine Question* (London: SCM, 1989). It is particularly interesting to see how virtually indistinguishable Hengel's John the elder is from the Bible's son of Zebedee (see esp. 130-32).

[16]Not only because of the lack of comparative data, but because of the literary unity of its current form. See Gilbert van Belle, *Les parentheses dans l'Évangile de Jean* (SNTA; Leuven: Leuven UP, 1985); E. Ruckstuhl, *Die literarische Einheit des Johannesevangeliums* (Göttingen: Vandenhoeck & Ruprecht, 1987); Carl J. Bjerkelund, *Tauta Egeneto: Präzisierungsätze im Johannesevangelium* (Tübingen: Mohr, 1987).

[17]John Ashton, *Understanding the Fourth Gospel* (Oxford: Clarendon, 1991) 163-6. Only slightly less complicated is the scenario sketched by John Painter (*The Quest for the Messiah: The History, Literature and Theology of the Johannine Community* [Edinburgh: T.&T. Clark, 1991] 72) following the early Barrett.

mines the Fourth Gospel for every possible sign of Old Testament quotation or allusion to demonstrate, surely successfully in the main, the preponderance of Jewish exegetical, and especially midrashic techniques, particularly in the discourses of Jesus.[18] Yet this consistently convinces Hanson of the historical unreliability of the material, when surely logic should lead in the opposite direction. If, for example, the Bread of Life Discourse (Jn. 6:26-59) is a tightly knit midrash on Exodus 16,[19] why should this not *enhance* the case that Jesus, the Jewish teacher, originally uttered it in something like the form in which it is now preserved?

It is interesting, too, that all the evidence that convinced a previous generation about John's Hellenistic origins and influence can now be so substantially jettisoned, precisely when the only recurring external evidence from antiquity ascribes the Fourth Gospel to the proto-Gnostic world of Christianity in Ephesus. The standard critical solution to this dilemma, of course, has been to posit successive Jewish and Hellenistic stages of John's Gospel and/or the Johannine community. But why should this reconstruction be inherently more plausible than one which sees this work, composed for the first time in largely its finished form, as addressed to a Christian community in Asia toward the end of the first century that was troubled by vehement attacks by local Jews (*cf.* Rev. 2:9, 3:9), and tempted by a syncretistic heresy similar to that known from Colossians and the Pastoral Epistles with elements of both Judaism and incipient Gnosticism? D.M. Smith's survey of Johannine research, apparently completed in about 1984 though not published until 1989, discusses the resurgence of interest in the Jewish origins of certain branches of Gnosticism and observes, 'a Jewish gnosticism in the Johannine milieu is a factor to be reckoned with.'[20] Yet it seems that few in the last decade have in fact reckoned with it. Two who have considered it in a different context are R.C. and C.C. Kroeger, in their study of the religious world of Asia Minor, which enables them to place 1 Timothy into a credible *Sitz im Leben* in Ephesus during Paul's life.[21] How much more plausible, then, might the case be for locating John in a similar milieu twenty or thirty years later? The

---

[18] A.T. Hanson, *The Prophetic Gospel* (Edinburgh: T.&T. Clark, 1991).
[19] See already Peder Borgen, *Bread from Heaven* (Supp NovT 10; Leiden: Brill, 1965).
[20] D. Moody Smith, 'Johannine Studies', in Eldon J. Epp and George W. MacRae (eds.), *The New Testament and Its Modern Interpreters* (Atlanta: Scholars, 1989) 279. On the dating of the essay, *cf.* Smith's bibliography (288-96) with the editors' preface (xxv).

answer awaits someone willing to flesh out the details of such a hypothesis.

2. Paul and the Law

Although seventeen years have elapsed since Sanders' ground-breaking work,[22] there is no end in sight of studies on Paul and the law. The amount of confusion that still exists on the topic and the foundational nature of the theological issues at stake surely justify continuing attention, not least on the part of Evangelicals. More so than in many areas of biblical research, the field seems to be dominated by major protagonists repeatedly reworking much of the same material, and each proposing credible but one-sided theses. What is needed is a synthesis of the work done that avoids numerous false dichotomies.

Thus we are forever indebted to Sanders for debunking the caricature of first-century Judaism that unfortunately continues to afflict the average Christian conception of Jews in New Testament times. But it seems clear that Sanders' own portrait does not do justice to the strands of merit theology that remain in both rabbinic and intertestamental literature.[23] M.A. Seifrid's recent thesis begins to redress this imbalance, but what is needed is a wholesale rereading of the material Sanders surveyed (and the material he did not survey) to create a more balanced perspective.[24]

Similarly, we may thank J.D.G. Dunn for repeatedly stressing that circumcision, Sabbath and the dietary laws in particular, like Torah more generally, often functioned in an exclusive way as Jewish badges of national righteousness.[25] Many passages in Paul are profitably illumined when we see this exclusivism lurking behind references to 'the law' or 'the works of the law.' But it is not at all obvious that this

---

[21]Richard C. Kroeger and Catherine C. Kroeger, *I Suffer Not a Woman: Rethinking 1 Timothy 2:11-15 in Light of Ancient Evidence* (Grand Rapids: Baker, 1992), although they do not always differentiate the varying ages of the data they amass; on Jewish Gnosticism more generally, *cf.* especially Birger Pearson, *Gnosticism, Judaism and Egyptian Christianity* (Minneapolis: Fortress, 1990).

[22]E.P. Sanders, *Paul and Palestinian Judaism* (London: SCM, 1977).

[23]See already the programmatic comments in D.A. Carson, *Divine Sovereignty and Human Responsibility* (London: Marshall, Morgan & Scott, 1981) 86-109.

[24]Mark A. Seifrid, *Justification by Faith: The Origin and Development of a Central Pauline Theme* (Supp NovT 68; Leiden: Brill, 1992); see especially his treatment of the Psalms of Solomon (109-32); also the unpublished thesis of Mark A. Elliott, *The Survivors of Israel* (Aberdeen, Ph.D., 1993).

[25]See especially the collection of essays in James D.G. Dunn, *Jesus, Paul and the Law* (London: SPCK, 1990). *Cf.* also *idem, Romans,* 2 vols. (WBC 38; Dallas: Word, 1988); and *idem, The Epistle to the Galatians* (BNTC; London: Black, 1993).

interpretation can be imposed unilaterally on the data. Romans 4:4-5, Galatians 3:10-14 and Philippians 3:7-10, among other texts, still read more naturally as contrasting faith and works in the more traditional Reformation sense of those terms.[26] And given the unity of Torah in Paul's thought, limitation of his criticism of the law to legalism (as, *e.g.*, in Cranfield[27]) or nationalism (as particularly in Dunn) overly plays down the major salvation-historical shift which Paul has come to believe has occurred with Christ's death and resurrection.[28]

As in all of his writing, N.T. Wright brings a refreshing perspective to the table.[29] Among the strengths of his approach to Paul are his insistence that we interpret developing Christology within the framework of Jewish monotheism, a monotheism which, as L.W. Hurtado and A.F. Segal have helpfully stressed, allowed more for 'two powers in heaven' than did later Judaism.[30] Wright's synthesis of previous views which allows for a trajectory in Paul's thought from 'plight to solution to plight' is also compelling, though it is not clear if one can talk about an initial corporate plight to the exclusion of an individual's sense of being under God's judgement. What is more, one still senses a little too much Lutheran-bashing in Wright's overall agenda. Why can one not affirm Wright's central thesis, with God's covenant faithfulness as the central category under which justification by faith is subsumed, without denying that Paul's critique of the first-century human condition may, by an appropriate logical outworking, be extended to take in the almost universal tendency toward self-justification? And nagging doubts remain as to just how much of Paul's theology can be reduced to the 'monotheism plus election lead to everything else' formulas he repeatedly invokes. But we nevertheless look forward to his fuller work with whetted appetites.

The work on Paul and the Law which encourages me the most, however, is T.R. Schreiner's quite recent monograph.[31] Here I think we come closest to preserving the valid insights of both Luther and Calvin,

---

[26]*Cf.* Moisés Silva, 'The Law and Christianity: Dunn's New Synthesis', *WTJ* 53 (1991) 339-53.

[27]C.E.B. Cranfield, *A Critical and Exegetical Commentary on the Epistle to the Romans*, Vol. 2 (ICC rev. ed.; Edinburgh: T.&T. Clark, 1979) 845-62.

[28]As helpfully stressed throughout Stephen Westerholm, *Israel's Law and the Church's Faith* (Grand Rapids: Eerdmans, 1988); and Richard N. Longenecker, *Galatians* (WBC 41; Dallas: Word, 1990).

[29]N.T. Wright, *The Climax of the Covenant* (Edinburgh: T.&T. Clark, 1991).

[30]Larry W. Hurtado, *One God, One Lord* (Philadelphia: Fortress, 1988); Alan F. Segal, *Two Powers in Heaven* (Leiden: Brill, 1977).

[31]Thomas R. Schreiner, *The Law and Its Fulfilment* (Grand Rapids: Baker, 1993).

preserving the unity of Torah and the salvation-historical shift of the ages which permeates Paul's thought, while nevertheless incorporating the equally valid insights of the new perspective on Paul. If Schreiner disappoints at all, it is in his return to the well-worn categories of moral, civil and ceremonial law. The problem is not that Paul (or the New Testament more generally) does not hint at such distinctions but that we probably need even more of them to make sense of the diversity both of the original Mosaic Law and of the New Testament applications of the Torah. I think, for example, of C.J.H. Wright's helpful fivefold division into categories of criminal, civil, family, cultic, and charitable law,[32] and I suspect that these, too, could be subdivided and refined. We need to find increasingly sophisticated ways of affirming with Paul and the other New Testament writers that all of the Torah (like all of the Old Testament) applies to Christians, but that none of it applies apart from its fulfilment in Christ.[33]

Not a few monographs thus cry out for composition: a reworked Sanders, a reworked Pauline theology more generally, à la H. Ridderbos (preserving his salutary emphasis on salvation-history but incorporating into it the legitimate insights of a post-Sanders, post-Dunn era),[34] a full-scale discussion of the various uses of the law in Paul (both positive and negative), a theology of the law in the New Testament more generally that demonstrates how similar categories of promise and fulfilment permeate all the major corpora, notwithstanding diversity of detail,[35] and related works.

I for one am particularly grateful for the detailed exegetical work of D.J. Moo on a variety of these fronts, most recently in his major two-volume commentary on Romans still in progress.[36] There is no little irony that J.A. Fitzmyer's new Anchor Bible volume on that Epistle, from the perspective of a Jesuit priest, is closer to the overall positions of the Reformers than Sanders, Dunn, Wright or even, in some ways, Cranfield.[37] But there are still specific passages which the new look on

---

[32]Christopher J.H. Wright, *Living as the People of God* (Leicester: IVP, 1983) 153-9.

[33]*Cf.* William W. Klein, Craig L. Blomberg, and Robert L. Hubbard, Jr., *Introduction to Biblical Interpretation* (Dallas: Word, 1993) 280.

[34]Herman Ridderbos, *Paul: An Outline of His Theology* (Grand Rapids: Eerdmans, 1975).

[35]*Cf.* Schreiner's 'soundings from the rest of the New Testament' (*Law*, 205-40).

[36]Douglas J. Moo, *Romans 1-8* (WEC; Chicago: Moody, 1991); *cf.* especially *idem*, 'The Law of Christ as the Fulfilment of the Law of Moses: A Modified Lutheran View', in Wayne G. Strickland (ed.),*The Law, the Gospel, and the Modern Christian: Five Views* (Grand Rapids: Zondervan, 1993) 319-76.

[37]Joseph A. Fitzmyer, *Romans* (AB 33; New York: Doubleday, 1993).

Paul may helpfully influence in ways Moo and Fitzmyer do not appreciate. I think, for example, of the vexed questions surrounding Romans 2:6-10, 14-16, and 26-9. Surely Luther's hypothetical interpretation is unnatural and Cranfield's view that Paul speaks here of Christians misses the pre-Christian context of this part of his argument. Despite important criticism which it has received, I believe the line of interpretation set out by K. Snodgrass and developed in more detail by G.N. Davies holds promise: these are pre-Christian Jews, and possibly even some Gentiles, who demonstrate not perfect righteousness but the obedience of faith which is adequate *for that age of salvation history* to make one right with God.[38] But with 3:21, and the coming of Christ, those doors are now closed.

In sum, we must get beyond both the old look *and* the new look on Paul to a fresh synthesis. But it should probably resemble Luther or Calvin a little more than Sanders or Dunn. Perhaps the ongoing translation of the Dead Sea scrolls fragments may facilitate this enterprise, as the usage of 'the works of the law' (מקצת מעשי התורה) in 4QMMT has already suggested. On the scholarly level, however, I am still concerned at the overly enthusiastic acceptance of the post-Sanders consensus. Here D.A. Hagner's recent caution proves timely:

> That some valid insights have emerged in the new perspective on Paul I do not wish to deny. I find myself doubtful, however, that the new perspective itself constitutes a breakthrough to a truer estimate of Paul and Judaism. This time Copernicus and his followers are taking us down the wrong path.[39]

3. An Eclectic Criticism

My first two major topics involved the two principal characters and corpora of the New Testament: Jesus and Paul, the Gospels and the major Epistles. My next two deal more with methods and cut across all branches and genres of New Testament study. The first of these calls for a reasoned eclecticism in evangelical use of critical methodologies.

---

[38]Klyne Snodgrass, 'Justification by Grace—to the Doers: An Analysis of the Place of Romans 2 in the Theology of Paul', *NTS* 32 (1986) 72-93; Glenn N. Davies, *Faith and Obedience in Romans* (JSNTS 39; Sheffield: JSOT Press, 1990) 53-71. For criticism, particularly of Snodgrass, see Brice L. Martin, *Christ and the Law in Paul* (Supp NovT 62; Leiden: Brill, 1989) 90-92; and Frank Thielman, *From Plight to Solution* (Supp NovT 61; Leiden: Brill, 1989) 93-4. More generally, both of these works are also important monographs on our subject.

[39]Donald A. Hagner, 'Paul and Judaism—The Jewish Matrix of Early Christianity: Issues in the Current Debate', *BBR* 3 (1993) 130.

As a cursory survey of topics at any annual SBL meeting will quickly confirm, ours is an age of methodological fragmentation and disarray. We must resist both the temptation to jump on the bandwagon of each latest disciplinary fad and the practice, for which Evangelicals are more commonly known, of mostly criticising or rejecting out of hand each new approach. The recent surveys edited by S. McKnight and by D.A. Black and D.S. Dockery set a good example for us, but the former does not address most of the newest methods and the latter is uneven in the quality of its summaries and critique.[40] The field is wide open for an updated work of the breadth and depth of I.H. Marshall's *New Testament Interpretation*, and expanded to include methods which were not yet commonplace in 1977.[41]

To be sure, some new approaches seem to be proving short-lived. Notwithstanding its vigorous advocacy by B.S. Childs and J.A. Sanders, canon criticism does not seem to have captured the fascination of a sufficiently large group of scholars to outlive its founders for long. Important exceptions include the ongoing efforts of evangelical scholars R.W. Wall and E.C. Lemcio,[42] but a careful reading of their collected essays confirms what is generally true of their predecessors: the valid insights of this discipline are duplicated in other methodologies, most notably redaction, literary, and midrash criticism. On the other hand, its most distinctive elements, as in Childs' emphasis on the post-New Testament canonising community, actually draw attention away from where legitimate hermeneutics should focus, that is, on the final form of the *individual* scriptural documents themselves.[43] Much work still remains to be done on the history of the development of both Old and New Testament canons, doubtless along the lines programmatically suggested by Beckwith and Bruce, respectively.[44] But that of course is a slightly different topic.

---

[40]Scot McKnight (ed.), *Introducing New Testament Interpretation* (Grand Rapids: Baker, 1989); David A. Black and David S. Dockery (eds.), *New Testament Criticism and Interpretation* (Grand Rapids: Zondervan, 1991).

[41]I. Howard Marshall (ed.), *New Testament Interpretation* (Exeter/Grand Rapids: Paternoster/Eerdmans, 1977).

[42]See their recent collection of essays: Robert W. Wall and Eugene C. Lemcio, *The New Testament Canon: A Reader in Canonical Criticism* (JSNTS 76; Sheffield: JSOT Press, 1992).

[43]Cf. Bruce M. Metzger, *The Canon of the New Testament: Its Origin, Development and Significance* (Oxford: Clarendon, 1987) 282-4.

[44]Roger Beckwith, *The Old Testament Canon of the New Testament Church* (London: SPCK, 1985); F.F. Bruce, *The Canon of Scripture* (Leicester: IVP, 1988).

A second discipline which has almost surely played itself out is structuralism,[45] though some of its legacy obviously carries over to post-structuralism, particularly in the two forms biblical studies know best: reader-response criticism and deconstructionism. I will risk predicting the ultimate demise of both of these methodologies as well, at least in their more radical forms, both because of their inherent instability (at root they are self-defeating) and because few real readers outside the rarefied airs of university departments of literature actually read books the way their practitioners do. S.E. Porter's lament that reader-response criticism has not caught on in biblical studies is misguided, as A.C. Thiselton has pointed out.[46] Nevertheless, several of the issues it has raised will persist, for example with respect to the locus of meaning: does it inhere in an author, a text, or a reader, or some combination of the three? Surely the correct answer is the last of these.[47] In fact, Thiselton's patient and detailed analysis of major developments in the history of hermeneutics, and especially its new horizons, is a model for all of us in its thoroughness, eclecticism and quest for metacritical models, generous treatment of views ultimately deemed inadequate, reworking of meaning-significance distinctions in terms of initial actions and truth-claims which are recontextualised, and use of speech-act theory to break down the false dichotomy between propositional and performative language. Now we need someone to popularise Thiselton's findings so that they can be accessible to more than just the most advanced student of hermeneutics.

Literary criticism is likely to continue to flourish, however, in at least three areas: narrative, rhetorical and genre criticism. Evangelicals will need to become increasingly conversant with the specialised terminologies and uses of these disciplines, as some are already doing. *A Complete Literary Guide to the Bible*, edited by L. Ryken and T. Longman III,[48] is scarcely that; most of its essays barely scratch the surface in terms of the literary features a narrative-critical reading of the various biblical texts might disclose. But it is a substantial improvement, as it set out to be, on its predecessor by Alter and Kermode,[49] and it points

---

[45]In New Testament studies it too was overly identified with one individual–Daniel Patte.

[46]Stanley E. Porter, 'Why Hasn't Reader-Response Criticism Caught on in New Testament Studies?', *JLT* 4 (1990) 278-92; Anthony C. Thiselton, *New Horizons in Hermeneutics* (Grand Rapids: Zondervan, 1992) 549.

[47]See my *Interpreting the Parables* (Downers Grove: IVP, 1990) 156-9, and the literature there cited.

[48](Grand Rapids: Zondervan, 1993).

the way forward for future collaborations, particularly if biblical and literary critics could write articles jointly, rather than alternating with one another as in this anthology.

Various evangelical works reflect an increasing appropriation of the possible insights of Greco-Roman rhetoric, for example, the numerous articles by D.F. Watson on the outlines of short Epistles or epistle portions, a major exegetical commentary like Wanamaker's on the Thessalonian letters, or L. Alexander's helpful discussion of Philippians as a family letter.[50] But to date, too few commentaries are appropriating these insights. Alexander's study impinges also on genre criticism, which I have recently surveyed in two different settings[51] and thus forego repeating here. The next step is to incorporate the best insights of these various literary-critical methods into more traditional historical and even theological analyses, rather than pitting each of these three spheres of study (history, theology, and literature) against each other.[52]

Also here to stay are the various sociological criticisms which have spawned an immense, recent bibliography.[53] An important distinction needs to be made between sociology as one component of historical study and the imposition of social-scientific grids developed in different times and cultures onto biblical texts which they may not fit.[54] But even if we limit ourselves to the former, many new illuminating interpretations of texts may still emerge, and others are presently available, which commentators again have not adequately noted. For

---

[49]Robert Alter and Frank Kermode (eds.), *The Literary Guide to the Bible* (Cambridge, MA: Harvard, 1987).

[50]*E.g.*, Duane F. Watson, 'Amplification Techniques in 1 John: The Interaction of Rhetorical Style and Invention', *JSNT* 51 (1993) 99-123; *idem*, 'A Rhetorical Analysis of 2 John according to Greco-Roman Convention', *NTS* 35 (1989) 104-30; *idem*, 'A Rhetorical Analysis of 3 John: A Study in Epistolary Rhetoric', *CBQ* 51 (1989) 479-501; Charles A. Wanamaker, *The Epistles to the Thessalonians* (NIGNT; Exeter/Grand Rapids: Paternoster/Eerdmans, 1990); Loveday Alexander, 'Hellenistic Letter-Forms and the Structure of Philippians', *JSNT* 37 (1989) 87-101.

[51]Craig L. Blomberg, 'New Testament Genre Criticism for the 1990s', *Themelios* 15 (1990) 40-49; *idem*, 'The Diversity of Literary Genres in the New Testament', in Black and Dockery (eds.), *New Testament Criticism*.

[52]As is being recognised by a few (*e.g.*, Mark A. Powell, *What Is Narrative Criticism?* [Minneapolis: Fortress, 1990]). This is one of the strengths of the massive five-volume project of N.T. Wright (see above, n. 11); as spelled out in Vol. 1, *The New Testament and the People of God* (London: SPCK, 1992) 6-28.

[53]See David M. May, *Social-Scientific Criticism of the New Testament: A Bibliography* (Macon: Mercer, 1991).

[54]See Klein, Blomberg, Hubbard, *Biblical Interpretation*, 443-50.

example, in 1987, D.M. May published an important study of Mark
3:20-35 on the implied patterns of kinship Jesus was establishing by
referring to his disciples as family members closer to him than his bio-
logical family.[55] Yet not one of the three major English-language
commentaries on Mark published in subsequent years reflects awareness of the article or its contents more generally.[56] Similarly, in my
research for my Matthew commentary, it was only in examining D.
Patte's structuralist work that I came across a sociological (!) interpretation of Matthew 8:17, and one which I found convincing: the
infirmities Matthew sees Jesus taking away, in fulfilment of the Isaiah
prophecy, are primarily neither spiritual nor physical but *ritual*, corresponding to the three categories of ritually impure and socially
ostracised people Jesus has just healed—the leper, the centurion's servant, and Simon's mother-in-law.[57] I am happy, though, to report seeing
a similar approach in D.E. Garland's new commentary.[58]

The recent compendium of perspectives reflected in Malina and
Rohrbaugh's social-scientific commentary on the Synoptics should
make such interpretations available to a wider audience.[59] Similar
works are needed on the rest of the New Testament, as are balanced,
evangelical critiques. Meanwhile, G.N. Stanton's words, penned in the
context of his contribution to the 'Parting of the Ways' symposium,
offer reasonable guidance in a variety of venues:

> Although I am an unrepentant redaction critic, I am convinced that
> the results garnered from this method of gospel criticism will be more
> compelling when they are supplemented by the insights drawn from
> the social sciences and from narrative criticism.[60]

---

[55]David M. May, 'Mark 3:20-35 from the Perspective of Shame/Honor', *BTB* 17
(1987) 83-7.

[56]Robert A. Guelich, *Mark 1-8:26* (WBC 34A; Dallas: Word, 1989); Morna D.
Hooker, *The Gospel according to Saint Mark* (BNTC; London: Black, 1991); Gundry,
Mark.

[57]Daniel Patte, *The Gospel according to Matthew: A Structural Commentary* (Philadelphia: Fortress, 1987) 117; *cf.* Craig L. Blomberg, *Matthew* (NAC 22; Nashville:
Broadman, 1992) 145.

[58]David E. Garland, *Reading Matthew* (New York: Crossroad, 1993) 107.

[59]Bruce J. Malina and Richard L. Rohrbaugh, *Social-Scientific Commentary on the
Synoptic Gospels* (Minneapolis: Fortress, 1992).

[60]Graham Stanton, 'Matthew's Christology and the Parting of the Ways', in James
D.G. Dunn (ed.), *Jews and Christians: The Parting of the Ways A.D. 70 to 135* (WUNT
66; Tübingen: Mohr, 1992) 101.

Substitute 'historical' for 'redaction' and we have a programmatic mandate for a reasoned eclecticism in the appropriation of scholarly methodologies for the decades ahead. But historical criticism must remain foundational. Once the text is loosed from its historical moorings it may mean anything or nothing.[61]

4. The Globalisation of Hermeneutics

Perhaps this final major category represents the most pressing need of the four. Life in a global village has made biblical interpreters aware as never before of the provincialism of their readings of texts. A burgeoning literature introduces us to Third World readings from a variety of theological perspectives.[62] Increasingly, the term 'globalization' is applied in hermeneutical discussions to reflect this diversity.[63] Definitions of the term vary, but five issues repeatedly come to the fore: a proper response to and appropriation of (1) liberationist hermeneutics, (2) feminist interpretation; (3) biblical teaching on wealth and poverty; (4) religious pluralism; and (5) the contextualisation of the gospel.[64]

Liberation theology early on challenged readers to see salvation in Scripture as not merely (or sometimes not at all!) a spiritual phenomenon but as one with major components of liberation in this life—from oppressive political, social and economic structures. A fair cluster of commentators now recognises that classic liberationist texts like Luke 4:16-19 and 6:20 cannot be limited to *either* physical *or* spiritual salvation but draw on the Old Testament use of עֲנָוִים to refer to those who were both religiously pious and materially impoverished.[65] Good work has been done in studying and applying Revelation 13 as a balance to Romans 13: the state can be a servant of God but it can also be

---

[61]See the appropriate cautions in Donald A. Hagner, 'The New Testament, History, and the Historical-Critical Method', in Black and Dockery (eds.), *New Testament Criticism*, 73-96.

[62]Particularly useful samplers include Priscilla Pope-Levison and John R. Levison, *Jesus in Global Context* (Louisville: Westminster/John Knox, 1992); and R.S. Sugirtharajah (ed.),*Voices from the Margin: Interpreting the Bible in the Third World* (London: SPCK, 1991). The results of five WEF conferences produced the valuable evangelical anthologies, all edited by D.A. Carson and published by Paternoster, on contextualisation, ecclesiology, prayer, justification and worship: *Biblical Interpretation and the Church* (1984); *The Church in the Bible and the World.* (1987); *Teach Us To Pray* (1990); *Right with God* (1992); *Worship: Adoration and Action* (1993).

[63]See, *e.g.*, *Biblical Interpretation* 1.1 (1993). In theological education, the discussion was spawned by Don S. Browning, 'Globalization and the Task of Theological Education in North America', *Theological Education* 23 (Autumn 1986) 43-59.

[64]See especially Alice F. Evans, Robert A. Evans, and David A. Roozen (eds.), *The Globalization of Theological Education* (Maryknoll: Orbis, 1993).

demonic.[66] But many other passages still call out for similarly intense but exegetically nuanced attention: the model of communal sharing in the early chapters of Acts, the principles of Christian stewardship enshrined in 2 Corinthians 8-9, and the implications of the contrasts between Nicodemus and the Samaritan woman in John 3-4.[67] More broadly, we need full-scale exegetical studies of major swathes of the New Testament which articulate what has been called an 'evangelical liberation theology'.[68]

In 1978 R.K. Johnston pointed out how otherwise responsible scholars regularly committed major exegetical gaffes when it came to studying biblical passages involving women's roles in home or church.[69] The vast majority merely found in the texts support for the positions to which they were already committed. It is doubtful if the situation has changed much in the last sixteen years. One has only to read the succession of increasingly implausible interpretations C.C. Kroeger has given for αὐθεντειν in 1 Timothy 2:12 to appreciate this situation: from symbolic murder to engaging in fertility rites to proclaiming oneself the author or creator of someone.[70] On the other hand, there are pleasant exceptions to this trend; the most notable recent one is surely C.S. Keener's carefully argued and thoroughly documented volume on *Paul, Women and Wives*.[71] Patient exegesis may shed still more light on the 'problem passages' in Paul. Interestingly, 1 Corinthians 11:2-16, 14:33b-38 and 1 Timothy 2:8-15 all contain a pair of features which has not yet been explained adequately: appeals to the order of creation that make it difficult to dismiss Paul's logic as merely culture-bound (against the prevailing egalitarian interpretations) and

---

[65]*E.g.*, C.H. Talbert, *Reading Luke* (New York: Crossroad, 1986) 70-72; John Nolland, *Luke 1-9:20* (WBC 35A; Dallas: Word, 1989) 197, 282-3; Robert H. Stein, *Luke* (NAC 24; Nashville: Broadman, 1992) 200-201.

[66]Valuable not only on this topic but on the Apocalypse more generally from key Third-World perspectives are Allan A. Boesak, *Comfort and Protest* (Philadelphia: Westminster, 1987); and Ricardo Foulkes, *El Apocalipsis de San Juan* (Buenos Aires/ Grand Rapids: Nueva Creación/Eerdmans, 1989).

[67]On the last of these see my forthcoming article, 'The Globalization of Biblical Interpretation: A Test Case--John 3-4'.

[68]*Cf.* Craig L. Blomberg, '"Your Faith Has Made You Whole": The Evangelical Liberation Theology of Jesus', in Joel B. Green and Max Turner (eds.), *Jesus of Nazareth: Lord and Christ* (Carlisle/Grand Rapids: Paternoster/Eerdmans, 1994) 75-93.

[69]Robert K. Johnston, 'The Role of Women in the Church and Home: An Evangelical Testcase in Hermeneutics', in W. Ward Gasque and William S. La Sor (eds.), *Scripture, Tradition, and Interpretation* (Grand Rapids: Eerdmans, 1978) 234-56.

[70]All of which are now collected in Kroeger and Kroeger, *I Suffer*, 87-104.

[71]Craig S. Keener, *Paul, Women and Wives* (Peabody: Hendrickson, 1992).

juxtapositions of ἀνήρ and γυνή that seem to require translation as 'husband' and 'wife' rather than just 'man' and 'woman' (against the prevailing hierarchical interpretations). Perhaps it is not too far-fetched to propose a mediating interpretation and application of these passages in which no role or ministry is forbidden to women unless it interferes with appropriate marital relationships.[72]

Evangelical appreciation of the feminist agenda, however, must get beyond preoccupation with the handful of major passages on gender roles and consider fresh readings of less scrutinised texts. One to which I became sensitised only recently involves seeing the Samaritan woman of John 4 as more of an innocent victim than an immoral slut. If women could only rarely initiate divorce in first-century Palestine, is it not more likely that this woman's first four husbands divorced her and that the fifth may have simply left, refusing to grant a legal divorce, and forcing her to seek the protection of a man to whom she was not married?[73] There are of course pitfalls for both traditionalist and feminist approaches, whether we are exegeting the classic 'problem passages' or merely rereading texts through women's eyes. Too much hierarchical exegesis employs hermeneutics which, if applied to the issue of slavery, would have us re-institute it. Too much egalitarian exegesis uses logic which, if applied to the issue of homosexuality, would have us condone it. The latter topic will likely be one of the next to explode in evangelical circles, where it has not already. The careful work of D.F. Wright on this topic sets a good model for some of the rest of us to elaborate in detail.[74]

It is doubtful if First-World Evangelicals on the whole have yet come to grips with the radical nature of New Testament teaching on wealth and poverty, that is, with what Vatican II misleadingly called God's 'preferential option for the poor'. The few that do recognise it easily get carried away and enamoured with the latest secular programmes, even after they have played themselves out in that realm.[75]

---

[72]See especially E. Earle Ellis, *Pauline Theology: Ministry and Society* (Grand Rapids: Eerdmans, 1989) 53-86.

[73]Alice Mathews, *A Woman Jesus Can Teach* (Grand Rapids: Discovery House, 1991) 24-6. *Cf.* Kenneth Grayston, *The Gospel of John* (Philadelphia: Trinity, 1991) 42: 'This is a case of a woman's socio-sexual dependence on the manipulation of men.'

[74]See especially David F. Wright, 'Homosexuals or Prostitutes? The Meaning of Arsenokoitai (1 Cor. 6:9, 1 Tim. 1:10)', *VC* 38 (1984) 125-53; *idem*, 'Homosexuality: The Relevance of the Bible', *EQ* 61 (1989) 291-300.

[75]See the critique by Humberto Belli and Ronald H. Nash (*Beyond Liberation Theology* [Grand Rapids: Baker, 1992]); though it is not clear that Belli's and Nash's economic alternatives are any improvement.

G.A. Getz has produced a semi-popular treatment of a biblical theology of material possessions (almost entirely devoted to New Testament teaching) from a very conservative perspective.[76] What is needed now is a corresponding scholarly treatment which does greater justice to the diversity of scriptural teaching on the topic, arguably summed up by the proverb, 'Give me neither poverty nor riches...' (Prov. 30:8).[77]

Issues of religious pluralism quickly move us again into the realm of biblical and even systematic theology. I, for one, am grateful for the willingness of Evangelicals at last to discuss publicly, and with at least some openness to a variety of answers, the questions about the fate of the unevangelised, redemptive analogies in other religions, Rahner's anonymous Christians, and even the issue of annihilationism.[78] I am rather surprised how closed some of us are to the possibility of God acting redemptively in at least a few lives of those who have not had the chance to hear a credible presentation of the gospel *and* how open some of us are to rejecting hell—as conscious, eternal separation from God.[79] Both trends I believe could have serious, damaging consequences for evangelism.[80] But what is important in this context is that it is clear that we have only scratched the surface when it comes to the detailed exegesis required of the relevant New Testament passages in these various debates. L. Newbigin's magisterial theological treatment of pluralism[81] needs to be matched by equally sophisticated biblical study. This becomes uniquely urgent in

---

[76]Gene A. Getz, *A Biblical Theology of Material Possessions* (Chicago: Moody, 1990).

[77]For an already existing model approximating somewhat to the balance I have in mind, *cf.* Thomas E. Schmidt, *Hostility to Wealth in the Synoptic Gospels* (JSNTS 15; Sheffield: JSOT Press, 1987).

[78]See especially William V. Crockett and James G. Sigountos (eds.), *Through No Fault of Their Own?* (Grand Rapids: Baker, 1991); and John Sanders, *No Other Name* (Grand Rapids: Eerdmans, 1992). *Cf.* already, Don Richardson, *Eternity in Their Hearts* (Ventura: Regal, 1981).

[79]For the former, see several of the contributors to Andrew D. Clarke and Bruce W. Winter (eds.), *One God, One Lord in a World of Religious Pluralism* (Cambridge: Tyndale, 1991); the most famous example of the latter now of course is John Stott in David L. Edwards and John Stott, *Essentials: A Liberal-Evangelical Dialogue* (London: Hodder & Stoughton, 1988) 312-20.

[80]Not allowing that the dead relatives and friends of newly evangelised people groups might be saved alienates many would-be converts from the gospel; not believing in conscious eternal punishment leaves many in regions hostile to Christianity with inadequate incentive in the present to believe.

[81]Lesslie Newbigin, *The Gospel in a Pluralist Society* (Geneva/Grand Rapids: WCC/Eerdmans, 1989).

the arena of modern Jewish-Christian relationships, in which rightful concern to avoid anti-Semitism leads many to compromise biblical teaching and propose exegetically untenable alternatives—most notably the 'two covenants' theory which claims that Jews can reject Jesus and still be saved under the Old Testament economy.[82]

Contextualising the gospel must begin with a recognition of the New Testament's own role in that process: the varying speeches in Acts, 'the kingdom of God' in a Jewish milieu being transposed into 'eternal life' in a Hellenistic one, the differences between the life-settings of James and Galatians that diminish the tension between those two Epistles, and so on.[83] Particularly instructive as we move to the contemporary world are treatments of a theme or section of Scripture in light of modern-day cultures that are actually closer in some respects to biblical cultures than our technological First-World societies. In this vein, and though not agreeing with every detail, I find E. Tamez's and P.U. Maynard-Reid's expositions of James very challenging, precisely because of the parallels between the oppressive social and economic structures of Latin America and the situation in which James' Jewish-Christian community found itself.[84] Few traditional commentaries adequately discuss this *Sitz im Leben*.[85] Ironically, one of the contemporary cultures often most neglected in the current concern to contextualise is that of the traditional Middle-Eastern peasant village. Here is where I find K. Bailey's works on the parables so refreshing, specifically because they stand a good chance of recovering some of the original dynamics of Jesus' own context.[86] But who will take Bailey's place when he retires? And who is doing comparable work on other parts of the Bible?

---

[82]Balanced models of the way discussion should proceed include the two anthologies edited by Dunn (*Parting of the Ways*) and Craig A. Evans and Donald A. Hagner (*Anti-Semitism and Early Christianity* [Minneapolis: Fortress, 1993]).

[83]A theme appropriately stressed by an excellent African-American contextualiser, Cain H. Felder. See his *Troubling Biblical Waters* (Maryknoll: Orbis, 1989); and *Stony the Road We Trod* (Minneapolis: Fortress, 1991).

[84]Elsa Tamez, *The Scandalous Message of James* (New York: Crossroad, 1990); Pedrito U. Maynard-Reid, *Poverty and Wealth in James* (Maryknoll: Orbis, 1987). Less compelling but still useful is Elsa Tamez on justification by faith in Paul: *The Amnesty of Grace* (Nashville: Abingdon, 1993).

[85]An important exception, in the main, is Peter H. Davids, *The Epistle of James* (NIGNT; Grand Rapids/Exeter: Paternoster/Eerdmans, 1982).

[86]Kenneth E. Bailey, *Poet and Peasant: A Literary-Cultural Approach to the Parables of Luke* (Grand Rapids: Eerdmans, 1976) and *Through Peasant Eyes: More Lukan Parables, Their Culture and Style* (Grand Rapids: Eerdmans, 1980).

III. Additional Needs

1. Verbal Aspect in Greek

Probably the most significant development to emerge out of the last generation of study in linguistics is the appreciation of verbal aspect in Hellenistic Greek. Irrespective of the debate between Porter and Fanning over details,[87] the agreements reflected in the massive studies of these meticulous scholars should inaugurate a new era in our understanding of the significance of tense, in both indicative and non-indicative moods, in the Greek of the New Testament.[88] Unfortunately, it is not yet obvious that this is happening. Commentaries continue to perpetuate long-since disproved fallacies about the meanings of aorists, the tenses of imperatives, and so on. And recognition that tense shifts may reflect actions that are more or less heavily 'marked' has scarcely entered into the broader world of New Testament scholarship at all.

An important exception appears in Seifrid's recent thesis. In discussing the changes from past to present tense between Romans 7:7-13 and vv. 14-25, Seifrid notes that verbal aspect now supplies the grammatical support that was previously lacking for the suggestion that Paul is still talking about his pre-Christian life. The shift could reflect not change in time but movement from the narration of an event to description of a condition. But Seifrid rightly goes on to note that observations about verbal aspect must be combined with attention to deictic indicators, which he believes in this instance are sufficient to demonstrate that Paul has in fact shifted to a discussion of his present, Christian experience.[89]

2. The Use of the Old Testament in the New

In the early- to mid-1980s, several evangelical studies began to enumerate the various options for understanding the diverse ways Old Testament quotations are used in the New Testament.[90] Since then, no

---

[87]See Stanley E. Porter and D.A. Carson (eds.), *Biblical Greek Language and Linguistics: Open Questions in Current Research* (JSNTS 80; Sheffield: JSOT Press, 1993). For a mediating position *cf.* also K.L. McKay, 'Time and Aspect in New Testament Greek', *NovT* 34 (1992) 209-28.

[88]Stanley E. Porter, *Verbal Aspect in the Greek of the New Testament, with Reference to Tense and Mood* (Studies in Biblical Greek 1; New York: Peter Lang, 1989); Buist M. Fanning, *Verbal Aspect in New Testament Greek* (Oxford: Clarendon, 1990). *Cf.* now especially K.L. McKay, *A New Syntax of the Verb in New Testament Greek: An Aspectual Approach* (New York: Peter Lang, 1994).

[89]Mark A. Seifrid, *Justification by Faith*, 234.

one has taken up the task of applying these taxonomies in more detail. To be sure we have had several important collections of essays, especially the Lindars *Festschrift*, and two anthologies on Paul and Luke by Evans and Sanders.[91] But frustratingly absent from most of these works is discussion of the legitimacy of the various hermeneutical techniques employed. For Evangelicals, pressing questions ought to include: (1) Can the exegetical techniques of the New Testament writers be defended as valid? (2) If so, what does this do to the narrowness of our conventional modern historico-grammatical approaches? (3) If not, what does this do to our doctrines of the authority and inspiration of Scripture?

The appeal to an unrepeatable hermeneutic on the grounds that the New Testament writers were inspired[92] is an unfalsifiable approach and therefore surely a cul-de-sac. M. Wilcox has pointed out briefly and D.L. Bock in more detail how a number of the uses of different text-forms may involve passages in which the main point a New Testament writer wishes to make could still stand even in alternate translations.[93] As the Dead Sea Scrolls continue to emerge, we will become even more conversant with variant Old Testament text forms, and this line of study ought to yield further insights. No doubt several important theses in this area yet remain to be written.

3. New Testament Theology

In keeping with themes noted in various places above, we dare not allow methodological debates about historical vs. literary methods to blind us to the importance of continuing to do exegetically responsible biblical and specifically New Testament *theology*. It is a pity that D.A.

---

[90]See especially Moisés Silva, 'The New Testament Use of the Old Testament: Text Form and Authority', in D.A. Carson and John D. Woodbridge (eds.), *Scripture and Truth* (Grand Rapids/Leicester: Zondervan/IVP, 1983) 147-65; Darrell L. Bock, 'Evangelicals and the Use of the Old Testament in the New', *BSac* 142 (1985) 209-23, 306-19; Douglas J. Moo, 'The Problem of *Sensus Plenior*', in D.A. Carson and John D. Woodbridge (eds.), *Hermeneutics, Authority, and Canon* (Grand Rapids/ Leicester: Zondervan/IVP, 1986) 175-211.

[91]D.A. Carson and H.G.M. Williamson (eds.), *It Is Written: Scripture Citing Scripture* (Cambridge: CUP, 1988); Craig A. Evans and James A. Sanders, (eds.), *Paul and the Scriptures of Israel* (JSNTS 83; Sheffield: JSOT Press, 1993); Craig A. Evans and James A. Sanders, *Luke and Scripture* (Minneapolis: Fortress, 1993).

[92]As notably in Richard N. Longenecker, 'Can We Reproduce the Exegesis of the New Testament?', *TynB* 21 (1970) 3-38.

[93]Max Wilcox, 'Text Form', in Carson and Williamson (eds.),*It Is Written*, 193-204; Darrell L. Bock, *Proclamation from Prophecy and Pattern* (JSNTS 12; Sheffield: JSOT Press, 1987).

Hagner felt unable to make the thorough revision to George Ladd's eminently useful textbook he originally intended to, though we remain grateful for the up-to-date additions of articles by R.T. France and D. Wenham.[94] Someone who *is* up to the task of a full-scale evangelical work of Ladd's format would provide us with an invaluable service. On an even grander scale I commend N.T. Wright's vision of a five-volume work on Christian origins.[95] I suspect some of the rest of us need to dream similarly big dreams and then set an agenda for our study over several decades that will make sterling results possible.

Also needed, however, are individual works on the theologies of specific writers or corpora and of themes which are traced throughout the various New Testament witnesses. Particularly crucial for the latter will be an assessment of the proper balance of unity and diversity among those witnesses. For an article-length model which approximates this balance, I laud D.L. Peterson's work on 'Worship in the New Testament' in the WEF symposium.[96] I am encouraged, too, by the plans for a series to be published by IVP and Eerdmans, entitled *New Studies in Biblical Theology*, along precisely these lines and in somewhat conscious imitation of some of the earlier volumes in the old SCM series with a similar name.[97]

4. The Book of Acts

As one who participated in several stages of the Tyndale House Gospels Project,[98] I am delighted to see how competently its successor on the Book of Acts is developing. There may never be another Colin Hemer,[99] but the six volumes in the series, *The Book of Acts in Its First Century Setting*, show promise of addressing with remarkable comprehensiveness the issues surrounding a correct interpretation of this portion of the New Testament.[100] I hope that plans are finalised to pro-

---

[94]George E. Ladd, *A Theology of the New Testament*, (rev. ed.; Grand Rapids: Eerdmans, 1993).
[95]See above, n. 11.
[96]David L. Peterson, 'Worship in the New Testament', in D.A. Carson (ed.),*Worship*, 51-91. *Cf.* now his book-length treatment, covering both Old and New Testament: *Engaging with God: A Biblical Theology of Worship* (Leicester: IVP, 1992).
[97]The series editor is to be D.A. Carson.
[98]With articles in *Gospel Perspectives*, Vols. 3, 5 and 6, and as co-editor of Vol. 6.
[99]See above, n. 13.
[100]Published as of this writing are Bruce W. Winter and Andrew D. Clarke (eds.), *The Book of Acts in Its Ancient Literary Setting* (Carlisle/Grand Rapids: Paternoster/Eerdmans, 1993); and David W.J. Gill and Conrad Gempf (eds.), *The Book of Acts in Its Graeco-Roman Setting* (Carlisle/Grand Rapids: Paternoster/Eerdmans, 1994).

duce a one-volume digest more accessible to the wider public, much as my *Historical Reliability of the Gospels* did for the Gospels Project,[101] though I am not hereby requesting an invitation to perform that task!

Somewhere along the way, too, I hope that the issues raised by M. Hengel's and C. Hill's recent works can be tackled in some detail.[102] It seems to me that a synthesis is needed between their thesis and antithesis, namely, that the Hebrews and Hellenists of Acts 6 were more theologically diverse than most commentators have admitted but that one important strand of Hellenistic Jewish Christianity, particularly exemplified by Stephen, did provide important precursors to Paul's more radical law-free mission to the Gentiles. Such a synthesis presumably could be produced without jettisoning the odd portions of Acts which Hengel finds historically unreliable or the more major chunks which Hill rejects.

5. Corinth and Charisma

Still in keeping with recent contributions by members of our Fellowship, I wish to express appreciation for the numerous works on the social setting and make-up of the Corinthian church by D.W.J. Gill, B.W. Winter, and A.D. Clarke.[103] Of immense value, too, is B. Witherington's sociological commentary on 1 Corinthians.[104] With all this groundwork complete, it seems that the next logical step is to reconstruct in detail a Pauline ecclesiology which lays to rest once-and-for-all the numerous false dichotomies between institutionalisation and charisma. Perhaps this can be a springboard to re-evaluating the nature of the communities addressed by the allegedly deutero-Pauline literature on a number of theological fronts, which in turn should shed new light on the rather stagnant debates about the authorship of those letters.[105]

As Clarke has pointed out, the implications of feuding patrons and the relationships with their clients may explain almost every

---

[101](Leicester/Downers Grove: IVP, 1987).

[102]Martin Hengel, *Between Jesus and Paul* (London: SCM, 1983); *idem*, *The Pre-Christian Paul* (London: SCM, 1991); Craig C. Hill, *Hellenists and Hebrews: Re-appraising Division within the Earliest Church* (Minneapolis: Fortress, 1992).

[103]*E.g.*, David W.J. Gill, 'In Search of the Social Elite in the Corinthian Church', *TynB* 44 (1993) 323-37; Bruce W. Winter, 'Theological and Ethical Responses to Religious Pluralism—1 Corinthians 8-10', *TynB* 41 (1990) 209-26; and especially Andrew D. Clarke, *Secular and Christian Leadership in Corinth* (AGAJU 18; Leiden: Brill, 1993).

[104]Ben Witherington, *Conflict and Community in Corinth* (Grand Rapids: Eerdmans, 1994).

debate which Paul addresses in 1 Corinthians, even though Clarke has developed this thesis in detail only for the Epistle's first six chapters.[106] It would be good, therefore, to extend his treatment to cover the rest of the letter. And if Winter is right that sophistry, rather than proto-Gnosticism or Hellenistic Judaism of some other kind, is the dominant ideology behind the problems of Paul's opponents,[107] then we need a published version of this thesis applied to each of the theological issues encountered. Might new illumination still appear, for example, on what the women of 1 Corinthians 11 and 14 were doing in their preaching, prophesying and asking of questions?

6. Epistolary Pseudonymity

Little significant has been done in this area since R.J. Bauckham's provocative treatments of 2 Peter in detail and of 'pseudo-apostolic letters' in brief.[108] And while Bauckham argues for a form of pseudonymity (the testamentary genre) which should be in principle acceptable to Evangelicals, the question remains open as to whether or not the early church would have admitted it.[109] Significantly, en route to his conclusions Bauckham has also provided a robust defence of the traditional authorship of Jude and has hinted at the same for James, 1 Peter and Colossians.[110] D.G. Meade's book showed how pseudonymity probably would have functioned had it been acceptable in early Christianity but did not actually demonstrate the plausibility of that premise.[111]

We have tended to defer greatly to the prevailing scholarly consensus concerning the authorship, date and setting of books like

---

[105] I think particularly of a work like Philip H. Towner, *The Goal of Our Instruction: The Structure of Theology and Ethics in the Pastoral Epistles* (JSNTS 34; Sheffield: JSOT Press, 1989).

[106] See n. 103.

[107] Bruce W. Winter, 'Are Philo and Paul Among the Sophists?' (Ph.D., Macquarrie, 1988), forthcoming in SNTS from CUP; *cf.* Stephen M. Pogoloff, *Logos and Sophia: The Rhetorical Situation of 1 Corinthians* (SBLDS 134; Atlanta: Scholars, 1992).

[108] Richard J. Bauckham, *Jude, 2 Peter* (WBC 50; Waco: Word, 1983); *idem,* 'Pseudo-Apostolic Letters', *JBL* 107 (1988) 464-94.

[109] As has been reasserted by Donald Guthrie, *New Testament Introduction* (Leicester: IVP, 1990[4]) 1011-28; E. Earle Ellis, 'Pseudonymity and Canonicity of New Testament Documents', in Michael J. Wilkins and Terence Paige (eds.),*Worship, Theology and Ministry in the Early Church* (JSNTS 87; Sheffield: JSOT Press, 1992) 212-24; and Tommy D. Lea, 'Pseudonymity and the New Testament', in Black and Dockery (eds.),*New Testament Criticism*, 533-59.

[110] See n. 108. *Cf.* also Richard Bauckham, *Jude and the Relatives of Jesus* (Edinburgh: T.&T. Clark, 1990).

[111] David G. Meade, *Pseudonymity and Canon* (Grand Rapids: Eerdmans, 1987).

Ephesians and the Pastoral Epistles; perhaps it is time to tackle those questions head on. What we need is a work of at least the scope of A.T. Lincoln's commentary on Ephesians[112] which explores in detail the possibility of Pauline authorship and relates the resulting *Sitz im Leben* to the contents of the book at each stage of the argument, so that we can judge which reading is more persuasive. We all look forward to Marshall and Towner on the Pastorals;[113] perhaps they will help us determine more definitively whether Pauline authorship of these three letters is indeed viable.

7. A New Look on Hebrews?

In an age that has re-established Jesus, John and Paul in their Jewish contexts, it is somewhat ironic that a similar new look has yet to affect as markedly the one book in the New Testament traditionally entitled 'to the Hebrews'. To be sure, Lane's detailed commentary places this Epistle well within the framework of pre-70 Jewish-Christianity in Rome.[114] But Lane, like Ellingworth, Attridge, and every other recent major study on this Epistle, assumes that the boundaries between Judaism and Christianity are already clearly defined.[115] Thus the overwhelming trend among exegetes is to take Hebrews' well-known warning passages as implying that the author believed some in his audience were genuinely in danger of losing their salvation, though the point is not always stated as baldly as that. Perhaps evangelical biblical theology has not yet adequately emerged from the shadows of systematic theology to realise the equally important role that *both* disciplines play.[116] But unless one is prepared to argue that Paul and John also see perseverance from a perspective compatible with Arminianism, serious problems remain for the Evangelical who would interpret Hebrews in that direction.[117]

But laying both systematic theology and the witness of the rest of the New Testament to one side for a moment, is it so obvious that the

---

[112]Andrew T. Lincoln, *Ephesians* (WBC 42; Dallas: Word, 1990).

[113]In the revised ICC series (Edinburgh: T.&T. Clark, forthcoming). Suggestive pointers in the right direction appear in the historical studies of Clinton E. Arnold; see especially his *Ephesians—Power and Magic* (Cambridge: CUP, 1989).

[114]William L. Lane, *Hebrews*, 2 vols. (WBC 47A and B; Dallas: Word, 1991).

[115]*Cf.* Paul Ellingworth, *The Epistle to the Hebrews* (NIGNT; Carlisle/Grand Rapids: Paternoster/Eerdmans, 1993); Harold W. Attridge, *The Epistle to the Hebrews* (Hermeneia; Philadelphia: Fortress, 1989).

[116]For pointers in the right direction from the perspective of a biblical scholar, see D.A. Carson, 'Unity and Diversity in the New Testament', in Carson and Woodbridge (eds.), *Scripture and Truth*, 65-95.

author of Hebrews believes he is writing exclusively or even predominantly to Christians? The data of 6:4-6 and 10:26-39 are notoriously susceptible to both Calvinist and Arminian interpretations.[118] But I have looked in vain for a treatment of 4:2 which convinces me that the author of this letter believed the Israelites to whom he compared his congregation truly believed. Notwithstanding the various possible readings, the NIV makes the point adequately: 'For we also have had the gospel preached to us, just as they did; but the message they heard was of no value to them, because those who heard did not combine it with faith.' Is it not inherently more likely that this Epistle was addressed to a community of Jewish people for whom the boundaries between Judaism and Christianity were far more fluid than we normally assume? And the more we appreciate covenantal nomism and related trends in first-century Judaism, is it so improbable that our author might have addressed Jews whom he had suspected had not yet fully embraced Christianity with the terminology of enlightenment, sharing in the Holy Spirit, sanctification, and so on? I am intrigued by the research of D. Stoutenburg in Winnipeg who is compiling a commentary of largely rabbinic materials relevant to the exegesis of Hebrews and is suggesting precisely such a background. But the slow pace at which it is proceeding suggests that there is plenty of room for others to undertake a similar task.[119]

8. Revisioning the Apocalypse

In the last fifteen years, six major critical English-language commentaries on Romans have appeared,[120] but none on Revelation. The mid-level works of the mid-seventies by Mounce and Beasley-Murray, and to a lesser extent Ladd, still prove profitable,[121] but a major work from

---

[117]Such compatibilism is of course possible; see already I. Howard Marshall, *Kept by the Power of God* (London: Epworth, 1969). Whether or not it is fully persuasive, however, is another matter.

[118]*Cf.* especially Roger Nicole, 'Some Comments on Hebrews 6:4-6 and the Doctrine of the Perseverance of God with the Saints', in Gerald F. Hawthorne (ed.), *Current Issues in Biblical and Patristic Interpretation* (Grand Rapids: Eerdmans, 1975) 355-64; with Scot McKnight, 'The Warning Passages of Hebrews: A Formal Analysis and Theological Conclusions', *TrinJ* n.s. 13 (1992) 21-59.

[119]Dennis Stoutenburg, *Hebrews: In Jewish Perspective* (manuscript in preparation, no publisher definitely committed as of this writing).

[120]Cranfield, Dunn, Moo, Fitzmyer (see nn. 25, 27, 36, and 37 above); and, in translation, Ernst Käsemann, *Commentary on Romans* (Grand Rapids: Eerdmans, 1980) and Peter Stuhlmacher, *Paul's Letter to the Romans. A Commentary* (Louisville: Westminster/John Knox, 1994).

an Evangelical fully abreast of recent research on apocalyptic still awaits us. Aune's contribution to the Word Biblical Commentary series will surely be outstanding but it is unclear how evangelical it will be.[122] R.L. Thomas' work in progress is obviously evangelical but reflects an old-line dispensationalist hermeneutic which is out of touch even with developments within that tradition, to say nothing of the broader world of scholarship on Revelation.[123] What is needed is a balance between futurism and preterism, between prophecy and apocalyptic, which affirms that Revelation points to genuinely future events, even in some detail, but with imagery that is intelligible only in the light of its original thought world and cannot be correlated in advance with any unfolding scenario of contemporary events.[124]

Alongside the necessary exegesis are needed ongoing discussions of Revelation's theology. I am particularly encouraged by Bauckham's two recent volumes, both big and small, though I wonder about his innovations dealing with 'the conversion of the nations';[125] at any rate, we need other works to complement his. I am distressed that the two most useful introductions to the topic for the level of students I regularly teach, by D. Guthrie and G. Goldsworthy, are both out of print, at least in the United States, though neither is yet ten years old.[126] Responsible evangelical handling of Revelation will become all the more crucial, I fear, as we near the intriguing year 2000, and as irresponsible grass-roots date-setting and popular prophecy handbooks increasingly embarrass all Evangelicals in the public eye via guilt by

---

[121]Robert H. Mounce, *The Book of Revelation* (NICNT; Grand Rapids: Eerdmans, 1977); George R. Beasley-Murray, *The Book of Revelation* (NCB; London: Oliphants, 1974); George E. Ladd, *A Commentary on the Revelation of John* (Grand Rapids: Eerdmans, 1972).

[122]*Cf.*, *e.g.*, the brief remarks in David E. Aune, *The New Testament in Its Literary Environment* (Philadelphia: Westminster, 1987) 226-52.

[123]Robert L. Thomas, *Revelation 1-7* (WEC; Chicago: Moody, 1992). Contrast Thomas with Craig A. Blaising and Darrell L. Bock, *Progressive Dispensationalism* (Wheaton: Victor, 1993); and Robert L. Saucy, *The Case for Progressive Dispensationalism* (Grand Rapids: Zondervan, 1993).

[124]Note, *e.g.*, how Frederick D. Mazzaferri's work re-emphasises the prophetic nature of Revelation against a prevailing imbalance in the apocalyptic direction (*The Genre of the Book of Revelation from a Source-Critical Perspective* [BZNW 54; Berlin: de Gruyter, 1989]). I am told that Gregory K. Beale's forthcoming NIGNT volume on Revelation (Carlisle/Grand Rapids: Paternoster/Eerdmans) may fill this niche.

[125]Richard J. Bauckham, *The Climax of Prophecy: Studies on the Book of Revelation* (Edinburgh: T.&T. Clark, 1993); *idem*, *The Theology of the Book of Revelation* (Cambridge: CUP, 1993).

association. Fourteen years ago, E. Schüssler Fiorenza suggested that 'the theological-doctrinal and the historical-critical paradigms of interpretation need to be integrated into a new literary paradigm that could do justice to the symbolic-mythopoeic language as well as historical communicative situation of the book.'[127] That work remains to be written; how exciting if it could be done from an evangelical perspective! A balanced view of Christian social ethics might even follow as a corollary.[128]

IV. Conclusion

I conclude with a plea for relevance. I would hope that it goes without saying that all evangelical scholarship, at whatever level, should have service to the church and the larger interests of God's kingdom clearly in view. We cannot take it for granted, however, that anyone else will perceive as relevant what we see as such, so we must explicitly articulate the connections. Concluding chapters on the contemporary application of technical research can help in this respect, as in the books by D. Hill on New Testament prophecy or R. Latourelle on Jesus' miracles.[129] We should probably refuse to participate in all new commentary series on the New Testament, at least until the current round is complete, except where they help readers focus on applications which have not previously been stressed. Zondervan's forthcoming NIV Application Commentary series holds out the potential, at least, of making a significant contribution on this front.[130]

---

[126]D. Guthrie, *The Relevance of John's Apocalypse* (Grand Rapids: Eerdmans, 1987); G. Goldsworthy, *The Gospel in Revelation* (Nashville: Thomas Nelson, 1985). Partial replacements, though in less helpful formats, are Bruce M. Metzger, *Breaking the Code: Understanding the Book of Revelation* (Nashville: Abingdon, 1992); and J. Ramsey Michaels, *Interpreting the Book of Revelation* (Grand Rapids: Baker, 1992). But neither focuses as much on the *theology* of the book.

[127]Elisabeth Schüssler Fiorenza, 'Revelation', in Epp and MacRae (eds.),*The New Testament*, 420 (where the editors indicate the manuscript was completed in 1980).

[128]*Cf.* Adela Yarbro Collins (*Crisis and Catharsis: The Power of the Apocalypse* [Philadelphia: Westminster, 1984] 174-5) on the appropriation of the political theology of Johannes Metz.

[129]David Hill, *New Testament Prophecy* (London: Marshall, Morgan & Scott, 1979) 193-213; René Latourelle, *The Miracles of Jesus and the Theology of Miracles* (New York: Paulist, 1988) 299-333.

[130]The two inaugural volumes, on 1 Corinthians and Galatians, are due to appear in 1995.

The requirements of doctoral theses alone will ensure that Evangelicals, as long as they continue to proliferate in biblical studies, will produce scholarly tomes. There also seems to be no lack of popular writers in our midst, though we scholars often need to help them gain access to the most reliable research. What arguably could use some bolstering is the body of mid-level, semi-popular works, written by responsible scholars, often as an outgrowth of their own more technical work, to help bridge the gaps between town and gown, church and seminary. I think here of works like C.E. Arnold's *Powers of Darkness* or D. Wenham's *Parables of Jesus*.[131] Some might even consider a calling to this level of writing.

Most challenging of all, we must find ways in this 'information age' to disseminate the results of evangelical biblical scholarship to people in countless cultures who do not have the myriad of resources in their own language which we have, and to get our views even in the English-speaking world into the hands of a biblically illiterate population. Particularly with increasingly large numbers of foreign and home missionaries retiring, we need a new generation of scholars willing to sacrifice certain pleasures for the sake of teaching overseas, translating good books (or advising others who do so), mastering the latest computer and media technology, developing innovative forms of education by extension, supporting indigenous biblical scholarship in non-Euro-American cultures and, more generally, seeking to integrate biblical studies with a wide variety of other religious and academic disciplines. That should keep all of us sufficiently occupied for years to come!

---

[131]Clinton E. Arnold, *Powers of Darkness: Principalities and Powers in Paul's Letters* (Downers Grove: IVP, 1992); David Wenham, *The Parables of Jesus: Pictures of Revolution* (London: Hodder & Stoughton, 1989).

CHAPTER 4

'Written for Us': Paul's View of Scripture

Brian S. Rosner

Summary

This essay considers the question of the nature and purpose of Scripture according to Paul. Although he has little to say directly on the subject Paul's view may be discerned from the way in which he refers to and cites Scripture. Paul regarded the Scriptures as the very words of God which were written for the ethical instruction of Christians and as a testimony to the gospel. Paul's view has much in common with the Jewish views of his day and may be summed up in his own words: Scripture was 'written for us'.

I. Introduction

The relationship between Paul and the Jewish Scriptures has been explored at many different levels and has long been recognised as a key to understanding his thought. High on the agenda of research on this subject are the following questions: What is the extent of Paul's canon of Scripture? Why does Paul cite Scripture explicitly in some cases and not in others? Why are the quotations numerous in only four of his letters? What is the purpose of the quotations of and allusions to Scripture in Paul's letters? Why does the wording of such quotations often differ markedly from all known versions of the biblical text? How does Paul's exegesis of Scripture compare with contemporary Jewish practice? Does Paul engage in allegorisation? Is his interpretation of Scripture largely non-contextual? What is Paul's attitude to the law of Moses? While all of these questions represent valid and fruitful avenues of enquiry, our concern in this essay is to ask a more fundamental question. It is not, what does Paul do with Scripture, but how does Paul conceive of Scripture? According to Paul, what is Scripture and what are its major functions?

It is surprising that this question, which after all concerns a presupposition for all other questions in the area, has not been given more attention. Modern discussions of the New Testament view of the Old Testament Scriptures usually concentrate on the two classic texts, 2 Timothy 3:16-17 and, outside the traditional Pauline corpus, 2 Peter 1:19-21. Even the vast literature spawned by the controversy about the inspiration and authority of the Bible in the USA in the 1980s did little with Paul's view of Scripture. In particular, this literature virtually ignored Paul's historical context, that is, the way in which first-century Jews viewed Scripture.[1] The *Dictionary of Paul and his Letters,* accurately subtitled, *A Compendium of Contemporary Biblical Scholarship*, has substantial articles on 'Law', 'The Old Testament in Paul' and 'Paul the Jew', but omits any substantial discussion of our question.[2] Pauline theologies and studies of Paul's use of the Old Testament likewise say very little. The late nineteenth-century Princeton theologian B.B. Warfield was, to my knowledge, the last to take seriously the Jewish context

---

[1]Scot McKnight makes this point in a review of Kern Robert Trembath, *Evangelical Theories of Biblical Inspiration: A Review and Proposal, CBQ* 50 (1988) 738: 'T.'s work reflects a very typical historical weakness of modern discussions of Scripture: *i.e.,* how did 1st-century Jews and Christians conceive of Scripture?'

[2]Edited by Gerald F. Hawthorne, Ralph P. Martin and Daniel G. Reid (Downers Grove/Leicester: IVP, 1993).

for New Testament views of Scripture. The study of early Judaism has of course moved on since his day, the two most obvious developments being the revival of interest in the Old Testament Pseudepigrapha and the discovery of the Dead Sea Scrolls.

Perhaps the subject has been neglected because of a dearth of relevant primary source material. Paul makes very few explicit comments on his view of Scripture, especially in the undisputed letters. As Clark H. Pinnock has written, 'Paul can write Romans and Galatians without bothering to discuss a doctrine of Scripture.'[3] Pinnock suggests that 'Paul does not discuss the nature of inspiration or the degree to which the Scriptures are reliable... He is simply not interested.'[4] Is Pinnock right in this assertion?

Just as serious an objection to this investigation would be that Paul's view of Scripture is too obvious to warrant attention. One could argue that his was a very high view, and that this is not in dispute. R.P.C. and A.T. Hanson express a widely held view when they state: 'The New Testament writers *like all devout Jews* in their time believed that the Old Testament scriptures were inspired writings.'[5] What could be worse for an essay than to have no data to investigate and no opponents to refute? Let us consider these two objections.

First, the sociology of knowledge cautions us not to expect Paul necessarily to expound directly every subject that is important to him. The Jewish Scriptures are a vital part of the symbolic world of Paul and the churches to which he wrote. Luke T. Johnson explains what sociologists mean by this term:

> A symbolic world is a system of shared meaning that enables us to live together as a group... it involves in particular the fundamental perceptions that ground the community's existence and that therefore do no need debate or justification... the symbolic world shared by a group can be discerned from the things that *go without saying*.[6]

That Paul does not tell us his view of Scripture may indicate, then, not that it is unimportant to him but that it is too important to call for comment. The argument from relative silence carries no weight here.

---

[3]*The Scripture Principle* (San Francisco: Harper & Row, 1984) 40.
[4]*The Scripture Principle*, 40.
[5]*The Bible Without Illusions* (London/Philadelphia: SCM/Trinity, 1989) 57 (italics added).
[6]*The Writings of the New Testament: An Interpretation* (London: SCM, 1986) 13 (italics added). Thanks are due to Roy Ciampa for drawing my attention to this and the following book.

Central to understanding any group, then, is the notion of 'shared understandings'.[7] A certain view of the Scriptures is a presupposition for Paul. The occasional nature of his letters, which largely address specific problems in the communities, supports this supposition. If the churches did not question Paul's view of Scripture then we should not expect it to receive extended treatment. We shall argue, however, that there are numerous implicit and incidental indications of his view which repay careful attention. Even if a particular conception of Scripture is assumed by Paul when writing to his churches, this may be given expression as it were indirectly when he refers to or cites Scripture.

Secondly, some scholars cast doubt on the impression that Paul regarded Scripture as highly as we might suppose, 'like all devout Jews' (to recall the words of the Hanson brothers). Christopher M. Tuckett has observed that at times Paul disregards scriptural teaching in a starkly un-Jewish fashion. Paul is willing to 'criticize and even reject' biblical laws.[8] Tuckett insists that 'Paul's attitude goes far beyond that of a Jewish teacher adapting the Law to a changed situation'.[9] James D.G. Dunn, in expounding his notion of Scripture, both Old and New Testaments, as the living word, argues that in 'abandoning' biblical teaching on food, the Sabbath and circumcision Paul 'was a heretic', at least in the eyes of 'any good Jew'.[10] Pinnock writes in a similar context:

> Thus it is not the Judaic Scripture principle that they [Christians] accept but a Christian one in which the Old Testament is a premessianic trajectory finding fulfillment in the gospel and not possessing absolute and independent authority. Of course each Old Testament provision was the Word of God in a historical sense, but it is not necessarily a Word addressed to us. The text is 'infallible' in this special sense for us, but not in the sense that it was infallible for Jews.[11]

Would Paul have agreed that Scripture is not a word addressed 'to us'? Others have pointed to the way Paul actively shapes the wording of his quotations from Scripture, which are seldom verbatim, to indicate that, as a Christian, Paul holds a somewhat diminished view of the author-

---

[7] Howard Clark Kee, *Knowing the Truth: A Sociological Approach to New Testament Interpretation* (Minneapolis: Fortress, 1989) 67.
[8] 'Paul, Tradition and Freedom', *Theologische Zeitschrift* 47/4 (1991) 310.
[9] *Ibid.*, 313.
[10] *The Living Word* (London: SCM, 1987) 60.
[11] *The Scripture Principle*, 44.

ity of the Jewish Scriptures. Still others, including A.T. Hanson and B.S. Easton, have asserted that the high regard for scriptural tradition in the Pastoral Epistles, especially in 2 Timothy 3:16-17, is a distortion of the freer attitude we find in Paul.[12] Indeed, Frances Young has observed that:

> A number of Christian scholars have asked in recent decades whether the Bible has not been asked to bear too much weight, whether the appropriate place of scripture in Christianity may not be quite different from its place in... Judaism.[13]

Several scholars for a variety of reasons distance Paul from Jews on the subject of Scripture.

Is Paul's view of Scripture identifiably Jewish? Or did the Damascus road experience drastically alter his view? The question of the Jewishness of Paul's theology in general has returned to centre stage in recent Pauline scholarship. Whereas scholars such as W.D. Davies saw Paul as essentially Jewish, E.P. Sanders' influential work portrayed him as something fundamentally different. Since the publication of Sanders' *Paul and Palestinian Judaism* in 1977 comparisons of aspects of Paul and his thought with early Jewish thought have abounded. Much recent work has stressed the Jewish matrix of Paul's thought and his scriptural inheritance. We shall note some of these contributions, limiting the discussion with one exception to books published since 1989.

Paul's identity has received fresh treatment in three books: Martin Hengel's *The Pre-Christian Paul*, one goal of which is to demonstrate 'how deeply his gospel is moulded by the language and spirit of the old people of God';[14] Karl-Wilhelm Niebuhr's *Heidenapostel aus Israel: Die jüdische Identität des Paulus nach ihrer Darstellung in seinen Briefen*, which examines the four points in Paul's letters that discuss his Jewish past (Gal. 1:13f; Phil. 3:5f; 2 Cor. 11:22f; Rom. 11:1) and concludes that Paul considered himself to be in a central rather than an extreme position within Judaism;[15] and Karl O. Sandnes' *Paul—One of*

---

[12]A.T. Hanson, *Studies in the Pastoral Epistles* (London: SPCK, 1968) 46; B.S. Easton, *The Pastoral Epistles* (London: SCM, 1948) 68.

[13]*The Art of Performance: Towards a Theology of Holy Scripture* (London: Darton, Longman & Todd, 1990) 62.

[14]London/Philadelphia: SCM/Trinity, 1991. The quotation is from p. xii. Many of the books listed below are published in series edited by Martin Hengel, a great advocate of the importance of the Jewish background for understanding the New Testament.

the Prophets? A Contribution to the Apostle's Self-Understanding, which argues that Paul understood his apostleship in terms of the Old Testament prophetic tradition.[16]

Four works stress the continuity between Paul's moral teaching and biblical/Jewish antecedents. The titles give an indication of the contents: G.P. Carras, *Paul, Josephus and Judaism: The Shared Judaism of Paul and Josephus;*[17] Peter J. Tomson, *Paul and the Jewish Law: Halakha in the Letters of the Apostle to the Gentiles;*[18] Ekhard Reinmuth, *Geist und Gesetz: Studien zu Voraussetzungen und Inhalt der paulinischen Paränese;*[19] and my own *Paul, Scripture and Ethics: A Study of 1 Corinthians 5-7.*[20]

Irene Taatz, *Frühjüdische Briefe: Die paulinischen Briefe im Rahmen der offiziellen religiösen Briefe des Frühjudentums,* contends that Paul's letters exhibit a marked continuity with Jewish epistolary tradition.[21]

Paul's view of the law, Christology, teaching on suffering and mystery language have all been considered anew from a Jewish standpoint. Frank Thielman, *From Plight to Solution: A Jewish Framework for Understanding Paul's View of the Law in Galatians and Romans,* attempts to understand Paul's view of the law on the basis of early Jewish expectations of an eschatological purification of Israel.[22] David P. Capes, *Old Testament Yahweh Texts in Paul's Christology* argues that Paul's Christological use of κύριος stands within the religious milieu of first-century Jewish practice.[23] James M. Scott, *Adoption as Sons of God: An Exegetical Investigation into the Background of υἱοθεσία in the Pauline Corpus,* argues that there is a unified and specific Old Testament/Jewish background which builds upon 2 Samuel 7:14 for Paul's notion of 'adoption as sons'.[24] Scott J. Hafemann, *Suffering and the Spirit: An Exegetical Study of II Cor 2:14-3:3 within the Context of the Corinthian Correspondence,* considers that the best backdrop for Paul's thinking about suffering is the tradition of the suffering of the righteous in the Old Testament and Judaism.[25] And Markus N.A. Bockmuehl, *Revelation and Mystery,* has focused attention on Jewish wisdom and apocalyptic literature, and

---

[15]WUNT 62; Tübingen: Mohr, 1992.
[16]WUNT 2.43; Tübingen: Mohr, 1991.
[17]Ph.D., Oxford, 1989.
[18]CRINT III.1; Assen/Maastricht/Minneapolis: Van Gorcum/Fortress, 1990.
[19]Berlin: Evangelische Verlagsanstalt, 1985.
[20]AGAJU 22; Leiden: Brill, 1994.
[21]Göttingen: Vandenhoeck & Ruprecht, 1991.
[22]Supp NovT 61; Leiden: Brill, 1989.
[23]WUNT 2.47; Tübingen: Mohr, 1992.
[24]WUNT 2.48; Tübingen, Mohr, 1992.

Qumran as the proper background for understanding Paul's use of 'mystery' language.[26]

On a grander scale Peter Stuhlmacher's New Testament theology firmly grounds Paul's thinking in the Old Testament and Judaism;[27] Jurgen Becker's *Paulus: Der Apostel der Völker* stresses continuity between Paul the Pharisee and Paul the Christian;[28] and Tom Wright's *Climax of the Covenant* takes the Jewish categories of monotheism and election, redefined in the light of Christianity, to be crucial for understanding Paul.[29]

To be fair, comparisons between Paul and Judaism have not of course all stressed continuity. Timo Laato, *Paulus und das Judentum: Anthropologische Erwägungen*, for example, argues that they differ radically in terms of anthropology, Judaism having a far more optimistic view of the human condition and free will than Paul does.[30] And Mark A. Seifrid, *Justification by Faith: The Origin and Development of a Central Pauline Theme*, compares Paul's soteriology with that of 1QS and the Psalms of Solomon and concludes that after his conversion it underwent a radical change.[31]

Several authors have connected Paul with Judaism in more general terms. Some recent articles, without reviewing the above-mentioned studies, stress Paul's Jewishness: according to D.J. Harrington, 'Paul the Jew', Paul never disavowed his identity as a Jew;[32] and for W.R. Stegner, 'A Jewish Paul', Paul fits more comfortably today into 1st-century Judaism than two decades ago.[33]

Whether or not we accept every detail of these studies, the general thrust is difficult to miss. It is that Paul is 'Jewish to the roots', to use Morna Hooker's words.[34] The present attempt to define Paul's

---

[25]WUNT 2.19; Tübingen: Mohr, 1986. *Cf.* also K.T. Kleinknecht, *Der leidende Gerechtfertigte: Die alttestamentlich-jüdische Tradition vom 'leidende-Gerechten' und ihre rezeption bei Paulus* (WUNT 2,13; Tübingen: Mohr, 1984).

[26]WUNT 2.2; Tübingen: Mohr, 1990.

[27]*Biblische Theologie des Neuen Testaments, I: Grundlegung: von Jesu zu Paulus* (Zurich/Göttingen: Vandenhoeck & Ruprecht, 1992)

[28]Tübingen, Mohr, 1989; see especially p. 297.

[29]*The Climax of the Covenant: Christ and the Law in Pauline Theology* (Edinburgh: T.&T. Clark, 1991).

[30]Åbo: Åbo Academy Press, 1991.

[31]Supp NovT 68; Leiden: Brill, 1992.

[32]*Catholic World* 235 (1992) 68-73.

[33]*Asbury Theological Journal* 47/1 (1992) 89-95. *Cf.* also H. Frankemölle ('Apostol Pawel i jego interpretacja smierci Jezusa Chrystusa', *Collectanea Theologica* [Warsaw] 61/2 [1991] 5-16) who argues that, even with his faith in Jesus as messiah, Paul remained fundamentally a Jew (See *NT Abstracts* 36/13 [1992] 361).

view of Scripture is set in the context of this recent rediscovery of the Jewishness of Paul. It would indeed be surprising if what is a crucial, defining feature of what it meant to be Jewish in Paul's day,[35] namely, a particular view of the Scriptures, was not true of Paul. Nonetheless, this conclusion must not be assumed without further investigation.

In the rest of this chapter two aspects of Paul's view of Scripture will be considered: the nature of Scripture (under this heading we are not concerned to discuss so much the how or the mode of inspiration as the result or fact of inspiration); and the purpose of Scripture. Where possible the results will be compared with early Jewish views. In the interests of space we shall restrict the enquiry to the *Hauptbriefe*.

II. The Nature of Scripture

The formulae Paul uses to introduce scriptural quotations are largely stylistic, telling us little about his use of Scripture. There is no correlation between how accurate the quotation is or the hermeneutical moves it employs and the words used to introduce it. However, many of the introductory formulae do reveal Paul's high regard for Scripture. Paul introduces quotations from Scripture in a variety of ways, most of which have Jewish precedents. The most frequent introductory formulae are those including perfect tense γέγραπται, 'it stands written', which, as in LXX usage (*e.g.*, 2 Ch. 23:18) and in Philo and Josephus denotes the authority and validity of what is written. Qumran documents prefer the verb to say, אמר, although to write, כתב, is not infrequent. That which is quoted as γέγραπται was given in the past but has continuing significance. The words introduced by such formulae are not merely of antiquarian interest. As we shall see one thing that is abundantly clear about Paul's and the Jewish view of Scripture is the undoubted relevance of Scripture.

This notion of the contemporary significance of the citation is even more clear in those introductory formulae which use the present tense of λέγω. It is not just that Scripture (Rom. 10:11; 11:3; *cf.* 1 Tim. 5:18), David (Rom. 4:7-8; 11:9-10), Moses (Rom. 10:19), Isaiah (Rom.

---

[34]'Paul—Apostle to the Gentiles', *Epworth Review* 18/2 (1991) 85. In this article Hooker argues that 'the popular picture of Paul as anti-Jewish is false' (89).

[35]*Cf.* P.M. Casey's eight factors of Second Temple Judaism (his identity scale), which includes Scripture (*From Jewish Prophet to Gentile God; The Origins and Development of New Testament Christology* [Louisville/Cambridge: Westminster/John Knox/James Clarke, 1991] 12).

10:16; 15:12) or God (Rom. 10:21; 2 Cor. 6:2) *spoke*. Rather, Paul affirms that in effect these subjects *speak* to his present situation. Romans 4:3 is particularly striking, where Genesis 15:6 is introduced with the question, 'What does the Scripture say (λέγει)?' Since the word 'Scripture' means 'what is written', to ask what Scripture 'says' is to personify it and to regard it as a living entity. Or is this perhaps to read too much into an innocent question?

Paul is certainly capable of personifying Scripture. In Galatians 3:8 and 3:22 Scripture foresees the justification of Gentiles by faith and consigns all things to sin respectively. The basis of this personification is the idea that it is God himself who speaks through Scripture. After all, it is a safe inference that Paul believed that it is the activity of God to foresee something and to consign all things to something. As D. Moody Smith has observed: 'in introducing an OT quotation Paul can simply say, "as God said" (2 Cor. 6:16), and there are a few other places at which God is the likely subject understood of the verb (Rom. 9:25; 2 Cor. 6:2, especially).'[36]

That the Scriptures are for Paul the work of God is also evident in three places where Paul adds λέγει κύριος, 'says the Lord', for no apparent reason: in Romans 12:19; 1 Corinthians 14:21 and 2 Corinthians 6:17. (In two other places, Rom. 14:11 and 2 Cor. 6:18, the same addition appears as 'part of a brief excerpt from a specific verse in the LXX'.)[37] The additions are puzzling. Whereas E.E. Ellis sees in these passages the influence of early Christian prophets,[38] David Aune argues that they simply make it explicit that the speaker is God.[39] Either way, the phrase at the very least indicates that Paul regarded the texts in question not merely as what the prophets spoke in the past, but as what God says to his own day. Isaiah 28:11-12 in 1 Corinthians 14:21 is especially noteworthy since it is clearly the prophet Isaiah's words and not divine speech that is reported. Thus we have some basis here for the dictum 'what Scripture says, God says'.

---

[36]'The Pauline literature', in D.A. Carson and H.G.M. Williamson (eds.), *It is Written: Scripture Citing Scripture. Essays in Honour of Barnabas Lindars*, (Cambridge: CUP, 1988) 281.

[37]Christopher D. Stanley, *Paul and the Language of Scripture: Citation Technique in the Pauline Epistles and Contemporary Literature*, SNTS Monographs 74 (Cambridge: CUP, 1992) 173.

[38]*Paul's Use of the Old Testament* (Edinburgh: Oliver and Boyd 1957; repr. Grand Rapids: Baker, 1981).

[39]*Prophecy in Early Christianity and the Ancient Mediterranean World* (Grand Rapids: Eerdmans, 1983) 339-46.

There is also indication that what God says, Scripture says, to reverse the familiar formula. In Romans 9:17 Paul introduces his quotation of God's words to Pharaoh in Exodus 9:16 with 'Scripture says to Pharaoh' and in Romans 10:19-21 the words of God are ascribed to Moses. It appears that God, the human authors and Scripture are so closely identified in his mind that Paul is able to refer to one as the utterance of the other and vice versa. B.B. Warfield was right to draw attention to a similar phenomenon in rabbinic Judaism:

> Whatever stood written in these Scriptures was a word of God, and was therefore referred to indifferently as something which 'Scripture says' ('amar qara', or 'amar hakkethibh, or kethibh qera') or 'the All-Merciful says' ('amar rachmana'), or even simply 'He Says' (wekhen hu' 'amar or merely we'amar); that God is the speaker in the Scriptural word being too fully understood to require explicit expression.[40]

The terms Paul uses to denote the Scriptures are also revealing. Holiness is something Paul regards as a defining attribute of God and his Spirit which is to be communicated to his people: ἅγιος most often has a personal rather than a cultic emphasis for Paul. Romans 1:2 is remarkable in this light, for there Paul asserts that the gospel was promised beforehand in the 'holy scriptures' (cf. Rom. 7:2; 'the law is holy'). Though we may be used to seeing it on the cover of many Bibles (compare the title of Tyndale's little book, A Pathway into the Holy Scripture), only twice in the New Testament is Scripture described as holy. This designation was not, however, uncommon in Jewish circles, being found in various forms in Philo, Josephus and in equivalent Hebrew or Aramaic titles in rabbinic literature.[41] Jews contemporary with Paul described the Scriptures as 'the holy scriptures', 'the holy records', 'the most holy oracles', and 'the holy word'. As C.E.B. Cranfield states, Paul's use of ἅγιος in Romans 1:2 'reflects Jewish usage, both Rabbinic and Hellenistic'.[42]

---

[40]The Inspiration and Authority of the Bible (Philadelphia: Presbyterian and Reformed, 1948) 229-30.

[41]See Roger Beckwith, The Old Testament Canon of the New Testament Church and its background in Early Judaism (London: SPCK, 1985) 105-9; idem, 'Formation of the Hebrew Bible', in M.J. Mulder (ed.), Mikra. Text, Translation, Reading and Interpretation of the Hebrew Bible in Ancient Judaism and Early Christianity (Assen/Maastricht/Philadelphia: Van Gorcum/Fortress, 1988) 39-86, esp. 40-41.

[42]The Epistle to the Romans, Vol. 1, (ICC; Edinburgh: T.&T. Clark, 1975) 56. Cf. H. Seebass, s.v. 'Holy', NIDNTT, Vol. 2, 228, who places Rom. 1:2 with 'a number of passages [which] remain entirely within the framework of OT tradition'.

Assuming the normal connotations of holiness, to call the Scriptures holy is to point to their uniqueness and perfection. It suggests their divine origin, that they belong to God. Roger Beckwith asserts that for Jews 'one of the corollaries of the holiness of the Scriptures was that they were especially suitable to be kept and used in holy places'.[43] There is widespread evidence that not just the Law, but the Prophets and Writings also,[44] belonged to a holy collection in the Jerusalem temple in Paul's day, a practice begun with the laying up of the Ten Commandments and the book of Deuteronomy in and beside the ark of the covenant in the tabernacle (Ex. 25:16,21; 40:20; Dt. 10:1-5; 31:24-6). This fact may well have reinforced in Paul's mind the notion that the Scriptures are holy.

Whereas we share with Paul in modern usage the title of Holy Scripture, Paul does not refer to the Bible as the Word of God, as many do today. For Paul these words usually refer to his own preaching or to the proclamation of the gospel generally (cf. 2 Cor. 4:2; 1 Cor. 14:36; 1 Thes. 2:13 ['when you received the word of God, which you heard from us']; 1:5; 2:5).

A short phrase with which Paul does refer to Scripture, τὰ λόγια τοῦ θεοῦ, 'the oracles of God' (Rom. 3:2), sheds considerable light on his conception of it. Although these words have been variously understood as certain portions of the Old Testament or as the Law, the Jewish Scriptures as a whole are probably in view.[45] In Philo, Josephus and Aristeas τὰ λόγια, 'oracles' or 'utterances', is often used to refer to the Scriptures in general. Furthermore, in context Paul refers in Romans 3:2 to the basis for his condemnation of the Jews: in spite of certain privileges they have been disobedient to God's will. They are a peculiar people because God has spoken to them. Their unfaithfulness to those instructions, which are contained in the Scriptures, is Paul's point. Thus it is not unlikely that 3:2 broadens the repeated reference in 2:17-29 to Jewish failure to keep the law (note the repetition of νόμος) to include all the Scriptures. To refer to the Scriptures as the 'oracles of God' is to regard them as divine utterances, oral communication from God himself. The phrase need not be restricted to those places where Scripture reports divine speech, for as already noted in Jewish usage it was not limited to this and as we saw with Paul's flexible use of intro-

---

[43]'Formation', 41.
[44]Ibid., 41-45.
[45]Cf. Beckwith, 'Formation'; Warfield, 'Inspiration and Authority'; and the commentaries of Dodd, Barrett, Käsemann, Lagrange, Murray and Morris ad loc.

ductory formulae, be seems to regard the whole of Scripture as of
divine origin.

Another indication of the divine character of Scripture is implicit
in Romans 15:4-5. Scripture, Paul says in 15:4, gives believers patience
and comfort. In the following verse he describes God as the God of
patience and comfort! Apparently God and the Scriptures work to the
same end.[46]

Thus, there are several traces of evidence to indicate that Paul
regarded Scripture as the very words of God. Most of these traces recall
contemporary Jewish usage. How does this picture compare with the
views of Scripture characteristic of the Judaism of Paul's day? Does
Paul's view operate within 'the constraints of history', to recall A.E.
Harvey's phrase from another context? In other words, is Paul's view
the standard Jewish one? Did such a thing exist?

Is it necessary to confine the comparison of Paul's view of Scripture to one area of Judaism? What was Paul's place in Judaism? Rather
than needing to limit Paul's background to one corner or another of
first-century Judaism, there are good reasons to believe that his exposure was broad indeed. The information about his pre-Christian career
in Acts connects him both with Jerusalem and the Diaspora. According
to the sole surviving witness to Paul's education, Acts 22:3, Paul was
educated at the feet of the honoured Rabbi Gamaliel (possibly the
grandson of Hillel).[47] Though trained in Palestine he maintained a
living connection with Tarsus, his hometown (see Acts 9:30; 11:25),
wrote his letters in Greek and used the Greek Bible. Indeed, in Acts
21:37ff., Paul is depicted as able to speak both Greek and Aramaic.

It is certainly the case that the normal first-century Jewish experience included considerable instruction in the Scriptures in the context
of both home and synagogue (cf. Josephus, Against Apion 2:178, 204).
Philo wrote that the Jews 'consider their laws to be divine revelation
and are instructed in them from their youth' (Legatio 210; cf. 115).
According to Aboth 5:24 'at five years old one is fit for the Scripture'.
In 4 Maccabees 18:10 there is intimation that the model Jewish father
gave much instruction in the Scriptures to his sons. The educational
character of the synagogue service is stressed by Josephus (Against
Apion 2:175): Jews 'gather together to listen to the law and learn it

---

[46]Steve Walton drew my attention to the implication of these verses.

[47]On Paul's relation to Pharisaic-Rabbinic tradition see W.D. Davies, *Paul and Rabbinic Judaism: Some Rabbinic Elements in Pauline Theology* (2nd. ed.; London: SPCK,
1955); D. Daube, *The New Testament and Rabbinic Judaism* (London: Athlone, 1956);
and Hengel, *The Pre-Christian Paul*, 46-8, 133, n. 232.

accurately'. To be Jewish in any sense was to have a knowledge of the Scriptures.

Nonetheless, talk of the Jewish position on any subject is likely to meet with scepticism. Judaism in the first century was characterised by a wide variety of religious belief and practice. In the case of Jewish views of Scripture, however, amidst the inevitable differences of expression, there is remarkable uniformity in terms of substance. A brief survey of a range of Jewish sources will set Paul's view in its proper context.

There is no doubting the absolute loyalty of the Qumran covenanters to Scripture; their whole existence was centred upon the Bible. As in Paul it is taken for granted that in Scripture God's word may and must be heard. The community was committed to the diligent study and practice of the teaching of Scripture, having assembled in order to rectify Israel's failure to keep the law. The 'Book of Hagu', a rather enigmatic title in the Scrolls, which is spoken of with such reverence at Qumran and is unique to the community, is almost certainly a reference to the Scriptures.[48]

Philo considered all of Scripture to be divine oracles. In On Moses 2:188 he states: 'Now I am fully aware that all things written in the sacred books are oracles (χρησμοί)'. He uses both χρησμός and λό-γιον in similar statements throughout his writings. He also repeatedly asserts the trustworthiness and truthfulness of Scripture.[49] Other ways of referring to Scripture in Philo stress its divine origin and also the holiness of Scripture. In Questions about Genesis 4:140 he wrote that the Scriptures are 'not monuments of knowledge and vision, but are the divine commands and divine words'. He has more to say than Paul about the mechanics of inspiration. Many believe that Philo conceived of the biblical authors as not having any idea of what they said or wrote; operating 'not so much as prophets [but] as mediums'.[50] In On the Special Laws 4:49 he states: 'For no pronouncement of a prophet is ever his own, but he is an interpreter prompted by another in all his utterances.' Philo commonly introduces passages from Scripture without expressing the subject of the verb. Warfield has plausibly suggested that this is 'in harmony with his fundamental viewpoint—which looked on the Scriptures as a body of oracular sayings'.[51] It is

---

[48]See N. Wieder, *The Judean Scrolls and Karaism* (London: Horowitz, 1962) 215ff.

[49]*Hypothetica* is an accessible point of entry into his vast corpus for his view of Scripture.

[50]Hanson, *Studies in the Pastoral Epistles*, 45.

[51]'Inspiration and Authority', 341.

possible to place too much stress on Philo's references to ecstasy and the prophetic passivity of the human authors of Scripture. Helmut Burkhardt insists that such comments in Philo must be seen as an expression of his desire to vindicate the divine origin of human prophecy.[52] Philo also stresses the moral qualifications for prophecy, especially with reference to Moses. It is open to debate whether Philo excludes personality from the process of inspiration. Nonetheless, the divine character of Scripture could not be more marked in Philo.

Josephus' view of Scripture is especially noteworthy since according to his own account he studied Scripture with the Pharisees, Sadducees and Essenes (Life 10-12). His was a broad exposure to Judaism. Josephus apparently saw no difference between the words of a prophet and words of God. He can write that God prophesied something, when referring to an Old Testament prophet's words (e.g., Antiquities 9:145; 10:126) and can supply the name of a prophet for God's words (Antiquities 7:72, 294, 371; 8:197; 9:139).[53] In Against Apion, which deals among other things with the reverence with which all Jews regarded the Scriptures, Josephus supplies a direct comment on our subject which we are lacking in Paul. Josephus states that the prophets alone wrote under divine inspiration (ἐπίπνοια) and as a result they present an accurate and consistent account (1:37-8). He talks of 'the inspiration which they owed to God'. Concerning the Scriptures Josephus contended that it is an instinct with every Jew, from the day of his birth, to regard them as the decrees (δόγματα) of God (Against Apion 1:42). Even allowing for an apologetic purpose and some hyperbole in these statements the basic point of a universally high regard for Scripture among Jews is here given strong support.

Rabbinic literature presents no lesser a view of Scripture. David Instone Brewer's exhaustive study of the exegesis of the predecessors of the rabbis before 70 AD concludes that they regarded Scripture as 'a legal document drawn up by God'.[54] In the talmudic b. Sanhedrin 99a, an explanation of Numbers 1:31, 'because he has despised the word of the LORD', is given as follows:

---

[52]*Die Inspiration heiliger Schriften bei Philo von Alexandrien* (Giessen/Basel: Brunnen, 1988). Cf. the short review by W. Horbury, *VT* 40 (1990) 503-4.

[53]Cf. Wayne A. Grudem, 'Scripture's Self-Attestation', in D.A. Carson and John D. Woodbridge (eds.), *Scripture and Truth* (Leicester: IVP, 1983) 36-7.

[54]*Techniques and Assumptions in Jewish Exegesis before 70 CE* (TSAJ 30; Tübingen: Mohr, 1992) 170.

This refers to him who maintains that the Torah is not from heaven. And even if he asserts that the whole Torah is from heaven, excepting a particular verse, which (he maintains) was not uttered by God but by Moses himself, he is included in 'because he has despised the word of the LORD.

To say something is from heaven is to say it is from God, the phrase being used out of respect for the divine name, as in 'the kingdom of heaven' and the prodigal's confession, 'I have sinned against heaven'.

The documents of the Old Testament Pseudepigrapha, which are related, according to James H. Charlesworth, because they are all 'exegetically rooted in the Old Testament', reinforce the impression that 'the life of the early religious Jews was defined and circumscribed by the Book'.[55] Whereas the documents of the Pseudepigrapha are diverse in terms of language, genre, provenance and at many points theology, there is no mistaking that they all assume without question that the Scriptures contain God's will and truth concerning sin and evil, the messiah, the afterlife, and whatever else exercised their interest.

It is not that Jews did not differ with regard to the interpretation of Scripture. On the contrary, in terms of both method and the results of biblical exegesis, we must speak of Jewish views. But with respect to the basic conception of Scripture there was only one basic Jewish view. Moshe Goshen-Gottstein does not exaggerate when he states: 'All testimonies from the tannaitic era indicate that the Bible was regarded as absolute authority.'[56] Even so-called non-mainstream Judaisms have no other view. We have already noted the Qumran sect. It may be added that though the Sadducees accepted only the five Books of Moses, this was because they felt that as God's word it was entirely sufficient and needed no supplement.[57] The Samaritan rejection of the Prophets and the Writings (the non-pentateuchal canon) has a more historical explanation: they were not involved in the Babylonian Exile when many of these books entered the canon. The Jews who produced

---

[55]'The Pseudepigrapha as Biblical Exegesis', in Craig A. Evans and William F. Stinespring (eds.), *Early Jewish and Christian Exegesis: Studies in Memory of William Hugh Brownlee* (Atlanta: Scholars Press, 1987) 139-152; the quotations are from pp. 141 and 151 respectively. *Cf.* Leo Baeck, *Das Wesen des Judentums* (Cologne: Melzer, 1960) 16: 'In der Bibel hat das Judentum sein sicheres, unverrückbares Fundament.'

[56]'Scriptural Authority—Biblical Authority in Judaism', in D.N. Freedman (ed.), *The Anchor Bible Dictionary*, Vol. 5, 1019 (New York/London: Doubleday, 1992).

[57]*Cf.* Hyam Maccoby, *Judaism in the First Century* (London: Sheldon, 1989) 4.

esoteric literature should not be seen as an exception. What may seem to us bizarre exegesis was produced on the assumption that it was the divine character of Scripture that made the search for hidden meanings possible

Before concluding that Paul stands within this broad Jewish tradition we must ask whether or not Paul's evident freedom with the wording of the passages of Scripture he quotes and his apparent flouting of certain biblical laws, such as circumcision, betray a lowering of the Jewish view of the nature of Scripture? A comparison with the behaviour of other Jews on these two scores may prove enlightening. Christopher D. Stanley recently produced the first full-length monograph on the subject of Paul's citation technique, *Paul and the Language of Scripture*.[58] He rightly points out that the problem of divergent wording cannot be explained fully by appealing to the use of a text different from the ones we now have or to the result of (bad) memory quotation (well known texts are sometimes quoted inaccurately and obscure texts appear verbatim). He believes that Paul actively adapted the wording of his biblical quotations to communicate his own understanding of the passage in question and to exclude other possible readings of the text. While the extent of this adaptation is open to debate case by case, his basic point seems to be established. In fact, Paul makes no attempt to conceal changes from his readers. In Romans 10:11 he quotes Isaiah 28:16 in a different form from Romans 9:33 and in 1 Corinthians 15:27 the verb in the citation changes from the aorist to the perfect in the same verse. Some changes are so obvious that no-one familiar with the original text would fail to notice (*e.g.*, Gal. 4:30; Rom. 10:6-8).

Apparently Paul thought his readers would not be perturbed by such interpretative renderings. How does Paul's rather loose practice square with the warning of Deuteronomy 4:2 or 12:32 where adding to or subtracting from God's commands is prohibited? These were popular texts in early Judaism (*cf. e.g.*, Josephus, Antiquities 1:17; also 4:197; 8:56; 10:218). Having studied the literary landscape of antiquity including the Jewish works of Philo, the Dead Sea Scrolls and the Apocrypha and Pseudepigrapha, Stanley concludes that in offering such interpretative renderings of the biblical text, Paul was working 'within the accepted literary conventions of his day'.[59] In conforming the biblical wording to the grammar of the new context, in eliminating irrelevant

---

[58]See n. 37.
[59]*Paul and the Language of Scripture*, 29.

material, and in incorporating interpretative comments, thereby recasting the text to show his understanding of it, Paul acted no differently from other Jews in his day, who esteemed Scripture highly. As James Scott argued with impressive documentation in 1875, 'truthful representation, and not verbal accuracy, was all that was required or sought from quotations in any era'.[60] The concern for 'dead-accurate' quotation is not only a modern invention, but it is limited to the academic context. Paul's practice is closer to the citation technique of a sermon than a scholarly monograph. And we all know that despite free quotation sermons often maintain a higher view of Scripture than scholarly monographs.

What of Paul's open abrogation of some parts of Scripture? Does not his disregard for laws concerning circumcision, food, festival days and the Sabbath render him decidedly un-Jewish in his view of the need to obey Scripture? To quote E.P. Sanders: 'How could a Jew of Paul's antecedents, while still viewing Scripture as Scripture, and quoting it to show God's plan and intention, say that some of its commandments are optional?'[61] At this point we confront the vexed question of Paul and the law, which we have not the space to explore in detail. No doubt Paul's views are tied up with his understanding of Christians living in the new age and under the new covenant inaugurated by the coming of Jesus Christ and the Spirit, and with his own mission which refused to restrict the people of God to the Jews by signifying distinctions between Jews and Gentiles. It is also worth nothing that in Hellenistic-Jewish literature like Joseph and Asenath, Pseudo-Phocylides and the Testaments of the Twelve Patriarchs the cultic-ritual laws including circumcision do not play any role, perhaps for pragmatic rather than theological reasons. As Traugott Holtz explains:

> The cult of the temple was indeed not a living reality for Judaism outside of Jerusalem and Judea, especially in the diaspora. According to the experience of that part of Judaism the practice of the cult was not a necessary part of life according to the order of the Law.[62]

---

[60] *Principles of New Testament Quotation: Established and Applied to Biblical Science* (2nd ed.; Edinburgh: T.&T. Clark, 1877) 84-100 (cited by Stanley, *Paul and the Language of Scripture*, 27).

[61] *Paul, the Law and the Jewish People* (Philadelphia: Fortress, 1983) 162.

[62] 'The Question of the Content of Paul's Instructions', translated by George S. Rosner and Brian S. Rosner, in Brian S. Rosner (ed.), *Understanding Paul's Ethics: Twentieth Century Approaches* (Grand Rapids: Eerdmans, 1995) 66 (German original: 'Zur Frage der inhaltlichen Weisungen bei Paulus', TLZ 106 [1981] 385-400).

This of course does not settle the issue. The most that can be said at this stage is that in playing down certain laws in the Torah Paul is not as far from all parts of Judaism as we might suppose.

III. The Purpose of Scripture

It is often asserted that Paul's understanding of Scripture altered dramatically after his call/conversion on the Damascus road and as he grew in his understanding of Christian existence. His journey took an unexpected detour as he now read Scripture Christocentrically, not unlike the disciples on the road to Emmaus. Doubtless he disagreed with Jews over the interpretation of numerous texts, as Acts and his letters, especially Galatians and Romans, attest. However, does Paul's view of the purpose to which Scripture speaks, the use to which one may validly put Scripture, set him apart from other Jews? Once again we are limited to 'off the cuff' remarks and other incidental hints in order to construct Paul's view of the purpose of Scripture. We shall see that when these are assembled, a clear two-fold purpose emerges, to which many Jews in Paul's day would have subscribed.

First, in 1 Corinthians 10:11 he states that Scripture was 'written for our instruction'. The Greek word in question, νουθεσία, is a standard pauline term which denotes moral appeal leading to amendment (1 Cor. 4:14; Rom. 15:14; Eph. 6:4; Col. 1:28; 3:16; 1 Thes.5:12,14; 2 Thes. 3:15; Tit. 3:10; cf. Acts 20:31). In context Paul is claiming that the exodus events recited in 1 Corinthians 10:1-10 (in a manner reminiscent of Ps. 78; Dt. 32; Ne. 9 and Acts 7) were written down for the purpose of the ethical instruction of Christians, in this case to keep them from idolatry, immorality and grumbling. In spite of Paul's explicit claim numerous authors deny that the Law or Scripture was in fact important for Paul's moral teaching, the most influential this century being Adolf von Harnack. More recently others have expressed such views, including the following:
John Barton (1986):

> Paul... does not take much trouble to derive his ethical teaching from scripture.[63]

Andreas Lindemann (1986):

---

[63]*The Oracles of God: Perceptions of Ancient Prophecy in Israel after the Exile* (London: Darton, Longman & Todd, 1986) 190.

> [Paulus] versteht aber das Alte Testament, seine Bibel, gerade nicht
> mehr als Tora in eigentlichen Sinne; sie ist ihm nicht mehr die Quelle
> der Weisungen Gottes für das Verhalten der Menschen, soweit sie
> Christen sind.[64]

R.G. Hamerton-Kelly (1990):

> The Mosaic Law played no constructive role in his [*i.e.*, Paul's]
> ethics.[65]

Such authors point to other sources and factors as more crucial to the
formation of Paul's ethics, such as the words of Jesus, the non-Jewish
ethics of his day, the influence of eschatology, the Spirit, love, social
conditions and the gospel itself. Nonetheless, 1 Corinthians 10:11 is not
the only place where Paul underscores the relevance of the Scriptures
for ethics. In a group of rather neglected texts, 1 Corinthians 4:6; 9:10;
10:6,11; 14:34 and Romans 7:12; 15:4, similar assertions are made. In
context these six verses refer to the value of passages found in Exodus,
Numbers, Deuteronomy, Job, Psalms, Isaiah and Jeremiah for Christian conduct. No wonder Paul can say in Romans 15:4 that 'whatever
was written in former days was written or our instruction'. And this
seems to be true of Paul's practice, at least in the case of 1 Corinthians
5-7, a sample from his ethics which I have investigated in another
place, where the major lines and many of the details of Paul's teaching
on a variety of subjects including sexual immorality, discipline, law-
suits and marriage and singleness can be traced to his scriptural and
Jewish inheritance.[66] There is good evidence from both his precept and
his practice that Scripture for Paul is 'written for our (ethical)
instruction'.

　　Paul speaks just as clearly about a second purpose of Scripture in
Romans 3:21, about which there is less controversy, where Scripture is
said to function as witness to the gospel concerning Jesus Christ. The
Jewish Scriptures testify (note the present tense of the participle μαρ-
τυρουμένη) that the righteousness of God has been manifested with the
coming of Christ. In other words, Scripture testifies to Jesus Christ.

---

[64]'Die biblischen Toragebote und die paulinische Ethik', in *Studien zum Text und
der Ethik des Neuen Testaments: Festschrift zum 80. Geburtstag von Heinrich Greeven*,
263-4.
[65]'Sacred Violence and "Works of the Law." Is Christ Then an Agent of Sin?', *CBQ*
52 (1990) 55-75.
[66]*Paul, Scripture and Ethics*. See also the studies of Carras, Reinmuth and Tomson
mentioned earlier.

Romans 3:21 makes explicit the principle upon which Paul operates throughout Romans. Similar thoughts are found in 1:2; chapter 4 *passim*; 9:25-33; 10:6-13, 16-21; 11:1-10, 26-9; 15:8-12.[67] It is no passing, trivial thought. Indeed, as Cranfield insists:

> that this attestation of the gospel by the OT is of fundamental importance for Paul is indicated by the solemn way in which he insists on it here in what is one of the great hinge-sentences on which the argument of the epistle turns.[68]

1 Corinthians 15:1-4 is comparable, where the main events of the gospel message are 'in accordance with the Scriptures'.

A.T. Hanson contrasts this New Testament view with contemporary Jewish views. Whereas Pharisees looked for guidance for daily life, Qumran sectarians for prophecies about their sect, Philo for allegorical truths, 'Christians on the other hand searched the scriptures in order to find prophecies of Jesus Christ'.[69] This purpose of Scripture is the focus of the vast majority of studies of Paul's use of Scripture, and it is captured in the title of Dietrich-Alex Koch's impressive study, *Die Schrift als Zeuge des Evangeliums*, an allusion to Romans 3:21.[70]

This twofold purpose of Scripture is signalled by the same words in Romans 4:23-4 and 1 Corinthians 9:10. In both places Paul insists that Scripture ἐγράφη δἰ ἡμᾶς, 'was written for us'. In Romans Paul contends that Genesis 15:6b was written not only for Abraham's sake but to encourage us to believe that God has raised Jesus from the dead. And in 1 Corinthians the words affirm that an obscure Torah text about fair treatment to oxen is applicable to the regulation of Christian behaviour. The words 'written for us' in these two contexts underscore a fundamental of Paul's view of Scripture, namely, its relevance. Paul is not put off by the fact that Scripture is culture-bound and historically relative. As we saw with the introductory formulae, Scripture not only stands written, it continues to speak. Christians, Paul says, are to do two things with Scripture: believe it, for it testifies to the gospel, and obey it, for it instructs them concerning proper conduct. Jews in Paul's

---

[67]Paul's use of 'witness' here is similar to Jn. 5:39, where the Scriptures bear witness to Christ.
[68]Cranfield, *Romans*, Vol. 1, 202-3.
[69]*The Living Utterances of God: The New Testament Exegesis of the Old* (London: Darton, Longman & Todd, 1983) 42.
[70]*Die Schrift als Zeuge des Evangeliums: Untersuchungen zur Verwendung und zum verständnis der Schrift bei Paulus* (Beiträge zur Historischen Theologie 69; Tübingen: Mohr, 1986).

day shared his presupposition about the relevance of Scripture. The vast body of Jewish literature preserved from the Second Temple Period and the Rabbinic corpus shares Paul's belief that Scripture was 'written for us'.

Jews also agreed unanimously that a major function of Scripture is the determination of ethical conduct, how one ought to walk. This is true of every surviving genre of Jewish literature to a lesser or greater extent. In the Apocrypha catechetical material appears in Tobit (*e.g.,* 4:3-18), The Wisdom of Solomon (*e.g.,* 4:24ff.) and especially Ecclesiasticus. In the Old Testament Pseudepigrapha practical teaching based on Scripture is found most readily in instructional material like Pseudo-Phocylides (esp. 3-8, 9-41, 177-94) and 4 Maccabees (*e.g.,* 2:4-16), but it also forms a primary focus in apocalyptic texts including the Sibylline Oracles (esp. 3:36-45, 185-91, 235-45, 377-80; 594ff., 726-66; 4:31-4; 5:165ff., 386-93, 430ff.),1 and 2 Enoch (*e.g.,* 2 Enoch 10:4ff.; 42:6-14), the Testament of Abraham (*e.g.,* [a]/10; [b]/12) and the Apocalypse of Abraham (*e.g.,* 24:5-8) and in testaments like the Testaments of the Twelve Patriarchs (*e.g.,* T. Reu. 3:3-6; T. Gad. 3:1-3; T. Levi 14:5ff.; T. Jud. 18:2-6; T. Iss. 3:3-8; 4:2-5; 7:2-6; T. Dan. 5:5-7; T. Ben. 4:1-5; 6:2-5; 8:1ff.; T. Ash. 2:1-10; 4:2-5) and Jubilees (*e.g.,* 7:20). Pseudepigraphic poetry such as the Psalms of Solomon (*e.g.,* 8:9-13; 4:2-5) and Pseudo-Menander (esp. 9-15) present no exception. Biblically based ethical prescriptions are also common among the sectarian documents of the Dead Sea Scrolls (see especially the Damascus Document, the Community Rule, the Temple Scroll and wisdom texts in the 4Q series, such as 4Q370). Moral teaching that is built upon Scripture is scattered throughout Philo's apologetic writings and commentaries, with a concentration in Hypothetica, and is equally diffuse in Josephus (see especially Against Apion). Rabbinic literature is of course taken up primarily with practical issues. The Jewish Greek Scriptures themselves also witness to the moral function of Scripture in their occasional pietistic and moralising additions (in Proverbs, Daniel and Esther, and the expanded ending to Job).

The explicitness of the relation to Scripture in this Jewish moral teaching varies from case to case, but in each case a major function of Scripture is to determine ethical conduct. This is the thrust of Karl-Wilhelm Niebuhr's impressive study, *Gesetz und Paränese*, that the traditional stereotypical form of early Hellenistic Jewish paraenesis was shaped largely by the Torah.[71] Niebuhr traces the formative influence of Exodus 20-23, Leviticus 18-20 and Deuteronomy 27 upon a host of texts, beginning with passages from Pseudo-Phocylides (2-41, 177-

91), Josephus' Against Apion (2:190-219) and Philo's Hypothetica (7:1-9), which are remarkably similar in content. Niebuhr is convinced that this Torah-dependent type of paraenesis was widespread in early Judaism, being understood in synagogues in Greek-speaking communities as the application of God's will to the practical problems of everyday life ('die praktische Lebensführung').[72] Niebuhr's conclusions may be extended to include texts from Qumran and the Rabbinic corpus as listed above. In the Prologue to Ecclesiasticus the ancient translator describes his grandfather, the author of the book, as a man steeped in the Scriptures and concerned to secure obedience to their moral teaching. His description captures a common Jewish sentiment in Paul's day which Paul shared:

> My grandfather Jesus, after devoting himself especially to the reading of the law and the prophets and the other books of our fathers, and after acquiring considerable proficiency in them, was himself also led to write something pertaining to instruction and wisdom, in order that, by becoming conversant with this also, those who love learning should make even greater progress in living according to the law.[73]

Virtually without exception, Judaism presents a powerful demonstration of Paul's notion that Scripture was written to teach us how to live. There is no distance between Paul and his Jewish contemporaries on this matter.

In general, therefore, scholars agree that all Jews expected Scripture to supply rules for living, but they have been much less ready to accept that Scripture has this function in Paul. The situation is reversed with regard to the Christological interpretation of Scripture: it is agreed to be present in Paul, but not so widely recognised in the writings of other Jews. Many Jews of course saw Scripture as containing texts of messianic import.[74] However, only in the Qumran community do we find Jews who shared the eschatological consciousness which drove Paul to hear Scripture's testimony on this score. It is true that Paul read Scripture in a fundamentally different light in view of the Christ-event. This reading, however, and the expectation that Scrip-

---

[71]*Gesetz und Paränese: Katechismusartige Weisungsreihen in der frühjüdischen Literatur* (Tübingen: Mohr, 1947).
[72]*Ibid.*, 241.
[73]The last sentence of the Prologue is also noteworthy: 'live according to the law'.
[74]For a handy survey see Jacob Neusner, William Scott Green and Ernest S. Frerichs (eds.), *Judaisms and their Messiahs at the Turn of the Christian Era* (Cambridge: CUP, 1987).

ture would speak to such an event, was not inconsistent with his Jewish roots. Rabbi Akiba's application of Scripture to Bar Kokhba in the second century is further proof of this.[75] According to y. Ta'an 4.8.68a Akiba declared Bar Kokhba the Messiah with reference to Numbers 24:17:

> R. Simeon b. Yohai taught, 'My teacher Akiba used to expound, *"There shall step forth a star out of Jacob*—thus Koziva steps forth out of Jacob!" When R. Akiba beheld Bar Koziva, he exclaimed, "This is the King Messiah."'

The double purpose of Scripture which we discovered in Paul corresponds loosely to David Instone Brewer's taxonomy: he distinguishes, on the one hand, the exegesis of the predecessors of the rabbis who regarded Scripture as fixed law, which he terms the nomological approach; and, on the other hand, the exegesis of Josephus, Philo and Qumran, who regarded it as a living prophecy, which he labels the inspirational approach.[76] Instone Brewer admits traces of these two conceptions in both camps, especially the nomological in the latter group. It is clear that Paul's views on the purpose of Scripture fits comfortably within both traditions of interpretation, the nomological corresponding to our first purpose and the inspirational to our second.

IV. Conclusion

Paul's view of Scripture is thus in large measure the standard Jewish view. With regard to its nature, like other Jews he regards Scripture as God's holy Word, as oracles of God. He sees it as both sacred and central. Like all Jews he expects Scripture to speak to the questions of daily conduct in the present. Like those at Qumran he looks to Scripture to testify to God's decisive eschatological and revelatory act. His view is, it must be said, also basically in line with and may be seen as an extension of Scripture's view of itself. Much, though not all, of the Old Testament claims to be the words of God and much is written about the high regard with which this word is to be held, in reverence, awe, and so on.[77] Furthermore, as regards its purpose, the Old Testament view of itself is in a nutshell that Scripture is to be believed with respect to

---

[75]Professor Alan Millard drew my attention to this fact.
[76]*Techniques and Assumptions in Jewish Exegesis.*
[77]See the summary in Grudem, 'Scripture's Self-Attestation', 19-36.

the messianic promises, *etc.*) and obeyed in the present
ncerning conduct). That Jesus also stood within this tradi-
...on regarding Scripture is also true, but it is a subject worthy of
another chapter.

These conclusions ought not to surprise us given that Paul was
by his own confession a Pharisee and a Hebrew of Hebrews. They also
ought not to be underestimated, for as Scott Hafemann has recently
written:

> The fundamental issue still to be resolved in Pauline studies is the
> determination of the *primary* religious and theological context within
> which Paul's thought is to be understood… whether one interprets his
> letters primarily against the Greco-roman philosophical and religious
> world of Paul's day, as Bultmann argued over fifty years ago, or in the
> light of the Hellenistic-Jewish world of the 1st century and its Scrip-
> ture, as Adolf Schlatter proposed in the early decades of this
> century.[78]

This essay is a small contribution to the debate in favour of recognising
Paul's fundamental Jewishness.

The implications of our results for two other areas may be noted.
How does Paul's view as we have sketched it from the four main letters
compare with that of the Pastoral Epistles? Are the two noticeably different?[79] As it turns out 2 Timothy 3:15-17 is not unpauline (*contra*
Hanson, Easton, *et al*). Rather, it is a fair and accurate summary of
Paul's view of Scripture. There Scripture also has a divine character, it
is inspired by God, and it is said to have the same double purpose: it is
able to 'make you wise for salvation', which corresponds to Paul's 'witness to the gospel'; and it is 'profitable for teaching, reproof, correction,
training in righteousness, that the men of God may be complete,
equipped for every good work', which is a good explanation of Paul's
notion that Scripture was 'written for our (ethical) instruction'.

Secondly, our results have relevance to modern theories of the
inspiration of the Bible. These may be attractive in important respects.
One cannot deny a valid place to the disciplines of systematic and historical theology in formulating a doctrine of Scripture. However,
unless modern theories do justice to the divine character of Scripture

---

[78]'Paul and his Interpreters' in Hawthorne, Martin and Reid (eds.), *Dictionary of
Paul and His Letters*, 678.
[79]Benjamin Paul Wolfe, 'The Place and Use of Scripture in the Pastoral Epistles'
(Ph.D., Aberdeen, 1990) makes a thorough comparison and concludes that they are
not.

and its immediacy in addressing contemporary concerns they cannot claim Paul's support. There is sometimes debate on which side Paul would have stood in modern discussions about the authority and place of Scripture. While it is true that Paul says little about the trustworthiness, truthfulness and sufficiency of Scripture, many Jews of his day did, and from every indication Paul maintains the Jewish view, which can be summed up in his own words: Scripture was 'written for us'.[80]

---

[80]Thanks are due to Professor Howard Marshall for his helpful comments on this paper, which was first delivered as the 1994 Tyndale New Testament Lecture.

CHAPTER 5

Authority and Hermeneutics: Some Proposals for a More Creative Agenda

Anthony C. Thiselton

Summary

These proposals for escaping the repetitiousness which blunts arguments about authority draw on hermeneutics, Christology, eschatology, Trinitarian theology, and speech-act theory. Tyndale anticipated a speech-act approach to scripture. Hermeneutics facilitates functional engagements with texts but moves beyond functionalism by evaluating the validity of textual effects. I compare 'absolutist' and 'functional' approaches respectively with Christologies 'from above' and 'from below'. Eschatology can integrate these, and can relate hermeneutics to 'authority'. Participation in Trinitarian conversation may provide a wider model than that of 'prophetic oracle'. Hermeneutics strives to disentangle manipulative appeals to authority to serve prior interests from actions in which the text shapes the reader.

I. Introduction: the Seeds of a Repetitive Agenda and Debate

Certain of the more conservative approaches to the nature of the authority of the Bible have, since the era of Warfield and Orr, reflected what may charitably be described as recurring themes. Less charitably some may suggest that debate has simply fallen into over-worn grooves from which it seems unable to escape.

Part of the problem lies with an unhealthy obsession which perceives the task of theology as that of mapping 'positions'. Often this constitutes a prelude to attacking those of other people and defending one's own. But under the dead weight of over-generalized survey and over-aggressive polemic, creativity becomes stifled and an agenda may become fixed and sterile, in this case for nearly a century. There is some justice in Paul Tillich's lament that dividing all theologians into pre-determined categories too often provides 'a cheap and clumsy way... of shelving somebody'.[1]

Warfield rightly perceived that issues of authority may entail the issue of truth, or even questions about knowledge and being. James Orr rightly perceived that the cutting edge of issues about authority lay in the functional effect of the Bible on human life and thought. But the particular ways in which these issues were formulated and handed down has resulted in some central points being lost from view, in a series of mutually polemical and even recriminatory debates.

This unhealthy repetitiousness also stems from another source, namely a dispute about method. The conflict may be explained by comparing a parallel controversy about method in modern Christology. Ever since Kant left a dualism of phenomenal knowledge and noumenal absolutes, theologians have felt a supposed need to distinguish between Christologies which build 'from below', and those which often form part of Trinitarian theology 'from above'. Harnack and much twentieth-century British Christology begin with the Jesus of history; Hegel and Barth expound Christology within the context of the nature and being of God.

The debate about the authority of the Bible runs along parallel lines. Largely in the Warfield tradition, some view the language of the Bible 'from above', as a specific instance of the speech of God. Others, largely in the tradition of Orr, ask questions about the specific functions of the biblical text, primarily on the basis of examining these texts

---

[1]Paul Tillich, *The Protestant Era* (London: Nisbet, 1951) xxviii.

as historical, literary and linguistic phenomena which mediate to readers a saving experience of God. But since each adopts a different
method, each tends to talk past, rather than with, the other. Each often
accuses the other of loss of nerve: in one case, of nerve to construct a
full-blooded system of theological doctrine; in the other, of nerve to
face the implications of phenomena which may serve as counter-exam-
ples to any uniform ontological model of texts which function in
practice in diverse ways. Almost against my will, I agree at this point
with a writer whose views on this subject I do not normally otherwise
share. Denis Nineham warns us that questions about the authority of
the Bible are seldom simple. He observes, 'Beware of all who claim to
have a simple answer... They are almost certainly guilty of serious,
and dangerous, oversimplification.'[2]

Later in this paper I shall appeal to a further parallel with the
Christological debate. Those few theologians who have gone part of
the way towards dissolving the conflict of methods 'from above' and
'from below' are those who rightly perceive that in the biblical traditions themselves divine transcendence less frequently and less
characteristically draws on a spatial metaphor which divides 'above'
from 'below' (although this certainly occurs) than on a temporal contrast between 'now' and 'then'. We shall develop the part played by
futurity and by eschatology as we proceed.

There is yet one more reason, also based on a confusion, why the
old debate wearily staggers on without signs of resolution. The unfortunate term 'propositional', which I should like to see banned from
discussion as a chameleon word, has tended to be commandeered by
one side. This has had two disastrous consequences. First, it may be
taken to imply that while Warfield values propositions, functional
views of authority do not. But this is false. More precisely expressed,
the Warfield tradition stresses propositional content; the tradition
associated with James Orr calls attention to propositional force. Certainly functionalists do not restrict their interest to propositions alone;
they rightly see that shouts of praise, acclamations, decrees, and acts of
electing, naming, or promising, and many other types of utterance may
enjoy divine sanction within Scripture. But this does not make them
advocates of a 'non-propositional' views. If we apply the hermeneutics
of contextual enquiry to historical theology, as we should, we discover

---

[2]D.E. Nineham, 'Wherein Lies the Authority of the Bible?' in Leonard Hodgson *et
al.*, (eds.),*On the Authority of the Bible* (London: SPCK, 1960) 81-96; the quotation is
from p. 95.

that the term became institutionalized as a slogan when dialectical theology, in which both Barth and Bultmann for a period in the 1920s shared, stressed 'event' and 'will' in a different context of debate.

The second consequence is that those who associated themselves with Warfield's view fell increasingly under the spell of regarding revelation primarily under the single model of information. Warfield himself must take some of the blame here. Among his various essays on the subject between 1880 and 1910, one of his most characteristic appeared in 1899 under the title '"It Says:" "Scripture Says:" "God Says"'.[3] He insists here that Scripture is 'an oracular book', and that the New Testament writers see and assume a 'double identification of Scripture with God and God with Scripture'.[4] His earlier essay of 1893 confirms that for him its authority is an issue of being, and only secondarily of function, when he writes of 'the whole doctrine that underlies... treatment of Scripture'.[5] What is at issue is 'the trustworthiness of the apostles as deliverers of doctrine'.[6]

James Orr was so close to Warfield that he invited him to write the article on 'inspiration' in his *International Standard Bible Encyclopedia*, and contributed a booklet to the series *The Fundamentals* (1910-15) from which the term 'fundamentalism' later derived its currency.[7] But in his book *Revelation and Inspiration* (1910) he regarded Warfield's stress on verbal and historical inerrancy as 'a most suicidal position'.[8] Rather than beginning with a pre-packaged doctrine of truth and being, Orr urged that the trustworthiness and authority of Scripture could be proved ever anew 'by those who rest themselves upon it'.[9]

The contrast between Warfield and Orr concerns not only the difference between propositional content and propositional (or other linguistic) force, but also a distinction between the proposition as formal descriptive statement, or a report about a state of affairs, and self-involving propositions (or other language) which may perform multi-functional tasks. I regularly illustrate this point with reference to the example 'this is poison'. This may serve as a descriptive report

---

[3] B.B. Warfield, *The Inspiration and Authority of the Bible* (Philadelphia: Presbyterian and Reformed, 1948) 297-348.
[4] *Ibid.*, 348.
[5] *Ibid.*, 197.
[6] *Ibid.*, 195.
[7] James Barr, *Fundamentalism* (London: SCM, 1977) 2 and 269; see further, Jack B. Rogers and Donald K. McKim, *The Authority and Interpretation of the Bible. An Historical Approach* (San Francisco: Harper & Row, 1979) 385-8 and 401, n. 36.
[8] James Orr, *Revelation and Inspiration* (London: Duckworth, 1910) 197-8.
[9] *Ibid.*, 218.

about the contents of a bottle; it may represent a cry for help: 'Quick! Fetch a doctor!'. It may constitute a reproach: 'You know I ought to keep off whiskey.' But it may perform a multiple function: 'this bottle contains poison' (descriptive proposition); 'don't you drink it' (warning); 'avenge me' (self-involving directive).

We may also note that James Orr's approach more readily takes account of the temporal context and conditioning of biblical language than Warfield. This does not detract from propositions. Few contemporary theologians have emphasized the importance of the proposition less uncompromisingly than Wolfhart Pannenberg. Yet Pannenberg rightly discerns the role of propositional force, self-involvement, and time, in the biblical traditions. He therefore declares, 'The truth of God must prove itself anew... True being is thought of not as timeless... It proves its stability through a history whose future is always open'.[10]

We shall return to these issues, but at this point our purpose is to suggest that these false starts, behind each of which lay positive and important concerns, initiated a debate which has, in effect, chased its tail for nearly a century. The development of the debate from 1880 to the 1970s has been traced most helpfully by Mark A. Noll (1986) and by George Marsden (1991) in their excellent historical reviews, as well as (more critically) by James Barr (1977) and others.[11] If we pass over the period up to the late 1950s, we find the same themes constantly re-emerging from the 1950s onwards. E.J. Young, for example, insisted in 1957 that the authority of Scripture entailed freedom 'from the errors which adhere to mere human compositions. Not alone to moral and ethical truths but to all statements of fact does this inspiration stand.'[12] By now not only has the prophetic model and propositional content come to be accorded privilege over other modes of discourse and over issues of propositional force; the model of revelation has become informational rather than primarily transformative.

---

[10]Wolfhart Pannenberg, *Basic Questions in Theology*, Vol. 2 (ET; London: SCM, 1971) 8 and 9; see further his *Theology and Philosophy of Science* (ET; Philadelphia: Westminster, 1976) and *Systematic Theology*, Vol. 1, (ET; Edinburgh: T.&T. Clark, 1991) chapter 1.

[11]Mark A. Noll, *Between Faith and Criticism: Evangelicals, Scholarship, and the Bible in America* (San Francisco: Harper & Row, 1986) and George M. Marsden, *Understanding Fundamentalism and Evangelicalism* (Grand Rapids: Eerdmans, 1991) 9-84 and 122-52; cf. also some of the essays in Nathan O. Hatch and Mark A. Noll (eds.), *The Bible in America. Essays in Cultural History* (New York/Oxford: OUP, 1982), esp. 139-62 by Richard J. Mouw; also James Barr, *Fundamentalism*.

[12]E.J. Young, *Thy Word is Truth* (Grand Rapids: Eerdmans, 1957) 48.

Some attempts were made to relate the functional to issues of being or doctrine. For example, in 1958 in a volume edited by Carl Henry, J.N. Geldenhuys addressed both aspects. But he began with the Warfield approach, almost as a self-contained system, and the functional aspect was tacked onto it.[13] I shall try to show in a later section that the reverse direction offers more hope of advance. In the same volume Everett F. Harrison attempts to discourage any pre-packaged doctrine which does not take full account of diversity and multiform modes of discourse within the Bible.[14] I am glad that Ernest F. Kevan, who was my uncle, brings together issues of authority and interpretation within the horizon of time. Illustrating the issue with reference to the Levitical prescriptions, he distinguishes 'what is of permanent validity from what belongs to a stipulated period'.[15]

In the next section I propose to trace how the same pendulum ceaselessly swings between Berkouwer and Lindsell, between Lindsell and Rogers and McKim, between Rogers and McKim and Woodbridge, between Woodbridge and Dunn, between Dunn and Grudem, and so forth. But it is high time to introduce a suggestion about the role played by hermeneutics in this debate.

II. The Role of Hermeneutics in the Repetitive Debate

Once the debate about authority has become mired in these grooves, it is understandable that among more conservative writers a sharp divergence about the nature, status and role of hermeneutics should come to the surface. Put simply, for those whose approach to biblical authority finds its centre in identifying the relevance of the Scriptures for daily life, hermeneutics becomes fundamental. It precisely concerns an active and transforming engagement between the biblical text and the life and thought of readers of our own day. But for those who approach the subject 'from above' only in terms of absolutes, the discipline appears to expose a painful nerve: if the definitive Word of God reaches human understanding, even under the guidance and initiative of the Holy Spirit as divine agent, through processes of enquiry, testing, judgment, and interpretation, does not hermeneutics provide the

---

[13]J. Norval Geldenhuys, 'Authority and the Bible' in Carl F.H. Henry (ed.), *Revelation and the Bible* (London: Tyndale, 1959 [American ed. 1958]) 371-86.
[14]Everett F. Harrison 'The Phenomena of Scripture', *ibid.*, 237-50.
[15]Ernest F. Kevan, 'The Principles of Interpretation' *ibid.*, 285-98; the quotation is from p. 297.

one fallible link in what may be thought of as an otherwise infallible chain? For is it not good Reformation and Protestant theology to acknowledge the fallibility of all interpretation, not least the interpretation of the church? In Anglican parlance, even general councils may err.

The positive view of the relation between authority and interpretation is expressed most strongly by G.C. Berkouwer.[16] He adopted a primarily but not exclusively functional approach to authority, and an entirely positive and constructive approach to hermeneutics. He declares: 'There is no more incisive question concerning our relation to Scripture than the one regarding the sharpening of our listening and obedience to that Scripture.'[17] Berkouwer spoke of its 'concrete authority' and rejected a 'formalized' approach on the grounds that this authority operates 'not in separation from, but rather in connection with, the understanding of Holy Scripture'.[18]

Berkouwer was fully aware of the blockage to understanding with which hermeneutics is concerned. Citing Paul's warning about the fruitlessness of reading Scripture 'with a veil over the heart' (2 Cor. 3:14-18), he asks how Scripture can have its way with us if 'various more or less impressive presuppositions can block our path to understanding it?'[19] Without hermeneutics appeals to authority remain in the realm of theory and hypothesis. Berkouwer is fully aware, standing as he does in the Dutch Reformed tradition, of the illusory nature of value-neutral enquiry concerning the texts, and the problem which, since the era of Schleiermacher, had come to be known as the problem of 'pre-understanding', namely the concepts, stances, attitudes, and interests which engender either a readiness to hear and to understand Scripture or a pre-disposition not to hear it for what it is. He thus rightly declares: 'To confess Holy Scripture and its authority is to be aware of the command to understand and to interpret it.'[20]

The very year after Berkouwer's work had been published in English, however, Harold Lindsell produced his polemical book *The Battle for the Bible* (1976), followed by its sequel, *The Bible in the Balance* (1979).[21] Nothing more effectively served to put the clock back and to deepen over-worn grooves of debate. I have already expressed sympa-

---

[16]G.C. Berkouwer, *Studies in Dogmatics: Holy Scripture* (ET; Grand Rapids: Eerdmans, 1975) 105-38.
[17]*Ibid.*, 107.
[18]*Ibid.*, 106.
[19]*Ibid.*, 110.
[20]*Ibid.*, 137.

thy with those in the Warfield tradition who find themselves
dissatisfied with a merely functional approach to authority. But Lindsell did not simply redirect attention from function and effect to being
and truth. With colossal oversimplification, he went further than Warfield in pressing the model of revelation as knowledge or information
in abstraction from other modes of discourse and from the logic of self-
involvement and transformation. For here the central nerve of the issue
becomes: 'Does that knowledge come from reason, the church, or from
the Bible?'[22]

One polemic always invites another, and a new escalation of the
old conflicts now followed. Jack Rogers and Donald McKim argued in
1979 that, in accordance with mainstream Reformed tradition which
went back to Calvin himself, 'the authority of scripture resided in its
function of bringing people into a saving relationship with God
through Jesus Christ'.[23] In two studies written in 1980 and 1986 John
D. Woodbridge questioned the accuracy of their reading of Calvin's
writings on grounds of historical and textual interpretation, and this
critique met with sympathy and support from Don Carson.[24]

A more functional view of authority, however, does not depend
on Calvin scholarship. In 1982 my friend James D.G. Dunn launched a
full-scale attack on the Warfield tradition in a lengthy and closely-
argued two-part article on the basis of an exegesis of all the biblical passages to which this tradition regularly appealed.[25] In 2 Timothy 3:16,
for example, a key verse for the debate, the writer speaks of Scripture
as divinely inspired in the context of its being 'profitable (ὠφέλιμος) for
teaching, for reproof, for correction and for training in righteousness'.[26] Dunn examines each of the relevant passages one by one in
painstaking detail.[27]

---

[21]Harold Lindsell, *The Battle for the Bible* (Grand Rapids: Zondervan, 1976); and *The Bible in the Balance* (Grand Rapids: Zondervan, 1979).
[22]Lindsell, *The Battle for the Bible*, 205.
[23]Rogers and McKim, *Authority and Interpretation of the Bible*, xvii.
[24]John D. Woodbridge, 'The Impact of the "Enlightenment" on Scripture' in D.A. Carson and John D. Woodbridge (eds.), *Hermeneutics, Authority and Canon*, (London/Grand Rapids: IVP/Zondervan, 1986) 241-70; esp. 243-5; and *idem*, 'Biblical Authority: Towards an Evaluation of the Rogers-McKim Proposal', *Trinity Journal* 1 (1980) 165-236. See further D.A. Carson, *Hermeneutics, Authority and Canon*, 10-11.
[25]'The Authority of Scripture according to Scripture', *Churchman* 96 (1982) 104-22 and 201-25.
[26]*Ibid.*, 108.
[27]*Ibid.*, especially 108-17 and 203-14.

Almost simultaneously, however, and apparently independently of Dunn, in a chapter in the volume, edited by Don Carson and John Woodbridge, Wayne Grudem wrote at almost the same length on almost the same topic under the title 'Scripture's Self-Attestation and the Problem of Formulating a Doctrine of Scripture'.[28] Grudem insists that no historical detail in Scripture can be 'contrary to fact', although he appears cautiously to concede that this applies primarily to the genre of historical statement.[29] Yet in contrast to Dunn he re-states the Warfield position that 'to restrict the areas in which Scripture is reliable and truthful will surely fail'.[30]

Must we continue for ever with this dualism of approach between being and truth on one side, and function and effect on the other? I believe that hermeneutical theory and the philosophy of language can offer certain clarifications which may begin to draw these divergent approaches more closely together.

This task cannot be achieved unless, first, functionalists perceive hermeneutics to concern not simply processes or principles of interpretation but also their ontological foundations. If the hermeneutical tradition reflected in Gadamer and others is valid, namely that operative understanding rests on pre-judgments even more than on conscious processes of judgement, we cannot avoid asking ontological questions about the basis on which given language-functions rest. It is not enough to say that the Bible is authoritative because a reader *feels* liberated, forgiven, or commissioned by reading the biblical texts. Is that effect based on a state of affairs which renders it valid? A phenomenological level of discussion alone can never answer such a question. Whether we like it or not we have entered the realm of theology and theological truth-claims.

On the other hand, it becomes logically odd to make the test of the validity of every possible kind of linguistic force depend on the supposed capacity of one given sub-set, namely that of historical report, to participate in a perfection otherwise reserved for the fulfilment of hope at the last day. Because the formulation of the theory reflects a seventeenth- and eighteenth-century concern with the mechanistic model of a universe and the theory of ostensive definition (not a theory of 'propositions') which went with it, it is as if a portrait by

---

[28]'Scripture's Self-Attestation and the Problem of Formulating a Doctrine of Scripture' in D.A. Carson and John D. Woodbridge (eds), *Scripture and Truth* (London/Grand Rapids: IVP/Zondervan, 1983) 19-59.
[29]*Ibid.*, 58.
[30]*Ibid.*

Van Gogh should somehow be considered 'less true' than a modern photograph. Anyone who ranks a modern photograph above a Van Gogh portrait simply has no soul, but has fallen captive to the mechanistic mind-set of the eighteenth century from which much of this thinking derives. The main issue is not whether all report carries an objectivism which even a photographer could not aspire to, but that biblical texts operate with functional authority because the states of affairs which they presuppose for the legitimation of their function are true in reality.

The cutting edge of the authority of the Bible is thus seen in its capacity to perform acts of salvation, liberation, forgiveness, renewal, authorization, appointment, commission, and above all acts of promise and pledges of love. But the story does not end there. The task of hermeneutics is threefold. First, it facilitates an engagement with the text in which the reader is not merely informed, but also addressed. Second, hermeneutics raises pointed questions about the basis and validity of communicative acts which purport to be scriptural. What basis in truth and reality does this linguistic activity depend upon? Third, far from relativising absolutes, hermeneutics, even through conflicts of fallible interpretation, makes possible the forward moving process of anticipating the divine verdicts which will be fully revealed only at the last judgment. There is nothing logically odd in holding together the notion of an inevitable and unrevisable divine pronouncement and the view that it is anticipated in principle in Christ and appropriated in practice in the daily advance of interpretative processes (and indeed even at times conflicts of interpretation); these processes, through subsequent correction and fuller corporate understanding, appropriate the definitive verdicts of divine revelation for daily life and thought in the present.

This principle finds support in the New Testament and in hermeneutical theory, although we must postpone elaboration of this point. In the Epistle to the Hebrews, by way of example, the fixed absolute in which the believer places hope is 'the city which has foundations, whose builder and maker is God' (Heb. 11:10). But each step of the journey of pilgrimage is not yet fully mapped out in advance: 'By faith Abraham obeyed when he was called to go to a place which he was to receive as an inheritance; and he went out, not knowing where he was to go' (Heb. 11:8). I have argued elsewhere in some detail that for the Reformers *claritas Scripturae* entailed sufficient certainty for the next active step, as well as some other issues which belonged distinctively to the epistemological and ecclesial agenda of the time.[31] The relation between relativities or corrigible knowledge and absolutes or certainty can be understood only in terms of the temporal dimension of eschatology, not in terms of spatial imagery of 'above' and 'below', or of theories of genetic origins of texts.

Further, since coming of age with Ast and Schleiermacher, hermeneutics perceives understanding as taking place in the interaction between the two dimensions of holistic vision, or a divinatory, anticipatory apprehension of the whole, and a painstaking study of parts and particularities, carried out largely by analysis and comparison. The divinatory axis reaches out, as it were, for the fuller understanding which lies ahead; but because of human fallibility and individual and corporate blindness and self-interest, a careful checking process of critical assessment operates interactively with a larger understanding of the whole. To press the metaphor, the glimpse of 'the city which has foundations' gains substance in the pilgrimage through the wilderness by constant critical checking of one's compass bearings.

III. Authoritative Communicative Acts and Interpretation from Tyndale to Recent 'Radical Hermeneutics'

On this occasion of the quincentenary of Tyndale's birth, together with the Jubilee celebrations of the research Fellowship which bears his name, we may recall the importance which William Tyndale accorded to the nature of Scripture as a series of communicative acts validated by the authority of God and to the need to interpret the language of these linguistic activities within the thought-world and life of the England of his day.

It would not go too far to suggest that Tyndale saw much of the importance and authority of Scripture to lie in its capacity to perform valid and effective linguistic activities. In the first few pages of his short treatise *A Pathway into the Holy Scripture* he expounds his central theme of Scripture as, above all else, promise. It conveys 'promises of God'; it 'maketh a man's heart glad'; it proclaims 'joyful tidings'; it 'nameth to be his heirs...'[32] Indeed within a dozen pages, Tyndale

---

[31] Anthony C. Thiselton, *New Horizons in Hermeneutics. The Theory and Practice of Transforming Biblical Reading* (London/Grand Rapids: HarperCollins/Zondervan, 1992) 179-86.

[32] William Tyndale, *A Pathway into the Holy Scripture*, included in his *Doctrinal Treatises and Introductions to Different Portions of the Holy Scripture* (Parker Society ed.; Cambridge: CUP, 1848) 7-29; see esp. 8-9.

specifies no less than eighteen distinct speech-acts as linguistic activities which Scripture performs: it promises, names, appoints, declares, gives, condemns, curses, binds, kills, drives to despair, delivers, forbids, ministers to life, wounds, blesses, heals, cures and wakes.[33]

It might seem predictable that I should compare Wittgenstein at this point, but his observations reveal so clearly how the issues addressed here by Tyndale differ radically from the tired modern debates about propositional content. Wittgenstein observes:

> The speaking of language is part of an activity, or of a form of life...
> Asking, thanking, cursing, greeting, praying... commanding,
> questioning... are as much part of our natural history as walking,
> eating, drinking.[34]

Simply to observe, Wittgenstein urges, may lead us to 'make a radical break with the idea that language always functions in one way... to convey thoughts...'.[35] Tyndale saw Scripture as 'unlocked and opened', not when it merely 'conveyed thoughts' but when it enacted contracts, changed life, bestowed status and appointment, and above all pledged promises.[36] Whereas thoughts may simply reflect or mirror being, promise brings new being to pass. A theology of promise, as the prophets and apocalyptists knew, and as Moltmann (among others) has reminded us afresh in our times, does not simply describe present or past states of affairs. Far from mirroring present reality and affirming it, it judges it deficient and seeks to change it.

Second, in his hermeneutics Tyndale considers the tradition of 'the Four Senses of Scripture' and attacks allegorical interpretation, other than as an illustrative device for what may be proven independently, as powerless and ineffective.[37] Looking to my own ancient city of Nottingham to make his point, he observes that if allegorical interpretation is not supported by the plain sense of other texts, 'then were the allegory... of no greater value than a tale of Robin Hood'.[38]

Tyndale's work on interpretation, however, runs deeper than this. He stresses the active role of the Holy Spirit in this fundamental

---

[33]*Ibid.*, 8, 9, 10, 11, 12, 15, 17, 18, 21, 22 and 23.
[34]L. Wittgenstein, *Philosophical Investigations*, (Oxford: Blackwell, 2nd ed. 1958 and 1967) sections 23 and 25.
[35]*Ibid.*, section 304.
[36]Tyndale, *A Pathway*, 27.
[37]Tyndale, 'Four Senses of Scripture' in *The Obedience of a Christian Man, op. cit.*, 305-14.
[38]*Ibid.*, 306.

and essential process.[39] More than this, by translation and interpretation he seeks on one side to preserve and respect the distinctiveness of the horizon of the biblical text; on the other, he seeks to enter the horizon of the life and thought of the English reader of his day. Centuries before the hermeneutical theory of Gadamer, he produces tables of correlative meanings in Hebrew, Greek and English which clearly anticipate Gadamer's point that in interpretation we must not 'cover up this tension', or distinctive difference, between the two horizons, but must avoid 'naive assimilation' with 'the horizon of a particular present'.[40] Only then may we aim at a 'fusion of these horizons', as an ideal or ultimate goal.[41] Tyndale and Gadamer join as one in rejecting the notion that this constitutes a merely mechanical linguistic process. For this reason Gadamer explicitly attacks the obsession with 'method' which he regards as an aberration of Enlightenment rationalism from Descartes to the beginning of the nineteenth century. We may note in passing how curious is the comment of Harold Lindsell that 'the new hermeneutics' [sic] has 'drunk the wine of German rationalism' [sic].[42]

Some of Tyndale's examples fall into the category of explanation. Thus 'the ark' is 'a ship made flat, as if it were a chest or coffer'; 'hell' may sometimes denote 'a place beneath the earth... a grave, sepulchre, or cave', or in other places 'Gehenna, a place of punishment... in Hebrew the valley of Hennon'.[43] But hermeneutics and theological interpretation enter the stage when he speaks of 'faith' as 'the believing of God's promises, and a sure trust in the goodness and truth of God'.[44] 'Grace' comes to mean 'favour'.[45] Because they remain semantically transparent terms, 'passover', 'scapegoat' and 'mercy-seat' remain to this day part of our theological and everyday vocabulary. But the same cannot be claimed for the translation of πρεσβύτερος as 'senior' rather than 'elder'; or for rendering ἐκκλησία as 'congregation' rather than as 'church'.[46] This is because within the horizons of readers from the Reformation to the present these words have positions on an agenda in

---

[39]cf. E. Flesseman-van Leer, 'The Controversy about Scripture and Tradition between Thomas More and William Tyndale' in *Nederlandsch Archief voor Kerkgeschiedenis* 43 (1959) 143-64, especially 158.

[40]Hans-Georg Gadamer, *Truth and Method* (ET; London: Sheed & Ward, 1975) 273 and 272.

[41]*Ibid.*, 273.

[42]*The Battle for the Bible*, 205.

[43]William Tyndale, 'A Table' in *A Prologue to the Book of Genesis, op. cit.*, 405, 407; and *A Prologue on the Epistle of St. Jude, op. cit.*, 531.

[44]*Ibid.*, 407.

[45]*Ibid.*

ecclesiology. While in semantic terms alone, πρεσβύτερος includes the meaning 'senior' and ἐκκλησία includes the meaning 'congregation', to an English-speaking reader who knows no Greek these translations exclude wider possibilities of meaning, which place 'elder' and 'church' as equal or perhaps better candidates.

This principle reveals not only that most translation is simultaneously interpretation, involving judgement rather than mechanistic rules alone, but also that all translation and interpretation offers scope for the possibility of manipulation. The interpreter chooses phrases or expressions which, within the horizons of the reader of a later age, remain congenial to a particular theology, interest or concern. As a major thesis of this essay we assert: *a greater and a deeper issue about the relation between authority and interpretation arises from the possibility of manipulative interests than from the more familiar questions about the fallibility and relativity of interpretation.*

We turn to this aspect of hermeneutics, which John Caputo distinguishes by the term 'radical hermeneutics' as a discipline 'only for the hardy', namely 'the great project of hermeneutical trouble-making'.[47] Since a detailed theoretical discussion would take us beyond the confines of this essay and also occurs in some measure in my *New Horizons in Hermeneutics*, I shall simply illustrate a little of what is at issue by citing some recent claims put forward by W. Dow Edgerton in his book *The Passion of Interpretation*.[48] He argues that 'One interprets in order to shape the story of the future by re-shaping the story of the past.'[49] That 'shaping' comes under the heading of conscious or unconscious manipulation of the text emerges when Edgerton calls interpretation 'theft'. Hermeneutics is 'where the theft occurs. The text is a pre-text... One interprets but claims only to repeat. That too is part of the fiction.'[50]

---

[46]For a wider discussion *cf.* Dean Freiday, *The Bible, Its Criticism, Interpretation and Use in 16th and 17th Century England* (Pittsburgh: Catholic and Quaker Studies no. 4, 1979) 24-34.

[47]John D. Caputo, *Radical Hermeneutics: Repetition, Deconstruction, and the Hermeneutical Project* (Bloomington: Indiana UP, 1987) 2. See further, B.R. Wachterhauser (ed.), *Hermeneutics and Modern Philosophy* (New York: Albany State University of New York Press, 1986).

[48]Thiselton, *New Horizons in Hermeneutics*, 145-7; *cf.* 84-132, 313-31, 379-405, 439-52, and 529-50; W. Dow Edgerton, *The Passion of Interpretation* (Louisville: Westminster/John Knox, 1992), esp. 11-42.

[49]*Ibid.*, 32.

[50]*Ibid.*, 34, 36.

Edgerton suggests that some proto-awareness of this emerges from the character of Hermes in the ancient Greek world as a liar, a thief, a cheat, and a master of deception, as well as messenger and spokesman of the gods.[51] For, he claims:

> Interpretation begins in impatience with the given, in restlessness and in hunger... You repeat what has gone before, accept its authority, carry the past forward, place the present under the sign of the past... sometimes out of love, sometimes out of self-interest, sometimes fear, sometimes faith.[52]

Self-interest and faith may equally motivate interpreters because they re-present the nature of human experience (past, present and future) as 'text', namely as that which can be understood in terms of patterns of narrative and relationship embodying character and temporal plot, and especially the 'point of view' of the interpreter. This is true both of a judicious biblical exegete, of a sensitive pastoral expositor, and of an authoritarian church leader who wishes to smuggle vested power-interests beneath the cloak of the authority of the biblical text.

The torment of this situation is fully and movingly acknowledged by Edgerton. He writes:

> I confess that I am a thief of the Author's words, who distorts them and erases them... I confess that this is what an interpreter does... God grant that I may nevertheless be one of the 'imposters who speaks the truth'(2 Cor. 6:8).[53]

Towards the end of his book Edgerton rightly perceives that hermeneutics concerns 'foundations of perception, thinking, experience, and community'.[54] Here he is not simply drawing on the hermeneutical tradition of Schleiermacher, Dilthey and Betti, but on the post-Gadamerian issues raised by Habermas and Ricoeur. In this respect the 'radical hermeneutics' of Caputo and Wachterhauser go further, embracing additionally the approaches of Roland Barthes, Jacques Derrida, Lacan, and Foucault. Here questions are raised not only about manipulation, interest, deceit, suspicion and 'theft', but also about the stability and givenness of texts themselves.

---

[51]*Ibid.*, 30.
[52]*Ibid.*, 31.
[53]*Ibid.*, 42.
[54]*Ibid.*, 139.

All this serves to show the degree of relative parochialism that characterized many internal debates in more conservative circles about the respective merits of two traditions that go back to Warfield and Orr. This is not where the action is, whether on issues of authority or of hermeneutics. There are indeed certain signs that some writers with unimpeachable conservative credentials have begun to perceive this point. As long ago as 1964 Carl F.H. Henry lamented the obsession with domestic issues and positional markers which led more conservative writers 'to neglect the frontier of formative discussion in contemporary theology'.[55] It is sometimes forgotten that James I. Packer's book *'Fundamentalism' and the Word of God* addressed an agenda of thirty-five years ago and was written at the beginning of his theological career.[56] More recently in an essay on Scripture and hermeneutics written in 1983 he observed: 'Divine revelation should not be thought of as if it were the kind of depersonalized conveying of information that one finds in official memoranda.'[57] Sinclair Ferguson writes in 1988 that *'Inspiration does not render redundant the necessity of interpretation.* No passage of Scripture discloses its meaning apart from actual exegesis.'[58] He acknowledges that even 'Scripture's view of itself' does not provide 'all the answers', but leaves questions and puzzles which it does not address.[59]

Nevertheless on the whole much of the thinking about authority and interpretation among conservatives appears, from the viewpoint of more recent fundamental issues about the very nature of textuality, linguistic action and reading processes, to be locked into a time warp, for all its good intentions. Strange anomalies remain. For example, Bernard Ramm produced constructive dialogue between theology and science and, expressing dissatisfaction with the nature of the inerrancy debate, moved in the direction of Karl Barth's conviction that biblical truth is to be found 'where and when God, by his activating, ratifying, and fulfilling of the word of the Bible and preaching lets it become true'.[60] Further, in Barth's words, 'The Word of God is itself the act of God.'[61] Nevertheless, even bearing in mind that it was published in 1970, the revised edition of Ramm's book *Protestant Biblical Interpreta-*

---

[55] Carl F.H. Henry, *Frontiers in Modern Theology* Chicago: Moody, 1964) 140.
[56] *'Fundamentalism' and the Word of God*, (London: IVF, 1958).
[57] 'Infallible Scripture and the Role of Hermeneutics' in Carson and Woodbridge (eds.), *Scripture and Truth*, 325-56; the quotation is from p. 335.
[58] 'How Does the Bible look at Itself?' in Harvie M. Conn (ed.), *Inerrancy and Hermeneutics* (Grand Rapids: Baker, 1988) 47-66; the quotation is from p. 58.
[59] *Ibid.*, 66.

tion still side-steps all the most important issues in modern hermeneutical theory, resorting to the pre-Schleiermacherian definition 'Hermeneutics is a *science* in that it can determine certain principles for discovering the meaning of a document.'[62] Hermeneutics remains as trapped by an innocent confidence in mechanistic models that also side-tracked earlier discussions about authority. By contrast, Grant Osborne's book *The Hermeneutical Spiral* attempts to incorporate the kind of agenda favoured by Ramm, but then advances to fundamental issues about the roles of texts, readers, and the sociology of knowledge in the era after Gadamer and Ricoeur.[63]

I believe that only as we address these issues that are fundamental to the questions of authority and interpretation will new conceptual frames and models emerge which will enable us to move beyond the polarisations of older debates in a new synthesis of issues about truth with questions about function. W.Randolph Tate is correct in his recent argument that, if what is at issue is an authentic communicative act, hermeneutical theory must work towards an integration of the three 'worlds', as he calls them, which lie behind the text, within the text, and in front of the text as textual effects. Tom Wright explores these issues with greater sophistication in his excellent book *The New Testament and the People of God*.[64] However, I should wish to add a further temporal dimension. Text and interpreters both betray a situatedness in time which raises questions about purposes and interests, whether manipulatory or born out of faith and love. Moreover, as I have already suggested, hope for a fixed anchorage against which relativity, fallibility and manipulation can be measured, lies in an openness towards both the Holy Spirit in the present and more especially the Spirit as the power of futurity, who transforms corrigible understanding, which is adequate for the present moment, into that which accords with final definitive verdicts of God at the *eschaton*.

---

[60]Karl Barth, *Church Dogmatics* I:1 (ET; Edinburgh: T.&T. Clark, 1975) 120; Bernard Ramm, *The Pattern of Religious Authority* (Grand Rapids: Eerdmans, 1959); *idem*, *After Fundamentalism: The Future of Evangelical Theology* (San Francisco: Harper & Row, 1983).

[61]Barth, *op. cit.* 143.

[62]*Protestant Biblical Interpretation* (3rd rev. ed.; Grand Rapids: Baker, 1970) 11.

[63]Grant R. Osborne, *The Hermeneutical Spiral. A Comprehensive Introduction to Biblical Interpretation* (Downers Grove: IVP, 1991) 366-415.

[64]W. Randolph Tate, *Biblical Interpretation. An Integrated Approach* (Peabody: Hendrickson, 1991); N.T. Wright, *The New Testament and the People of God* (London/Minneapolis: SPCK/Fortress, 1992) 29-144.

Even if Hermes is, as Edgerton reminds us, a thief and a liar, 'interpretation' constitutes no more a fiction, a theft, a fallible act of *hybris* than justification by grace constitutes a 'theft' when it appropriates by faith a verdict which strictly and properly belongs to the future as a public pronouncement of judgment at the last day. Its provisionality may appear to be softened when the functional effects of justification become present in terms of a changed life which points to Christ. Nevertheless its basis and validity lie in divine decree, or an institutional speech-act of verdict. But if justification by grace stands at the heart of the gospel and applies the authority of a divine verdictive utterance to daily Christian life, may we not apply the model of an authoritative divine verdictive, brought forward in faith, to issues of authority and interpretation? This model seems to offer a more promising way forward than unresolved debates about the accuracy of historical reports or about the merely functional effects of reading texts.

Luther's notion of faith as a glad and bold 'staking of one's life' on the grace of God suggests a link with the title of Claude Geffré's book *The Risk of Interpretation*.[65] Attempting to hold together the two sides, Geffré writes:

> Christianity becomes meaningless without permanent reference to the founding event of Jesus Christ himself. At the same time, it also ceases to be a way that is open to a... future without permanent creativity.[66]

Geffré regards this dialectic between a definitive divine act and an 'open' future as characterising the 'exodus' pilgrimage of God's people. Abraham both journeyed in venture, 'not knowing where he was to go', and journeyed to the city 'which has foundations, whose builder and maker is God' (Heb. 11:8,10).

IV. Christological and Theological Reformulations and Proposals

Few items on the theological agenda about authority have provoked non-conservative readers more than appeals to the model of classical

---

[65]Claude Geffré, *The Risk of Interpretation. On Being Faithful to the Christian Tradition in a Non-Christian Age* (ET; New York: Paulist, 1987).
[66]*Ibid.*, 215.

Chalcedonian Christology as a means of explaining and defending the status of the Bible as simultaneously 'divine' and 'human'. The use of the analogy is understandable. First, in considering the problem of 'absolute authority', G.D. Yarnold comments: 'Whereas the authority of God as known is absolute, yet our knowledge of the authority of God is not absolute.'[67] But if God reveals himself within the conditions of human life, the mediation of absolute authority is bound up with the revelation of God in Christ. Second, in his critical survey of Catholic theories of biblical inspiration, J.T. Burtchaell points out that the issue which 'confounds scholars' is 'the manner in which individual human events are jointly caused by both God and man'.[68] Third, James Smart recalls that whereas in the patristic period 'the church in its zeal to exalt the Scriptures so emphasized their divinity as to deny the actuality of the human element in them', the reverse happened with the rise of modernity:

> So obsessed... did scholars become with the importance of this discovery [of their human character] that in a very large degree they lost sight of the divine character of Scripture. It became for them the human story of man's religiousness and ethical achievements.[69]

Against this background, J.I. Packer, in the tradition of Warfield, expounded 'the analogy of the Person of Christ' in the context of patristic and Chalcedonian categories.[70] Thus, as against 'Monophysite' heresy, we should ascribe neither to Christ nor to the Bible a simple 'divine' nature divorced from humanness. As against 'Nestorian' heresy, the divine and the human should be held together as one, in such a way that the very identity of Christ entails this unity. 'Similarly', Packer writes, 'the right way to think of Scripture is to start from the biblical idea that the written Scriptures as such are the "oracles of God" and to study their character as a human book only as one aspect of their character as a divine book.'[71] This argument builds on Warfield's parallel.[72]

Three issues arise here. First, James Barr attacks the analogy on the ground that 'Jesus becomes, according to the picture, more like God dispensing eternally correct information through a human mouth

---

[67]G.D. Yarnold, *By What Authority?* (London: Mowbray, 1964) 9.

[68]*Catholic Theories of Biblical Inspiration Since 1810* (Cambridge: CUP 1969) 279.

[69]*The Interpretation of Scripture*, (London: SCM, 1961) 15.

[70]*'Fundamentalism' and the Word of God*, 82-4.

[71]*Ibid.*, 84.

[72]Warfield, *Inspiration and Authority of the Bible*, 160-65.

than a man speaking under the conditions of his time.'[73] I am not sure that the Warfield-Packer view entirely deserves this caricature. Second, in Paul Wells' critique of Barr's approach, a more careful statement of the difficulty emerges. Wells observes: 'The analogy with hypostatic union' hardly seems to make 'the character of the divine and human elements attributed to Scripture any clearer'.[74] Would we genuinely wish to place the Bible on the same level of veneration and worship as that which we accord to Christ? Here Karl Barth rightly shows a concern with parallel issues about the status of sacraments in much Roman Catholic theology. Are the Bible and the sacraments instantiations of an 'objectified deity' who awaits our disposal and manipulation?[75] Third, the analogy between the Bible and classical patristic Christology gives priority to Christology 'from above', and thereby loads the agenda in such a way as to cause biblical specialists and systematic theologians too often to talk past each other.

A different Christological model, especially one that begins with Jesus of Nazareth but leaves room for retrospective theological understanding in the light of the resurrection and the cosmic scope of Christian eschatology, may offer a more fruitful starting-point. The dualism implied by the Greek metaphysics which partly shaped early Christological and Trinitarian formulations became magnified and torn into two distinct realms after the three critiques of Kant. Schleiermacher took Kant's challenge seriously, and attempted to replace a moral absolute by a pietist 'given' of relationality. But in so doing he left a Christology in which Jesus represented the 'ideality' (*Urbildichkeit*) of a humanity in which 'God-consciousness' achieved a unique degree.[76] He explains:

> The Redeemer, then, is like all men in virtue of the identity of human nature, but distinguished from them all by the constant potency of his God-consciousness, which was a veritable existence of God in Him.[77]

Hegel's three-volume *Lectures on the Philosophy of Religion* respond to Kant in the very opposite direction. 'Nature is only appearance', and 'Spirit in its finiteness is consciousness.'[78] In other words, religion

---

[73]*Fundamentalism*, 171.

[74]*James Barr and the Bible. Critique of a New Liberalism* (Phillipsburg, N.J.: Presbyterian & Reformed Publishing, 1980) 348.

[75]*Church Dogmatics* I:1, 4-6, 42-4, 53-71, 111-20, 132-86, 190-98, and 375-83.

[76]*The Christian Faith* (ET [from 2nd German ed.]; Edinburgh: T.&T. Clark, reprinted 1989) sections 93, 378.

[77]*Ibid.*, section 385; *cf.* sections 96-9, 377-424.

which is more than a relative, finite, natural 'construct' belongs by sheer logical necessity to the non-finite realm of the Absolute or the Whole.

As against Schleiermacher, Hegel asserts that 'In its immediacy Spirit is still finite.'[79] 'It is not *our* reflection... which tells us that the finite... is founded on something that is true. It is not *we* who bring forward its foundation.'[80] By 'objective necessity', not by consciousness alone, 'we follow the object as it returns of itself to the fountain of its true being'.[81] In other words, the 'Absolute' in authentic terms belongs to a process which can be understood only 'from above'. 'Consciousness' must be distinguished from '*the necessary nature* of that which Spirit knows'.[82]

This 'necessity' takes the form of a historical and logical dialectic in which the Absolute as the divine Holy Trinity unfolds Godself in a process combining continuum and differentiation as Father (origin and goal), as Son (as 'other') and as Holy Spirit (as creatively open to the future).[83] Schleiermacher's reduction of the Trinity to a way of articulating experience or human consciousness offers an entirely different account. The doctrine of the Trinity in Schleiermacher forms a brief postscript to *The Christian Faith*, as that which arises from 'utterances concerning the Christian self-consciousness'.[84]

This radical contrast of method 'from above' and 'from below' came increasingly to dominate Christological debate. The story is too well known to require detailed rehearsal. D.F. Strauss took up Hegel's contrast between concept (*Begriff*) and pre-conceptual anthropo-morphic representations (*Vorstellungen*). The latter he associated with 'myth' as a mode of placing empirical data within the 'value' dimension which Kant linked with ethics, God or absolutes. Myth, in this sense, represents ideas in the form of historical account. Since in Strauss's view the historical dimension of Christology, in effect, collapsed, eventually he felt unable to sustain faith on the basis only of this value aspect.[85] Once again, however, the pendulum swung to the opposite side, and F.C. Baur alleged that theological ideas were gener-

---

[78]*Lectures on the Philosophy of Religion* (ET; London: Kegan Paul, Trench, Trübner, 1895) Vol. 1, 111.
[79]*Ibid.*
[80]*Ibid.*, 107.
[81]*Ibid.*
[82]*Ibid.*, 112.
[83]*Ibid.*, 106-15; *cf.* also 61-73, 156-209.
[84]*The Christian Faith*, 740; *cf.* 738-51.

ated in the main by social history or historico-sociological forces. Harnack placed his emphasis on a Jesus of history who taught basic ethical truths. For Kähler and for Bultmann the emphasis lay on the preached Christ as against the Jesus of history. Even if the Kantian legacy held less sway in Britain and in America, the problematic shape of the Christological discussion had been decisively set, effectively until Pannenberg and Moltmann, among others, began to re-shape it.

I contend here that debates about biblical authority and interpretation shared in a parallel pattern, with disastrous results. Three responses may be found to the above/below dualism. First, a false assumption is embraced that whatever is 'of God' must be characterized by a flawless and timeless perfection, of a kind which, as Kierkegaard bitterly complained of Hegel's system, cannot engage with human subjectivity and contingent existence without appearing to lose or compromise this absolute perfection. Second, in reaction against such a view of Scripture, a model similar to Schleiermacher's Christology becomes activated by way of reaction, in accordance with which the Bible is seen to share in the common humanness of all writings, except that it also stems from a uniquely full degree of consciousness of God. A third approach reflects the Christology of Strauss and Bultmann: the biblical writings allegedly reflect a precarious relation to history, but offer religious values through language of various kinds, and function, in effect, independently of history to initiate decision and faith.

Much of the underlying problem dissolves however, as soon as we pay adequate attention to the fact that the Bible does not portray reality in Platonic or Kantian terms. The biblical writings do not conceptualize divine perfection, divine transcendence, divine otherness or divine otherworldliness primarily, and certainly not exclusively, in spatial imagery at all. They more characteristically, and more constructively for discussions about Christology and about biblical authority and interpretation, express the issues in temporal terms. If, as it is entirely right to do, we wish to take account of the work of the Holy Spirit, for example, in the authority and interpretation of Scripture, we should do well to heed Oscar Cullmann's comment: 'The Holy Spirit is nothing else than *the anticipation of the end in the present*.'[86] Cullmann

---

[85]*The Life of Jesus Critically Examined* (ET; London: SCM, 1973). I have offered a detailed discussion in 'New Testament Interpretation in Historical Perspective' in Joel B. Green (ed.), *New Testament Interpretation Today* (Grand Rapids: Eerdmans, 1995).

[86]*Christ and Time* (ET; London: SCM, 1951) 72.

further observes: 'Primitive Christian faith and thinking do not start from the spatial contrast between the Here and the Beyond, but from the time-distinction between Formerly, Now, and Then.'[87] Virtually all acts of God in relation to humanity are bound up with time and the temporal process. This constitutes, Cullmann urges, a 'natural presupposition' of earliest Christian faith and practice.[88] Thus in the Epistle to the Hebrews the definition of faith as 'assurance of things hoped for' defines 'the conviction of things not seen' (Heb. 11:1). These are 'not seen' not because they belong to Plato's world of 'above' but because they have not yet taken place.[89] In a similar vein, Jürgen Moltmann also asserts:

> From first to last, and not merely in the epilogue, Christianity is eschatology, is hope, forward looking and forward moving and therefore also... transforming the present. [Eschatology] is the medium of Christian faith... the key in which everything in it is set.[90]

Moreover, eschatology becomes critical not only for Hebrews, but for the Gospels and for their Christology. The teaching of Jesus bears this out. Even if the Fourth Gospel from time to time in specific contexts uses language about 'coming down' (Jn. 3:31), in the Synoptic Gospels the stretching of language to denote the action of a transcendent God in the contingent world utilizes the temporal tension of language about the kingdom of God which is both here in Jesus, but is also yet to come. This kingdom of God has drawn near or is 'at hand' (ἤγγικεν, Mk. 1:15; cf. Mt. 4:33); some present will see the kingdom 'come with power' (Mk. 9:1; cf. Mt. 16:30; Lk. 9:27); the kingdom has 'crept up on you' (ἔφθασεν, Mt. 12:28; Lk. 11:20). If the kingdom of God has arrived in the person of Jesus, in what sense does Jesus invite his disciples to pray 'May your kingdom come' (ἐλθέτω, Mt. 6:10; Lk. 11:2)? Norman Perrin, Werner Kelber, and numerous other writers have compared different approaches to these passages.[91]

---

[87] Ibid., 37.
[88] Ibid., 49.
[89] Ibid., 37-8.
[90] Theology of Hope (ET; London: SCM, 1967) 16.
[91] Norman Perrin, The Kingdom of God in the Teaching of Jesus (London: SCM, 1963); Werner H. Kelber, The Kingdom in Mark. A New Place and a New Time (Philadelphia: Fortress, 1974); cf. also A.M. Ambrozic, The Hidden Kingdom. A Redaction-critical study of the References to the Kingdom of God in Mark's Gospel (CBQ Monograph Series, 2; Washington: Catholic Biblical Association of America, 1972); Morna D. Hooker, The Gospel according to St. Mark (London: Black, 1991) 55-8; and N. Perrin, Jesus and the Language of the Kingdom (London: SCM, 1976).

This temporal imagery does not necessarily invite the kind of debates about present and future time which we may associate perhaps with C.H. Dodd, J. Jeremias, or W.G. Kümmel. It is more fruitful to follow the line of thought emphasised by Bruce D. Chilton, my former Sheffield colleague, in his book *God in Strength*.[92] Chilton argues on the basis of its meaning in the Targum of Isaiah and on exegetical grounds that 'the kingdom of God' denotes God's self-revelation. Hence we may conclude with Chilton that Jesus presses into his service the language of temporal ambiguity in order to proclaim that God acts now, but will act fully and openly in strength in the future, as the kingdom of God reaches its consummation.

V. The Application of this Approach to Authority and Interpretation

If we now apply that temporal model to Christianity and to the biblical writings, certain confusions may be resolved. First, as Wolfhart Pannenberg stresses, it is possible to begin with the contingent phenomena of history, as it were 'from below', but to interpret their meaning in the light of past and future events, including 'the unsurpassable anticipation of the ultimate revelation of God'.[93] This has particular relevance as a hermeneutic which applies to, and makes sense of, Christology. We may begin with Jesus of Nazareth, but in the light of the resurrection and of eschatological promise, and thus re-read and interpret historical data both retrospectively and eschatologically in the light of the divine verdict pronounced publicly at the end but anticipated in the resurrection of Christ.[94]

Moltmann opens up a most fruitful and suggestive approach both for Christology and for our understanding of Scripture when he combines a theology of eschatology, hope, and promise, with a bold attempt to speak (like Hegel but in biblical terms) of 'the Trinitarian history of God'. Christology from Kant through Schleiermacher and Strauss to Troeltsch, he confirms, largely failed on the basis of its alternatives of 'from above' and 'from below'. In the light of eschatology, however, we may approach Christology both in terms of Jesus as the

---

[92]*God in Strength. Jesus' Announcement of the Kingdom* (Freistadt: Plöchl, 1979).
[93]'Historical and Theological Hermeneutics' in *Basic Questions in Theology*, Vol. 1 (ET; London: SCM, 1970) 137-81; the quotation is from p. 157.
[94]Pannenberg, *Jesus—God and Man* (2nd ed.; Philadelphia: Westminster, 1977) esp. 33-7 and 324-49.

One who comes in obedience to the Father, and equally and co-jointly as the event of the co-suffering of the crucified God.[95] Still more boldly, and also rightly, Moltmann asks not simply about the meaning of the cross for humanity, but 'what does Christ's cross really mean for God himself?'[96]

Such a question shows the limitations of the oracular model of biblical authority and inspiration offered by Warfield, even if he grasps one aspect of truth. For in the *perichoresis* of the Holy Trinity Moltmann perceives a reciprocity of love and of mutual-self-imparting, in which, through the love of God and the agency of the Holy Spirit, the people of God are also derivatively caught up. Therefore God's 'word' and God's linguistic actions are not confined to conveying information and commands, or even, though this is better, pledges of love and promises. For psalms and hymns which address God equally constitute part of Scripture. Thus by appropriating the praise and worship of the Psalmist and of Jesus and Paul, each new generation of believers joins in with the unfolding divine dialogue of loving promise, loving pledge, loving forgiveness, loving adoration and loving mutual acts of blessing.

This approach as the Trinitarian basis of prayer was affirmed in a recent report by the Church of England Doctrine Commission, on which I served as a member and Vice-Chairman. The report speaks of the Trinitarian nature of God not as a doctrinal construct remote from life, but as foundational for prayer and sanctification. We speak of 'the experience of being mysteriously caught up by divine dialogue into the likeness of Christ'.[97] Just as the Holy Spirit evokes from believers the cry of Jesus, 'Abba, Father' (Rom. 8:15), even so to pray *by* the Holy Spirit *through* the mediation of Christ *to* God as Father 'is to be re-modelled by the activity of God in the redeemed life of "sonship"'.[98] But if this is the experience of authentic inspired prayer, is it not also the experience of appropriating the prayer and praise of Scripture, of

---

[95]*The Crucified God. The Cross of Christ as the Foundation and Criticism of Christian Theology* (ET; London: SCM, 1974) 87-98 (on the difficulties of the usual modern approaches) and 98-107, 160-278, especially 248-9, 254, 277-8 and 294-6; *The Church in the Power of the Spirit* (ET; London: SCM, 1977) 50-65; and *The Spirit of Life. A Universal Affirmation* (ET; London: SCM, 1992) 248-67.
[96]*Experiences of God* (ET; London: SCM, 1980) 15.
[97]Doctrine Commission of the Church of England, *We Believe in God* (London: Church House Publishing, 1987) 118: *cf.* 104-21.
[98]*Ibid.*, 109.

entering biblical narrative worlds and indeed the work of Scripture in all its many modes of discourse?

Is it appropriate, then, to enquire whether such linguistic activity needs 'authority'? It is essential to raise the issue of authority in this wider context, precisely because words and deeds of love are often commissive, covenantal, or directive and therefore depend for their legitimacy on certain institutional states of affairs being the case. In the essay on Christology and speech-act theory which forms part of the *Festschrift* for I. Howard Marshall, I drew on a careful distinction in J.L. Austin, Donald Evans, and John Searle between illocutionary speech-acts and perlocutionary speech-acts to make a fundamental point about the authority of the speech-acts of Jesus.[99] As a rule of thumb, Austin defines illocutions as 'the performances of act in saying something', whereas perlocutions 'produce certain consequential effects upon the feelings, thoughts, or actions of the audience'.[100]

Jesus did not rely on mere causal power in language. Perlocutions operate by the causal power of psychology and rhetoric, and may readily be confused, especially in those churches which are sometimes called 'preaching shops', with the perlocutionary force of sheer assertiveness. This can degenerate into rhetorical wheedling or into verbal bullying, and stands a thousand miles away from the authority of Jesus. Illocutions depend on other factors, especially on the institutional role and authority of the speaker to perform the act.

The words of Jesus become effective as valid and operative speech-acts because he is the anointed one, appointed as God's elect to mediate divine forgiveness, divine judgment, divine commission, divine promise, divinely authorized freedom and pledges of divine love. Thus when he says to the paralytic 'Your sins are forgiven' (Mk. 2:5; Lk. 5:20; *cf.* Mt. 9:2), the speech-act operates with illocutionary force (*i.e.*, *in* the saying of it, not merely *by* the saying of it), because Jesus is who he is. Ahead of his time, Karl Barth was entirely correct to insist that speech of God is act, and act of God is speech, and that this is bound up with what linguistic theorists call institutional states of affairs but which Barth expounded in terms of divine decree, divine election and covenant promise.[101]

All of this serves to show, among other things, that each side in the Warfield-Orr debate offered some kind of contribution, but in a dis-

---

[99]Thiselton, 'Christology in Luke, Speech-Act, Theory, and the Problem of Dualism in Christology after Kant' in Joel B. Green and Max Turner (eds.), *Jesus of Nazareth, Lord and Christ* (Grand Rapids: Eerdmans, 1994) 453-72.
[100]Austin, *How to Do Things With Words* (Oxford: Clarendon, 1962) 99 and 101.

astrously one-sided manner and within a confused and unfruitful conceptual scheme. That a debate in which truth-claims and function appeared to oppose each other should never have occurred emerges in J.L. Austin's comment, which I have often repeated, that 'for a certain performative utterance to be happy, certain statements have to be true'.[102] To take up some of Austin's own examples, I cannot say 'I give to you' as an operative and valid illocutionary act if what I claim to give is not mine to give; nor can I say 'I appoint you' if I am not entitled to appoint; nor can I say 'I do' at a wedding service if I am in a prohibited degree of relationship or am already married to someone else (unless the utterance is contextualised in a polygamous culture).[103] That this touches the central nerve of what constitutes 'authority' for valid effective utterance becomes clear when Austin offers legal or sociological synonyms for examples of incapacity to perform illocutions, namely being *ultra vires*, or 'not a fit person to', or 'not entitled to'.[104]

I have pursued these matters with reference to more recent writers than Austin, especially Evans, Searle, and Recanati, first in *New Horizons in Hermeneutics* and then more recently in the essay in the *Festschrift* for Howard Marshall, *Jesus of Nazareth: Lord and Christ*.[105] In the earlier work I have drawn especially on John Searle's work on the logic of promise as an example of a speech-act in which language changes the world.[106] In the more recent essay I have focused on the very different notions of Christological 'authority' which illocutionary acts and perlocutionary acts respectively imply or entail. The former do not require displays of power, miracle, rhetoric or assertiveness; they may function with authority and validity, even if Jesus goes to the cross in humiliation, self-renunciation, and hiddenness, on the basis solely of his identity and duly appointed role. A merely functional approach to

---

[101]*Church Dogmatics*, I:1, esp. section 3, 111-20; section 6, 187-98; section 9, 375-83; I:2, sections 14 and 19; II:1, sections 26 and 31, esp. 298-9, 450-51 and 672-3; and II:2, sections 32 and 33, on election and covenant.

[102]*How to Do Things With Words*, 45.

[103]*Ibid.*, 34.

[104]*Ibid.*

[105]*New Horizons in Hermeneutics*, 283-307; *cf.* n. 99.

[106]*Expression and Meaning. Studies in the Theology of Speech Acts* (Cambridge: CUP, 1979) esp. 1-29; *cf.* also his *Speech Acts. An Essay in the Philosophy of Language*, (Cambridge: CUP, 1983); and F. Recanati, *Meaning and Force. The Pragmatics of Performative Utterances* (ET; Cambridge: CUP, 1987). Further literature is mentioned in the relevant sections in *New Horizons in Hermeneutics*, especially chapter 8.

the effects of language on readers does not of itself offer tools or criteria
for this fundamental distinction. Indeed perlocutionary acts may
become effective and operative, even if they remain invalid and illegitimate, through self-assertive or even self-deceptive manipulation.

The second severely limiting factor in the Warfield tradition has
been to accord undue privilege, even exclusive monopoly, to the mode
of discourse of prophetic oracle, as against hymns, psalms, projected
narrative-worlds of actual or fictive possibilities, deconstructionist or
other exploratory strategies in the wisdom literature, and pledges of
promise, liberation and love. If someone suffers deprivation and
oppression, and some agency holds them captive, to discover that
another has authority to offer them release is utterly to disengage the
notion of 'authority' from repression, and to understand it as a vehicle
for liberation. Yet, as the Epistle of James reminds us, some performative speech-acts may rest on mere illusion and pretence. If a person,
James observes, uses the language of giving without performing it as a
commissive which has practical consequences, it is a fraud. 'If... one of
you says "Go in peace, keep warm and eat your fill", and yet you do
not supply their needs, what is the good of that?' (James 2:16). This
brings us to our final sections on the two most fundamental problems
of hermeneutics, namely corrigibility, and self-deception or
manipulation.

VI. Two Key Hermeneutical Issues:

1. Corrigibility of Interpretation
In popular terms the difficulty of interpretation in the context of a concern for some absolute authority has often been expressed as the
problem of relativism. Since this term has become a value-laden catch-
all which is regularly used in undisciplined and loosely defined ways,
often even by writers who should know better, it is more accurate to
state this problem as that of corrigibility. An interpretation, because it
is fallible, may need to be corrected and revised. It is important to
remind ourselves that even if some or all Reformers ascribed infallibility to Scripture, the church's own understanding and use of Scripture
participated, for the Reformers, in the fallibility of all ecclesial and individual judgment. The Thirty-nine Articles of the Church of England
insist not only that 'it is not lawful for the Church to ordain anything
that is contrary to God's Word written...' (Article 20), but also that

'General Councils... may err, and sometimes have erred, even in things pertaining unto God' (Article 21).

Significantly, G.C. Berkouwer draws attention to the problem from within the Reformed tradition. In his chapter on 'Authority and Interpretation' he concedes:

> The true understanding of Scripture is not automatically guaranteed by pure theories and clear hermeneutical rules... This does not yet mean that the way of understanding will be free from danger and the possibilities of getting lost.[107]

This occurs partly, but only partly, because exegetes and interpreters are not

> neutral observers. Neutral observation might be conceivable if Scripture had been intended to inform us about various neutral tidbits of information. Real understanding acknowledges a necessary relationship between our life and the text.[108]

The text makes 'a claim (*Anspruch*)'.It wants 'engagement'. Berkouwer acknowledges all this while still holding a traditional view of textuality as 'the "given data"'.[109]

Some may wish to dismiss even Berkouwer's conservative approach as insufficiently conservative, in that it shares with Schleiermacher, with Dilthey, with Heidegger, with Bultmann, with Fuchs, with Gadamer, and with all major hermeneutical theorists the recognition of pre-understanding and the part played by a life-relationship to the text.[110] But an illusory appeal to the supposed value-free knowledge of the sciences will not help. Even as modified by his own second thoughts, the work of Kuhn, and certainly not only Kuhn, demonstrates that the sciences constantly stand in need of revision, and their methodological paradigms in need of development as knowledge and understanding advance.[111] Gadamer ruthlessly exposes a naively objectivist view of the sciences, including even statistics. Statistics, he

---

[107]*Studies in Dogmatics*, 117.

[108]*Ibid.*, 118.

[109]*Ibid.*, 119.

[110]Probably the most widely known example is Rudolf Bultmann's essay 'Is Exegesis Without Presuppositions Possible?' in *Existence and Faith: Shorter Writings of Rudolf Bultmann* (ET; London: Fontana; 1964) 342-51.

[111]Thomas S. Kuhn, *The Structure of Scientific Revolutions* (2nd rev. ed.; Chicago: Chicago UP, 1970); idem, *The Essential Tension. Selected Studies in a Scientific Tradition and Change* (Chicago: Chicago UP, 1977).

asserts, depend not on 'the facts', but on human judgements about what count as 'significant facts'.[112]

Should this disturb us? Is it merely to be accepted, or to be shrugged off, or what? It is of fundamental importance here to recall our re-formulation of the 'above' of absolute certainty and perfection and the 'below' of contingent change in terms of biblical eschatology and Trinitarian theology. In a lecture originally delivered as early as 1964, Pannenberg asserts that the 'anticipatory structure' which relates to the ministry and destiny of Jesus 'can become the key to solving a fundamental question facing philosophical reflection in the problematic post-Hegelian situation'.[113] He declares:

> It is possible to find in the history of Jesus an answer to the question of how 'the whole' of reality and its meaning can be conceived without compromising the provisionality and historical relativity of all thought, as well as openness to the future or the past of the thinker who knows himself to be only on the way and not yet at the goal.[114]

Pannenberg acknowledges the hermeneutical axiom that 'the parts themselves cannot attain any firm footing without knowledge of the whole... Only knowledge of the whole can make clear what significance the parts really deserve.'[115] In principle we need to understand the purpose and shape of all history before we can reach a definitive judgment about individual historical events. But as against Cullmann and those who restrict the focus of revelation to 'salvation-history', Pannenberg sees the whole process of world history, which will be fully understood only at the end, as focused in an anticipatory way in as far as Jesus Christ in his death and resurrection anticipates verdicts of the end-events.

We have already pointed out that in the day-to-day life of the Christian believer, justification by grace through faith alone operates on this basis. To formulate the principle more broadly to include biblical authority and interpretation: *I entrust my daily life to the consequences and commitments entailed in acts of promise, commission, appointment, address, directive and pledge of love spoken in the name of God or God in Christ in Scripture, even though the definitive corroboration of the validity of*

---

[112]Hans-Georg Gadamer, *Philosophical Hermeneutics*, (Berkeley: University of California Press, 1976) 3-17., esp. 10-11.
[113]*Basic Questions in Theology*, Vol. 1, 181.
[114]*Ibid.*
[115]*Ibid.*, 164.

these linguistic acts awaits final confirmation at the last judgment. Just as sanctification entails a process of transformation into the image of Christ, although through justification I already am 'in Christ', clothed in his righteousness, even so interpretation and understanding of Scripture entails a process of grasping more fully the implications, entailments, nuances, and perhaps further commitments and promises that develop what has been appropriated in faith.

There is a sense in which the Christian reader is like a person holding a bank cheque in their hands, bearing the words 'I promise to pay...' The believer, in trustful faith, draws on the financial credit which it promises, but its validity and ultimate authority will become fully evident, to translate the simile, at the last day. In this sense Luther spoke of 'faith' as 'staking one's life' on God's promises, and of *claritas Scripturae* as that which offered clear enough light for each next step. We must recall, as I have urged in *New Horizons in Hermeneutics*, that *claritas Scripturae* emerged primarily in the context of Luther's rejection of the claim of Erasmus that Scripture is too ambiguous to allow action of the kind Luther wished to take. For Erasmus its alleged ambiguity paralysed action.[116]

The authority of the Bible, then, derives from the operative statutory or institutional validity of transforming speech-acts in Scripture. These speech-acts remain temporally conditional, and engage with processes of understanding which are also temporal. But while corrigibility implies temporal relationality, it does not evaporate into what is often called radical relativism. For interpretation serves to advance the reading community towards those verdicts and corroboration of promises and pledges which will become public and revealed as definitive at the last judgement. In this corporate and historical process, we need not regard conflicts of interpretation with dismay. For they belong to a broad process of testing, correcting, and initiating readiness for fresh advance, even if from time to time they also enter blind alleys. But such is the nature of appropriating the gifts and grace of God which is both fallible and bold, touched by sin, yet empowered and directed by the Holy Spirit. 'Now we know in part (ἐκ μέρους)... Then shall I know, even as I am known' (1 Cor. 13:9,10).

2. Self-Deception, Interest, and Manipulation

Like the sacraments, the Scriptures belong to the intermediate period of time 'until the Lord comes' (1 Cor. 11:26). But just as Protestants look

---

[116]Thiselton, *New Horizons in Hermeneutics*, 179-85.

with distaste on periods of church history when the use, or withholding, of sacraments was used by a priestly establishment for the exercise
of its own interests of power, even so the history of Protestant communities has not remained entirely guiltless of using the Bible equally to
serve manipulative interests.

One reason why the debate which took up Warfield's work has
often proved to be unconstructive is that it remains largely defensive.
It operates in a context of polemic rather than enquiry. It serves to
negate any deviation from a specific formulation. But if we are to
assume the mode of polemic, nothing undermines the authority of
Scripture more destructively and seductively than interpreting it in
such a way that it becomes our own mouthpiece, or the mouthpiece of
our own community, to legitimate, by virtue of its status as the perceived Word of God, that which merely serves our interests.

In hermeneutical theory the introduction of issues about social
interest has been associated especially with J. Habermas, initially with
the implications of his book *Knowledge and Human Interests*.[117] The
issues also came to the attention of hermeneutical theorists through
Paul Ricoeur's major breakthrough on the need for a 'hermeneutic of
suspicion' in his *Freud and Philosophy: An Essay on Interpretation*.[118]
Dreams, according to Freud, may constitute 'disguised, substitutive,
and fictive expressions of human wishing or desire'.[119] Often the
recounting of the dream, or the dream-as-remembered may represent
a 'condensation' and 'displacement' or 'scrambling' of the dream-as-
dreamed.

Interpretation of the dream as a means to understanding the genuine wishes and concerns of the dream entails probing through the
disguises of unconscious self-deception by which the dream-as-
remembered protects the self. But this principle, Ricoeur argues,
embraces in part all interpretation. He rightly insists: 'Hermeneutics
seems to me to be animated by this double motivation: willingness to
suspect, willingness to listen; vow of rigor, vow of obedience.'[120] In
interpreting especially the Bible, Ricoeur, again rightly, sees the hermeneutic of suspicion as a process of destroying idols, which appear to be
sacred but in actuality represent no more than human constructs, or
projections of our own desires.

---

[117]*Knowledge and Human Interests*, (ET of 2nd ed.; London: Heinemann, 1978).
[118]*Freud and Philosophy: An Essay on Interpretation* (ET; New Haven: Yale UP, 1970).
[119]*Ibid.*, 5.
[120]*Ibid.*, 15.

The French edition of *Freud and Philosophy* appeared in 1965, and came from the matrix of thought in Paris with which his near-contemporary Roland Barthes was associated and from which Jacques Derrida's *Of Grammatology* (1967) and *White Mythology* (1971) came.[121] Barthes and Derrida drew not only on Freud, but also on Nietzsche and Heidegger. According to Derrida:

> Metaphysics—the white mythology of the West which reassembles and reflects the culture of the West—the white man takes... for the universal form of that he must still wish to call Reason.[122]

'Western' rationality depends on nothing more than being deceived by the metaphor of one's culture. Everything is a disguised construct of human wishes in which metaphor, to look back to Nietzsche, becomes a mobile army, or a shifting instrumental power-construct.

The power of self-deception for the sake of self-interest lays down its greatest challenge to theological hermeneutics when literary theory, sociology of knowledge, and post-modernism conspire to develop the combined work of Marx, Nietzsche, and Freud on suspicion into a sophisticated theory of textuality, interpretation, semiotics and the authority of communities. Reinhold Niebuhr's utterly devastating exposé of the nature of sin or corporate self-deception in societies and in communities in *Moral Man and Immoral Society* can be too readily forgotten.[123] Where the individual may become openly aware, and indeed shamed, by evidence of self-interest, self-interest within the nation may be readily disguised as patriotism; sharp practice in businesses as efficiency or benefits for one's loyal clients; self-aggrandizement in life-style as for the sake of the family.[124]

Churches and theological traditions, however, are not exempt from disguised forms of power-interests. They become all the worse when they commandeer traditions of biblical interpretation to impose their interests on others in the name of the Word of God. It is precisely here that hermeneutics performs one of its most essential and necessary functions. By drawing on, and by proposing and teaching habituated patterns of self-criticism and suspicion on one side, and patterns of openness and listening on the other hermeneutics assists in

---

[121]*Of Grammatology* (ET; Baltimore: Johns Hopkins UP, 1976) and 'White Mythology: Metaphor in the Text of Philosophy' in *Margins of Philosophy*, (ET; New York: Harvester Wheatsheaf, 1982) 207-72.
[122]'White Mythology', 213.
[123]*Moral Man and Immoral Society* (New York: Scribner, 1932) xi-xii.
[124]*Ibid.*, 18, 27, 45, 93, and 95.

restoring authority where it belongs, and thereby destroys idols of our own making.

A brilliant study of the early thought of Gadamer undertaken recently by Robert R. Sullivan shows how radically from the very start Gadamer sought to disengage a philosophical tradition of wisdom and understanding from mere knowledge and technical skill which can be manipulated in the service of prior interests.[125] Gadamer did not publish *Truth and Method* until he was sixty. In radical contrast to Heidegger, his former teacher, he did not blame Plato for many of the ills of the Western tradition. Rather, Gadamer saw in the dialogue form used by Plato a model of open, non-manipulative discourse, in which all sides began with, or came to see, an admission of ignorance and a need to discard pre-packaged assumptions and modes of questioning. Sullivan contrasts the will-to-power shared by Nietzsche, by Heidegger (in a particular sense) and by Nazism and Goebbels' manipulative propaganda, with Gadamer's disengagement from all this.[126] Gadamer suspects 'method', because Enlightenment sciences were obsessed with mastery, success and power. By contrast, Gadamer seeks to appropriate a tradition of 'wisdom' which underlies, and provides a continuum for, the supposed 'acts of reason', or 'uses of method' which appeared to acquire (spuriously) a status of foundational ultimacy from Descartes to the end of the Enlightenment.[127]

In this context Gadamer points out that there is nothing irrational about appealing to, and heeding, 'authority'. This 'rests on... an act of reason itself', for it arises from being 'aware of its own limitations' and accepting that someone else may 'have better understanding'.[128] This cannot but remind us of Paul's words: 'If you think that you are wise in this age, you should become a fool so that you may become wise' (1 Cor. 3:18).

This principle may perhaps serve to explain why so many irrationally regard hermeneutics as intrusive and inhibiting, and as overlaying the text with unnecessary and intimidating theory. We recall here Terry Eagleton's *bon mot* that antipathy towards theory usually means hostility towards other people's and oblivion of one's own. Hermeneutics, by exposing self-interest and the use of texts as instruments to serve a will-for-power, liberates them to speak not with the

---

[125]*Political Hermeneutics. The Early Thinking of Hans-Georg Gadamer* (University Park, PA: Pennsylvania State UP, 1989)
[126]*Ibid.*, 169-81.
[127]*Truth and Method*, 5-39, 73-152, 274-343, and xi-xv.
[128]*Ibid.*, 248.

perlocutionary force of a seductive Hermes who has 'thieved' the text, but with the illocutionary force of an authority appropriated in faith and validated finally at the last day.

Our proposals have not been offered as an alternative to other contemporary angles of approach. There is value, for example, in James Barr's point about the authority of the Bible residing analytically or by internal grammar in Christian identity. Barr states: 'Involvement with the Bible is analytic in being a Christian.'[129] There is value in James Smart's warning, 'Let the Scriptures cease to be heard, and soon the remembered Christ becomes an imagined Christ.'[130] David Kelsey rightly urges that the Bible functions to 'shape persons' identities' with 'self-involving force'.[131] The aim here, however, has been to explore the basis of this force. This is a task central to the role of hermeneutics.

---

[129]'Has the Bible any Authority?', in *Explorations in Theology 7: The Scope and Authority of the Bible* (London: SCM, 1980) 52.
[130]*The Strange Silence of the Bible in the Church* (London: SCM, 1970) 25.
[131]*The Uses of Scripture in Recent Theology* (London: SCM, 1975) 90 and 89; see also Frances Young, *The Art of Performance. Towards a Theology of Holy Scripture* (London: Darton, Longman & Todd, 1990) 173.

CHAPTER 6

God's Mighty Speech-Acts: The Doctrine of Scripture Today

Kevin Vanhoozer

Summary

The doctrine of Scripture explains how the Bible is related to the Word of God. The 'Scripture principle' affirms a direct identity of Scripture and the Word of God, as opposed to Barth's 'indirect identity' and Barr's 'non-identity' theses. The Scripture principle ultimately depends on divine sovereignty and ultimately founders, according to its critics, on the problem of evil. This article further explores the connections between the doctrines of God and Scripture, and in particular the relation between providence and inspiration. While contemporary theologians tend to construe God's involvement with Scripture in terms of only one biblical genre, a more promising approach, one which overcomes the dichotomy between personal and propositional revelation, views Scripture in terms of the diversity of divine communicative acts.

> And we also thank God constantly for this, that when you
> received the word of God which you heard from us, you
> accepted it not as the word of men but as what it really is, the
> word of God, which is at work in you believers (1 Thes. 2:13)

I. Why a 'Doctrine' of Scripture?

What does a doctrine of Scripture hope to achieve? If the task of Christology is to show how 'Jesus' is the 'Christ', we might say that the task of a doctrine of Scripture is to show how the Bible is, or is related to, the 'Word of God'. A doctrine of Scripture tries to give an account of the relation of the words to the Word and of how this relation may legitimately be said to be 'of God'. A doctrine of Scripture seeks to show how biblical language and literature participate in the Word of God. All such attempts presuppose, therefore, some understanding of the meaning and locus of 'Word of God'.

1. The 'Scripture principle'
The so-called 'Scripture principle' represents the historical orthodox view that the Bible is to be identified with the Word of God. Reformed Confessions often expressed their concern for biblical authority by devoting a separate article to the doctrine of Scripture.[1] Calvin's statement is representative:

> We have to do with the Word which came forth from God's mouth
> and was given to us... God's will is to speak to us by the mouths of the
> apostles and prophets... their mouths are to us as the mouth of the
> only true God.[2]

Various forms of biblical criticism since the Enlightenment have chipped away at such an identification of the Bible with divine revelation. The rootedness of the language and traditions of Scripture in human history became increasingly apparent, to the point that the

---

[1] *Cf.* Karl Barth: 'the Scripture principle is in fact expressed more or less sharply and explicitly at the head of all the more important confessional writings of the Reformed Church...' (*Church Dogmatics* [ET; Edinburgh: T.&T. Clark, 1975] I:2, 547).
[2] Calvin, in J. Haroutunian (ed.), *Calvin: Commentaries* (The Library of Christian Classics; Philadelphia: Westminster, 1958) 83. Calvin is expounding 1 Pet. 1:25: '"but the word of the Lord abides for ever". That word is the good news which was preached to you.'

Bible appeared to be a man-made rather than God-breathed product. In 1881, William Robertson Smith recommended the same methods of historical and literary analysis for the study of Scripture as those applied to other books, a suggestion that eventually led to his being put on trial in Scotland for heresy. In America during the following decade, the Presbyterian Church similarly charged Charles A. Briggs with heresy, largely because he rejected verbal inspiration. Briggs used both exegetical and historical arguments in his defence: neither the teaching nor the phenomena of Scripture supported the notion of verbal inspiration, nor did the notions of verbal inspiration or inerrancy reflect the views of the Fathers and Reformers. The General Assembly of the Presbyterian Church in the United States three times (in 1910, 1916 and 1923) declared, in response, that biblical inerrancy was an 'essential doctrine' of the church.[3]

One of the major factors in the demise of the Scripture principle was the rise of historical criticism. What is perhaps less well documented is the extent to which the dispute about the Scripture principle was essentially theological. For what is at stake in debates about Scripture is ultimately one's doctrine of God.[4] In this article, therefore, I propose to deal more with theological than with exegetical or historical arguments against the scripture principle.

Perhaps the single most important aspect of the doctrine of God which has a bearing on the doctrine of Scripture is divine providence. Indeed, Pope Leo XIII entitled his 1893 encyclical on Scripture and scholarship *Providentissimus Deus*. The encyclical states: 'All the books and the whole of each book which the Church receives as sacred and canonical were written at the dictation of the Holy Spirit.'[5] Leo XIII was simply repeating the simple identification of Scripture and revelation which characterised the confessions of the Protestant Reformation as well as the Council of Trent's Counter-Reformation *Decree on Scripture*

---

[3]See George Marsden, *Reforming Fundamentalism: Fuller Seminary and the New Evangelicalism* (Grand Rapids: Eerdmans, 1987) 112 and Jack B. Rogers and Donald K. McKim, *The Authority and Interpretation of the Bible: An Historical Approach* (San Francisco: Harper & Row, 1979) 348-61.

[4]Is it merely coincidence that biblical criticism arose, and flourished, when Deism was increasingly in vogue? Or that classical views of revelation and inspiration presuppose theism? In our time, theism appears to be giving way to various forms of panentheism (*i.e.*, the idea that God is not 'over' the world, as Lord, but rather that the world is 'in' God, who serves as its inner ground). Work on how this broader theological context affects the doctrine of Scripture is urgently needed.

[5]Cited in Baillie, *The Idea of Revelation in Recent Thought* (New York: Columbia UP, 1956) 31.

and Tradition (1546), from which Leo had borrowed the phrase, 'at the dictation of the Holy Spirit'. The fundamental issue in the doctrine of Scripture concerns the manner of God's involvement in the words of Scripture and thus the manner of God's activity in the world.

2. The nature of a 'doctrine' of Scripture

Doctrine, according to Alister McGrath, is an integrative concept with four essential elements: social, cognitive, experiential and linguistic.[6] First, doctrine arises in response to threats to a community's self-understanding or identity. Clearly, the doctrine of Scripture has indeed functioned as a means of social demarcation—and that with a vengeance! Fundamentalism, Evangelicalism, liberalism, post-liberal, orthodox, neo-orthodox, *etc.* are distinguished in large part on the basis of their respective stance towards Scripture. Evangelicals of one school have a difficult time doing justice to other kinds of Evangelicals. Gabriel Fackre's careful taxonomy of the various positions on biblical authority even finds several species of inerrancy.[7] The situation today is comparable to the Christological controversies of the fifth and sixth centuries, which saw an expansion in the vocabulary of Christology.

Second, doctrine arises in response to questions about the community's founding narrative. Doctrine provides a 'conceptual framework', suggested by the biblical narrative itself, for interpreting that narrative. There is a conceptual sub-structure to the biblical narrative that calls for thought—doctrine formulation. It is precisely this conceptual sub-structure that is in dispute in debates over the doctrine of Scripture. One hundred years ago, Warfield wrote: 'The subject of the Inspiration of the Bible is one which has been much confused in recent discussion.'[8] More recently, Edward Farley and Peter Hodgson write: 'we do not believe that an adequate reformulation of the doctrine of scripture has yet been achieved by contemporary theology.'[9] My thesis in what follows is that the concept of divine speech-acts may go some way in falsifying this judgement.

---

[6]Alister McGrath, *The Genesis of Doctrine: A Study in the Foundations of Doctrinal Criticism* (Oxford: Basil Blackwell, 1990) ch. 3

[7]See Gabriel Fackre, *The Christian Story: A Pastoral Systematics* (Grand Rapids: Eerdmans, 1987) Vol. 2, 61-75.

[8]Benjamin B. Warfield, *The Inspiration and Authority of the Bible* (Presbyterian and Reformed, 1979) 105.

[9]Edward Farley and Peter Hodgson, 'Scripture and Tradition', in Peter Hodgson and Robert King (eds.), *Christian Theology: An Introduction to its Traditions and Tasks* (2nd ed; Philadelphia: Fortress, 1985) 81.

3. 'Mighty speech-acts'

The doctrine of Scripture is only intelligible in the light of a whole network of other doctrines which includes revelation, providence and pneumatology. The concept of a speech-act is, I believe, a helpful one with which to integrate and interpret the classical categories of revelation, inspiration and infallibility. Above all, it allows us to transcend the debilitating dichotomy between revelation as 'God saying' and 'God doing'. For the category speech-act acknowledges that saying too is a doing, and that persons can do many things by 'saying'.

The biblical theology movement typically distinguished between God's acts and God's speaking. 'The New Testament has no authority which is not the authority of Jesus and the authority of the mighty acts of God involving him.'[10] Well and good—but disagreement arises over the nature of God's mighty acts. For many contemporary theologians, history is the arena of God's acts and, consequently, the proper category for understanding God's self-revelation. On this view, the Bible is only a witness to revelation, not the revelation itself. According to G.E. Wright: when 'the Word of God' is interpreted to mean 'that the centre of the Bible is a series of divinely given teachings, then it is certainly a misconception'.[11] This dichotomy turns up in other theologians too.

Whereas the biblical theology movement attended to the 'act of God' in a salvation-history *behind* the text, Barth argued that it is only through the singular history of Jesus Christ that God makes himself known. Pannenberg works yet another variation on the idea of revelation in history: because God is the 'all-determining reality', *all* of history is revelatory of God. Because Jesus' resurrection anticipates the end of history, however, God may be said to be revealed in Christ. For Pannenberg, the biblical texts are promissory, insofar as they anticipate the final shape of history and thus the nature and purpose of God. The Bible is an witness to (in the sense of anticipation of) the Word of God.

What these three approaches share is the conceptual distinction between Scripture and the mighty act(s) of God, located in a special, singular and universal history respectively. But just as the biblical theology movement earlier had difficulty articulating the notion of an 'act of God', so today there is confusion over the nature of the 'Word of God'. For Bultmann, the 'Word of God' is a communicative act of

---

[10]Oliver O'Donovan, *On the Thirty-Nine Articles: A Conversation with Tudor Christianity* (Exeter: Paternoster, 1986) 51.

[11]G.E. Wright, 'God Who Acts', in Owen Thomas (ed.), *God's Activity in the World* (Chico: Scholars Press, 1983) 25.

address shrouded in the deep recesses of human subjectivity. In Barth's theology, the Word similarly lacks definition, for the properly semantic moment of God's self-disclosure remains insufficiently analysed. At the same time, the emphasis on the Word being a "mighty act" of God must not be lost. Instead, God's Word and God's act must be thought together.

The notion of a divine speech-act addresses both the problem of the nature of God's activity and the problem of the nature of biblical language. Specifically, it explains how God is involved with the production of Scripture and so overcomes the ruinous dichotomy between historical-actualist and verbal-conceptualist models of revelation, that is, the dualism between 'God saying' and 'God doing'. Scripture is neither simply the recital of the acts of God nor merely a book of inert propositions. Scripture is rather composed of divine-human speech-acts which, through what they say, accomplish several authoritative cognitive, spiritual and social functions.

4. A pathway

'He will teach us his ways, and we will walk in his paths' (Mi. 4:2). Calvin's comment on this verse is instructive: 'the church of God can be established only where the Word of God rules, where God shows by his voice the way of salvation'.[12] The pathway into the doctrine of Holy Scripture is neither simple nor straightforward: it intersects with the doctrine of God—in particular, the doctrine of providence—and with theories concerning the nature of language and literature. This is only as it should be, if indeed the task of a doctrine of Scripture is to explain how and why the Bible is the 'Word' of 'God'. In what follows I first review the problems associated with the 'Received View' and some recent evangelical attempts to restate it. I then turn to consider the ways in which the doctrine of God is decisive for one's understanding of the doctrine of Scripture. Finally, I propose the model of communicative action for conceiving the Scriptures as the revelatory Word of God. The Bible, I shall argue, is a diverse collection of God's mighty speech-acts which communicate the saving Word of God.

The pathway I am proposing leads to three theses and a corollary. First, one's view of Scripture is always correlated to one's view of God: no doctrine of Scripture without a doctrine of providence. Most theologians, I argue, gravitate towards a particular genre of Scripture in their construal of how God is involved with Scripture.

---

[12]*Calvin: Commentaries*, 79.

Second, I shall defend a version of the 'identity thesis': Scripture is, in a sense yet to be defined, really the Word of God. Those who affirm biblical infallibility are often charged with holding a quasi-magical view of the Bible as a sort of talisman that reveals the secrets of the universe. The Scripture principle, it is true, can degenerate into a species of bibliolatry. However, I shall contend that identifying the Scriptures as the Word of God need not result in bibliolatry, so long as God's communicative acts are not mistaken for the divine being itself. The Word of God is God in communicative act, and there is no reason why some divine communicative acts cannot be verbal. This implies that the dichotomy between propositional and personal revelation is not as hard and fast as almost a century of debate has thought. We are not confronted with a stark choice of opting for the 'system' or the 'Saviour' in Scripture. There are, therefore, ecumenical possibilities for an evangelical view of Scripture that focuses on God's mighty speech-acts. This chapter will have succeeded if it enables Evangelicals of the left and of the right to discover a means for reconciling unnecessary differences.

Third, a number of theologians, prompted largely by Barth, see biblical authority in functional terms, as instrumental in leading us to Christ. Truth would, on this view, be a matter of faith and practice. The focus on God's mighty speech-acts is a bit broader: the Bible is, to be sure, no science textbook, but neither is it restricted only to serving as a witness to Christ. Neither cosmo- nor Christocentric, the Scriptures are rather centred on God's covenant. The covenant involves the cosmos, and Christ is at the centre, but 'covenantal efficacy' is the more comprehensive term to cover all the things that God does with and in and through the Scriptures. What we have in the Scriptures is therefore everything which God deemed necessary and sufficient for the doctrinal, moral and spiritual welfare of his covenant people.

We will find, finally, a corollary: why the doctrine of Scripture matters. Here it is perhaps more accurate to speak of a pathway *out* of the Scriptures: the scripture principle matters because it is the norm of both dogmatics and ethics. The task of Christian dogmatics is nothing less than 'the unfolding and presentation of the content of the Word of God'.[13] Likewise, the task of Christian ethics is nothing less than the unfolding and presentation of the content of the Word in individual and social practice. The doctrine of Scripture is far from being a theo-

---

[13]Barth, *Church Dogmatics*, I:2, 853.

retical abstraction. Those who 'identify Scripture as God's Word, are deeply concerned to submit to its authority in their lives'.[14]

II. The Doctrine of Scripture: Yesterday and Today

The Reformation understanding of Scripture has been variously interpreted. Some stress the elements of continuity with Protestant orthodoxy, others the discontinuity.[15] By the 'Received View', I am referring to Warfield's Princetonian doctrine of Scripture and its contemporary restatements.[16] I am more interested in the theological underpinnings of this position than in the historical question of whether or to what extent this represents the view of the Reformers themselves. In any case, the Received View was the form that the doctrine of Scripture had assumed at the end of the nineteenth century, when it was attacked and defended with equal vigour. The story of the doctrine's development in the twentieth century has, with few exceptions, been one of hardening nineteenth-century positions. One way or another, then, the Received View continues to function as the touchstone in debates about the doctrine of Scripture.[17] In this section I examine the development of the Received View, problems with the

---

[14]John Stott's definition of 'evangelicals', in David Edwards and John Stott, *Evangelical Essentials: A Liberal—Evangelical Dialogue* (London/Downers Grove: Hodder & Stoughton/IVP, 1988) 104.

[15]William J. Abraham, for example, claims that the Warfield-Packer view 'involves substantial innovations in theology' (*The Divine Inspiration of Holy Scripture* [Oxford: OUP, 1981] 16), as do Rogers and McKim. For an opposing point of view, see John Woodbridge, *Biblical Authority: A Critique of the Rogers/McKim Proposal* (Grand Rapids: Zondervan, 1982) and Richard Muller, *Post-Reformation Reformed Dogmatics, Vol. 2: Holy Scripture: The Cognitive Foundation of Theology* (Grand Rapids: Baker, 1993)

[16]The Received View was developed systematically by Warfield about one hundred years ago, and it was also a significant factor in the emergence of Evangelicalism in America in the 1940s and in the founding of the Tyndale Fellowship in 1944.

[17]Just how pervasive the Received View of revelation was may be illustrated by a comment from John Baillie. Referring to the nineteenth-century continental Protestant flight from the doctrine of revelation, Baillie writes: 'It is as if these thinkers felt revelation to be so universally understood as the verbal or conceptual communication of truth by divine authority that only by abandoning the term itself could they effectively retreat from this wrong [sic] meaning' (*Idea of Revelation in Recent Thought*, 15).

Received View and contemporary evangelical modifications and alternatives.

1. The 'Received View' stated: the Warfield-Packer position

The components of the Received View—propositional revelation, verbal inspiration and infallible authority—are doubtless familiar and may be briefly sketched.[18] At its heart is an 'identity thesis', namely, the belief that Scripture *is* the Word of God.

(1) Propositional revelation. Perhaps the most important, and contentious, claim is that God reveals himself verbally in Scripture. The emphasis is on God's self-communication through the revealed truths formulated in the canon. Revelation is largely a matter of doctrine or 'sacred teaching'. What makes the Bible authoritative is its cognitive content. Of course, one must be careful not to caricature the Received View. Packer, for instance, acknowledges that the Scripture principle is not self-standing: 'when this affirmation [viz., that Scripture is revelation] is not related to God's saving work in history and to the illumining and interpreting work of the Spirit, it too is theologically incomplete.'[19]

(2). Verbal inspiration. The Bible is the very Word of God itself. God so superintended the process of composing the Scriptures that the end result manifests his divine intention, and this without overriding the human authors and their intentions:

> The Bible is the Word of God in such a sense that its words, though written by men and bearing indelibly impressed on them the marks of their human origin, were written, nevertheless, under such an influence of the Holy Ghost as to be also the words of God, the adequate expression of His mind and will.[20]

We might call this the 'direct identity thesis' (as opposed to Barth's 'indirect identity thesis' and to James Barr's 'non-identity thesis'). It would be incorrect, however, to infer that a dictation theory necessar-

---

[18]For a comprehensive re-statement of this position, see Carl F.H. Henry, *God, Revelation, and Authority*, Vols. 1-3 (Waco: Word, 1976-79). *Cf.* the articles on Packer and Warfield in Walter Elwell (ed.), *Handbook of Evangelical Theologians* (Grand Rapids: Baker, 1993).

[19]J.I. Packer, 'Scripture', in S. Ferguson, D.F. Wright and J.I. Packer (eds.), *A New Dictionary of Theology*, (Leicester: IVP, 1988) 628.

[20]Warfield, *Inspiration and Authority*, 173.

ily follows from the 'identity thesis'. Indeed, Warfield makes two important qualifications to pre-empt just such a conclusion.

First, Warfield is cautious about drawing a Chalcedonian analogy to the doctrine of Scripture. 'There is no hypostatic union between the Divine and the human in Scripture; we cannot parallel the "inscripturation" of the Holy Spirit and the incarnation of the Son of God.'[21] Warfield acknowledges a remote analogy only: though both involve a union of divine and human factors, in the one 'they unite to constitute a Divine-human person, in the other they co-operate to perform a Divine-human work'.[22] Second, Warfield is careful to affirm the reality of human agency in the writing of Scripture. His view entails a conception of concursus rather than mechanical dictation.[23]

(3). Infallible authority. According to Packer, the Bible is the Word of God not only instrumentally (*e.g.,* functionally) but intrinsically (*e.g.,* materially). It follows that Scripture will be without error, for God cannot lie (Heb. 6:18), nor is God ignorant (Heb. 4:13). Gordon Lewis and Bruce Demarest claim that the human writers were kept from error by an 'epistemological miracle' which they attribute to the Spirit. They see the Spirit's influence, however, not like that of an impersonal machine but rather like 'worthy personal relationships'.[24] Nevertheless, the tendency of this view is to see all parts of the Bible as forms of teaching whose purpose is to make true assertions about God and the world. 'Hard' biblical authority claims the Scriptures speak truly on matters of history and science as well as on matters of faith.

2. Problems with the Received View
The Received View has been subjected to searching criticisms. I here focus only on criticisms that come from two opposing points of view: the neo-orthodoxy of Karl Barth and the neo-liberalism of James Barr.

(1) Theological problems with 'propositions'. According to Barth, to say revelation is to say 'The Word became flesh'.[25] The Received View errs in elevating propositions about a person above a personal encounter.

---

[21]*Ibid.,* 162.
[22]*Ibid.*
[23]'The Divine and Human in the Bible', *Selected Shorter Writings* (ed. John E. Meeter; Nutley, NJ: Presbyterian & Reformed, 1970, 1973) 2:547.
[24]Gordon Lewis and Bruce Demarest, *Integrative Theology,* Vol. 1 (Grand Rapids: Zondervan, 1987) 162.
[25]Barth, *Church Dogmatics* I:1, 119.

Revelation is a non-conceptual, personal encounter with Christ's person or with God's mighty acts. John Baillie: 'God does not give us information by communication; He gives us Himself in communion.'[26] Or, as he elsewhere puts it, revelation is always 'from subject to subject'.[27] The kind of knowledge that corresponds to divine revelation is, therefore, more like that of a personal relation (knowledge by acquaintance) rather than of a particular kind of data (knowledge about).

According to George Hunsinger's reading, Barth holds that scriptural language only refers to its revelatory subject matter (viz., the Word of God) by way of an analogy of grace. 'The incapacity of human language in itself and as such is what separates Barth's view from literalism [which] tends to assume that human language is intrinsically capable of referring to God.'[28] The worry, apparently, is that propositional revelation leads to a 'natural theology', as it were, of biblical language. If the Bible is itself revelation, then this revelation is ascertainable by human reason and the truth of Christ can be procured by historical and scientific investigation. Barth's attitude towards the identity thesis and natural theology alike is briefly expressed: *Nein!*.

From a wholly other perspective, James Barr believes that a perfectly good account of the Bible's status as Scripture can be given without appealing to the 'Word of God' at all. For him, the Bible is a record of the human attempt to understand and transmit the religious tradition of the people of God, not a movement from God to man.[29] Modern learning, with its rival descriptions of natural, social and historical processes, has dethroned the Bible as a document of propositional authority. Historical critical study of Scripture has led scholars to believe that the Bible manifests the same kind of historical and cultural relativity as do other texts. Is the Bible a human response to divine revelation?

> The real problem, as it seems to me, is that we have no access to, and no means of comprehending, a communication or revelation from God which is antecedent to the human tradition about him and which then goes on to generate that very tradition.[30]

---

[26]Baillie, *Idea of Revelation*, 47.
[27]*Ibid.*, 24.
[28]George Hunsinger, *How to Read Karl Barth: The Shape of his Theology* (Oxford: OUP, 1991) 43.
[29]James Barr, *The Bible in the Modern World* (London: SCM, 1973) 120.
[30]*Ibid.*, 121.

The message is clear: where human language is, God is not (though Barth allows, as Barr does not, for the possibility of a miracle which would render human language the Word of God).

(2). Theological problems with the prophetic paradigm. The Scripture principle is also thought to entail a 'prophetic paradigm' of verbal inspiration. A number of contemporary scholars believe that this paradigm tends towards a docetic view of the Word which denies both the humanity and spirituality of the Scriptures.

Barth objects to any 'materialising' of inspiration which ties down what the Spirit can say to what the human words say. Against the Received View of verbal inspiration, Barth posits a fundamental discontinuity between human speech and the Word of God. Barth acknowledges that the human authors were 'inspired' in the sense that they were immediately related to the content of revelation, Jesus Christ himself, as commissioned witnesses. Inspiration has more to do with the special content of the witness rather than its verbal forms.[31] The human witness only becomes the Word of God when the Spirit graciously appropriates the words for the purpose of self-revelation.

For Barr, the prophetic paradigm stands at the very centre of evangelical thinking about inspiration: the authors speak not their own words but those given him by God.[32] An initial difficulty is that the large portions of the Bible do not read as if they were composed in this fashion. The form of many biblical books 'is that of a man-to-man communication'.[33] John Barton observes that one cannot always paste a prophetic imprimatur on every passage: 'Samuel hewed Agag in pieces before the Lord in Gilgal: this is the Word of the Lord' creates an awkward moment in the liturgy.[34] Seriously to uphold the prophetic paradigm is, he argues, to subscribe to a dictation theory of inspiration. It is also to impose the same kind of truth claim on all parts of Scripture. But the Bible is manifestly composed of literature other than prophecy: wisdom, narrative, hymnody, apocalyptic, law, and so forth: 'Scripture contains genres which cannot be assimilated to the model of divine communication to men.'[35] If one must characterise

---

[31]Barth, *Church Dogmatics* I:2, 520-1.
[32]James Barr, *Escaping From Fundamentalism* (London: SCM, 1984) ch. 3, 'The Prophetic Paradigm'.
[33]Barr, *Bible in the Modern World*, 123.
[34]Barton, *People of the Book: The Authority of the Bible in Christianity* (London: SPCK, 1988) 71.
[35]*Ibid.*

Scripture by a central genre, then Barton believes that wisdom literature, rather than prophecy, is the better candidate.[36] The Bible is
people's reflection on their relationship with a God who is already
known.

Barr's hesitations about verbal inspiration are closely related to
his doctrine of God: 'We do not have any idea of ways in which God
might straight-forwardly communicate articulate thoughts or sentences to men; it just doesn't happen.'[37] Inspiration means that God
was 'in contact' with his people and 'present' in the formation of their
tradition: 'Today I think we believe, or have to believe, that God's communication with the men of the biblical period was not on any different
terms from the mode of his communication with his people now.'[38]
This 'soft' view of inspiration is like its poetic counterpart: as a result
of some experience, a writer's expression achieves sublimity and profundity but not, however, inerrancy or infallibility.

Must a doctrine of verbal inspiration presuppose the prophetic
paradigm? I do not see that it must. After all, the primary purpose in
stressing the verbal aspect of inspiration is to make a point about the
final product, not the process, of inscripturation. The process may well
involve free human agency, but the end result is what God intended.
Indeed, Barton cites Austin Farrer's concept of double agency as the
most satisfying account of how we should speak of Scripture if we did
wish to claim that the scriptural writers convey divine revelation,
though he fails to acknowledge that Warfield also espouses a similar
view.[39]

For all its valid caveats, Barr's understanding of the prophetic
paradigm (and thus of verbal inspiration) remains something of a caricature. He points out that, with regard to prophetic discourse, God's
judgements are not merely objective assessments, but conditional on
the people's response: 'What is said by a prophet, then, is characteristically not an absolute... the Lord does not through the prophets utter
perfect, final, ultimate and unchangeable statements.'[40] Yet the notion

---

[36]*Ibid.*, 56.
[37]Barr, *Bible in the Modern World*, 17.
[38]*Ibid.*, 17-18.
[39]Barton, *People of the Book*, 38. It is true, however, that Warfield sometimes speaks
as though the human authors were only instrumental agents. For example: 'the
completely supernatural character of revelation is in no way lessened by the cir-
cumstance that it has been given through the instrumentality of men... the Divine
word delivered through men is the pure word of God, diluted with no human
admixture whatever' (*Inspiration and Authority*, 86).
[40]Barr, *Escaping*, 24.

of verbal inspiration does not require that everything in Scripture be
treated as 'absolute' assertions, only that what is said is taken to be
divinely intended. To suggest that the prophetic paradigm implies that
everything in Scripture must be an absolute truth is to overlook the
semantics of biblical literature.[41]

(3). Theological problems with cognitive perfection. Is the Spirit's 'guidance' such that it overrides human fallibility, making the human
authors mouthpieces of infallible communication? Bernard Ramm
worries that the notion of propositional revelation 'is but an alternate
version of this Hegelian theory of a pure conceptual language'.[42] The
divinity of Scripture is not a stable property which it permanently possesses. Verbal inspiration, says Barth,

> does not mean the infallibility of the biblical word in its linguistic, his-
> torical and theological character as a human word. It means that the
> fallible and faulty human word is as such used by God and has to be
> received and heard in spite of its human fallibility.[43]

Many of the critics of the Received View prefer to locate the Spirit at
the point of the reception rather than production of the Scriptures. Bernard Ramm comments that, if the Bible could transform lives without
Christ and the Spirit, then its power would be magical and not spiritual.[44] Scripture is a medium for knowing Christ. The Bible is
authoritative and infallible not for any purpose whatsoever, but only
for the purpose of witnessing to Christ. James D.G. Dunn wonders,
'How *valid* is the proposition that inerrancy is *the necessary implication*
of scripture being God's word?' He believes that historical exegesis
must be open to the Spirit's prodding now. John Baillie agrees:

> The weakness of Protestant orthodoxy has been that it could show no
> convincing reason for insisting on the plenary nature of the divine
> assistance to the Scriptural authors while as firmly denying it to the
> mind of the Church in later days.[45]

---

[41]See my 'The Semantics of Biblical Literature', in D.A. Carson and J.D. Woodbridge (eds.), *Hermeneutics, Authority and Canon* (Grand Rapids: Zondervan, 1986)
53-104.
[42]Bernard Ramm, *After Fundamentalism: The Future of Evangelical Theology* (San
Francisco: Harper & Row, 1983) 90.
[43]Barth, *Church Dogmatics*, I:2, 533.
[44]Ramm, *Special Revelation and the Word of God*, (Grand Rapids: Eerdmans, 1961)
184.
[45]Baillie, *Idea of Revelation*, 112.

For Barr, the Bible's authority is not ontological, a matter of what it is, but functional, a matter of what it does. Specifically, the basis of biblical authority 'lies in its efficacy in the faith-relation between man and God'.[46] The Bible is the instrument of faith, not its object. It is not properties, but pragmatics, which render the Bible authoritative: the Bible is Scripture only when it proves itself fruitful in the life of the believing community. What makes the Bible efficacious? Why should the Bible rather than some other book function in this way? Does its functioning in this way have nothing to do with the kind of work it is? It is not yet clear how the words of Scripture are related to the Word of God. In a sense, the Christocentric understanding of infallibility is as reductive as the propositional. In both cases, infallibility is reduced to a single kind of communicative function: in the one case, asserting, and in the other, witnessing.

Does the Received View's affirmation of biblical infallibility deny the humanity of the Scriptures? Must humanity entail errancy? I do not see that it does. Fallibility need not entail actual fault. For example, it does not follow that, just because a maths textbook is written by a fallible human being, there must be mistakes in it! Of course, something more is being claimed for Scripture. Some—not all—defenders of the Received View draw a parallel with Chalcedonian Christology. To say that Jesus is sinless does not deny his humanity. Because of his real human nature, Jesus was tempted. Because of his divine personality, Jesus did not sin. The debate about biblical infallibility mirrors that concerning Jesus' 'impeccability'.[47]

(4). Theological problems with the Bible as the 'Word of God'. The words of Scripture are human words. For Barth, the Word of God is God in revelatory action.[48] Biblical statements must not, therefore, be directly equated with the revealed Word of God. Donald Bloesch here parts company with Packer: Scripture is not intrinsically revelation, 'for its revelatory status does not reside in its wording as such but in the Spirit of God, who fills the word with meaning and power'.[49] Similarly, the

---

[46]James Barr, *Explorations in Theology 7* (London: SCM, 1980) 54.
[47]Some maintain that impeccability is inconsistent with Jesus' humanity. The issue turns on how to define 'humanity'.
[48]See T.J. Gorringe, 'In Defence of the Identification: Scripture as the Word of God', *SJT* 32 (1979) 303-18.
[49]Donald G. Bloesch, *Holy Scripture: Revelation, Inspiration & Interpretation* (Carlisle: Paternoster, 1994) 27.

truthfulness of the Bible is not a property of the human words but of the Spirit who speaks through them.

The main problem with the identity thesis, according to its critics, is neither exegetical nor historical but theological: it falsely equates the human with the divine. Bibliolatry commits the most basic of theological errors, namely, that of identifying God with what is not-God. Dunn worries that the heirs of the Princeton theology are in danger of bibliolatry, for by affirming the infallible authority of Scripture, they are according an authority proper only to the triune God.[50] Dunn rejects the Chalcedonian analogy between the divine and human in Christ (effecting impeccability) and the divine and human in scripture (effecting inerrancy) and concludes that the Princeton doctrine is 'theologically dangerous'.

3. Whither an evangelical theology of the Word?

As a consequence of the above-mentioned criticisms, many recent evangelical works on Scripture have given greater prominence both to the humanity and to the spirituality of the Bible.

(1). New emphasis on the dynamic relation between the Word of God and Scripture. Bloesch sees three options: a rational Evangelicalism that equates Scripture with revelation understood as propositional (*e.g.,* principles or facts); an experiential liberalism that views the Bible as an illustration and intensification or human morality and spirituality; a spiritual Evangelicalism which views the Bible as 'the divinely prepared medium or channel of divine revelation rather than revelation itself'.[51]

On the hand are conservatives who swallow up the humanity of the biblical text in the notion of the Word of God and thus succumb to a kind of scriptural 'docetism'. On the other hand are liberals who evacuate the biblical text of divinity, thus creating a parallel with the Ebionite heresy that denied the divinity of Christ. In the middle are 'progressive' Evangelicals, Barth included, who seek some kind of Chalcedonian analogy which would permit them to affirm, however paradoxically, that the Scriptures are at once 'truly human' and 'truly divine'.

For Bloesch, the answer is a recovery of the 'paradoxical unity' of Word and Spirit. The Word must not be a dead letter but a living word.

---

[50]Dunn, *The Living Word*, 106.
[51]Bloesch, *Holy Scripture*, 18.

Bloesch espouses a sacramental model which sees revelation as God in action and Scripture as the means for encountering God. The Word of God must not be reduced to rational statements; it is rather God in action. The Word of God, to cite Calvin, is 'the hand of God stretching itself out to act powerfully through the apostle...'.[52]

Revelation is increasingly treated as bi-polar. One cannot properly speak of revelation without speaking of someone's receiving revelation. Here we may note Ramm's comment that the discipline of communication studies may well be the next challenge for a theology of revelation. The divine message is received by an addressee only if the Spirit accompanies the signs: 'The external letter must become an inner Word through the work of the Spirit.'[53] The knowledge of God is always assimilated through the work of the Spirit. The Spirit uses the forms of the Word of God to minister its content: Christ—the gospel of God. Ramm believes that fundamentalism loses this dynamic link between the Spirit and the Scriptures in its zeal to assert the authority of the letter.

(2). New emphasis on the humanity of the Scriptures. It is generally acknowledged that the Received View 'tended to ignore the human side' of Scripture.[54] What precisely is involved in such an admission? First, that the Bible may be read like any other book. The positive side to biblical criticism is that it serves as an antidote to a docetic interpretation of the Bible which reads it as if it had no human historical-cultural context. The Bible is a human text, with all the marks of human weakness. For instance, Pinnock says that its propositions 'fall short of expressing exactly what a speaker would wish'.[55] Moreover, the Bible is historically and scientifically 'flawed'. But God can use the 'weak' things of this world to communicate his wisdom. Inspiration for Pinnock is a 'dynamic' but 'non-coercive' work of God whereby he communicates his message in such a way that the human authors 'make full use of their own skills and vocabulary'.[56]

William Abraham argues that the Received View confuses divine inspiration with divine speaking, 'as if it were some kind of complicated speech-act of God'.[57] 'Inspiring' is not one independent activity

---

[52]Cited in Bloesch, *Holy Scripture*, 49.
[53]Pinnock, *The Scripture Principle* (San Francisco: Harper & Row, 1984) 155.
[54]*Ibid.*, 105.
[55]*Ibid.*, 98.
[56]*Ibid.*, 105.
[57]Abraham, *Divine Inspiration*, 37.

among others, but something one does by doing other activities. A teacher, for example, inspires his pupils through his lectures, his questions, his eagerness and so forth. For Abraham, God inspired the authors of the Bible through his revelatory and saving acts. Inspiration is a consequence of these other acts rather than an act in its own right. Divine speaking is only one of the acts by which God has inspired the biblical writers. Inspiration for Abraham is an effect (on the authors) of divine activity rather than a divine activity itself. (It is odd that Abraham is basing his theology of Scripture on an analysis of the ordinary usage of the term 'inspiration'. In the Received View, 'inspiration' operates as a technical term that refers to God's providential guidance of the authors in writing Scripture. Abraham, like others who appeal to a poetic model of inspiration, may be guilty of a variant of the word-concept fallacy.)

Kern Robert Trembath, following Abraham, argues that biblical inspiration refers

> to the enhancement of one's understanding of God brought about instrumentally through the Bible, rather than to the mysterious and non-repeatable process by which 'God got written what He wanted' in the Bible.[58]

Inspiration on this view is something that happens to readers, not the authors, of Scripture. The recipient of inspiration is not a book but a believer. Such an understanding corresponds more or less with Barr's 'soft' or 'functionalist' revision of the doctrine of inspiration: inspiration refers to the Bible's capacity to mediate God's saving intention to the world.

(3). New emphasis on the spirituality of Scripture. 'Progressive' Evangelicals tend to conceive of biblical authority in terms of the Bible's saving purpose. According to McKim: 'For neo-evangelicals, the purpose of Scripture is to bring people to faith and salvation in Jesus Christ.'[59] Note that this limits the various kinds of propositions and forms of literature in Scripture to one kind of authority: the soteric. This is, in its own way, as restrictive as the 'conservative' evangelical view which tends to conceive of biblical authority in terms of the Bible's proposi-

---

[58]Kern Robert Trembath, *Evangelical Theories of Inspiration: A Review and Proposal* (Oxford: OUP, 1987) 103.
[59]Donald K. McKim, *What Christians Believe About the Bible* (Nashville: Thomas Nelson, 1985) 91.

tional perfection. Infallibility is something we confess after the fact. It is as much, or more, a statement about our experience as it is about some property of Scripture.

It is pointless to affirm Scripture as God's Word apart from a living faith in Christ. For Berkouwer it is the content of the Bible—Jesus Christ—that legitimates its authority. Inspiration is not an a priori formal principle so much as a material principle: Scripture is authoritative insofar as it witnesses to its subject matter, Jesus Christ.[60] Biblical authority, we might say, is a correlate of faith in Christ—not its foundation. One must first have a personal relationship with Christ before one can recognise the authority of the Scriptures.

III. The Centrality of the Doctrine of God

The doctrine of Scripture is not self-standing but depends on one's concept of God and of the way God interacts with his people.

1. 'Construing' God

In his magisterial work, *The Uses of Scripture in Recent Theology*,[61] David H. Kelsey analyses the diverse ways in which theologians use Scripture and concludes that every theologian 'construes' (takes, interprets) the Bible *as* something or other (*e.g.*, *as* history, *as* literature, *as* doctrine, *as* narrative, *etc.*). The nature of biblical authority is a function of one's construal of Scripture: doctrines have one kind of authority, history another and narrative yet another. One's construal of Scripture, however, is determined not by the text, but by the conjunction of two extra-textual factors: the way Scripture is perceived to be used in the community and the way God is perceived to be present in the church.[62]

Darrell Jodock, following Kelsey, argues that our images of God's relation to the world are 'logically extra-biblical', for all such images 'assume a view of the world not found in the Bible itself'.[63] Does the Bible have no say at all over how it is to be construed? Not

---

[60]G.C. Berkouwer states: 'Every word about the God-breathed character of Scripture is meaningless if Holy Scripture is not understood as the witness concerning Christ' (*Holy Scripture* [Grand Rapids: Eerdmans, 1975] 166).

[61]David H. Kelsey, *The Uses of Scripture in Recent Theology* (Philadelphia: Fortress, 1975).

[62]Kelsey calls the conjunction of these two factors the 'discrimen'.

[63]Darrell Jodock, *The Church's Bible: Its Contemporary Authority* (Minneapolis/ Augsburg: Fortress, 1989) 66.

according to Jodock: our picture of how God relates to the world 'remains a theological judgement rather than a logical deduction from uniform biblical evidence'.[64] Kelsey's view is more nuanced; he admits that the Bible provides patterns for judging Christian aptness. There are logical patterns (between doctrines), symbolic patterns, historical patterns (*e.g.*, in salvation-history) and literary patterns (*e.g.*, type scenes). But the choice to make one pattern paradigmatic is, he insists, always an extra-biblical one. Neither historical nor literary criticism can tell us how to take Scripture today: only a study of how it functions in the church's life can do that.

Kelsey criticises 'God saying' as a comprehensive description for how God is related to Scripture. 'God saying' is only one imaginative construal. The Received View, in elevating the picture of 'God saying', makes the Bible the source of theology and reduces theology to mere translation. God is not only 'Revealer'. To construe the Bible as 'revelation' is to make the doctrinal aspect of Scripture the authoritative one. This fails to describe the way in which many theologians actually appeal to Scripture as authoritative, and so Kelsey rejects it. 'God doing', according to Kelsey, more adequately grasps the diverse ways in which God uses the Scriptures to 'shape Christian existence'. Further, 'shaping Christian existence' affirms God's presence with Scripture without specifying anything about the nature of Scripture itself. 'Inspiration' pertains to a text's efficacious use, not its nature. Kelsey preserves a link between God and the Bible, but it is to God the sanctifying Holy Spirit rather than to God the revealing Word. Significantly, Kelsey suggests that the doctrine of Scripture should be discussed under the heading of ecclesiology rather than revelation. In so doing, he gives voice to the spirit of post-modern philosophers and literary theorists who see knowledge and truth as a function of interpretative communities rather than of texts.[65] Kelsey fails, however, to consider saying as a kind of doing. In omitting this possibility, I believe Kelsey overlooks a most fruitful pathway into an understanding of the nature of Scripture. He also overlooks the possibility that God may be doing different things in Scripture.

2. God and Scripture: a brief typology

My purpose in this section is to suggest, with Kelsey, that theologians do often work a construal of God which affects their construal of Scrip-

---

[64]*Ibid.*
[65]I am thinking here of thinkers such as Stanley Fish and Richard Rorty.

ture (and vice versa). Specifically, I believe we can perceive a connection between one's construal of God and one's privileging a particular aspect, or literary genre, of Scripture.

(1). Classical theism. Warfield formulated his doctrine of Scripture on the basis of classical theism as interpreted by the Reformed confessions. Scripture is God's Word because God is in control of history:

> When we give due place in our thoughts to the universality of the providential government of God, to the minuteness and completeness of its sway, and to its invariable efficacy, we may be inclined to ask what is needed beyond this mere providential government to secure the production of sacred books which should be in every detail absolutely accordant with the Divine will.[66]

Kelsey claims that God for Warfield is present in an 'ideational' mode, that is, through the teaching of doctrine. This is a common description of Princeton theology. McKim describes fundamentalist theology as construing Scripture 'as proposition' and Protestant scholastic theology as construing Scripture 'as doctrine'. There is some merit in this interpretation. Charles Hodge portrayed the Bible as the 'storehouse of facts' for the theologian. God can be known because he has revealed himself in propositional form. Such a position tends to read Scripture as though everything were didactic literature, similar, say, to Paul's epistles. God thus becomes a rational communicator who is not self-revealing so much as revealer of information about himself and his plan. Scripture, as a cognitive Word of God, is more like a rule of faith than a means of grace.

(2). Christocentric theism. The situation is different in Barth, who reinterprets the sovereignty of God in terms of divine freedom. God's freedom entails that God's being is never merely a 'natural' given, never 'there' for the taking, but must be actively, 'graciously' given. Barth worries that the identity thesis which equates the Bible with the Word of God leads to a natural theology—to a knowledge of God that could be had apart from God's free and gracious activity.

For Barth, God's being is in God's acts. Specifically, God's being is revealed in the various acts that comprise the life and fate of Jesus Christ. Hunsinger calls this aspect of Barth's thought 'actualism'.

---

[66]Warfield, *Inspiration and Authority*, 157. Jodock labels this the 'supernaturalist' position because of its emphasis on the miraculous.

Kelsey says that, for Barth, God is present in the mode of concrete actuality. The biblical genre which best corresponds to such actualism, as Hans Frei has shown, is narrative. Narrative is the preferred literary form for rendering an agent. We know who a person is by what the person does. If Jesus Christ is the Word of God, then narrative is the most adequate form of witness to him, insofar as narrative recounts what agents do, and what people do to them.

(3). *Process theism/panentheism.* The doctrine of God is somewhat under-developed in the thought of James Barr. In general, however, he seems to fit into the broad category of 'liberal' theology, which McKim depicts as construing Scripture 'as experience' and George Lindbeck depicts as holding to an experiential-expressive view of doctrine. Jodock calls this the 'ecclesial developmentalist' position, for it bases biblical authority 'on an appeal to the historical continuity of the Christian community and the role played by the biblical documents in that history'.[67] In the tradition of Schleiermacher, Barr and other liberal theologians view both the Scriptures and theology itself as reflection on religious experience. God can only be known by his effects—through his 'contact' with the believing community.

 What biblical genre provides the paradigm for Barr's construal of Scripture as an inspiring record of religious experience? Is it historical narrative, with its emphasis on the development of religious traditions? Or is it, as Barton suggests, wisdom literature, with its emphasis on a people's reflection on the relationship with God?[68] In either case, the revelation or Word of God is what lies behind the Scriptures, not within it. The Bible is a historical record of human wisdom and human faith.

 What doctrine of God funds this notion of a (functionally) authoritative history of tradition? Neither Barr nor Barton constructs a full-fledged systematic theology, nor do they show much interest in metaphysics. Neither would, as far as I am aware, claim to be a follower of Whitehead or of process theology. However, by associating Protestant liberalism with process theism and panentheism, I wish to highlight the profound change in their understanding of divine activity from that of the Received View. Whereas Warfield and Barth stress the transcendence of God, the liberal view we are now considering affirms an immanent God who is known by reflecting on human expe-

---

[67]Jodock, *The Church's Bible*, 53.
[68]Barton, *People of the Book?*, 56.

rience. The God of process theology is not provident but only well-intentioned: his Word cannot rule, only woo. The process God is a dynamic; personal but non-coercive presence.

Such a doctrine of God seems to be what lies behind views of Scripture such as those of Barr and Barton. Revelation 'is both an *identity*-forming presence... and a *community*-forming presence'.[69] God is the shaper rather than the sovereign of Christian existence. God's active and purposive presence 'synchronizes with the active, purposeful response of human beings in a creative way'.[70] The Spirit is the ongoing presence of God who participates in the community's 'hunt for words' to articulate the divine presence. The Bible is authoritative only if, and to the extent to which, it actually reveals and inspires (*e.g.*, mediates the presence of God).

What makes the biblical texts efficacious? How do we account for their salvific function? Jodock answers that they have the capacity to mediate God's identity-forming presence. But why do just these words have this capacity? The reason is unclear. For Barr, texts other than Scripture can also mediate God's presence. For, if God is generally making himself available, his presence is confined neither to the canon nor to Christ. William Abraham correctly locates the weakness of this view: 'the key point is this: Barr has not told us enough about God's present mode of contact with his people for us to be clear about the past mode of contact.'[71]

3. Construing divine action and providence

> [W]e cannot believe that God, having performed His mighty acts and having illumined the minds of prophet and apostle to understand their true import, left the prophetic and apostolic *testimony* to take care of itself. It were indeed a strange conception of the divine providential activity which would deny that the Biblical writers were divinely assisted in their attempt to communicate to the world the illumination which, for the world's sake, they had themselves received.[72]

(1) Sovereignty and Scripture. Is it merely coincidence that, at several key points in his *People of the Book?*, Barton appeals to divine providence? He acknowledges that his view of the Bible as human reflection on religious experience 'entails some kind of theory about the providential

---

[69]Jodock, *The Church's Bible*, 93-4.
[70]*Ibid.*, 97.
[71]Abraham, *Divine Inspiration*, 54.
[72]Baillie, *Idea of Revelation*, 111.

character of the religion of Israel'.[73] He affirms, with Irenaeus, that 'we
should not have these books without divine providence'.[74] And yet,
when it comes to specifying why one should prefer his explanation of
divine action to Warfield's, Barton is reduced to silence: 'to untangle
the relation of divine and human causality here is a task of the utmost
intricacy—certainly not one for a biblical specialist to attempt.'[75]

The main reason for the demise of the Received View has been
the decline of classical theism. Indeed, Clark Pinnock's basic reproach
of the Warfield position is that it relies on a Calvinistic theology of the
sovereignty of God: 'The theology of a Warfield or a Packer, which
posits a firm divine control over everything that happens in the world,
is very well suited to explain a verbally inspired Bible.'[76] Pinnock himself prefers a 'dynamic personal model' that upholds both the divine
initiative and human response. Can God achieve his will in the world?
Pinnock opts, like the process theologians, for a softer view of divine
sovereignty: God may not have control over his charges but he can out-
think and out-play them: 'God is present, not normally in the mode of
control, but in the way of stimulation and guidance.'[77]

Just how different is Pinnock's conception from that of Warfield?
Warfield takes great pains to dissociate his position from a mechanical
inspiration view: while it involves the Spirit's guidance, inspiration is
a process 'much more intimate than can be expressed by the term "dictation"'.[78] However, at other times Warfield risks endorsing a quasi-
dictation view when he suggests that providence only aids human
capacities while inspiration imparts an immediate divine voice. 'Inspiration' thus becomes a *donum superadditum* which enables human
words to surpass human knowledge. Inspiration gives the books a
'superhuman' quality. Warfield comments: 'It will not escape observation that thus "inspiration" is made a mode of "revelation".'[79]

(2) The theological foundations of the 'identity thesis': Farley's critique. Perhaps the clearest recognition of how the doctrine of providence

---

[73]Barton, *People of the Book?*, 21.
[74]*Ibid.*, 40.
[75]*Ibid.*, 56.
[76]Pinnock, *Scripture Principle*, 101.
[77]*Ibid.*, 104.
[78]Warfield, *Inspiration and Authority*, 153. Warfield sounds almost contemporary
when he observes that the production of Scripture is a long process which involves
varied divine activities (156).
[79]*Ibid.*, 160.

supports the Scripture principle comes from a theologian who seeks to overthrow it. Edward Farley's *Ecclesial Reflection: An Anatomy of Theological Method*[80] is the most incisive theological attack on the idea of the Scripture principle to date. Farley exposes the most basic presuppositions that undergird the attempt to identify the Bible with the Word of God.[81]

Salvation-history, the first presupposition, expresses God's relation to the world in a kingly or 'royal' metaphor. The royal metaphor implies a 'logic of sovereignty' that says that God is able to accomplish his will through worldly means. Salvation-history refers to those particular events under special divine control. The second presupposition underlying the Scripture principle is the identity thesis itself. Farley asks, in the light of the distinction between Creator and creature, how anything worldly can be called 'divine'? How can we call the Scriptures 'holy'? The principle of identity affirms an identity between what God wills to communicate and what is brought to language by a human individual or community. However, Farley correctly acknowledges (in a way that other theologians do not) that what is in view is not an ontological but a *cognitive* identity. That is, the identity is between what God wants to communicate—the message—and the linguistic or literary expression of it. A creaturely medium for God's communication is thus regarded as a substitute presence not for the divine being but for a divine *work*. This can only be brought about because of divine causal efficacy, hence the royal metaphor. 'The principle of identity... is the basis for attributing infallibility and inerrancy to what appears to be human and creaturely.'[82]

The temptation is to extend further these 'identifications'—to a confession or a magisterium—and ensure the survival of the divine content. Farley points out that the later secondary representations tend to become dominant (*e.g.*, Chalcedonian Christology is now the framework for reading Scripture) and occasionally claim the same privileged status as the original (*e.g.*, biblical and papal infallibility). The end result of this principle is that the divine will becomes inseparable from human interpretation (*e.g.*, Scripture, doctrine). Farley worries that the divine-human identity is often claimed for the work of theology itself. Identifying human interpretation with the divine will mistakes vehicles of social duration for deposits of immutable truth. To identify

---

[80]Philadelphia: Fortress, 1982.
[81]A shorter version of his argument may be found in his 'Scripture and Tradition', in Hodgson and King (eds.), *Christian Theology*, 61-87.
[82]Farley, *Ecclesial Reflection*, 39.

Scripture and doctrine with the divine will violates the very essence of the church, whose role is to witness to revelation and redemption, not equate itself with them. Farley, like Barr, wants to locate the redemptive presence of Christ (the Word of God) in the continuing life of the church.[83]

The conjunction of these two presuppositions—the royal metaphor and the identity thesis—gives rise to what Farley takes to be an inescapable dilemma: either God controls or he does not control, and if he controls he controls something or everything. If we retain the royal metaphor (which salvation-history does) and say that God controls only a section of history, then we must conclude that God wills a non-salvific presence in most of human history. If we retain the royal metaphor and say that God's will and action are universal, then the horrors of history have the same relation to God's causality as salvific events. Both of these options fail to meet the problem of evil: either God is involved with only part of the world in a loving way, or he determines all creation and is thus a determiner of good and evil.[84]

In short, salvation-history—together with the Scripture principle that it supports—flounders on theodicy: either God is King or God is love. In order to say that God is love, Farley abandons the logic of salvation-history and the royal metaphor, and thus deprives the Scripture principle of its foundation. In short, Farley would have us choose between the Scripture principle and a loving God:

> To summarize, with the first alternative, salvation history, God's activity as heteronomous causality violates creaturely freedom and autonomy and therefore divine goodness and love are sacrificed. With the second alternative, these features are retained but salvation history goes. In my view there is really no choice.[85]

The three-stranded cord which binds together the doctrine of God, the nature of biblical authority and theological method in Farley's hands becomes a violent whip which has had its day. Farley prefers theological arguments that, like Scripture and divine activity itself, are persuasive rather than coercive. He ultimately rejects the Scripture principle because it relies on a picture of divine sovereignty which he

---

[83]Farley, 'Scripture and Tradition', 65.
[84]Farley, *Ecclesial Reflection*, 156.
[85]*Ibid.*, 157.

can no longer accept: if God is in control of everything, why has he acted/spoken only *here*, in Scripture and the life of Jesus, not there?

IV. A Way Forward: Divine Speech-Acts

A contemporary doctrine of Scripture neglects the issues raised by the identity thesis and the royal metaphor only at its own peril. The former pertains to the nature and location of God's being or presence, the latter to the nature and character of God's activity or providence. Both issues concern the relation between the Word of God and the human words of Scripture. This section briefly reviews the major problems and offers a pathway towards their resolution.

1. The current impasse

(1) The identity thesis. By far the major obstacle to ecumenical agreement about the doctrine of Scripture is the identity thesis. I have argued that the task of a doctrine of Scripture is to explain how the church can confess that the Bible is the Word of God. It may be helpful at this point to heed McGrath's reminder about the nature of doctrine: doctrines should be recognised to be 'perceptions, not total descriptions, pointing beyond themselves towards the greater mystery of God himself'.[86] The question is: does the identity thesis, which locates the Word of God in Scripture, constitute an accurate, and adequate, perception about the nature of God's Word?

Both Barth and Barton argue that only Christ is truly the Word of God. Both decry what they take to be an idolatrous elevation of the canon over Christ: Scripture cannot save, but points to the one who can. The most they will admit is an *indirect* identity between Scripture and the Word of God.

Does this mean that the Word of God is not a verbal phenomenon? Does the 'Word' of God have nothing to do with semantics (the study of verbal meaning)? Is it possible to articulate a biblically based, theologically sound and philosophically intelligible account of how the human words of Scripture can be or become the Word of God? What sense can it make to refer to Scripture as "God's Word written"? It is not clear how, or even whether, Barth accounts for the properly semantic moment of God's self-disclosure. In the last resort, Barth's doctrine of Scripture moves to Christ *too fast*. Our challenge will be to reinter-

---

[86]McGrath, *Genesis of Doctrine*, 17.

pret the identity thesis in such a way as to do full justice to the semantic
as well as personal dimension of God's self-revelation. The way forward for the doctrine of Scripture must be, I believe, to overcome the
dichotomy of personal/propositional revelation.

(2) The royal metaphor. Throughout this chapter I have claimed that
one's doctrine of Scripture depends on one's view of God and of God's
activity. Farley assumes that we must choose: *either* God controls history and manifests his control through his secondary presence in
Scripture-doctrine-church *or* humans are free and historically conditioned, in which case the Bible is only a human witness to antecedent
revelation. Farley, Kelsey and Barr prefer a more 'populist' metaphor:
God is not over his people but among them. This personal-relational
model of conceiving God's presence and activity is not, however, without its problems.

First, there seems to be a covert identity thesis at work here too,
though the locus of God's presence is not the canon but the community. For Farley and Barr, the people of God have become the real
authority for theological judgements. Farley and Barr assume that God
is best reflected in the ecclesia. As I have suggested, the emphasis on
the authority of interpreting communities is well-suited to the post-
modern intellectual climate.

It is far from clear, however, by what means one can discern
God's presence. The theological diversity in the Scriptures is nowhere
near as pronounced as the theological diversity of the believing community. Indeed, just as many biblical scholars insist that we must
speak of biblical theologies, so here too we must speak of believing
communities. In which community do we best see God's inspiring
presence? Should we include the German Christians who supported
Hitler? The main weakness in Barr's view, however, is that it does not
correspond to what we see in Scripture. Even a casual reading of the
Old Testament and New Testament discloses communities which are
primarily *unbelieving* for much of their histories. What kind of authority can interpreting communities have if they misinterpret God?

2. God's communicative action

'It is my conviction that the next impetus to rethink our evangelical
doctrines of inspiration and revelation is going to come from the
modern communications theory.'[87] I wish now to argue, in the light of
Ramm's suggestion, that the principal mode in which God is 'with' his
people is through speech-acts. I find it difficult to conceive how one

could discern God's presence, or know anything whatsoever about God, without a communication on God's part. Mere 'contact' is not enough. As William Abraham observes: 'Without His word, the alternative is not just a tentative, carefully qualified guessing at what God is doing, but a radical agnosticism.'[88]

(1) The God who speaks. Scripture portrays God as a speech agent. Much of what God does—warning, commanding, promising, forgiving, informing, calling, comforting—he does by speaking. As the speech-act philosophers J.L. Austin and John Searle have effectively shown, language is a productive force and a phenomenon of social interaction. I know of no compelling philosophical or theological reason not to take this depiction of the speaking God seriously. If God is a personal, albeit transcendent, agent, and if God can do some things, then there is no *prima facie* reason why God could not speak as well. Indeed, in the prophets the distinction between the one true God and the false gods is precisely the criterion of speech: false gods are dumb. The burden of proof lies with views that claim God, for some reason, cannot speak. I find it interesting that even theologians who eschew the notion of propositional revelation are often happy to talk about the promises of God and divine forgiveness. On my view, however, promising and forgiving are nothing if not speech-acts. One can only promise, for example, by uttering a sentence which counts as a promise—by performing a 'speech-act'.

(2) A verbal Word? Langdon Gilkey criticised the biblical theology movement for being only half orthodox and half modern. On the one hand it speaks of God's mighty acts in history, but on the other it affirms the modern assumption that God does not intervene in the natural-historical causal nexus. The 'acts of God' of which the neo-orthodox theologians spoke seem to be visible only to the eyes of faith. There is an uncomfortable dualism between these mighty acts and actual history. This leaves the notion of an act of God empty or equivocal.

I have precisely the same problem, in regard to literature rather than history, with Barth's notion of the 'word' of God. On the one hand this word is verbal, but on the other hand it is something that only

---

[87]Bernard Ramm, *The Evangelical Heritage: A Study in Historical Theology* (Grand Rapids: Baker, 1979) 163.

[88]William Abraham, *Divine Revelation and the Limits of Historical Criticism* (Oxford: OUP, 1981) 23.

becomes verbal when God freely and graciously decides that it does so. There is an uncomfortable dualism between the Word of God and the actual words of Scripture which threatens to render each equivocal. Barth apparently wants to have the Word both ways. On the one hand, he identifies the Word of God with Jesus Christ—a personal, not prop- ositional, communication. On the other hand, he writes: 'The personalizing of the concept of the Word of God, which we cannot avoid when we remember that Jesus Christ is the Word of God, does not mean its de-verbalizing.'[89] At one point, Barth actually calls reve- lation a divine 'speech-act' (Rede-Tat).[90] And, somewhat surprisingly, Barth says that 'We have no reason for not taking the concept "Word of God" in its primary and literal sense. "God's Word" means God speaks. "Speaks" is not a symbol.'[91]

What actually happens to the literal meaning of the human words when God graciously decides to disclose himself through Scrip- ture in a miracle whereby the Bible 'becomes' the Word of God? It would appear that the Word's 'being', like the being of God himself, is only in becoming. Barth fails to provide anything like a clear concep- tual analysis of this event. Even Hunsinger's generally helpful guide to Barth fails to clarify matters here: 'Although intrinsically incapable by nature, theological language has been made to correspond to its subject matter by grace.'[92] God's Word for Barth is a semantic miracle. We may recall that, for Barth, what is at stake is ultimately God's freedom. God's being is not a natural 'given', either in nature or in Scripture. While the human words are witnesses to the living Word, the Spirit is 'Lord of the hearing'. The phenomenon of a text that sometimes is and sometimes is not the Word of God prompts Clark Pinnock to ask: 'Is this Word of God... really the name for a personal experience?'[93]

---

[89]Barth, Church Dogmatics, I:1, 138.

[90]Ibid., 162.

[91]Ibid., 150.

[92]Hunsinger, How to Read Karl Barth, 44. Much has been said about the inadequacy of human words to speak of God. But in an important sense, we can say what lies beyond our words. While we may not have nouns that 'name' God, speaking is much more than a matter of 'labelling' the world. Indeed, the noun is not the basic unit of meaning in language. That privilege goes rather to the speech-act. Moreo- ver, the sentence has been described as the infinite use of finite means. Where individual words are unable to articulate the majesty and glory of God, sentences succeed in so doing. I do not wish to be misunderstood. I am not suggesting that sentences transcribe the divine reality without remainder, but rather that some sentences themselves contain a 'surplus of meaning' (Ricoeur) which is richer than any literal paraphrase.

Scripture, I suggest, is best viewed neither as a set of propositions nor as a sacramental story that mysteriously renders Christ, but rather as a set of human-divine communicative actions that do many different things. What one *does* by saying something is called an 'illocutionary act'. What the Bible does is not arbitrarily related to its nature, but rather a function of its illocutionary acts. What Scripture does follows from what Scripture is. It is vital, in this regard, to see the various literary genres in Scripture as diverse kinds of illocutionary acts. It is just here that biblical criticism provides an indispensable service. Biblical criticism should

> exercise its explanatory function in helping us to appreciate the letter of the biblical text in all its foreignness and complexity. It is to teach us to be close readers, straining to hear something other than our own voices.[94]

Biblical criticism best fulfils this task when it becomes literary criticism and explores the nature of the biblical genres. The most spectacular and damaging interpretative errors are mistakes about genre. To misidentify a literary genre is to mistake the kind of illocutionary act a text performs.

3. The Bible as polygeneric

(1) Speech genres. Everything we say or write belongs to some speech or literary genre. Every communicative act belongs to a particular kind— warning, greeting, statement, question, *etc.* What are the implications for a doctrine of Scripture of a view that sees the Bible composed of a variety of divine communicative acts? We may say, first of all, that there is no one kind of speech-act that characterises all of Scripture. The limits of Kelsey's approach, or at least of the construals he studies, are here exposed for the reductions they are. Any attempt to catch up what is going on in Scripture in a synoptic judgement must be careful not to reduce the many communicative activities to a single function, be it doctrinal, narrative or experiential. Even Barth's construal of Scripture as 'rendering an agent' is too narrow.

---

[93]Clark Pinnock, *Tracking the Maze: Finding our way through Modern Theology from an Evangelical Perspective* (San Francisco: Harper & Row, 1990) 56.
[94]Christopher E. Seitz, 'Biblical Authority in the Late Twentieth Century: the Baltimore Declaration, Scripture-Reason-Tradition, and the Canonical Approach', *Anglican Theological Review* 75 (1993) 484.

(2) Generic theology? Theologians typically construe the diversity of God's Word in terms of one kind of genre. Any doctrine of Scripture that levels its generic diversity is bound to be inadequate. Such a reduction of generic multiplicity to generic uniformity represents both a literary and a theological mistake: literary, for one has misread the nature of a particular communicative act; theological, because one has mistook the nature of God's involvement with the text.

Barton, we may recall, privileges the wisdom genre: 'what is written in the Bible, with rare exceptions such as certain prophetic oracles, is presented as human words about God, not as words of God to man.'[95] So too, I think, does Bultmann. For Bultmann theology is about the self-understanding of faith, which pertains more to existential possibilities that are always already present than to the significance of contingent historical events. Pannenberg, by according pride of place to anticipations of the end of history, makes the apocalyptic genre paradigmatic for Scripture and theology. And the list could go on. Kelsey himself opts for a broader vision of God 'shaping Christian existence' through Scripture, but he overlooks how the Bible achieves this out of his concern to elevate 'God doing' over 'God saying'.[96]

(3) Divine speech-acts and the identity thesis. What follows for the identity thesis from the model of God's Word as speech-act? Does the Bible only become God's Word or is it permanently God's Word? Does one's recognition of the Bible as God's Word make it so, or is Scripture the Word of God even if no one accepts it? It is, of course, important not to lose sight of the personal reference of the Word of God to Jesus Christ. No one claims that the Bible is a part of the Godhead. What is being

---

[95]Barton, *People of the Book?*, 56. On the same page, Barton acknowledges that revelation involves a complex relation between divine and human causality. Whereas Barton locates this relation behind the text, I wish to argue that the Bible itself suggests that it is a relation that characterises the scriptural texts themselves.

[96]Several scholars have now acknowledged the exegetical significance of the diverse literary genres in Scripture. Paul Ricoeur sees a theological significance as well and suggests that God is 'named' or revealed differently in the various biblical genres. The Word of God, far from being monolithic, is rather mediated through a host of literary forms. Barton cites Ricoeur as one who has taken seriously 'the need to make theological sense of the fact that Scripture contains genres which cannot be assimilated to the model of divine communication to men' (*People of the Book?*, 71). What Barton means, of course, is that not all biblical genres correspond to the prophetic paradigm. True enough. But I have argued that God's communicative agency involves not merely statements about the past, or future, but includes questions, warnings, hymns, stories, letters, and so on. God's Word written is not simply timelessly true propositions.

claimed is that the Bible is a 'work' of God. While Christ is a fully human and fully divine agent, all we are claiming for Scripture is that it is a fully human and fully divine *act*.[97] Does bibliolatry still remain a possibility?

What sort of temptation is bibliolatry? What many theologians find objectionable in bibliolatry is its elevation of biblical statements to the status of absolute truths—a 'paper pope'. The worry is that the identity thesis leads to a view of the Bible as a textbook of timeless truths and inerrant propositions which could be 'mastered' by students of divinity. Pinnock suggests that the appeal of such heaven-sent cognitive information is undeniable, for it offers 'an apparently safe refuge from the relativising effects of history'.[98] But there are two problems with the argument that the identity thesis caters to a (perhaps sinful) desire for epistemological certainty: first, what absolute truths there are in Scripture still have to be interpreted. If they were to become a possession, it would only be after careful (and humble) exegetical work, whose outcome remains provisional. Second, and more importantly: the Word is not a collection of timeless truths that can be either withdrawn or left on deposit. Scripture is composed not only of assertions but of commands, warnings, promises and so forth. One does not 'possess' a divine command; one obeys it. Insofar as the recurring theme of Scripture is Good News, its content is to be shared with the world, not hoarded in the Church.

(4) Divine speech-acts and the royal metaphor. A false view of 'word' has held us captive, namely, word as 'literal' truth claim. But, strictly speaking, letters (words, nouns) do not refer—only speech-acts (and speakers) do that. God does many things with human language besides assert truths. Against Farley, we need not conclude that the identification of Scripture with God's Word leads to authoritarianism in theology. Not all speech-acts assert timeless truths. One must first look to what is said/done in Scripture before equating 'saying' with 'making timeless truth claims'. Theologians must recognise, and respect, the divine communication action for what it is.

---

[97]Moreover, God's mighty speech-acts work through and with the human speech-acts of Scripture. God's action is communicative rather than coercive: 'If we are looking for a way of picturing God's action which indicates what sort of efficacy it has, we should consider the spoken word... Speech, too, is an action of sorts, but not the sort of action that can by itself deprive another of his freedom' (Robert King, *The Meaning of God* [London: SCM, 1974] 92).
[98]Pinnock, *Tracking the Maze*, 48.

(5) Covenantal communication. God's communicative action reaches its culmination in the Christ event. But this event needs to be interpreted. Even G.E. Wright acknowledges this principle: '[b]y means of human agents God provides each event with an accompanying Word of interpretation, so that the latter is an integral part of the former.'[99] God's diverse communicative action finds its unity in the end towards which it is variously directed: Jesus Christ, the supreme covenant blessing and crown of creation.

In his influential book which launched speech-act philosophy, *How to Do Things with Words,*[100] J.L. Austin cites 'making a covenant' as an example of a 'commissive' speech-act. God appears to his people as an agent who performs promissory speech-acts which commit him to continuous activity. Without this commissive communicative act, how would we know of God's intentions? According to speech-act philosophy, an agent signals an intention by invoking the appropriate linguistic or literary conventions. One's intending something is more than just randomly related to the meaning of one's sentence.

God is the agent who is true to his Word. 'I will be your God and you will be my people'—such is the fundamental covenant promise. It is by keeping his word that God reveals himself to be who he is. The Bible is God's covenant 'deed', in both senses of the term. It is an act and a testament: a performative promise wherein certain unilateral promises are spoken, and a written document that seals the promise. The canon is a collection of diverse speech-acts that together 'render' the covenantal God.

4. A Trinitarian theology of holy Scripture

The Bible is the 'Word' of God for it is the result of divine self-communicative action. I now want to show how God's being in speech-acts is Trinitarian.

(1) God's being in speech-act. Barth arrived at the doctrine of the Trinity by analysing God's self-revelation with the schema Revealer-Revelation-Revealedness. Can we similarly unfold the notion of verbal revelation in the light of speech-act theory? Such an attempt may contribute to that rethinking of revelation in terms of communication theory for which Ramm called more than ten years ago.

---

[99]Wright, 'God Who Acts', 26.
[100]2nd. ed., Cambridge, MA: Harvard UP, 1975.

The Father's activity is locution. God the Father is the utterer, the begetter, the sustainer of words. He is the agent who *locutus est per prophetas* in former times, and who now speaks through the Son (Heb. 1:1-2). God the Father's locution is the result of his providential involvement in the lives of the human authors of Scripture. God works in and through human intelligence and human imagination to produce a literary account that renders him a mighty speech agent. The Logos corresponds to the speaker's act or illocution, to what one *does* in saying. The illocution has content (*i.e.*, reference and predication) and a particular intent (a force) which shows how the proposition is to be taken.[101] It is illocutionary force that makes a speech-act *count* as, say, a promise. What illocutionary act is performed is determined by the speaker; its meaning is therefore objective.

The third aspect of a speech-act is the perlocutionary. This refers to the effect an illocutionary act has on the actions or beliefs of the hearer. For example, by 'arguing' (illocution) I may 'persuade' (perlocution) someone. The great benefit of this analysis is that it enables us clearly to relate the Spirit's relation to the Word of God. First, the Spirit illumines the reader and so enables the reader to grasp the illocutionary point, to recognise what the Scriptures may be doing. Second, the Spirit convicts the reader that the illocutionary point of the biblical text deserves the appropriate response: 'But these are written that you may believe that Jesus is the Christ' (Jn. 20:31).

The Spirit does not alter the semantics of biblical literature. The locution and illocution as inscribed in Scripture remain unchanged. The Spirit's agency consists rather in bringing the illocutionary point home to the reader and so achieving the corresponding perlocutionary effect—whether belief, obedience, praise and so on. The testimony of the Spirit is nothing less than the effective presence of the illocutionary force. Thanks to the Spirit's testimony, these biblical words *deliver*. They convey illocutionary act and so liberate. Historical-critical scholarship alone cannot achieve a perlocutionary effect.

Is such a view similar to Barth's insistence that God the Spirit remains 'Lord of the hearing', and that the Bible only 'becomes' the Word of God when the Spirit illumines the reader? That depends on how one views communicative acts, and on how one defines 'Word'. Here Evangelicals disagree: 'People do not have to receive the Bible for it to become the Word of God. It *is* the Word of God objectively

---

[101]See John Searle, *Speech Acts: An Essay in the Philosophy of Language* (Cambridge: CUP, 1969) ch. 2.

whether received as such or not';[102] 'The presence of the living Word
in Holy Scripture is not an ontological necessity but a free decision of
the God who acts and speaks.'[103] Speech-act theory gives us a better
purchase on Barth's Trinitarian explication of divine revelation.
According to the analysis I have just given, we may say that the Bible
is divine-human communicative action: its locutions and illocutions
are the result of a double agency, what Austin Farrer calls the 'causal
joint'. The warnings, promises, assertions, prophecies, songs and so
forth in Scripture are divine as well as human communicative acts.
God's Word is really written. However, whereas human discourse
relies on rhetoric to achieve the intended perlocutionary effects, Scripture's perlocutionary effects depend on the Spirit's agency.

Is the Bible a divine communicative act, then, if a reader fails to
respond to its illocutions? This is a subtle query. In the context of a trial,
is the testimony of a witness true only if it is judged to be so? No, for a
jury can err. Testimony can be true even though it is not accepted. The
answer to my query depends on whether one includes the reader's
response (*i.e.*, the perlocutionary effect) in the definition of 'communicative act'. Interestingly, the Oxford English Dictionary includes both
possibilities under its first entry: 'communication' may be 'the act of
imparting propositions' or 'the proposition communicated'. Perhaps
the solution is to affirm both that Scripture *is* the Word of God (in the
sense of divine locution and illocution) and that Scripture may *become*
the Word of God (in the sense of achieving its intended perlocutionary
effects).

(2) *Personal or propositional?* The doctrine of Scripture has been much
damaged by an over-estimation of the dichotomy between 'God saying' and 'God doing', between propositional and personal revelation.
Paul Helm offers a salutary reminder: 'There is no antithesis between
believing a proposition and believing a person if the proposition is
taken to be the assertion of some person.'[104] Propositions need not
always be taken as assertions. *Every* illocutionary act involves a proposition, but not all illocutions have the force of assertions. Promises
have propositional content too (*e.g.*, sense and reference), but are
marked by commissive rather than assertive force.

---

[102]Lewis and Demarest, *Integrative Theology*, Vol. 1, 168.
[103]Bloesch, *Holy Scripture*, 26.
[104]Paul Helm, 'Revealed Propositions and Timeless Truths, *Religious Studies* 8
(1972) 135-6.

Barr is therefore partly right and partly wrong when he suggests that the real issue in propositional revelation is that of genre and function.[105] He is right in saying that genre-mistakes cause the wrong kind of truth values to be attached to biblical sentences; he is wrong in thinking that all propositional revelation must be assertive (and thus that some biblical sentences are false).

Against the dichotomy between personal and propositional revelation, I am inclined to say that *all* our encounters with persons are 'propositional', in the sense of involving communicative action. Revelation, as Ramm puts it, is both a meeting and a knowing. An encounter with a person may be 'propositional'. Not all propositions need to be characterized as 'rationalistic'. Not all propositions are put forward as claims of precise correspondence to reality. To suggest so is to caricature the notion of propositional revelation. Again: all illocutionary acts have a propositional element. The point to remember is that propositions may be taken, or given, in various ways (*i.e.*, as assertions, questions, commands, *etc.*).

God identifies himself by his speech-acts. Better: what God does with language reveals God's identity, just as our actions reveal who we are. The way we encounter a person is largely through his or her speech-acts, and a person's identity is largely a function of whether, and how, they keep their word.[106] God identifies himself as the one who utters words on our behalf, and as the one who keeps his words. God's Word is utterly reliable, whether that word is a command, a warning, a promise, forgiveness or, yes, even an assertion.

The neo-orthodox emphasis on the self-revelation of God is faulty only in its neglect of the semantic means by which this disclosure takes place. Scripture is itself a mighty speech-act by which God reveals himself in his Son Jesus Christ. The Scriptures do not become a substitute for Christ but are the means by which the memory of Christ is given substance. God's personal identity is rendered in language and literature. Behaviour without verbal interpretation is too ambiguous to reveal anything. It is precisely the fuzziness of the tie between illocutionary act and verbal meaning that ultimately makes Barth's account of the Word of God unsatisfactory. Is God so free that God's speech is exempt from the normal obligations which accrue to the uttering of a promise? It is difficult to see how Barth can talk about the

---

[105]Barr, *Bible in the Modern World*, 125.
[106]See Paul Ricoeur, *Oneself as Another*, (London: University of Chicago Press, 1992), chs. 5, 6.

divine promise if he were not prepared to acknowledge divine speech-acts, such as promising, to which God holds himself accountable. As Austin put it: 'our word is our bond'.[107] God too, therefore, is 'tied' to these texts.

V. Conclusion: the Humility of the Word

Does God speak in Scripture? Calvin refers both of the majesty of God's Word and to the divine stammering. To say that God's Word is 'majestic' is to say that his illocutionary acts are mighty. It is to invoke, in explicit fashion, the royal metaphor. On the other hand, God's mighty speech-acts are clothed in the form of human speech genres. In order to communicate with humanity, God has accommodated himself to creaturely media, to human language and literature, to human flesh and blood. God's Word, incarnate and inscripturate, is God in communicative action. The might of God's speech is hidden by the divine lisp as the might of God's saving act is hidden in Christ's cross. God's power is revealed in weakness; this applies to God's speech-acts too.[108] A word of forgiveness can be ignored, or it can be accepted. The divine speech-acts, though humbly clothed, are nevertheless powerful enough to liberate the captive, empower the weak, fill the empty and sustain the suffering.

The word that goes out from God's mouth will not return empty but will accomplish its purpose (Is. 55:11). What is this purpose? I suggest it is *embodiment*. Jesus Christ is the unique and definitive embodiment of God's Word, the divine foundation and fulfilment of the covenant. The Church, as the body of Christ, is a secondary and derivative embodiment—the human response to the covenant of grace. The written Word seeks, in the power of the Spirit, to be embodied in the life of the people of God. Scripture's warnings demand attention, its commands obedience, its promises faith. The Word must be continually 're-contextualised'—'embodied in the lives, words and actions of contemporary human beings'.[109] As literary style generates a corresponding lifestyle, so the biblical genres engender a culture—the

---

[107]J.L. Austin, *How to Do Things with Language*, 10.

[108]Need weakness, need *humanity*, for that matter, imply fallibility, and beyond that, actual failure? Perhaps fallibility, but not actual fault. Many books—textbooks, phone-books, cookbooks—contain no error. Fallibility means only 'capable of making mistakes', not that mistakes have actually been made.

[109]Jodock, *The Church's Bible*, 143.

kingdom of God.[110] To follow *these* words is to be cultivate true freedom.

God is indeed involved in shaping Christian existence, through biblical law, wisdom, song, apocalyptic, prophecy, narrative and the other literary forms of Scripture. These are the ordained means of rendering, by the testimony of the Spirit, the meaning, the reality and the implications of God's act in Christ. The message of the Scriptures may be errant foolishness to some, 'but to those who are being saved it is the power of God' (1 Cor. 1:18). A doctrine of Scripture is therefore right to conceive of the Bible as God's mighty speech-acts:

> not merely as the record of the redemptive acts by which God is saving the world, but *as itself one of these redemptive acts*, having its own part to play in the great work of establishing and building up the kingdom of God.[111]

[110]See my 'The World Well-Staged? Theology, Culture and Hermeneutics', in D.A. Carson and J.D. Woodbridge (eds.), *God and Culture* (Grand Rapids: Eerdmans, 1993) 1-30.
[111]Warfield, *Inspiration and Authority*, 161 (emphasis mine).

CHAPTER 7A

The Role of Biblical and Theological Research in the Church Today: A View from the Church

A. Morgan Derham

I. Introduction

My brief is to deal with the subject from the point of view of the church-man rather than the scholar, the man at the coal-face rather than the technician in the Coal Board's laboratory, so to speak. My qualifications for doing this are: membership of the Tyndale Fellowship Biblical Theology group almost from its beginning, twenty years at the coal-face as a local pastor, twenty years as editor of Scripture Union Bible-reading publications, and a spell as vice-chairman of the World Evangelical Fellowship.

II. The Early Days of the Tyndale Fellowship

I begin exactly forty summers ago. The Biblical Theology group assembled in the original Tyndale House under the chairmanship of Dr. Martyn Lloyd-Jones. (Operating under his chairmanship in a discussion was an almost perfect demonstration of how divine sovereignty and human free-will can be reconciled: he gave us absolute freedom to take the discussion wherever we willed, but the conclusion was the one which he had had in mind all along.) The subject that year was 'Immortality', and papers were read by John Wenham, E.F. Kevan, Stafford Wright, Michael Farrer, and Philip Hughes, among others. (Incidentally this preponderance of Anglicans presided over by Martyn Lloyd-Jones with no sign of the subsequent strains and stresses of the 1960s can only cause us to regret that the separatist controversy of 1966 was ever allowed to erupt, to the detriment of that unity which has been effectively embodied in the life and work of the Tyndale Fellowship—a unity which in those early days not only took in the widest spectrum of British Evangelicalism, but spanned the Atlantic also with the attendance of such distinguished Americans as Cornelius Van Til and Wilbur Smith. I still sometimes wonder if the Tyndale Fellowship could have made some attempt to prevent that tragedy.)

I begin, however, with Dr. Lloyd-Jones. He opened the 1954 Biblical Theology Conference with a review of Tyndale Fellowship history. He recalled the early conference at Kingham, called by Douglas Johnson in the blackest period of the Second World War to consider post-war Evangelicalism, and which among other consequences, led to the founding of the Tyndale Fellowship. In what sounds like a précis of his contribution to that conference he noted how there had been a significant change in Evangelicalism in the period 1870-80—related he suggested, to the appearance on the scene of D.L. Moody and the Keswick Convention. Evangelicals became 'less and less interested in theology', even 'fearful of theology and distrustful of any emphasis upon the intellect'. He described how Alan Stibbs, a regular attender at Tyndale Fellowship conferences, asked an evangelical leader for advice as to what he should read when he went up to Cambridge in the 1920s. 'Anything but theology', was the response. As a result, said Dr. Lloyd-Jones, 'Evangelicals have been counting for less and less in all branches of the church.' At Kingham this failure of theological nerve was questioned and challenged, which is one reason why we are here.

Moving on to consider the position in 1954, Dr. Lloyd-Jones noted that things had become both more difficult and more complex. The liberal 'opposition' had shifted its ground in relation to the doctrine of Scripture in a way which meant that 'you could hold the message while you let go of the facts'. (He did not actually mention the name of Karl Barth.) So Evangelicals were being asked why they could not go along with all the rest and stop being the ecclesiastical awkward squad. Lloyd-Jones' response to this shift was typical: 'This is more than ever the time for scholarly Evangelicals.'

Furthermore, he suggested that there were other trends needing attention. These included a new interest in spiritual phenomena, the rise of movements and cults offering 'peace, happiness, power in life, along with an individualistic emphasis arising out of "pseudo-psychology"', with too much emphasis on results. The cross was being bypassed. Ultimately it was a question of authority. 'We need men who can contend for the truth,' he said.

From this it is clear that the early vision for the Tyndale Fellowship took in a broad spectrum of interests, ranging across the whole area of church life, with particular attention to the Bible and its authority. It existed to further and encourage sound scholarship of a quality that would stand alongside any that existed in the church as a whole, and to put competent men and women in positions of influence in the churches, including, of course, Theological Colleges and University faculties.

III. The Fellowship's Achievements

I shall return to this theme, but would like, first of all, to put in a word for the ordinary, run-of-the-mill pastor and church leader. I was at college in the 1930s and became a minister in 1940. What was so serious then was the dearth of up-to-date evangelical theological resources. As a young Crusader, facing the challenge of rampant liberalism, I had to rely largely on the Schofield Bible, *Can a Young Man Trust His Bible?* by Arthur Cook, and Marshall's Shilling Series of devotionals. Thin gruel for a hungry learner. With the birth of the Tyndale Fellowship and the inter-related launch of the IVF's publishing programme, a new day began. And it was not so much the appearance of specific titles which made the difference. It was the feeling of confidence engendered by the knowledge that there were competent scholars of repute who were working at the highest levels and who were known to be people for whom the Bible was the final authority, the inspired Word of the living God.

How this has worked out in practice may be judged by reference to the contents pages of the *Tyndale Bulletin* in the past ten years. Some of the articles are in the category of the detailed and rather esoteric—for example, a discussion of a possible reference to a slain Messiah in a fragment from the Dead Sea Scrolls[1]—hardly likely to provide the harassed pastor with an inspirational sermon for Mothering Sunday! But it was in fact very relevant: the discovery of the fragment led to a burst of misleading and sensational publicity suggesting, so to speak, that Judaism had anticipated Christianity. It was important that a corrective and authoritative statement should be available, even if it did not follow the original tendentious comments into the popular press.

But as I suggested above, the original vision was for the Tyndale Fellowship to be a 'resource centre' in the areas of biblical and theological studies; and this calls for a much broader agenda than a discussion of Qumran fragment 4Q285, relevant as this proved to be. Further study of the contents of *Tyndale Bulletin* suggests that this need has not been ignored. The same volume includes the first part of a study of how the teaching of the Old Testament is being applied to ethical concerns. It brings us right up to date with its critique of various modern schools of thought, including the work of Jubilee Centre in Cambridge—from Marcion to Michael Schluter, so to speak.[2] There is such

---

[1]M.N.A. Bockmuehl, 'A "Slain Messiah" in 4Q Serekh Milhamah (4Q285)?', *TynB* 43 (1992) 155-69.

a dearth of serious interest in contemporary theological issues in the churches of our day that one is tempted to ask if there is anyone out there listening; but if they are, they have been given two useful studies of some of the ideas of E.P. Sanders,[3] not to mention an assessment of Barth as a biblical theologian.[4] That the Fellowship has its feet on the ground is confirmed by such features as a study of the ethical problems associated with euthanasia[5] and ecology.[6]

The breadth and depth of Tyndale Fellowship members' interests is confirmed by looking through the list of members' publications—books and articles and work in progress. By contrast with the virtual famine of fifty years ago, it represents an extraordinary diversity of interests, pursued by an international community of like-minded scholars and students. Subjects noted range from 'The Music of the Old Testament Reconsidered' to a book on *Sane Sex* published in New Zealand.

IV. The Continuing Need

However, there remains a question, asked by me on behalf of the working minister or Christian leader who is not a member of the Fellowship. It arises from the definition of the aims of the Fellowship as set out in the founding document—'to advance the Christian faith by promoting biblical and theological studies and disseminating the useful results of such study for the public benefit.' It is this last clause which bothers me. Is the Fellowship really taking this task seriously enough? Learned articles in specialist journals are better than nothing. But should there not be a more deliberate and organised effort to disseminate some of the more relevant research findings?

When I was serving as Information Officer of the United Bible Societies, responsible for a global information network, our slogan was: 'Information is the lifeblood of partnership, but information only

---

[2]C.J.H. Wright, 'The Ethical Authority of the Old Testament: A Survey of Approaches. Part I', *TynB* 43 (1992) 101-20; 'The Ethical Authority of the Old Testament: A Survey of Approaches. Part II', *TynB* 43 (1992) 203-31.
[3]B.D. Chilton, 'Jesus and the Repentance of E.P. Sanders', *TynB* 39 (1988) 1-18; D.R. de Lacey, 'In Search of a Pharisee', *TynB* 43 (1992) 353-72.
[4]C.A. Baxter, 'Barth—a Truly Biblical Theologian?', *TynB* 38 (1987) 3-27.
[5]D.J. Atkinson, 'Causing Death and Allowing to Die', *TynB* 34 (1983) 201-28.
[6]D.A. Hay, 'Christians in the Global Greenhouse', *TynB* 41 (1990) 109-27; F.W. Bridger, 'Ecology and Eschatology', *TynB* 41 (1990) 290-301.

flows if someone pumps it.' Defenders of capitalism talk about the 'trickle-down' effect of creating wealth, and I suspect that the Fellowship is working on the same principle, with the useful help of IVP. Simplified versions of some at least of the *Bulletin* features might well be prepared and placed in the more popular publications of our time. For example, Chris Wright's articles on the way we use the Old Testament as a basis for ethical teaching (referred to above) are surely very relevant in an age when superficial and indiscriminating use of Bible texts is increasingly widespread. Paul does not mention a 'gift of sound hermeneutics' in his list of spiritual gifts, and if there is such a thing it seems to be somewhat neglected, to say the least. But that is no reason for not emphasising the need for it and demonstrating how it should be put into effect.

Such a popularising task would need to be done by someone with a flair for, and experience in, journalism, along with sufficient scholarly qualifications to be able to discern what is crucial and what is not. Taking the matter one stage further, and bearing in mind the speed with which issues are liable to become matters of public concern these days, what about a telephone help-line (not continuously manned, of course)? Who knows what electronic network lies in wait to enmesh us? Perhaps we shall celebrate our centenary sitting at home and watching a two-metre wall screen. Who knows?

CHAPTER 7B

The Role of Biblical Research in the Church Today: A View from the Academy

H.G.M. Williamson

I. Introduction

The relationship between the church and the academy in matters concerning biblical and theological research has frequently been a stormy one. The expectations of each side have often been misunderstood by the other and the issues at stake have had a sad tendency to become personalised instead of being discussed, as they should be, on the basis of their own inherent validity. It is for this reason that I welcome the agreement given to the suggestion that this topic should be treated by two writers in the present volume. By first allowing each side of the relationship independently to articulate its own self-awareness of the situation, the discussion may be able to move forward with a greater, and hence more charitable, understanding of the situation within which each interested party finds itself.

I recognise, of course, that there is an element of artificiality about this distinction. All Christian scholars are members of the church, and many of them play an active role in ministry of all sorts. Conversely, many church members, be they in full-time ministry or not, take a great interest in the academic enterprise and contribute to it as time permits. So most of us find ourselves wearing both hats at one time or another, and the very fact that this can give rise to personal tensions is a witness to the truth that our subject is by no means to be lightly dismissed. Nevertheless, on the assumption that research has a part to play within the rich diversity of the body of Christ with its many members, I shall here approach our topic resolutely and exclusively from the side of the academy.

II. The Scene Transformed

So far as the world of evangelical biblical scholarship today is concerned, we need first to recognise how completely the situation has changed over the past fifty years. At least until the Second World War, we were effectively nowhere. The giants of the nineteenth century were men of the past, and on the British side of the Atlantic, at least, there were virtually no evangelical scholars in academic institutions. Of course, there were those who continued to teach in other contexts, but even among them it is hard to think of any who contributed significantly to research *per se*.

Fifty years on the position is totally different, and the role of the Tyndale Fellowship, whose jubilee we celebrate with this volume, should not be overlooked when seeking to explain what has happened. I well remember that when I was secretary of the Fellowship more than twenty years ago the committee used regularly to receive figures of how many of its members were now in university positions in Britain, and there was a great sense of satisfaction when at that time the figure of twenty-five was reached. Such statistics would be meaningless today, for not only is the Fellowship far more international than it used to be, but the very term 'evangelical' is more elastic than it then was. It thus becomes misleading to use the arbitrary yardstick of the member-ship of a Fellowship, however prestigious, as the exclusive measure of evangelical strength.

Even without detailed statistics, however, it is clear that the situ-ation today is unrecognisable by comparison with what it was, and this has led to what in other contexts is often called a 'feel good' factor. Evangelical biblical scholarship has advanced, and increasingly it is having to be taken more seriously by other Christians, if for no other reason than that it relates to the increased strength of the evangelical wing of the church at large.

At the same time, however, it should be recognised that the ground itself has shifted considerably over the years in ways that have a significant bearing on the role that biblical scholarship sees for itself. This is almost bound to be the case if research is doing its stuff prop-erly. Pure research in any field opens up new avenues and perspectives, and as these become assimilated by the wider commu-nity, so the questions that are asked and the expectations which are fostered move on. Some avenues and lines of thought which once held centre stage turn out to be dead ends; others open up new vistas and horizons which simply could not have been envisaged a generation ago. By definition, research means pressing forward into the unknown, so that it has to work to a developing agenda if it is to be true to itself.

This can perhaps be illustrated in our field by the three founding projects for which the Tyndale Fellowship offered particular support in the area of Old Testament studies. They were: the unity of Isaiah; the date of Daniel; and the interpretation of Genesis 1-11. These are reveal-ing of the outlook and approach to biblical scholarship at that time. First, two of the trio, at least, suggest, if they do not presuppose, a dog-matic approach to critical issues. Second, they imply that the role of biblical research should be defensive, and its purpose apologetic. And third, scholarship's agenda should be set by the church: it should fur-nish the church with ammunition in order to hold the present line of understanding rather than allowing itself the possibility of being in the

vanguard of questioning whether that understanding is itself legitimate and profitable.[1] It was rather as though medical research should
endlessly reaffirm the value of penicillin rather than setting itself the
new challenge of cancer research.

III. The Role of Biblical Scholarship

Paradoxically, this has changed in the modern world by significant
shifts both in the expectations of the church towards biblical scholars
and (of more importance for my immediate purposes) in the agenda of
the wider community of biblical scholars itself. To illustrate the first
point briefly, the guidelines for the recently published 21st Century
edition of the *New Bible Commentary*[2] were explicit that contributors
should concentrate their attention on a positive interpretation of the
text and not on the furnishing of technical information that students
might need for their narrower academic engagement with critical
issues. Conversely, in the scholarly realm the move towards post-crit-
ical methods means that it is now quite normal to read, for instance, of
the unity of Isaiah, and indeed I have a monograph about to appear on
precisely this theme.[3] Of course, this unity is conceived today in ways
quite different from those of the founding fathers of the Tyndale Fellowship, but the point I wish to stress remains unaffected: both what
the evangelical wing of the church is asking of its scholars and the academic atmosphere in which we work today as scholars mean that our
agenda can no longer continue to be set by precisely the same programme of work which dominated the scene fifty years ago. We stand
proudly and firmly in the same tradition, but our immediate tasks have
moved forward as circumstances have changed.

All this, I suggest, opens up new possibilities for biblical research
to serve the church, but in ways that are not, perhaps, obvious at first
sight. In my opinion, it will fulfil these best by being true to itself rather

---

[1] I am conscious at this point of having over-simplified for the sake of clarity. In
addition to the accepted variety of views within the Fellowship from its earliest
days (on which see F.F. Bruce, 'The Tyndale Fellowship for Biblical Research', *EQ*
19 [1947] 52-61), there are also regional variations to be taken into account; *cf.* D.F.
Wright, 'Soundings in the Doctrine of Scripture in British Evangelicalism in the
First Half of the Twentieth Century', *TynB* 31 (1980) 87-106.
[2] D.A. Carson, A. Motyer and G.J. Wenham (eds.), *New Bible Commentary: 21st Century Edition* (Leicester: IVP, 1994).
[3] H.G.M. Williamson, *The Book Called Isaiah. Deutero-Isaiah's Role in Composition and
Redaction* (Oxford: Clarendon, 1994).

than subservient to some alternative programme, however well intentioned. If it is to open up new avenues of understanding of the Scriptures and to correct those which may be false, it will never succeed by casting its role in terms of propping up the intellectual *status quo*. Not all that is mistaken in current interpretation of the Bible comes from outside evangelical circles. Indeed, it may fairly be said that there is as much diversity of opinion within Evangelicalism as between it and others. Far from being always a comforter, biblical research must often find itself in what is popularly called a 'prophetic' role, challenging error in this realm quite as much as offering reassurance that is not soundly based. All too often the questions which the church asks of the Bible (and by extension, therefore, of those who give their lives to its study) are inappropriate to the material; only free and uninhibited research will allow the right questions to be asked in the first place.[4]

In order to pursue this role aright, and in the light of the 'feel good' factor to which I referred earlier, I envisage, then, that evangelical scholarship will continue to develop its progress towards an increasing engagement with the mainstream of the discipline which embraces a variety of religious commitments and none. All too often in the past, evangelical scholarship has given only the appearance of such an engagement. In reality, there was little intention of dealing with whole swathes of critical issues with any real sense of commitment. It seems to have been done more for the sake of appearances in order to justify a rejection of what scholarship was investigating while the intention all along was to pursue a wholly separate agenda. Hence it became necessary to establish separate publishing imprints, not only to retain the confidence of the wider constituency but also because there was a likelihood that material might otherwise not be published at all. Evangelical scholarship was thus a discipline of its own which only made use of wider research in so far as it could be turned to serve its own interests. The selectivity of citations to give a semblance of scholarly respectability has often been pointed out.

In the new situation, much of this has changed, and you will not be surprised to learn that I see this as part of the right way forward. Evangelical scholars are increasingly working as part of the wider academic community, which inevitably means employing its methods

---

[4]A clear example of this necessity is rightly stressed elsewhere in this volume when K. Vanhoozer points out that 'the most spectacular and damaging interpretative errors are mistakes about genre' and affirms that a vital task of biblical criticism is to clarify the nature of the genres within the biblical text 'in all its foreignness and complexity' (p. 173).

and seeking to engage with it on its own terms. Publication is therefore by no means always immediately recognisable as distinctively evangelical at all. Scholarship is scholarship, and it stands or falls by its own excellence or otherwise.

IV. Scholars' Expectations of the Church

What does all this mean for the nature of the relationship between the academy and the church? Let me first address the issue of what scholars might reasonably expect of the church before turning to the other side of the coin—the question of accountability.

In the first place, those engaged in research would ask for an appropriate level of trust and understanding on the part of the wider constituency. This is not a request for particular privilege any more than it is a statement of lofty superiority. It is, rather, a recognition that in this as in all research there is a conventional mode of discourse and a set of shared assumptions which can hardly be understood (but can all too easily be misunderstood) by those without the necessary technical training. Specifically when evangelical scholars are engaged on this aspect of their work, they should be free to undertake research without having to qualify or justify every remark for the benefit of an audience for whom their words are not in that context intended.

Secondly, it needs to be recognised that most research proceeds by the accumulation of many small pieces of new data. It is given to only a few to synthesise all this into some major new hypothesis that may lead to what is often called a paradigm shift in the discipline. Yet such a shift could not occur without the prior build-up of a mass of minor elements. Students embarking on research, and the churches or others who support them, often seem to expect too much, so that what starts out as an attempt to settle once and for all the question of 'the historical Jesus', for instance, is likely to end up as the study of a single saying or parable. The analogy of cancer research again suggests itself. We need to learn to see the study of such minutiae in the context of the doctrine of the body of Christ with its many members—it makes its contribution, but is not itself the whole body. To puzzled onlookers it may seem an extravagance, a profligate use of resources with little to show for itself. Taken in isolation, such a charge might be justified, but Christians above all should know better than to regard any such enterprise in isolation. Biblical scholars look to the wider church for encouragement, especially for those in the lonely and arduous years of research leading to a first doctorate, not the crushing rebuke that it is all a waste of time and talents.

Thirdly, scholars tacitly accept that there is a hypothetical element in much of what they do, not least because they often have to move behind the text to its literary pre-history, or from the narrative presentation of events, with all that that includes by way of interpretation and portrayal for other than historical purposes, to the social and political hinterland of the text. Scholars, in their calmer moments, acknowledge this; the rest of us need to do so too, and not expect every word written in that context to be an attempt to say the last word.

Finally, and in conscious development of this last point, scholarship advances by the proposing and testing of hypotheses. In the past, under pressure from the church for the reasons I have set out above, evangelicals have generally concentrated on 'testing', but in the new situation they are moving towards the front in the more positive role of proposing.[5] Such exploratory work is surely essential if evangelicals are to contribute in the long run to the task of re-awakening a sense of expectancy and excitement in the church at large when it listens to the Bible, even though, as already indicated, it may entail some painful rethinking of cherished and long-held opinions. In some circles the response may only be unpopularity at best. Among thoughtful Christians with minds open to the possibility that they may yet have things to learn, however, those who undertake such work deserve our support and trust in their explorations.

V. Scholars' Accountability to the Church

If scholars seek so much from the church by way of support and understanding, it is only right that they should in their turn accept the need for some sort of accountability. The question here, however, is how such accountability may appropriately be rendered. This is a problem with which British academics in particular have been rudely confronted in recent years because so much of their support comes from public funding, and there has been much discussion and unease about the methods which have been imposed upon them. One point, how-

---

[5]In my own field, I think, for instance, of the splendid recent books of Walter Moberly, *The Old Testament of the Old Testament. Patriarchal Narratives and Mosaic Yahwism* (Minneapolis: Fortress, 1992), and of Gordon McConville, *Judgment and Promise: An Interpretation of the Book of Jeremiah* (Leicester/Winona Lake: Apollos/ Eisenbrauns, 1993).

ever, seems now to be agreed, and it applies well to one aspect of
evangelical biblical scholarship's accountability to the church. That is,
the principle of so-called peer review. For reasons which I have briefly
outlined already, excellence in scholarship can only adequately be
tested by those with a full understanding of the methods and procedures of the discipline. Too much pain has been caused in the past by
hasty pronouncements concerning the results of research from those
outside the academic discipline. Part of the academy's request for trust
on the part of the church, therefore, should include the confidence in
the members of the evangelical academic guild to appraise the work of
one another, including its doctrinal propriety.

I am not, of course, suggesting the establishment of some official
watchdog committee. Rather, such appraisal is already an automatic
part of the continuing work of scholarship as publications are regularly
reviewed and evaluated, conferences are convened and groups such as
the Tyndale Fellowship are established to provide a forum within
which assessment goes forward in both formal and informal discussions. If scholarship is to advance, then allowance has to be built into
the system for trial and error. Proposing, testing, evaluating, accepting
and rejecting are all valid facets of the common enterprise. But it stands
to reason that this can only be done appropriately by those who are
themselves active participants in the work.

There is, however, another side to accountability which the
church also has a right to seek, not least because of the heavy investment which serious scholarship entails. Crudely stated, the church can
reasonably ask whether biblical scholarship is producing the goods;
are the results of all this activity leading towards the enrichment of the
people of God? Naturally, the ultimate test in this is a matter which
others must evaluate. But the basis for such an evaluation needs to be
clearly understood. It is often assumed that it should be conducted on
the basis of the willingness of academics to provide popular and accessible works, commentaries, reference books and other writings which
make their findings available to those who are not specialists. Of
course, this sometimes happens, and when scholars also have the facil-
ity to communicate effectively it is to be welcomed. But two caveats
must at once be entered: not all scholars are by any means gifted in this
separate enterprise, and even if they are they are really wearing
another hat when they engage in it. An alternative, and in many cases
more appropriate, approach is once again by way of the multifaceted
diversity of ministries within the church. Alongside research scholars,
there are others with sufficient training to profit by the results which

scholars produce but whose principal gift is teaching and communication. They may not have the ability or the vocation themselves to pursue research, but they feed quite properly off those who do. Thus it is through the effectiveness of *their* work that the church benefits from the initial input of the academic. It is my opinion that there are many examples of publication on record which demonstrate the truth of this,[6] and the church would do well to remember that such publications would not have been possible in the first place without the prior investment in research which has led to such beneficial results.

In other words, accountability in terms of results must be based on a realistic assessment of the complementary ministries of research and teaching within the church at large. If that is done, scholars will have greater freedom to pursue their own vocation, which is both demanding and time-consuming. To put pressure upon them to render an inappropriate form of accountability for their labours will be counter-productive. Appropriate accountability, on the other hand, will encourage them to continue in their work, confident that their efforts are appreciated and effective, to the ultimate benefit of the church as a whole.

---

[6]It is unnecessary to try to document this assessment fully. In the present context, however, and with due allowance for the fact that all series are uneven, it is appropriate to mention the Tyndale and 'The Bible Speaks Today' commentary series. Some of the latter are outstanding examples of the kind of process which I have chiefly in mind.

CHAPTER 8

Climbing Ropes, Ellipses and Symphonies: the Relation between Biblical and Systematic Theology

Howard Marshall

Summary

Systematic or dogmatic theology is the faithful expression of the theology inherent in the biblical revelation in a form which is appropriate for the changed situation of our world. It has to combine identity and development. The relationship between biblical and systematic theology is in some ways similar to that between the theologies of the Old and New Testaments, and various analogies may throw light on it. The essay explores this relationship in terms of the strands of a rope which are not identical throughout its length; the way in which a more developed and abstract general mathematical system may include a simpler one; and the ways in which 'doing theology' may resemble a musical composition and its performance.

I. Introduction

During the early years in the history of the Tyndale Fellowship and its associated institution, Tyndale House, it was recognised that resources were limited and that therefore it was necessary to draw up a set of priorities for the development of evangelical theology. Accordingly, it was resolved that the right strategy was to concentrate attention on biblical studies and to leave theology in the broader sense to take care of itself, at least for the time being. Those who took this decision presumably felt that it was essential to lay a firm foundation for future building. The main battles for the future of evangelical theology would take place at the level of biblical studies, by demonstrating that the Bible was a reliable basis for the erection of Christian theology and by interpreting its theological message more truly. Thankfully there were never lacking some people with an interest in historical and systematic theology and the practical outworking of theology in ethics to ensure that these vital areas received attention. Today we rejoice that it is now possible for them to receive much more of the resources that they need. But basically the history of the past fifty years illustrates the evangelical conviction that the foundation of its theology is biblical studies. But in what ways is biblical study foundational to theology, and how is the Bible related to theology? Our present task is to explore the relationships between these two broad areas.

There are welcome signs at present of fresh attention being given to these relationships, and not only by scholars belonging to the professedly evangelical wing of theology. Within the biblical area the prior question of whether there is such a thing as a biblical theology has been attracting the attention of a number of scholars,[1] and the question of the relation between such a biblical theology and systematic theology is also again becoming a live issue. At the annual conference of the Scottish Evangelical Theological Society the 1994 Finlayson Memorial Lecture was given by Dr. Kevin Vanhoozer under the title 'From Canon to Concept: the "Same", the "Other" and the relation between

---

[1]It must suffice here to mention the work of P. Stuhlmacher and B.S. Childs. On a more local level the work of the Biblical Theology Study Group of the Tyndale Fellowship deserves honourable mention, and especially the work recently done under its aegis. See especially C.H.H. Scobie, 'The Challenge of Biblical Theology (Part 1)', *TynB* 42.1 (1992) 31-61; 'The Structure of Biblical Theology', *TynB* 42.2 (1992) 163-94. The present paper is a development from one given at a seminar at the Study Group in 1992, when I was asked to discuss 'the problems of biblical interpretation with specific relevance to the development of an integrated biblical theology'.

Biblical and Systematic Theology', in effect the same topic as concerns us.[2]

One difference between us that may be fruitful is that Dr. Vanhoozer approaches the subject from the angle of the systematic theologian, whereas I come at it from biblical studies. I am not equipped to discuss the nature of systematic theology at anything more than a superficial level.[3] Nevertheless, the outside observer like myself can detect the difference between the theology of the Reformers, which appears to be essentially a biblical theology, expounding Scripture and basing itself on Scripture at every point, and the kind of theology represented, for example, by a Paul Tillich where reference to the Bible is minimal. I doubt if there is any great value for us in this context in discussing too deeply what exactly is going on in the kind of theological tradition represented by such as Tillich. I think that much the most valuable thing for us will be primarily to examine our own neck of the woods and do some self-examination and criticism.

II. Systematic and Dogmatic Theology

Let us begin with some preliminary definitions and demarcations of our fields which may help to set the agenda for the discussion. A *prima facie* description of our procedures might be to say that biblical theology, in the sense of a theology of the biblical writings (as, for example, has been done for the New Testament by Bultmann or Goppelt or Ladd), and as opposed to a systematic theology which is biblically based over against one which is not, is ideally a systematic presentation of the biblical teaching or of the 'system' which may be presumed to underlie the biblical writings, such as might have been written by a writer in biblical times. By contrast systematic theology is the endeavour to write a theology for our own times which will be based on and true to the biblical revelation.

---

[2]The lecture will be published in *Scottish Bulletin of Evangelical Theology* 12 (1994). I have to confess that I had hoped to complete my preparation of this lecture before hearing Dr. Vanhoozer, so that my own contribution, while lacking in quality, might at least be free from plagiarism; in the event, I did not succeed, and therefore I can take this opportunity to express my grateful appreciation of his stimulating insights while hoping that there is still something more that is worth saying.

[3]For anybody else in my position a strongly recommended guide is S.J. Grentz and R.E. Olson, *20th Century Theology: God and the World in a Transitional Age* (Carlisle: Paternoster, 1992).

I have so far used the term 'systematic theology', in accordance with the assignment given to me. But it may be helpful if we bring in another term which is, if anything, more important, and that is the term dogmatic theology or dogmatics, a word for ever associated in my mind with the thick guttural German accent of Otto Weber lecturing in Göttingen on 'Dawg-ma' (as he pronounced it). The connotation of dogmatics is that its concern is with what ought to be believed in the Christian church. It is the formulation of an *authoritative* theology, as compared with a biblical theology which may be nothing more than a description of the theology held by the biblical writers, or a systematic theology which similarly may be nothing more than an orderly account of the theology held by a Christian group or individual. Our interest is surely in dogmatic theology. Our concern is not simply with a description of evangelical theology, but with an understanding of what we should believe and whether our belief is coherent and defensible. This means that dogmatic theology can be properly carried on only in the context of the Christian church and never as a purely academic exercise.

As I have suggested, the question of the relationship between dogmatic and biblical theology may appear to be settled fairly quickly for Evangelicals. The major classics of evangelical theology are in effect largely textbooks of biblical theology. This requires no argument for those books that stand in the succession which runs from John Calvin's *Institutes* to Karl Barth's *Church Dogmatics*. By contrast you may feel that you are hunting in vain for any decisive influence of Scripture on F. Schleiermacher's *The Christian Faith*. Nevertheless, there are some obvious differences between a biblically-based systematic theology and a biblical theology. Let me try to list them.

(1) Systematic theology includes *topics*, or aspects of them, which are not treated (or scarcely treated) in Scripture. We shall not find a discussion of the so-called proofs for the existence of God in Scripture, even though there may be hints of some of them. We shall be anachronistic if we look for a discussion of 'person' in relation to God in the Bible. We shall hunt in vain in the Bible for a treatment of the relation between natural and revealed theology, even if there may be some material relevant to a modern discussion of these topics.

(2) Systematic theology tends to have a 'shape' or *structure* which is not necessarily that of biblical theology. It is structured under themes such as the Trinity, the atonement and the sacraments. It is obvious that none of these topics has influenced the 'shape' of the biblical material; none of them is the subject of thematic treatment in the Bible—

certainly not in the Old Testament and to a limited extent in the New Testament. Nobody doubts that the 'raw materials' for doctrine are there, but not expositions of the doctrines themselves. Equally, the structural themes of the biblical writers—the purposes of God with reference to Israel's foreign neighbours (*e.g.*, Je. 46ff.), the pattern of Christian mission (Mt. 10), or visions and revelations (2 Cor. 12)—are generally not those of systematic theology. Either discipline suffers if it is subject to the constraints of an alien structure. For example, it is a justifiable criticism of Donald Guthrie's *New Testament Theology* that it organises the biblical material in accordance with the categories of systematic theology instead of asking whether the New Testament provides its own structures for expounding its content.[4]

(3) Systematic theologians are inevitably affected by the *general culture and philosophy of their own time*, and this influences the way in which they understand and organise the biblical material. The influence is twofold.

On the one hand, the systematic theologian has a duty to relate biblical teaching to the thinking of the time, *e.g.*, by attempting to formulate a Christian doctrine of creation and of the nature of humanity in relationship to what scientists may be saying on these matters, so that the doctrine is developed in critical dialogue with modern knowledge and culture.

On the other hand, theologians cannot avoid being constrained by the ways of thinking that are shared with the culture to which they belong, *e.g.*, by thinking against an Aristotelian or Kantian philosophical framework. Here one may think of the way in which the doctrine of the atonement was understood to some extent in terms of feudalism in the Middle Ages and in legal categories at the Reformation.[5]

(4) Equally the work of the theologian is affected by developments in the *life of the ongoing Christian church* and by personal *Christian experience*. These play a significant role. If I may be allowed a personal allusion, I remember how, when I wrote a brief outline of *Christian Beliefs* in the early 1960s, it said next to nothing about the gifts of the Spirit, but when I came to revise the book in the 1970s the changing experiences of many Christians made it necessary to tackle that topic

---

[4]*New Testament Theology* (Leicester: IVP, 1981).
[5]It is also the case that biblical theologians will be influenced by the thought-forms of the modern world, but in their case the problem will be not so much to relate biblical thinking to the modern world as to attempt—and it can only be an attempt—to present the biblical material on its own terms and within its own framework of thinking.

more directly and fully. This may be an example of fresh contemporary experience leading one back to neglected passages of Scripture. At the same time, it also illustrates how our limited experience does lead us to ignore some elements in Scripture; for example, the demonic occupies a much greater place in the Synoptic Gospels than in contemporary western works on theology, but a theologian in some Third World countries would more quickly recognise its prominence in the Gospels and its contemporary relevance. Despite the criticism I made above about the structure of Donald Guthrie's work, it is to his credit that he gave the demonic a proper place in his discussion of 'Man and his world'.[6]

In the light of these points none of us would want to claim that it would be sufficient for an evangelical systematic theologian to write a biblical theology in the limited sense of a systematic account of what the Bible says, nor would any of us argue that our problems would be solved if we were to do simply this and ignore the passing of the centuries and the contemporary situation. It is not enough merely to find out what the biblical writers believed and wrote and reproduce it in a way that is intelligible for today. Nor is it sufficient to go a stage further and attempt to uncover an underlying theology which they severally held and to make it our own, so that we can say that, whatever we believe and teach, it was believed and taught by the biblical writers, or that it underlay their thinking. More generally we sometimes talk of 'recovering a biblical world-view'. But in what respects do we go along with the biblical world-view and in what respects do we go beyond it or abandon certain aspects of it? How can we be the same and yet different? That is the crux of the problem! What then is the relation between biblical theology and contemporary biblically-based theology, or, if you like, between the Bible and contemporary theology?

III. Problems in Biblical Theology

It may help us to tackle this problem if we devote some attention to the questions that arise when we try to write a biblical theology. It will not surprise you if I suggest that a large part of our main problem lies at this basic level, and that there are similarities between the relationship of the theologies of the two Testaments and the relationship of biblical and systematic theology.

---

[6]*New Testament Theology*, 122-30.

How does one write a biblical theology in the sense of a theology of the Bible as a whole? In principle the question is no different from that of how one writes a theology of the Old Testament or a theology of the New Testament. At whatever level one makes the attempt the same related problems are present. There are basically two difficulties to be faced, but the second one has two aspects.

The first difficulty is that each Testament consists of a number of separate books which are not textbooks of theology but have a wide variety of genres and contents; we thus face the problem of turning material which is not couched in the form of 'systematic theology' into a different form. For example, how do we get theology out of narrative passages as opposed to explicit, authoritative teaching?

The second difficulty lies in the twofold fact that the biblical books were, firstly, written over a considerable period of time and over a wide geographical area by writers who were largely independent of one another; and, secondly, may contain differing and, as many would say, mutually inconsistent or contradictory understandings of matters theological.

It is this second difficulty or cluster of difficulties which is generally regarded as being really the key one, and we can sum it up by saying that the problem is one of development and diversity. However, the first difficulty, the variety of genres, is also extremely important and we shall have to include it in our discussion.

Moreover, the problem arises on more than one level. There is first the question of whether the *surface teachings* throughout the Bible are the same and can be fitted together harmoniously. Thus one might gather together some pieces of jigsaw that have been found in different boxes in a cupboard and see whether they all belong together and can be joined up to form a unified picture. Can one draw ideas from Paul and John and James and fit them together to get a total picture to which they each make their contributions?

Another appropriate analogy might be that of a reservoir or pool occupied by a shoal of fish. The shoal represents a collection of ideas from which each biblical author has drawn on occasion and which we can reconstruct by putting together the contents of their various individual trawls.

The analogy is complicated by the fact that a reservoir may contain a lot of different species of fish that do not stand in any particular relationship to one another, whereas we might want to claim that the doctrinal ideas in the Bible are somehow related to one another in a structure. This leads over into the second question as to whether there is some kind of *implicit structure* of thought which comes to expression spasmodically in the literature but which is not actually stated.

And, third, there is the question whether there is *development* in understanding—and even retrogression on occasion. In terms of my analogy, is the reservoir a place where young fish are born and older ones die over a period of time, so that inevitably different fishers will produce rather different catches from one another, even if they throw their catch back into the pool after they have examined it? Have we to reconstruct a natural history of the fish pool rather than describe a static situation? Here I am trying to take into account the ways in which there is manifestly development in the New Testament over against the Old Testament, but there may also be retrogression in that it is arguable, for example, that the writings of Paul show greater theological profundity than those of Luke written at a later point.[7]

All this suggests, firstly, that the goal of simply pooling scriptural texts and trying to impose some kind of systematic order on them is over-simplistic, and, secondly, that we have to take into account change and development.

The point can be made more sharply by remarking that the analogy is not to be applied merely to the Bible as a whole or even to the two Testaments each considered on its own. The same problem arises within the writings of one person. The candidate for illustration here is Paul who has at least seven and possibly as many as thirteen separate writings to his credit. All the points that I have made or the questions that I have raised can be placed against his writings. Do his surface teachings form a coherent whole? Is there any underlying framework or structure that can be deduced from the surface? And are there signs of change and development so that we are dealing with a living, developing entity rather than something static and complete? Here the kind of questions raised by J.C. Beker are involved, with his important suggestion that Paul's theology has a coherent centre expressed variously in different contingent situations.[8]

---

[7]We shall do well, of course, not to be pushed into an over-emphasis on development. Some contemporary NT scholars want to see a development over a period of time as theological thinking goes on from a very simple, primitive beginning, whereas some of us may want to give rather more credit to Jesus or the earliest church for the same ideas: a case in point is the theology of the Lord's supper where I have been criticised for ascribing so much to the mind of Jesus himself that there is not enough development in the early church to keep speculative minds employed in tracing it. Nevertheless, once we start talking of the Bible as a whole the question of development over a lengthy period of time becomes of major importance.

And, of course, the problems are accentuated as soon as we try to move on from biblical to dogmatic theology. To take just one example, there is the question of underlying structure. Suppose we take up again that old chestnut, the doctrine of the Trinity. It is a cliché to observe that no New Testament author explicitly teaches the doctrine in the way in which it may be found in a textbook, but nevertheless the New Testament provides the data which need to be explained. (Nevertheless, it is worth comment that the amount of explicit expression of a functional Trinitarian understanding of the nature of God in the New Testament is greater than is often admitted.[9]) It follows accordingly that one fundamental criterion for a successful doctrine of the Trinity is whether it adequately accounts for the New Testament data. A modern theologian, then, would hold a doctrine of the Trinity which gives some explanation of the biblical materials in terms of what is meant by three Persons and how their mutual relationship is to be expressed. But now, even if this doctrine is regarded as necessary to explain the New Testament data, we would agree that there is no sense in which this doctrine was held by the New Testament authors, even as an implicit doctrine which they do not teach explicitly. Are we then to say that the later theologians were discovering something about the nature of God which was not known in New Testament times, still less in Old Testament times? And what is the status of this doctrine as compared with the statement of some doctrine for which direct biblical evidence is forthcoming (*e.g.*, that God is loving)? When the Doctrinal Basis of this Fellowship is regarded as binding on its members and they express their subscription to it, are they giving their assent to something more than Scripture teaches? Would some (or all?) biblical writers, if they were brought back to life, refuse to assent to it because they could not understand it? Or would it be possible to devise a first-century AD or a sixth-century BC equivalent that would have been comprehensible and binding? Nobody would presumably want to exclude Paul from the Tyndale Fellowship because, if he came back, he would not be able to understand where theology had reached since the first century, and, as an honest person, would not want to sign the Doctrinal Basis because he simply could not understand it.

The question is thus partly at least one of language, concepts and structures which had not developed, whether in biblical times as com-

---

[8]J.C. Beker, *Paul the Apostle: The Triumph of God in Life and Thought* (Edinburgh: T.&T. Clark, 1980).

[9]See J.B. Green and M. Turner (eds.), *Jesus of Nazareth: Lord and Christ* (Carlisle: Paternoster, 1994), where several essays make this point.

pared with post-biblical, or even at one stage of biblical history compared with another.

IV. The Climbing Rope

In order to try to understand what is happening in a way that may shed light on how we go about writing theology, I want to explore the problem in terms of a number of further analogies that may be helpful to various degrees.

The first picture is that of a climbing rope which is made up of various strands that are twisted together and run along the length of the rope. Some strands go through the whole length, while others run for limited stretches, but the effect is that it is the same rope throughout because there is continuity from one part to the next (even if the actual connecting links are not identical throughout its length), there are no breaks, and the rope can do much the same things at any point in its length. The strands running the whole length are the major locus of the rope's identity and unity, but shorter ones also do duty over limited periods.

The application of the analogy is fairly obvious. The rope represents the chronological course of biblical revelation. There is a unity in that there are strands which go right through the rope, and others which stretch for considerable distances. There are various theological beliefs and concepts which run right through the course of the biblical revelation. The belief in one God, creator and righteous ruler of the universe, is obviously one. The fact of the Son of God coming as Saviour is very obvious throughout the latter part of the revelation, although it is not obvious earlier on, and is not present or is at best hidden at many points in the Old Testament; it certainly does not bear the strain in the earlier stages. The Holy Spirit functions likewise. Some strands are woven in at a late stage, *e.g.*, baptism and the Lord's supper or the concept of the body of Christ; others which once were important disappear, like the ritual prescriptions and the food laws or the requirement of physical circumcision. The vital stress on 'the land' is metamorphosed. One example that might be singled out for brief discussion is the characteristic belief that God is to be understood in terms of Fatherhood. We can see that the characteristics of divine fatherhood are there in embryo in the earlier part of the revelation but the actual term is rather infrequent; in the teaching of Jesus there is, in effect, explicit revelation that God is a Father, indeed a personal Father, to individual disciples who can call on him in prayer as Jesus did; and the result of the teaching of Jesus is that in the writings of Paul and John the point needs no argument, and 'Father' is now taken for granted as the appropriate term for addressing and describing God. The theme is thus present throughout the revelation, although the crucial exposition of it is not reached until Jesus.

The analogy then suggests that the task of biblical theology is to tease out, identify and describe the different strands and show how they are interwoven at any given point. It encourages the belief that the various strands have been woven together into a unity and it demonstrates that there can be change over a lengthy period of time accompanied by a basic unity. A biblical theology will accordingly analyse the thought of the biblical writers over the whole period of revelation, setting out the characteristic content and arrangement of their beliefs at different times and showing how there is harmony and unity between them.

I suppose that, so far as actual ropes are concerned, we could have one in which the original strands came to an end at different stages and fresh strands were likewise inserted piecemeal, so that the end of the rope consisted of entirely different strands from those at the beginning. I think that we would have to say that if no strands run right through the biblical rope then there would not be the kind of unity that we would regard as necessary. In short, the analogy would break down, because at the end of the day the considerations that apply to ropes are inadequate when dealing with doctrine.

A related analogy may take us further. I am thinking of the proverbial axe which we still keep for chopping wood. Years ago, the wooden shaft broke, and we replaced it with another, and then not so long ago the metal head became too blunt and bent for further sharpening to be any use, and so we replaced it. We still have an axe that looks much the same as it did when it was originally bought, but is it the same axe? There has always been an object composed of shaft and head, and it has done the same tasks, and we recognise it as 'the axe'. But really it is no different from a new axe that we might have bought to replace the old one in one stage rather than in two. The difference between it and a totally new axe is that there is a certain 'institutional' continuity, such as there might be in the case of Aberdeen Grammar School which has different teachers and pupils from those which it used to have, which occupies different buildings from those with which it started centuries ago, which teaches different subjects from different textbooks, and which has changed its name from that which it originally had; nevertheless, there is an institutional continuity and there is a basic functional continuity. You might then want to speculate as to what is essential in that continuity and what changes over time might make you want to say 'The school calls itself the Aberdeen Grammar School but in no way is it what is used to be.' Or, again, if we shift our attention from institutions to persons, then we might want to claim that there must be some kind of 'immortality of the soul' to create continuity between the John Brown whose 'body lies a mouldering in the grave' and the John Brown who will share in the world to come.

The point of these comments is to raise again this question of whether it is a condition for doctrinal continuity that there must be some strands which are present throughout the length of the rope. This does not mean that all the basic strands must run through each and every passage. That is manifestly not the case. There would, however, be a unity constituted by the various passages belonging within the same community of faith—so that the broad theology of the community might be presumed to form the framework of the writers and they would be developing different themes within it.

A further question that arises and that is not answered on this analogy is whether there is in fact a real unity between different writers and passages. Have we grounds for believing that, in terms of our analogy, the Bible is like one rope rather than several such as several separate lengths tied or spliced together at various points or a number of pieces laid loosely side by side and perhaps leading off in different directions? How different can the parts of the rope be and yet remain parts of the same rope? What makes the faith of Rahab the harlot part of the same rope with Abraham and Paul and James? That is perhaps not the best example because Rahab is not a biblical writer. Maybe, then, we have to ask about the author of an imprecatory Psalm and the author of Romans 12:19-21: could they have agreed with one another that they were both uttering what could be parts of a unified, harmonious Scripture?[10]

How, then, do we deal with apparent contradictions and disharmonies? Are there points where we seem to be dealing with different or broken ropes rather than with different-coloured strands of the

---

[10]Here may be the place to make yet another important point, which is that we must beware of thinking of the biblical writers as professional theologians who had pondered the problems of theology at deep intellectual levels; Amos does not claim to have been more than a countryman whom the Lord called to be a prophet. We must not expect a fully fledged systematic theology from each and every writer.

same rope? Is it simply a matter of faith that the various passages are ultimately in harmony? Or have we grounds for arguing that this is the truth of the matter? Is it not the case that in principle we can never know all the reasons which may yet be offered for believing passages to be contradictory and therefore can never say that final proof of harmony has been offered?

Whatever be the answers to these questions, the point of this analogy has been to show that there are ways in which we may find a unity in the biblical revelation in terms of the coherence of the strands of thought at any given time or in terms of a coherence from one point in time to another.[11]

We could then go on to say that the same analogy might fit the extension of theologising beyond the biblical period into our own time. It would indicate that we are dealing with the same rope as our biblical forefathers and that therefore the same basic strands of the rope must continue to run through it and any fresh ones that are added must cohere with them. Where the analogy fails us is in that is not able to show, firstly, whether the strands actually do cohere in unity at any given time and across the centuries and, secondly, how the composition of the rope may legitimately vary at different stages. A further analogy needs attention.

V. The Circle and the Ellipse

A second analogy that might be fruitful here would be to consider the kind of simple mathematical system which we learned fairly early on at school. It included the geometry of the circle, but it had not progressed any further. Within its limits it had a full and accurate knowledge of the circle and its properties, the nature of tangents, chords and so on. Later on a student might become familiar with the more advanced mathematical system which includes the geometry of the ellipse and of conic sections generally. The crucial point for us is that mathematicians working with the latter system are then able to regard the ellipse as a particular example of the larger family of conic sections and the circle as a special case of an ellipse in which the two foci coincide.[12]

---

[11]It may be that I am really repeating in a different way the kind of approach taken by W. Eichrodt in his *Theology of the Old Testament* (London; SCM, 1961), where he took 'cross-sections' of the theology at various points and exposed the theme of the covenant as the basic strand linking together these points.

We might say that the circle is a simplification of the ellipse. Thus within a system which knows only circles, all that is said about circles—their radii, areas and so on—is true and complete. But it is only part of the theory of conic sections, where we have a larger and more complex system in which all that we previously knew about circles is still true but is only part of the truth; and new vistas open up which could not have been imagined by somebody who knew only of circles.

So too, it might be argued that within biblical theology the—to us—rather limited conceptualisation of his knowledge of God possessed by Amos was true within the theological system which he had, and it remains true within the more complex systems found in Paul and John but is now seen to be only part of the truth.[13]

The analogy might then be applied to biblical theology in relation to the later developments of systematic theology, so that the biblical material about the nature of God is seen to be a simple statement of what is expressed on a different conceptual level in later theology and vice-versa.

The analogy may be taken a bit further. I do not know the history of mathematics, but it is presumably the case that the geometry of the circle was discovered and developed before the geometry of conic sections and certainly before the development of the algebraic representation of geometry in co-ordinate geometry; if so, the geometry of conic sections did not exist at the time when people were first familiar with the circle, and therefore, the later geometry is a new discovery giving a picture of reality that did not previously exist. The reality has not changed, but perception of it has widened and deepened.[14]

---

[12]The general equation of an ellipse (with its centre at the origin of co-ordinates) is $x^2/a^2 + y^2/b^2 = 1$, where $b^2 = a^2(1 - e^2)$ and e is the eccentricity or distance between the foci; when the foci coincide, the eccentricity $e = 0$, and the equation then simplifies to $x^2 + y^2 = a^2$, which is the corresponding general equation for a circle. There is also, of course, a general equation for conic sections which simplifies to the equation for the ellipse when the appropriate conditions are fulfilled.

[13]The analogy, like all analogies, has its limitations and dangers. It therefore needs to be emphasised that we are thinking of the analogy between the 'theology' of a particular writer and one specific circle which can be regarded as a special case of one particular ellipse. The analogy is not meant to suggest that there are many possible circles (the theologies of the Bible, the Koran, the Buddhist scriptures and so on) and many possible ellipses (the theologies of the 'death of God' school, of liberal Protestantism, *etc.*) all of which might be equally valid. It is meant to suggest that there can be different levels of understanding of the same reality which are in harmony with one another.

So too it could be argued that the understanding of God as Trinity was not known in Old Testament times, but this is how God really was, and equally the later ontological understanding of the Trinity goes beyond what the New Testament teaches in more functional terms[15] but expresses what was true all the time.

To put it otherwise, there is fresh truth about God not known in the time of Amos, although what he was doing was valid in its own setting, even if it was dim and limited. So the invitation to us is to go beyond the Bible to explore theological ellipses and even theological conic sections.

We thus have an analogy which enables us to see how there can be 'progress in doctrine' beyond the biblical apprehension of it.[16] It is possible to grasp reality on different levels of understanding so that we get a fresh picture which goes beyond anything that could have been envisaged earlier. To revert to our previous analogy, it is not just a case of extending the strands of the rope or of weaving in new ones but rather of changing the composition of the rope in some way. In terms or our earlier analogy of a pool of concepts, it is not saying that the biblical writers trawled in the shallows for their ideas but left important depths unplumbed, whereas we are able to explore more deeply (and, it must surely also be said, more shallowly in many cases); we are talking about a different degree of understanding of the same concepts rather than simply a different choice of concepts.

But now an important question arises. It may be illustrated by a further mathematical example. Clearly one test of whether the more complex systems which we have considered are true is whether they include the simpler ones. If the equation for the ellipse did not simplify to that of the circle, then our understanding of the circle as a special case of an ellipse would break down. But we can think of cases where a simple system might be replaced by a more complex one which would show that the simpler system was in certain respects inadequate or merely an approximation to the truth. For example, the Ptolemaic

---

[14]We do not need to discuss here whether mathematicians discover new aspects of reality that previously were not known but were 'there' all the time (like an observer with a more powerful telescope seeing fresh stars), or create new realities that formerly did not exist (like an artist painting a new picture).

[15]In putting the matter in this simplified way I am not intending to rule out the existence of some level of ontological understanding of God as Trinity in the New Testament. A *purely* functional understanding does not square with the evidence.

[16]*Cf.* such a title as J. Orr, *The Progress of Dogma* (London: Hodder & Stoughton, 1901).

understanding of the solar system with its cycles and epicycles based on circles was in fact erroneous in detail even if it was adequate for an approximate description of the movements of the planets. Likewise, we are told, the Newtonian understanding of gravitation can be seen to be an approximation to an Einsteinian understanding rather than a simplification of it; it is good enough for most practical purposes but not where extreme accuracy is required. By contrast, what is true of circles in the context of elementary mathematics is in no way in need of correction in the context of conic sections. In short, one test of whether the geometry of conic sections is valid is whether or not it can accommodate the simple geometry of the circle; but a corresponding test of the validity of Einsteinian physics would simply be whether it can accommodate Newtonian physics as being a near approximation to the truth.

Similarly, we must ask whether the more developed theological insights must be in complete harmony with the less developed ones. Evangelicals would doubtless want to say that the analogy is with circles and ellipses rather than with Newtonian physics. It is affirming that the later, deeper understanding must be of such a kind that the hypothesised reality would have generated the earlier understanding in its time. Traditional upholders of biblical authority are not happy with suggestions that the biblical teaching was only an approximation to the truth or wrong in certain particulars. The criterion for the validity of modern theology is its relation to Scripture rather than vice versa. If the so-called development has the effect of showing that Amos was wrong, then so much the worse for the modern theologian.

But of course the analogy cannot *prove* that any aspect of biblical theology at its more elementary level of understanding and expression will be 'true' when seen in relationship to systematic theology. In other words, it cannot dismiss so-called *Sachkritik* as inappropriate; the case against that must rest on other grounds. Equally, it cannot prove the case that, so far as upholders of biblical authority are concerned, the criterion for the validity of a developed system of theology is that it can accommodate the biblical material as a true expression in its own time.

The value of this analogy in the present context is rather that it gives us some grounds for moving boldly on from biblical theology to a systematic theology that uses post-biblical concepts and enables us to do our theologising in a different frame of reference and to relate our theology to other currents of thought.

In an earlier attempt elsewhere to compare the theology of three New Testament figures, I made the suggestion that it could be helpful to consider three aspects of their thought: the basic presuppositional framework within which they conducted their thinking; the central theme or cluster of themes which gives direction to their thought; and the specific, characteristic elements which they develop more broadly.[17] What we are now saying is that we are at liberty to adopt other frameworks of thought than those of the biblical writers in order to develop our theological systems. To be sure, it is not possible to make a rigid distinction between the framework and the content, and it may well be that adoption of a biblical framework will lead us to question the validity of certain aspects of a modern framework. A framework which is entirely materialistic, for example, is clearly unacceptable in terms of biblical criteria, and a theology developed to fit into such a framework will be a false development from the Bible. Granted this important caveat, however, it remains true that we are at liberty to look at the adequacy and the fruitfulness of other intellectual frameworks.

VI. The Symphony and the Fairground Organ

I now want to take up a third main analogy which may take us further in a number of ways. We come to the symphony, always bearing in mind that an analogy with an artistic composition in a different medium may be misleading. The analogy may be developed in different ways.

Consider then, first, the comparison between the performer and the composer of a musical work. The performers of a symphony are in a sense attempting to discover what is 'there' in a particular composition, to reproduce what the composer intended. They may find things that are 'new' in the sense that previous performers and interpreters did not find them but the composer nonetheless intended them; they may find things that are 'new' in the sense that the composer did not realise that they were there.[18]

My question is whether later theologians discover what was true in the time of Amos or create new ideas. But this is not a very good way of posing the question. Would it be fair to say that the biblical theologian is like a performer, attempting to extract and present what was there in the biblical material, explicit or implicit, but that the systematic theologian goes beyond this and becomes something like a composer

---

[17]I.H. Marshall, 'Jesus, Paul and John', in *Jesus the Saviour: Studies in New Testament Theology* (London: SPCK, 1990) 35-56.

who produces something that is 'new' in comparison with the Bible
but is not 'new' in the sense that it is a discovery of an aspect of what
has always been true about God? The analogy is a limited one, and in
particular it cannot do justice to those vital ideas of continuity which
were brought out in the rope and geometrical analogies.

However, my main purpose in introducing the musical analogy
is to make a second, quite distinct application of it. Here we return at
last to Vanhoozer who reminds us that we must pay attention to the
different genres in the Bible and co-ordinate the varying perspectives
that they offer.

To say this is to go beyond the equally important fact that we
learn as biblical theologians to appreciate Jesus from four portraits in
the Gospels and also from the varied pictures in the rest of the New
Testament. These give us different styles of perception of him, and the
systematician must try to bring together these varied insights—which
can be of very different kinds. Here, then, we have the insight that different compositions may tackle the same theme from different aspects.

But what Vanhoozer was emphasising is rather the variety of
kinds of material in the Bible: poetry, story, letter, homily, all the different types of oral tradition discovered by form criticism, psalms and
proverbs, law-codes, and much else. These do not all work in the same
kind of way. We see different kinds of things happening in the biblical
story, such as personal encounter and flashes of mental insight, and we
see different literary effects, such as story, metaphor, analogy, evoca-
tive symbolism, and so on. The task of the theologian is to consider
their individual contributions and somehow to bring them together in
synthesis. The analogy with different kinds of musical instrument, producing sounds by different principles (strings, wind, percussion,
electronic gadgets, *etc.*) is helpful.

Something important is being said here, and it is that theology
may be conveyed and expressed by different kinds of literary medium,
and the various media may say something about the nature of the the-

---

[18]Readers will appreciate that I have shifted to the musical analogy because, as
noted above, I am not competent to deal with the philosophical question of
whether mathematicians create 'new things' or simply discover what was always
there. Presumably the composer who produces a new symphony produces something that was not there before, even if it is only a rearrangement of existing
musical notes in the available repertoire; there is also a sense in which the performer produces something 'new' by a fresh rendering of the symphony. But we
must not let ourselves be enticed into the discussion of 'authorial intention' at this
point.

ology. The fact that much of the Bible is narrative or story is a point whose significance is much under consideration at present, although I will not attempt here to develop this point. Equally, the fact that there is poetry and not just straight prose is highly important.

This leads me, thirdly, to ruminate on the fact that textbooks of theology are just that—textbooks of theology, collections of propositions. How far, then, can the theological textbook really do justice to the variety of biblical material? Does the theologian kill the animal by dissecting it?

Perhaps not, one may think. A musical composition can be reduced to propositional form in a score. Pushing the point further, it can be reduced to the kind of material that would have been input in the past to a fairground organ or a pianola or nowadays to a computer equipped with sound, so that not only the individual notes but also their individual volume and length can be specified. Even with much less sophisticated technology than is available today, a good pianola rendering can be hard to distinguish from a good solo rendering. It would seem that music can be reduced to propositional or digital form; or can it?

But of course it is not *music* unless it is both played and heard by human ears.[19] The propositional form is not the same as the performance. It must be played. And then things happen in terms of emotional, intellectual and aesthetic effect that you would not get by simply reading the score.

Does this lead us to the conclusion that theology must be 'played' to become theology? It is certainly suggesting that the goal of the theologian must be something more than producing a textbook of theology. It suggests that other media may be possible and necessary. It may justify the belief that Charles Wesley was as much a theologian as John Calvin, and that both were really being theologians when they were 'playing' their theology, Charles singing his hymns and John preaching his sermons. It explains why I should find myself totally frustrated as a New Testament scholar if I never preached or never tried to express my understanding of the New Testament in exposition rather than pure exegesis.

---

[19]Or unless something similar occurs: what about the deaf Beethoven?

VII. Conclusion

We now attempt to draw the threads together. I have tried to suggest that biblical theology is the attempt to express in an appropriate, systematic way the theological ideas implicit and explicit in the biblical writings. We have seen that we are dealing with a developing entity, and therefore a unified synthesis is not possible; but we can trace lines of continuity and follow these through at different stages. In this way we can discover a unity with diversity at any given stage and a unity with diversity between the different stages. We can then go on to argue that systematic theology is the attempt to trace these same lines into our own time and to formulate a theology that will deal with the questions that face us in terms of the biblical message. It is the extension of the strands of doctrine beyond the biblical period. Perhaps what we have been discussing here is not so much the making of theology as rather the ways in which we might critically assess the theology of the church at different times and stages. For certainly one task of the systematic theologian is the critical assessment of what the church and its theologians have taught and still teach in the light of Scripture: has the church, or have its theologians, inserted alien strands into the rope, cut off the genuine strands, or even jumped, like an acrobat in the gymnasium, from one rope to another? Our first analogy, therefore, has much to do with the critical task of the theologian.

Second, we saw that even within the Bible there is a developing conceptuality, which means that there is growth in depth of understanding and sometimes transition to different conceptual frameworks. We argued that the systematic theologian likewise must be ready to move to a different level of conceptuality in order to express the biblical truths in a way that is more adequate for a particular culture, and that the problem which has to be faced is that of maintaining continuity so that the biblical expression remains normative in determining whether the new expression is true and valid. The force of the second analogy, therefore, is to justify the theologian in using a new conceptuality that will help to understand the realities to which the Bible bears witness in a different way. The vital question is whether the new conceptuality is able to 'contain' the old or be translated into it.

Third, we argued that the biblical material is presented in a variety of ways, not only by different writers in different centuries but also in a variety of different literary genres. The biblical theologian must treat these genres seriously, for they may be saying different kinds of thing. Equally the systematician must take them seriously when listening to the biblical message and attempt to do justice to their various contributions. We saw that the danger of systematising is the reduction of all this gloriously variegated material to the flatness of propositional prose, and argued that somehow theology must not only be written but also 'played' in a performance in which each instrument has its distinctive part.[20]

To say all this is to give an exposition and some defence of what we do when we act as systematic theologians. It does not solve our problems, nor does it prescribe in any detail how we go about our business, but it may act as a first step in bringing us to critical self-awareness.

---

[20]The word 'performed' has come into vogue in some quarters in connection with Christian living. I am not sure that it is entirely appropriate in that setting. For its use in connection with Scripture see Frances Young, *The Art of Performance* (London: Darton, Longman & Todd, 1990).

CHAPTER 9

Scripture and Confession: Doctrine as Hermeneutic

Gerald Bray

Summary

Traditionally, Christian doctrine has been understood as the Church's hermeneutic of the Bible. Under the pressure of modern biblical criticism, coupled with Enlightenment scepticism, this position has now been abandoned, and the disciplines of biblical studies and systematic theology have gone their separate ways. Recently, there have been attempts to counteract this tendency, which ought to be encouraged and developed. There is a core of basic beliefs which unites the Scriptures into a single theological tradition, which is more important than the diversity of its parts. The Old Testament is concerned with monotheism and creation, whereas the new Testament reveals the Trinity and the divine plan of redemption. These four subjects are the pillars of biblical theology. It may no longer be possible or desirable to devise a specific confession of faith, in the Reformation sense, but Evangelicals ought to work towards a common statement of beliefs which can serve as the Church's 'mission statement' for the present age.

I. Introduction

Has the study of Christian doctrine any bearing on the way in which we read the Bible? For many centuries, such a question would have seemed absurd. It was obvious to the Fathers of the church, as it was to the mediaeval schoolmen, that the Bible was the ultimate source of Christian teaching, and that the dogmatic pronouncements of the church were designed to be the authorized guide to its interpretation.[1] Even at the time of the Reformation, this belief was held in common by all sides. Defenders of the Roman position knew that they had to support their case from Scripture, and Protestants intended their confessions to be normative for the teaching ministry of the whole church. The argument was largely over the interpretation and sufficiency of the Bible. Protestants claimed that the tradition of the church was not an authoritative supplement to Scripture, which did not teach such Roman doctrines as the universal jurisdiction of the papacy, the power of the church to remit sins, the existence of purgatory, and so on.

At first, Protestants saw little difficulty with their *sola Scriptura* position, but as we all know, they soon fell out among themselves, largely over questions of worship, church government and sacramental practice, where the biblical evidence was inadequate or could be used in more than one way. Modern research has generally shown that the early church was more catholic in these matters than many Protestants would wish, but a number of key issues remain unresolved. For example, we do not know whether the New Testament church baptized infants or not, and both views continue to find scholarly advocates today. But in spite of these problems, all Protestants continued to believe that the doctrine they taught was what the Bible said, either explicitly or implicitly. In the latter category were doctrines like the Trinity, which was not obvious at first sight but could be deduced from clear Scriptural statements without doing violence to their meaning.[2]

---

[1]This was particularly evident at the Council of Chalcedon, where the assembled bishops prefaced their definition of the two natures of Christ with the words 'Following the Holy Fathers', by which they meant supremely, the writers of the New Testament. Intense debate over the precise meaning of Scripture was characteristic of every major theological quarrel. Athanasius, for example, wrote three *Discourses against the Arians*, which are almost exclusively concerned with Biblical texts, and Augustine's classic work on the Trinity begins with a discussion of the New Testament evidence for the divinity of Christ. These examples can easily be reproduced throughout the Middle Ages and the Reformation period.

The traditional Christian consensus on the relationship between Scripture and doctrine lasted until the eighteenth century, when it broke down because of pressures which came from two quite different directions. On one side were the evangelical pietists, who thought that the various doctrinal orthodoxies which emerged as a result of the Reformation obscured the plain teaching of Scripture and did nothing but provoke divisions among people who shared a common spiritual experience. On the other side were the rationalistic philosophers of the Enlightenment, who believed that simple and universal truths had been forgotten by theologians, who bickered over matters which were both unknowable and unimportant. In this respect, they adopted the same position towards Protestant scholasticism as the Reformers had done towards its late mediaeval ancestor. Questions like whether Adam had a navel were presented as the stuff of theological argument, and were caricatured as trivial and irrelevant beside such issues as the fatherhood of God and the brotherhood of man.

Matters came to a head when biblical scholars started to demand the academic freedom which they thought necessary for the pursuit of their discipline. Church officials, and many powerful lay people too, were frightened when unorthodox theories (like the multiple origin of the Pentateuch) were put forward, because they thought that acceptance of such ideas would undermine the authority of Scripture and therefore also the confessional basis of the church. In Germany there appeared a conservative, confessionally-based biblical scholarship, led by E.W. Hengstenberg (1802-69) and developed by others, including K.F. Keil (1807-88) and F. Delitzsch (1813-90), who fought what can only be called a losing battle against the tide of liberalism which swept through German academic life in the nineteenth century.[3]

Conservative confessionalism was also present in the English-speaking world, but except at Princeton Theological Seminary, it was seldom creative. In Britain, textual study of the Bible was kept within a conservative doctrinal framework by the Cambridge trio of Lightfoot, Westcott and Hort, but none of them made any substantial contribution to systematic theology. British textual criticism retained a conservative bent for two generations, and may have it still, but this may have little to do with commitment to a conservative theological position. In at least one famous case, that of the late Bishop John Rob-

---

[2]For a modern discussion and re-affirmation of the evidence, see A.W. Wainwright, *The Doctrine of the Trinity in the New Testament* (London: SPCK, 1952).
[3]On this subject, see *e.g.* John Rogerson, *Old Testament Criticism in the Nineteenth Century* (London: SPCK, 1984).

inson (1919-83), conservative biblical exegesis was combined with the most radical theological assumptions, something which would hardly have been possible in Germany or the USA, where biblical conservatism has generally implied theological conservatism as well.[4]

II. Theology and Biblical Studies

Whether this is still the case though, may be open to doubt. Thanks to the explosion of information and specialisation, there is now such a gulf between biblical studies and systematic theology as academic disciplines, that experts in the one do not need to know much about the other and may fail to see any meaningful relationship between them. Biblical scholars may easily regard systematics as irrelevant and potentially dangerous, because in their minds it is liable to distort or limit the use which can be made of exegesis. On the other side, systematic theologians often do not want to be tied to the Bible, which for many of them is but one witness, albeit an important one, to universal spiritual realities. At the extremities, when biblical studies gets immersed in archaeology and systematic theology fades into philosophy, the two disciplines end up having no more in common than archaeology and philosophy have!

But whereas archaeology and philosophy can survive as independent and largely unrelated disciplines, biblical studies and systematic theology are not so fortunate. It is not just that they often have to co-exist within a single university department; each of them also has a direct relationship to the preaching ministry of the church, which has to attempt some kind of integration between them. At the time of the Reformation, this point was made quite clear by Thomas Cranmer, when he placed the creed immediately after the gospel and before the sermon—an order which made it plain that preaching was meant to be the message of Scripture governed by the doctrine of the church. It is interesting to note that modern liturgists have displaced the creed, putting it after the sermon, which may suggest that they see the preaching as helping to interpret the doctrine, rather than being an exposition of it. Or perhaps the doctrine is really meant to be a corrective for theologically deficient sermons!

The need for theologians and biblical scholars to come to some understanding has recently been stated quite forcefully by Brevard

---

[4]See S. Neill and N.T. Wright, *The Interpretation of the New Testament 1861-1986* (Oxford: OUP, 1988).

Childs, in his book *Biblical Theology of the Old and New Testaments*.[5] As one would expect, Childs takes the canon of Scripture as the theological norm for interpretation. This has the great merit of treating the biblical text as a whole, even if Childs is not entirely clear what the limits of the Old Testament canon should be. It also enables Childs to integrate the findings and theories of modern scholarship without worrying whether these are in accord with a theological system devised before the invention of the historical-critical method. In many ways, his is the solution of a biblical scholar, who wants to make sure that whatever insights can be gleaned from systematic theology, they will be interpreted in categories familiar, and therefore presumably acceptable, to his colleagues. Childs evidently believes that his solution also stands a chance of being accepted by systematic theologians, who (he thinks) should be able to relate their own concerns to a framework which presupposes a theological principle undergirding the canonical selection of the texts.

Childs' canonical approach has come under fire from some of his colleagues, not least because it presupposes that there was an organised scholarly activity among ancient Jewish rabbis and early church leaders, of which there is little evidence. From what we can tell, authorship seems to have played more of a role in shaping the canon than theological content, at least in the case of the New Testament, though one was obviously linked to the other, and apostolic origin was not necessarily by itself a guarantee of orthodoxy. We must not forget, for example, that the New Testament tradition records the fact that Paul had to set Peter right on the question of the admission of Gentiles into the church.

The problem is that there are too many historical uncertainties for Childs' theory to be demonstrable with any degree of assurance. He himself has been rather weak at providing exegetical examples to back it up, and several canonical books do not figure in his *Theology* at all—Ruth, Esther, Song of Songs, Obadiah, Jonah, Nahum, Zephaniah and Malachi in the Old Testament, and 2 Peter and 2 and 3 John in the New. Admittedly, many of these books are slight and might easily have been overlooked, but given Childs' thesis, it would seem appropriate to have included Ruth, Song of Songs, Jonah and Malachi at least, since they all have a direct bearing on traditional New Testament interpretation.

---

[5]London: SCM, 1992.

But in spite of these problems, Childs' basic instinct appears to be sound. He has correctly perceived that biblical studies and systematic theology need to be brought back into a fruitful relationship with one another, and that the only way to do this is to re-establish both the validity and the necessity of deriving theological principles from the biblical text. But rather than try to discern these principles in the process of canon formation, it is better to begin elsewhere—with the need of the church to hear the Word of the Lord in our time. This does not really contradict Childs' approach, which is also very much concerned with the church, but tackles the same basic issues from another angle.

III. The Crisis in the Church

It has become a commonplace to say that the contemporary church is in crisis, but it is less often recognised that this crisis is basically one of the preaching ministry. The sermon, which the Reformers thought should be the centrepiece of Christian worship, has long been the most embarrassing part of most church services. Congregations have a tendency to fall asleep during the preaching, or to let their thoughts wander. Preachers are often ill-prepared, repetitious and predictable in what they say. Increasingly, we find that other activities are taking up the sermon slot—a presentation designed for children, perhaps, or 'sharing' from different members of the congregation. If the overall worship time is too long, we can be sure that the sermon will be blamed, and that its length will be cut. In some cases, it may even be omitted altogether!

Fuelling these developments are pressures which come from two quite different sources. On the one hand, there is the academic establishment, which contributes to the preaching ministry by way of commentaries on the Bible. The practical uselessness of most of these commentaries is immediately evident to anyone who tries to preach from them. Either he will end up regurgitating information which has no application to the life of the congregation, even if it makes a good lecture on biblical history and archaeology, or he will quickly abandon the attempt to relate what he says to the text and resort to unconnected 'blessed thoughts' instead. Both of these tendencies, sometimes in combination with each other, are readily observable on a Sunday morning, and easily discredit the whole preaching exercise. Biblical scholars may reply, with some justification, that their commentaries were never intended to be guides for preachers, but why else would most people want to buy them?

The second source of pressure on the modern church comes from what might be called 'popular spirituality', which sees no need for an academically-trained ministry. Spiritual life wells up from inner resources, which may be present in anyone. Once this is recognised, there is nothing to stop a 'word of knowledge' from appearing in the most unlikely places. There are just enough examples from church history—Francis of Assisi and John Bunyan spring to mind—to support this way of thinking, and to make it extremely difficult for a spiritually-sensitive pastor to try to suppress what might turn out to be another great outpouring of divine power.

Once forces of this kind are unleashed, almost anything might happen. Quite often a number of eloquent teachers may emerge, who can hold their audience spellbound and, in extreme cases, exercise dictatorial influence over them. These teachers invariably have a theology of sorts, though it may be characterized by an unbalanced insistence on matters which most Christians have regarded as peripheral. Thus we find that eschatology, charismatic gifts and sometimes a rather simplistic morality take the place of more central issues like the person and work of Christ, though these things would probably not be denied. It is almost as if traditional theological concerns have been pushed to one side—taken for granted perhaps, or thought of as irrelevant—so that room can be made for the real interests of the congregation!

Few academic scholars have much time for this sort of thing, but it does at least reveal one simple fact. This is that preaching is grounded in theology, whether the preacher recognises it or not. Merely expressing an opinion about the meaning and applicability of a given text is making a theological statement—however crude and unsophisticated it may be. The challenge which we face today is to demonstrate that truly anointed preaching can only be rooted in good theology, which is essential if spiritual enthusiasm is to be nourished and sustained over the longer haul.

IV. What Theology?

Where is this theology going to come from? If it is to stay faithful to the Christian message, it can only come from the Scriptures, which convey that message to us. But here the minister of the church comes up against the reluctance, or inability, of biblical specialists to present their subject in theological categories which would give their material overall system and coherence. Modern biblical study, even when it takes a conservative form, is a child of the Enlightenment, which was intrinsically hostile to theological formulations. As soon as the subject is raised, the old objections resurface—theology is an unwarranted attempt to systematize, and therefore reduce, the many-faceted meaning of a diverse set of texts. Theology is also divisive, and theologians never seem to agree among themselves—though biblical scholars are hardly in a position to throw the first stone on this score!

In answer to this, the would-be biblical theologian ought to admit that there is some truth in these arguments. There have indeed been times when theologians have gone off in pursuit of trivialities, at the expense of central doctrines. The result has been division, when the biblical evidence has been pressed too far. There are things which the Bible does not tell us, and which we shall never know this side of eternity. No theological system can be exhaustive for the simple reason that no knowledge is exhaustive, and claims to comprehensiveness or infallibility ought to be rejected from the start. But even when all that is said, there remains a central core in the biblical message which is consistent, and which gives the canon a spiritual and intellectual unity which is more fundamental than its evident diversity. In this sense, those who stress the diversity of Scripture over its unity are being superficial. The diversity is immediately obvious to anyone who cares to look, whereas the unity is more subtle and requires greater attention to the substance of the message being conveyed by each of the diverse parts.

Christian biblical theology rests on four basic principles. The first, and most fundamental of these, is the belief that there is only one true and living God. This is so obvious that it is often overlooked, but it is essential. Monotheism is a belief which Christians share with Jews and Muslims, and were our Bible confined to the Old Testament, with no revelation from Jesus Christ, our faith would presumably be a form of Judaism. But because of Jesus, our knowledge of God—the way in which we perceive him—differs from that of other monotheists. It is this difference which determines everything else, and which lies at the root of our religious identity. The New Testament indicates that the one God has revealed himself to us as Father, Son and Holy Spirit, and that Jesus Christ identified himself as the Son. This is the second basic principle of Christian theology. God is a Trinity of three Persons in one substance, and Jesus Christ is the second Person of the Trinity, who has been revealed to us in two natures—one divine and one human.[6]

The third basic principle is that the divine work of creation is common to all three Persons of the Trinity without distinction, and the fourth is that the divine work of redemption is shared among them in a way which allows us to distinguish one from another. In the work of creation there is only the one God, who sustains everything by the word of his power. But in the work of redemption, each of the Persons plays a distinct part. The Father sends the Son; the Son dies in obedience to the Father's will and is raised to life by the Father on the third day; the Holy Spirit bears witness in our hearts to the reality of God's saving love and makes it relevant to us both now and in the future.

These four principles form the essential framework of all Christian theology, and provide the key to our interpretation of the Bible. Diagrammatically, they can be related to each other as follows:

	OT		**NT**
1.	One God	2.	Trinity/Christ
3.	Creation	4.	Redemption

The Old Testament, a revelation of the one God, belongs together with a corresponding emphasis on creation. The importance of creation is not confined to the Genesis narrative and a few Psalms, but runs through the entire text. It is the basis of the Wisdom tradition, which is deeply concerned with the providential ordering of God's universe. It underlies the promises which are made to the obedient in the Old Testament—long life, many children, material prosperity, security and dominion over the lower creatures. These things crop up all over the place, in blessings, in visions and even in the Ten Commandments, where the Israelites are told to honour father and mother, that their days may be long in the land which God has given them!

But magnificent as the creation is, and great though its blessings are, it contains a basic inadequacy. This is its finitude, its inability to lead us either to moral awareness or to eternal life—the two gifts which God withheld from his creatures in the garden of Eden. But Adam, who was created in the image and likeness of God, was not content with this, and transgressed the bounds imposed by God on his creaturely finitude. Because of this, creation turned sour. Instead of long life, Adam became subject to death. His children took to killing one another. Material prosperity became a tale of poverty and want, relieved only by backbreaking labour. Insecurity replaced the safety of

---

[6]See G.L. Bray, *The Doctrine of God* (Leicester: IVP, 1993).

the garden, and Adam's descendants began to worship the beasts, rather than to exercise dominion over them.

Into this tale of sin and rebellion came the Word of God, proclaiming judgement on the posterity of Adam, but promising that in spite of everything, a remnant would be redeemed—not by their own efforts, which could never correct the wrong which had been done, but by God's free grace and favour. As a sign of this coming redemption, God chose for himself a people, descended from the patriarch Abraham, whose duty it was to bear witness to this eschatological principle. They were told what was coming, and were promised that if they obeyed God's commands, they would share in it. These commands were expressed in the law, which was designed to set forth the principles under which a divine society would operate.

The law then set out the signs of the coming redemption in terms which made sense only in a creational context. God's presence among his people was tied to a physical location, which eventually became the temple, and the sphere of his operations was defined as the promised land. Within these parameters the people of Israel would be a light to the nations, sending forth the law out of Zion, and drawing all nations to itself.[7] At this point we come face to face with the first of the great, unresolved problems of biblical theology—to what extent did the Jewish people share in the promise of divine redemption? Is it appropriate to speak, as the Puritans often did, of Old Testament saints, who were members of an Old Testament church? Can Exodus be taken as a Christian model for the liberation of oppressed peoples today?

If our understanding of the Old Testament is valid, the answer to both of these questions would have to be negative. The Old Testament must be read in its own context, and not in that of the Christian church. To speak of 'saints' and the church before the coming of Christ and the sending of the Holy Spirit is to distort the witness of Scripture, and to make it more (not less) difficult to see the relevance of the Old Testament to us today. The finished character of the law must also be respected—Christians cannot turn to it now for answers to modern social and political problems.[8] This applies to Sabbath observance as much as to peasant liberation—a new dispensation has come and the

---

[7]Is. 2:3; Mi. 4:2.

[8]At least not without considering the fundamental differences between ancient Israel and modern states, and the way in which Christ has fulfilled the promises made to the former. Of course there are patterns within Israel which have parallels today, and these may still be helpful; trouble arises only when the Israelite pattern is made *normative* for modern conditions.

old has passed into history. Of course, Christians have long disagreed about this, and this disagreement underlies a number of other theological discussions, like the justification of infant baptism on the basis of covenant theology, for example. There is certainly a lot of room here for a fruitful exploration of theological themes in biblical studies!

When we turn to the New Testament, we find that the promises of the Old are fulfilled in the revelation of Christ and the redemption which he brings. These two things belong together—without Christ there can be no redemption, which in turn makes no sense apart from Christ. Paul's whole polemic against the Jews and the law is based on this fundamental premiss. Now that the reality has come, the symbols of the old dispensation have become superfluous. They are not wrong in themselves, but they are no longer necessary, and it is wrong to impose them on new converts. But here we run into the next great area of controversy among Christians. Granted that the shadow of redemption has faded in the presence of the reality, what place does creation now occupy in the life of the Christian? Can it still be used to symbolize redemptive themes, or must it now be transcended? Behind this question lie most of the major differences between Catholics and Protestants, especially in the sphere of sacramental theology. In what way do the sacraments present redemption to the believer? Is there a transformation of created elements such as is implied by a doctrine of transubstantiation, and (in a somewhat different way) by baptismal regeneration? If not, what is the importance of the material element in the sacraments? Do we have to bother with them at all, if faith is all that is needed?

Popular perception is that Catholics generally tend to affirm the role of the material creation in redemption, and Protestants to downplay or even deny it. This is not entirely true of course; many of the most world-denying ascetic practices are closely associated with Catholicism, and it is not right to say, as some Catholic theologians have done, that Protestants have an inadequate doctrine of creation. What is true is that Protestant practice has tended to desacralise creation by avoiding elaborate rituals and symbolism in worship, and by putting its emphasis on internal, spiritual and heavenly rewards and prosperity. The Protestant work ethic can perhaps be presented as contrary to the witness of the Old Testament, because it glorifies labour (which the Old Testament regards as a curse) but castigates material enjoyment of its fruits (which the Old Testament regards as a blessing). But such contradictions are more apparent than real. The common element between Protestantism and the Old Testament is the desacralisation of creation, which gives mankind a new freedom to exploit its potential. Many Catholics take a different line, claiming that as creation was used to herald redemption in the Old Testament, so it is used to confirm and extend it in the New. To them, all creation is 'God-bearing', reflecting the pattern established in the incarnation of Christ, which is the beginning of our salvation. Here there is another challenge to biblical scholars—what part does creation play in the New Testament vision of redemption? Can we hope to resolve differences among Christians by tackling this great question?

To do this effectively, theologians have to take into account the eschatological dimension, which has figured so prominently in modern biblical studies. In the new heaven and earth, creation and redemption will come together. In the breaking of the bread we show forth the Lord's death 'until he comes': the eschatological perspective is present at the very heart of the church's life.[9] Furthermore, we who are still on earth in the flesh, who continue to bear the responsibilities and the burdens of the first Adam, are nevertheless a new creation in Christ, called to bear witness to this eschatological redemption. What does that mean? To what extent does the eschaton break into our present reality? Some would say that it does not, even that it cannot, without losing its eschatological character. In their view, the church *in via* walks in faith, believing in what is as yet unseen. Others would claim that the eschaton is partially realized in our spiritual experience, so that it is possible for us, as it was for Jesus and the apostles, to experience the healing miracles of the kingdom, even if the kingdom itself is not yet fully present.

How do we reconcile these things? Does the earthly life of Jesus have any direct bearing on the life of the church now? Can Christians model their spiritual lives on that of Jesus, as if he were somehow the first Christian? If not, what are we to make of the earthly life of Jesus? Here are theological questions which are basic to the life of the church, as well as to the study of the Bible.

V. Confessions?

Finally, does a theological analysis of Scripture lead inevitably to a binding confession of faith? Can we subscribe *ex animo* to an existing confession of faith, do we need a new one, or are we better off without

---

[9] 1Cor. 11:26.

any? As far as existing confessions are concerned, modern research has conclusively demonstrated that they are conditioned by the period and culture in which they were composed. However, it is a fallacy to conclude from this that they represent an alien intrusion into the Christian faith; generations of scholars have shown that the church borrowed terms and concepts from the Greek-speaking world in order to make the gospel message clear in the face of pagan and heretical attacks. Considering that the New Testament writers themselves borrowed Greek for a similar purpose, it would be hard to claim that this was unbiblical!

Nevertheless, we may freely recognize that the creeds of the ancient church are no longer fully adequate as statements of belief, because in so many ways theological discussion has moved on since that time. Even within their own context, the creeds occasionally represent an outdated theology. The opening line of the Apostles' Creed is a case in point. It reads: 'I believe in God the Father Almighty, Maker of heaven and earth.' This was a faithful reflection of the church's expressed belief in the second century, when the Old Roman Creed, the probable ancestor of the Apostles' Creed, was originally composed, but it was superseded as a result of the Arian controversy. The point is not that it is untrue, but that what is said of the Father (and only of the Father) in this creed is now said of all three Persons of the Trinity. Furthermore, we would now no longer define the Father in this way, in relation to the other members of the Godhead, but distinguish him as 'unbegotten'.[10]

Turning to the major confessions of the English Reformation, everyone now accepts that the Thirty-nine Articles of the church of England are not a comprehensive statement of Christian belief. To say that they were never intended as such is perhaps going too far; there is some evidence that Archbishop Cranmer wanted to be systematic in his presentation of Anglican beliefs, and the Articles are decidedly better organised in this sense than any document which predates them.[11] However, leading Anglicans soon recognized that more needed to be said, and various projects were undertaken to revise the Articles. These failed mainly for political reasons, and it is unfortunate that by the time a comprehensive replacement was produced, the cir-

---

[10]See J.N.D. Kelly, *Early Christian Creeds* (3rd. ed.; London: Longman, 1972).
[11]See G.L. Bray (ed.), *Documents of the English Reformation* (Cambridge/Philadelphia: James Clarke/Fortress, 1994).

cumstances were such that a royalist church of England could not
accept it.

The Westminster Confession aimed to be both scriptural and
comprehensive, and in the context of its time, it did remarkably well.
Of course, we may wish to dissent from parts of it now, just as some
believers did then, though perhaps not always for the same reasons.
For example, there can be no doubt that not all the scriptural support
cited for the various articles of the Confession is of equal weight, and
some revision in the light of modern biblical research would seem to
be desirable.

Unfortunately, political and ecclesiastical circumstances would
now make such a move difficult or even impossible, and it is probably
wiser to leave such documents as monuments to the theology of the
age in which they were composed, rather than try to tinker with them
now. Realistically speaking, Evangelicals can now do little more than
devise an unofficial confession which might serve as a general indication of our theological position, without being absolutely binding on
anyone. The main challenge to such an endeavour is to find a way in
which a confession could be written which would be comprehensive
without being unnecessarily exclusive. A major weakness of denominational confessions is that they inevitably unchurch true believers
because of what have come to be called 'denominational distinctives'.
Sadly, these 'distinctives' are often more keenly felt than the main
points of agreement are!

That leaves us with the third possibility—no confession at all!
Many Evangelicals are attracted by this option, and in a sense it can be
said to be a feature of Evangelicalism from its beginnings in pietist
revivalism. In the perfect world, it would be unnecessary to devise special confessions setting out our beliefs with great precision, since
everyone would understand them and agree. But in the imperfect
world in which we are called to live, confessions of faith are statements
of theological engagement both inside and outside the church. Such
engagement is part of our evangelistic purpose, and could be thought
of as our 'mission statement', to use a contemporary expression! That
would make it possible to express our evangelical distinctiveness as a
form of clarification, rather than as a threat of excommunication,
though no doubt it would act as the latter in certain cases.

The ultimate issue at stake is whether the Bible is a book about
God or not. If it is, then it must have a theology, which can be
expressed in rationally coherent terms. That means doctrine. The
Christian church lives on the basis of what the Bible says about God,

and about his marvellous acts. If we lose sight of that, we lose not only the Bible, but the church as well. No doubt there will always be people who will want to use the Scriptures for other purposes, and who will develop ways of reading it which seem strange to most Christians. That ought not to matter, provided that we are free to maintain our own perspective as believers, and continue to live by it. It will not persuade everyone, but at least it will be able to claim continuity with the Bible's past, and above all, with its origins. That ought to ensure that it will not be extinguished in the academic world, however much pluralism of interpretation we find ourselves living with. Biblical scholars who are Evangelicals stand in a privileged position in this respect. It is up to them to do their part, as it is to theologians to do theirs, to ensure that the Bible and theology grow together, not apart from each other, in the coming generation.

CHAPTER 10

Scripture and Criticism: Evangelicals, Orthodoxy and the Continuing Problem of Conservatism

Nigel M. de S. Cameron

Summary

Until the rise of historical criticism in the nineteenth century, the churches and their theologians generally held that the Bible was infallibly true. In the second half of that century the British churches were riven by a succession of controversies, focused especially in the debate around Essays and Reviews *and the Robertson Smith case, which finally resulted in general acceptance of the methods of historical criticism—though many of its widely held conclusions were repudiated by 'conservatives' who in some measure sought to maintain the traditional understanding of biblical inspiration and authority. Since then, evangelical approaches to Scripture have been crucially conditioned by those debates, and continue to reflect an ambivalence towards the general methods of historical criticism while typically holding to conservative conclusions in particular matters of interpretation.*

I. Introduction

In an oft-quoted aphorism which surely let slip more than he intended, George Adam Smith, doyen of 'believing critics',[1] opened the twentieth century with a ringing declaration: 'Modern criticism has won its war against the traditional theories. It only remains to fix the amount of the indemnity.'[2] As that century draws to a close, the negotiation continues; a protracted and confused exercise that holds the attention of the world-wide theological community. What will be the final cost to the Christian tradition of the steady abandonment of its historic rooting in 'God's Word written'?[3] The uneasy conscience of twentieth-century Protestant theology suggests that the optimistic assessment of Adam Smith and his contemporaries, that 'modern criticism' would leave the essentials of the faith intact, was as groundless as early conservative expectation that it presaged the imminent collapse of the

---

[1]'Believing criticism' refers to the ready acceptance given to the tenets of higher criticism by a group of pious biblical scholars in the Scotland of the late nineteenth century. William Robertson Smith and A.B. Davidson were the other most prominent believing critics. See R.A. Riesen, *Criticism and Faith in Late Victorian Scotland* (Lanham, Md: University Press of America, 1985). As to the term 'criticism', conservative protagonists in the nineteenth century, as today, use it both pejoratively (as designating an inappropriate method which would lead to the abuse of Scripture) and in a neutral fashion (so as to include proper methods). Then as now the context is generally sufficiently lucid as to obviate misunderstanding. Contemporary evangelical approaches to particular 'critical' questions, as indeed to the general question of the relevance of historical criticism to the study of Holy Scripture, reflect a wide spectrum of conviction. Yet the central significance of affirmations of biblical 'infallibility' and 'inerrancy' in the doctrinal statements of representative evangelical organisations points up the problematic of those positions most congruent with mainline scholarship; for these terms testify above all to the fact that bibliology is indeed a doctrine; that part of orthodox Christian faith is to believe certain things about the Bible, a book which, by virtue of its character as the revelation of God, cannot be known solely as other books are known, but a book which may be properly read in the light of this self-testimony.
[2]*Modern Criticism and the Preaching of the Old Testament* (London: Hodder & Stoughton, 1901) 72. While serious historical awareness in the interpretation of Scripture is to be carefully distinguished from the 'modern criticism' of which Adam Smith writes, the origins of 'historical criticism' lie in the rationalistic critique of Holy Scripture which goes right back to pagan interaction with Hebrew and Christian religion in the ancient world, and continues through the middle ages. Of special significance are Richard Simon's *Histoire critique du vieux testament* (1678) and Baruch de Spinoza's *Tractatus Theologico-Politicus* (1670). Spinoza stands more plainly in the sceptical tradition. Spinoza and Simon substantially anticipate what was to become the nineteenth-century 'historical-critical' agenda. See L. Strauss, *Spinoza's Critique of Religion* (New York: Schocken Books, 1965).
[3]Article 20 of the Thirty-nine Articles.

broad structures of orthodoxy. Instead we have had a century of ambiguity and ambivalence: mainline theology clings with remarkable tenacity to the principle of the canonical justification of theological proposals;[4] while resurgent conservatism, once zealous to wage the paradigm war, evidences growing support for the view that the indemnity may not, after all, be the Danegeld it once appeared. The question whether the depth of unease within the mainstream—manifest perhaps most tellingly in the work of Brevard Childs,[5] but also, and increasingly pervasively, in the broad fresh focus on 'literary' approaches to the Bible[6]—should be taken by conservatives to suggest that there is an emerging possibility of consensus along the lines of a reconstructed 'believing criticism', or rather as an encouragement to return to the development of their own traditional position *tout court*, confronts the conservative community with growing urgency. How it is finally resolved will be fateful for the future of evangelical Christianity.

There can be no doubt that the explosion of interest in approaches to Biblical studies which side-step, even though they do not deny, the historical-critical method, underscores the failure of critical history to deliver to the church the enlightened, new consensus of which the 'believing critics' of a century ago were so persuaded. This failure is now widely acknowledged by scholars who have no quarrel

---

[4]The problem for the mainline, of course, is that of the canonical identity of Christian theology; how else than 'according to the Scriptures?'. Which is not to say that the use of Scripture to that end has consistency, as David H. Kelsey has shown in *The Uses of Scripture in Recent Theology* (London: SCM, 1975). For a complementary evangelical discussion which takes Kelsey as a point of departure, see Robert K. Johnson (ed.), *The Uses of the Bible in Theology: Evangelical Options* (Atlanta: John Knox, 1985).

[5]*Introduction to the Old Testament as Scripture* (Philadelphia: Fortress, 1979); *The New Testament as Canon: An Introduction* (Philadelphia: Fortress, 1985); *Old Testament Theology in a Canonical Context* (Philadelphia: Fortress, 1985); and his programmatic *Biblical Theology in Crisis* (Philadelphia: Westminster, 1970) which reflects on the failure of neo-orthodoxy to recover a proper use of the Bible in the church.

[6]So, most significantly, Hans Frei, *The Eclipse of Biblical Narrative* (New Haven: Yale UP, 1974); Northrop Frye, *The Great Code: The Bible and Literature* (New York: Harcourt Brace Jovanovich, 1983); Robert Alter and Frank Kermode (eds.), *The Literary Guide to the Bible* (Cambridge, MA: Harvard UP, 1987); Regina Schwartz (ed.), *The Book and the Text. The Bible and Literary Theory* (Oxford: Blackwell, 1990); and, for example Martin Warner (ed.), *The Bible as Rhetoric. Studies in Biblical Persuasion and Credibility* (London/New York: Routledge, 1990); Sandra M. Schneiders, *The Revelatory Text. Interpreting the New Testament as Sacred Scripture* (San Francisco: Harper, 1991); and, with a special interest in preaching, Mark Ellingsen, *The Integrity of Biblical Narrative* (Minneapolis: Fortress, 1990).

with its actual conclusions for, they would say, it is not *qua* historical criticism that it has failed; its failure lies in the limitations of such an exercise, whether in the elucidation of any text, or the reading of this particular text which the church confesses as its canon. As one recent writer has put it:

> Basically, the argument goes, historical-critical means of interpretation are inadequate to the task when applied as the primary tool to Scripture. The critical method focuses on the historicity of Scripture or its genesis—what goes on 'behind' the text. But the purpose of exegesis is to discern what the text actually means for the contemporary Christian community, so the question of historicity is only of secondary importance. What a text means is not entirely revealed through an understanding of its historical development. The fact that historical-critical scholarship has failed to realize this helps explain the fragmentation that exists within the biblical guild. It also partially explains why historical criticism has had relatively little impact on the churches.[7]

It is immediately evident that, from a conservative evangelical perspective, these developments constitute something of a curate's egg. What some would read as the success of the conservative critique of, as it were, the usefulness of Holy Scripture after the 'critics' have done their work has resulted in a declaration on the part of the mainline scholarly community that there are other ways of recovering that usefulness than what would be characterised as the wilfully 'pre-critical' stance of the conservatives. Yet the provocative title of Gerhard Maier's book, *The End of the Historical-Critical Method*,[8] begins to ring at least a little true. While neither of these approaches—literary or canonical—heralds a return to pre-critical interpretation, the steady dethroning of historical criticism on the ground that it is uninteresting and unproductive offers the most significant development in biblical studies since Adam Smith. Yet, even as it has given new heart to the conservative cause, it has raised fresh questions about its rationale.

---

[7]Ellingsen, *The Integrity of Biblical Narrative*, 9.
[8]St. Louis: Concordia, 1977; ET of *Das Ende der historische-kritische Methode* (Wuppertal: Brockhaus, 1974).

II. Our Story: Evangelicals as Scripture Conservatives

The centrality of the doctrine of Holy Scripture to evangelical theology was vigorously re-asserted in the context of the recent debate over biblical 'inerrancy', which offered a trenchant reminder of the unique place of bibliology in contemporary evangelical identity.[9] This has not, of course, always been the case. Until the debates of the nineteenth century (first in Europe, then in Britain, and finally towards the end of the century in the United States) our evangelical forebears defined themselves in other ways, since what is now the characteristically 'high' view of the Bible held by Evangelicals as their most distinctive theological conviction was generally shared within the church at large. Evangelicals' chief distinguishing mark lay in their concern for personal religion, for twice-born Christianity. While there have been attempts at revisionist re-writing of the history—not least by more liberal Evangelicals seeking an historical rationale for their own position—there remains a general scholarly consensus as to the framework of belief about the Bible prior to the rise of historical criticism. The consistently conservative character of eighteenth- and nineteenth-century bibliology is widely admitted, albeit somewhat unwillingly. Indeed, the grudging character of, for example, Alan Richardson's testimony in the *Cambridge History of the Bible* actually strengthens its weight, since it is plain that he would much rather argue something else. He writes that 'the claim, so frequently made, that the conservative evangelicals are maintaining the historic or traditional position is only formally true'. By that he means that conservative Evangelicals (together with some others, we should add, including many conservative Roman Catholics) reject the evidence and arguments which in the nineteenth century were widely held to overthrow the traditional view. That is, since mainstream scholarship shifted its position, it is illegitimate (he argues) for conservatives today to claim continuity

---

[9]See, for example, Norman L. Geisler (ed.), *Inerrancy* (Grand Rapids: Zondervan, 1979), one of a series of volumes associated with the International Council on Biblical Inerrancy, whose Chicago Declaration (reproduced *ibid.*, 493-502) is a considered statement of the conservative position; and D.A. Carson and John D. Woodbridge (eds.), *Scripture and Truth* (Grand Rapids: Zondervan, 1983) and *Hermeneutics, Authority and Canon* (Grand Rapids: Zondervan, 1986), the two most important volumes to result from the controversy. Jack B. Rogers' and Donald K. McKim's *The Authority and Interpretation of the Bible: An Historical Approach* (San Francisco: Harper and Row, 1979) proved a spark that found dry tinder; see the well-argued rejoinder in John D. Woodbridge's *Biblical Authority: A Critique of the Rogers/McKim Proposal* (Grand Rapids: Zondervan, 1982).

with the earlier mainstream, whatever the 'formal' degree of agreement between the two. He speculates that earlier writers, such as Bishop Butler, would have changed their mind had they lived later. Yet he acknowledges that in Butler's *Analogy of Religion* (1736)—arguably the most important product of English eighteenth century theology— 'it is everywhere assumed that the Bible is throughout divinely and infallibly inspired'.[10] In less grudging terms, we have this admission of Kirsopp Lake, liberal New Testament scholar and budding radical theologian of the early twentieth century:

> It is a mistake, often made by educated men who happen to have but little knowledge of historical theology, to suppose that Fundamentalism is a new and strange form of thought. It is nothing of the kind: it is the partial and uneducated survival of a theology which was once universally held by Christians. How many were there, for instance, in Christian churches, in the eighteenth century, who doubted the infallible inspiration of all Scripture? A few, perhaps, but very few. No, the Fundamentalist may be wrong; I think he is. But it is we who have departed from the tradition, not he, and I am sorry for the fate of anyone who tries to argue with a Fundamentalist on the basis of authority. The Bible and the corpus theologicum of the church is [*sic*] on the Fundamentalist side.[11]

---

[10]S.L. Greenslade (ed.), *Cambridge History of the Bible* (Cambridge: CUP, 1963-70) III, 310. The fatuity of Richardson's contention is worth illustrating, for while it may bring comfort to liberals who cannot quite disown Christian tradition (Anglicans are a good case in point) it has implications for our view of history and, indeed, epistemology, which are outrageous. It would imply, for example, that believers in the *homoousion* could have claimed only 'formal' continuity with orthodoxy during the Arian ascendancy. And it would also suggest that mainstream leaders, like E.B. Pusey, who maintained their conservative convictions during the period of paradigm shift could themselves only 'formally' be claimed as conservatives, since they could well (like Butler) have taken another view had they been born later. This was in fact the case with Pusey's successors: Charles Gore, who took over leadership of the Anglo-Catholics and later penned the scornful *Doctrine of the Infallible Book* (London, Student Christian Movement, 1924); and S.R. Driver, whose *Introduction to the Literature of the Old Testament* (Edinburgh: T&T Clark, 1891) was soon the standard critical introduction, who succeeded him as Regius Professor of Hebrew at Oxford, which chair had been Pusey's for more than half a century. For that matter, since every major figure in the church had once been an infallibilist, so would have been Gore, Driver, and every non-infallibilist since (including Richardson) had they flourished as contemporaries of the great Bishop Butler; are they then only 'formally' of the post-infallibilist, 'critical' position? Which is of course to suggest that Richardson's distinction rests on the assumption that intellectual change on the part of the mainstream community is necessarily in the direction of truth.

Richardson goes on to draw special attention to the work of William Sanday, who in his Bampton Lectures on *Inspiration* (1893) developed and popularised what Richardson candidly terms 'the new view of inspiration'. Sanday offers his own evidence, outlining the 'traditional' theory and setting it over against his 'inductive' or 'critical' alternative.[12] The traditional theory was 'the common belief of Christian men, at least in this country' just fifty years before;[13] 'it is found to be substantially not very different from that which was held two centuries after the Birth of Christ'; and two centuries before that, 'the full conception of the Bible as a Sacred Book was already formed', and was 'recognized in the sayings of Christ Himself'.[14] The solidity and uniformity of this conviction in the churches is particularly striking, and worth some reiteration since it sheds its own light on the significance of contemporary evangelical reflection on the doctrine—and, in particular, on the wide evangelical judgement, significant not least for the formation of the Tyndale Fellowship, to raise generally practical and often principled objections to the historical-critical project since it was judged to be subversive of Christian orthodoxy. However we might now wish to footnote that choice, it would be hard to exaggerate its significance, not least in defining the claim that Evangelicalism is the standard-bearer of the tradition of orthodoxy.

A striking example of the earlier orthodoxy is found in William Van Mildert, Bishop of Durham and a High Churchman of the old school, who was chosen to deliver the bellwether Bampton Lectures in 1814, and who chose biblical interpretation as his subject. The 'authenticity, authority, and truth' of the Scriptures 'are assumed as axioms or postulates, on which the whole inquiry is founded. It is presumed also, that truth, and truth only, can issue from this Divine source of knowledge';[15] for 'it emanates immediately from the Fountain of divine wisdom'.[16] So one historian can write that the nascent historical criticism of the early and mid-nineteenth century confronted as its 'chief obstacle' the

---

[11]*The Religion of Yesterday and Tomorrow* (Boston/New York: Houghton Mifflin, 1925) 61f.

[12]W. Sanday, *Inspiration. Eight Lectures on the Early History and Origin of the Doctrine of Biblical Inspiration* (London: Longmans, 1893; third ed., 1896) xxviii.

[13]*Ibid.*, 392.

[14]*Ibid.*, 393.

[15]W. Van Mildert, *An Enquiry into the General Principles of Scripture-Interpretation* (Oxford: OUP, 1815) 11.

[16]*Ibid.*

traditional view of the Bible as a volume inspired throughout from cover to cover, whose statements, whether they related to science, or history, or religion, were to be accepted without questioning. The Bible was treated as something apart from other writings. Its various books were regarded as being all on the same level of inspiration, and as having proceeded under a divine superintendence, which protected them from any material error.[17]

That obstacle, of course, was surmounted in the course of the century. From an evangelical perspective, it makes a dispiriting story; since as the century progressed most conservatives—including Evangelicals— gave up in some measure their commitment to the traditional position. They generally did so in order, as they saw it, to engage their opponents more effectively. But what began as an *ad hominem* debating ploy had the unintended effect of withdrawing the conservatives from their commitment to the relevance of doctrine to the debate. That is, in their concern to engage the 'critics' on the merits of their historical-critical arguments, the conservatives unwittingly evacuated their own distinctive position.[18] They engaged in detailed historical discussion as they sought to establish the unreasonableness of critical reconstructions. Sometimes they succeeded, sometimes they did not; but the net result of their tactical decision to abandon the defence of distinctive theological warrants for their view of Holy Scripture was the collapse of their position. What began as apologetics was transformed, for many, into hermeneutics; in place of maintaining the traditional view of inspiration and infallibility they entered vigorous historical argument for conservative conclusions on particular issues. This metamorphosis

---

[17]V.F. Storr, *The Development of English Theology in the Nineteenth Century, 1800-1860* (London: Longmans, 1913) 177. *Cf.* C.J. Abbey and J.H. Overton, *The English Church in the Eighteenth Century* (London: Longmans, 1887²) 243: 'the doctrine of unerring literal inspiration was almost everywhere held in its straitest form.' The range of reaction to 'criticism' itself illustrates the point. Willis B. Glover writes that 'England and Scotland really constituted a single religious public of remarkable homogeneity. Particularly in regard to higher criticism denominational and party lines meant little or nothing; even the Anglo-Catholics are not distinguishable as a group from the general body of English religious opinion on critical issues.' *Evangelical Nonconformists and Higher Criticism in the Nineteenth-Century* (London: Independent Press, 1954) 9.

[18]The present writer has argued this at length in his *Biblical Higher Criticism and the Defense of Infallibilism in Nineteenth Century Britain* (Lewiston, New York: Edwin Mellen, 1987); see also his 'Inspiration and Criticism: The Nineteenth-Century Crisis', *TynB* 35 (1984) 129-59. One way of expressing the shift is to note the move from infallibilism held *ex hypothesi* on dogmatic, or perhaps traditional, grounds; and *de facto* infallibilism which was, and had to be, the fruit of historical argument.

went largely undetected until, by the end of the century, the remaining conservatives found themselves marooned in a new consensus in which appeal to dogmatic or traditional considerations was no longer possible; and in which their attempts at the historical-critical defence of particular positions no longer carried any weight. As Harvey observes, to 'enter the lists of the debate and to attempt to vindicate the truth of the sacred narrative', it was necessary 'to pay a costly price... to accept the general canons and criteria of just those one desired to refute. This', he continues, 'was fatal to the traditionalist's cause, because he could no longer appeal to the eye of faith or to any special warrants. The arguments had to stand or fall on their own merits.'[19]

III. Two Soundings in the Nineteenth Century

1. Prologue to Criticism: the *Essays and Reviews* Debate

The publication in 1860 of this modest volume[20] marked the beginning of the long debate about the Bible—and much else theological—which would climax toward the end of the century in general acquiescence in the abandonment of the traditional conception of inspiration. Its interests were broader than criticism, but the longest and most important of its seven essays was that of Benjamin Jowett 'On the Interpretation of Scripture'. Jowett's argument was, in short, that the Bible must be studied 'like any other book'; and while that maxim (which was hardly original) can be pulled and pushed in different directions, in the context of *Essays and Reviews* it served as a manifesto for the adoption of a fundamentally non-dogmatic approach to the reading of Scripture. So, Jowett writes, in a characteristic false dichotomy, the work of biblical interpretation 'has nothing to do with any opinion respecting [its] divine origin.'[21] The interpreter should seek to

> recover the original [interpretation], the meaning, that is, of the words as they first struck on the ears or flashed before the eyes of those who heard and read them... The history of Christendom is nothing to him, but only the scene at Galilee or Jerusalem... All the after-thoughts of theology are nothing to him... His object is to read Scripture like any other book.[22]

---

[19]Van Austin Harvey, *The Historian and the Believer* (London: SCM, 1967) 105f.
[20]*Essays and Reviews* (London: John Parker & Son, 1860).
[21]*Ibid.*, 350.
[22]*Ibid.*, 338.

In other words, 'The meaning of Scripture is one thing; the inspiration of Scripture is another.'[23] The doctrine of inspiration, like the rest of the church's theological development, could have no relevance to the task of the interpreter of Scripture. There are no special principles of interpretation, which the doctrine of Holy Scripture requires the believing student to bring to the study of the text. Scripture should be studied simply as are the other texts of classical antiquity.

The significance of *Essays and Reviews* lies chiefly in the vigorous debate which it initiated. Among a number of replies, John William Burgon's *Inspiration and Interpretation*[24] offered an energetic restatement of the traditional doctrine of Scripture, in the most coherent and systematic of any conservative rejoinders to the emerging criticism. Burgon is insistent that the Bible must be allowed to interpret itself; and while on one reading the 'like any other book' principle could encompass such a concern, it is plain that this is not how Jowett intends his maxim to be taken. So, Burgon writes:

> in order to interpret the Bible, our aim must be to ascertain how the Bible interprets itself... How then does Scripture interpret Scripture? That is the only question! for the answer to this question must be held to be decisive as to the other question which Mr. Jowett raises... [Is] the Bible to be interpreted as no other book is, or can be interpreted; and for the plain reason, that the inspired writers themselves (our LORD himself at their head!) interpret it after an altogether extraordinary fashion.[25]

And that, of course, remains the central question for those who would interpret Holy Scripture.

2. L' Affaire Robertson Smith

The central figure, and the most celebrated case, in the nineteenth- century controversies over biblical criticism was undoubtedly William Robertson Smith (1846-94).[26] The controversy turned chiefly on the question of pseudonymity in the case of the book of Deuteronomy, though this was sampled from Smith's general acceptance of the new orthodoxy of Continental critical scholarship because it presented a seemingly straightforward example of the Bible's testimony to itself

---

[23]*Ibid.*, 338.
[24]London and Oxford: John Parker and Son, 1861. It is interesting to note that Burgon was no Evangelical. On the remarkable uniformity of conservative responses to criticism, see note 18 above.
[25]Burgon, *Inspiration and Interpretation*, clxiii.

being overturned by the like-any-other-book methods of critical scholars.

Robertson Smith was born a child of the Disruption of the Scottish church, which in 1843 had split the Presbyterian establishment down the middle, the 'Free' Church of Scotland departing with most of the Evangelicals into a church which became a byword for orthodoxy among conservatives far from Scotland. Smith's father had left the establishment and with it his head- teacher's job in Aberdeen, and entered the parish ministry of the Free Church; so his precocious, argumentative, and soon famous son was born in a country manse. The young man made rapid progress through the Scottish universities, and spent important periods of study in Germany. By 1870 he had been elected to the chair of Hebrew at the Church's Aberdeen college. During the following years, Robertson Smith's views on criticism and the study of the Bible were subject to a process of development, which led finally to his open adoption of what were in Britain regarded as highly innovative and suspect positions. It should, however, be noted that as early as November, 1869, he had shared with the Theological Society of the Free Church's New College in Edinburgh his conviction that the 'real restorers of believing theology' in Germany were 'followers mainly of Schleiermacher'; that 'the only way to escape the wave of violent unbelief which has already swept over the German Churches is frankly to recognise the need for progress in our theological conceptions'.[27] In the light of what followed, these and other such statements, modest though they seem, take on new significance.[28]

By the year 1875 he had contributed several articles to the great ninth edition of the *Encyclopaedia Britannica*. The appearance of 'Bible' in Volume 3 in December of that year signalled the start of the case, ini-

---

[26]The standard biography is J.S. Black and G.W. Chrystal, *The Life of William Robertson Smith* (London: A.&C. Black, 1912). A helpful dissertation is R.R. Nelson, 'The Life and Thought of William Robertson Smith, 1846-1894' (University of Michigan, 1971). The present writer discusses Robertson Smith's position, and his trials for heresy, in his *Biblical Higher Criticism and the Defense of Infallibilism in Nineteenth-Century Britain*, 204-62.

[27]William Robertson Smith, *Lectures and Essays* (ed. J.S. Black and G.W. Chrystal; London: A.&C. Black, 1912) 148, 150. Apparently the weather was poor and few attended the meeting.

[28]This and other early essays remained unpublished during Robertson Smith's lifetime. Other evidence of his changing position emerges in his correspondence to and from Germany, and his manuscript lecture notes. So in 1870-71 he declares that certain considerations 'are part of the many proofs that... [Moses'] work is such as the Torah describes to us'; in 1876 he returns to the subject, omitting this sentence from his notes; see Nelson, 'Life and Thought of William Robertson Smith', 101f.

tiating controversial reviews to which (characteristically) Smith replied with vigour. The central question, which remained at the heart of six years of ecclesiastical proceedings and which still poses a vital problem in contemporary discussion of faith and criticism, is focused on the Mosaic authorship of Deuteronomy. The first official review of Smith's position was that of the committee which supervised the Church's theological colleges. Smith assured the committee of his belief in the doctrine of Scripture taught in the Westminster Confession of Faith. The committee write in these terms:

> The question remains, no doubt, whether Professor Smith has maintained critical opinions which, in their own nature, subvert the doctrine he professes. It is in this connection that those of Professor Smith come into consideration, of which his theory of Deuteronomy is the leading instance. The Committee have freely stated their view of that theory, that it appears liable to objection, and is fitted to create apprehension. The objection to it is, that it ascribes to the author of the book the use of the device, or as Professor Smith prefers to term it, a literary form, which to many thoughtful minds, familiar with the subject in all its aspects, appears unworthy and inadmissible in connection with the Divine Inspiration and Divine Authority of such a book as Deuteronomy. The apprehension felt in connection with it is, that the theory of an inspired and non-deceptive personation will not generally command assent; and then the admission that the statements of the book regarding Moses are not true in the obvious sense will operate, it may be feared, in the way of unsettling belief.[29]

The committee actually concluded that there were no grounds for further process, however uneasy Smith's work made them. Others, however, took another view, and after much further process the General Assembly of 1878 served on him (by one vote!) a Libel, charging that he held that:

> the book of inspired Scripture called Deuteronomy, which is professedly an historical record, does not possess that character, but was made to assume it by a writer of a much later age, who therein, in the name of God, presented, in dramatic form, instructions and laws as proceeding from the mouth of Moses, though these never were and never could have been uttered by him,—an opinion which contradicts or is opposed to the doctrine of the immediate inspiration, infallible

---

[29]Cited Black and Chrystal, *Life*, 208-9.

truth, and Divine authority of the Holy Scriptures as set forth in the Scriptures themselves, and in the Confession of Faith as aforesaid.[30]

Successive attempts to convict Robertson Smith proved unsuccessful, but in May of 1881, even now only 34, he was dismissed from the chair of Hebrew at the Church's Aberdeen college, on the ground that he had thrown 'grave doubt on the historical truth and divine inspiration' of Scripture.[31] That brought to an end six years of highly public controversy in the most extraordinary manner possible: despite two lengthy trials, which involved hearings at several levels in the Byzantine structures of nineteenth-century Presbyterianism, that most conservative of Christian churches had found itself unable to convict him of heresy; but dismissed him nonetheless. And through this three-fold combination of granting brilliant publicity to Smith's position, showing itself unable to convict him of heresy, and finally demonstrating expedience in dismissing him unconvicted, the Free Church of Scotland made the greatest and most ironic of contributions to the dissemination in Britain of the new 'higher criticism'—especially among Evangelicals. And it exemplified the problems of definition and identity which would thereafter confront Evangelicals, and confront them still.[32]

IV. Dogma and History

These samples from the generation of debate which finally won over the mainstream of the British churches to a set of particular critical theories and, more important, to a post-orthodox view of inspiration and infallibility, remind us that the questions we face today are but sophisticated versions of those which troubled the churches in the nineteenth century. Central to their debates was the question of the relation of history and dogma: that is, whether scholarly study required an approach to Scripture as merely an ancient text, on the unfettered principles of critical historical and literary study; or whether Christian study offered a context of dogma within which historical and literary claims would be otherwise assessed.

---

[30]Cited Black and Chrystal, *Life*, 324.

[31]Black and Chrystal, *Life*, 425.

[32]Glover comments, 'Unquestionably, the most important single factor in forcing upon English evangelicals the realization that higher criticism was consistent with evangelical theology was the trial of Robertson Smith by the Free Church of Scotland' (*Evangelical Nonconformists and Higher Criticism in the Nineteenth Century*, 110).

Thus to set the warrants of history over against those of dogma suggests, of course, that Christian dogma cannot be squared with biblical history, which threatens to lead us ineluctably into the kind of historical discussion in which we must abandon dogma in order to take part; and which proved so fatal to the doctrine of Scripture in the nineteenth century—in which orthodox bibliology was lost altogether to the mainline theology which in the early part of the century held it so dear, and almost lost even to Evangelicalism. It is not, however, our intention to imply the converse, either—that orthodoxy should be maintained through an obscurantist embrace, in willing ignorance of the incontestable facts of history (like the Victorian who prayed that if Darwinism were indeed true it might not be widely known). While the tactics adopted by the conservatives in the nineteenth-century battle for the Bible proved ultimately to be disastrous, and while their growing lack of interest in their own dogmatic warrants for Holy Scripture steadily undermined the logic of their own position, their underlying confidence that Scripture could stand the test of historical scrutiny was not of itself misplaced. What was needed was critical reflection on the nature of the dogmatic warrants, as on the character of the historiography against whose results, *prima facie*, Christian belief found itself pitted. Discussions of the historiography of 'historical criticism' are exceedingly rare.

1. Doctrine

Though they share a common authority in the teaching of canonical Scripture, the sources of Christian beliefs are many. From one perspective they simply come out of tradition, the tradition of a given community which thus confesses its faith. The community will have reasons for what it believes, and its account may or may not find its final resting-place in a bed of canonical Scripture. We need only to mention the *homoousion*, or the *Filioque*, to be reminded that the genealogy of particular heads of doctrine is complex. And this is true of none more so than bibliology, partly because its development until so recently has been largely implicit; for the reason that, historically, the church has only engaged in elaborate definition of doctrine where that doctrine has been the focus of controversy. Though the Reformation saw some such reflection, and Protestant scholasticism continued it, it was not until the nineteenth century that the attention of the theological community was focused foursquare on the question of Holy Scripture. Because the context of that attention was the unleashing of intellectual forces which worked to subvert every Christian doctrine, while clarification of the doctrine did indeed result (from Gaussen to Warfield,[33] and beyond), in the theological academy the consequence was the delineation of an avowedly new doctrine of a fallible and suddenly 'human' Holy Scripture.[34] Indeed, the lasting result of the historical-critical programme was to focus attention everywhere but on the text of Scripture itself—on earlier reconstructions; on the 'inspired' writers; on the history which might be discerned behind their text; and, especially, on the 'acts of God' in that history, the revelatory landmarks of 'salvation-history'. What all these had in common, of course, was their lack of interest in canonical Scripture as such; and, by way of reaction, both 'literary' and 'canonical' approaches today are attempts to recover a role for the text, but without the need to return to the old belief in inspiration and infallibility which once secured a single, undivided, place in Christian doctrine for the Bible story, the Bible text, and the Bible received as the revelation of God.

And, in the old system, these were held to be mutually supportive. It was because Scripture was held to be inspired and revelatory that it could be trusted as a narrative account of what happened. Which raises, of course, the question of historiography. For the dogmatic warrants themselves—as we have noted in a succession of mainline figures in early nineteenth-century theology—had been central to the historiographic task. To that we shall return.

2. History

Historical warrants, of course, are the creatures of historiography, a tradition all of its own, no stronger or weaker than the presuppositions according to which history is being practised; and so to say is immediately to suggest the fundamental point of contact between what we have called dogmatic and historical warrants. For the older tradition did not neglect historiography as such, it engaged in the project of biblical history according to special canons which were informed by prior dogmatic warrants as to the nature of Holy Scripture, which was a book like other books, but also a book unlike other books. In the nineteenth century a new historiography came to be applied to Holy Scripture, the secular history-writing which had proved so successful in recovering other ancient civilisations. Yet the very reason for its suc-

---

[33]L. Gaussen, *Theopneustia* (ET; London: Samuel Bagster & Sons, 1841); reprinted as *The Divine Inspiration of the Bible* (Grand Rapids: Kregel, 1971); Benjamin B. Warfield, *The Inspiration and Authority of the Bible* (Philadelphia: Presbyterian and Reformed, 1948) and elsewhere.
[34]So, as we have noted, Sanday *et al.*

cess elsewhere was the ground of its problematic here: its development was on firmly naturalistic principles, in which the analogy of present experience was considered to be compelling. It was inevitable that the application of naturalistic method to a *prima facie* supernaturalistic account would yield a reconstruction in which anything beyond the merely natural was squeezed out. That is the function of historiographical method. And while some of the particularities of nineteenth-century approaches have long since been disowned, the principles of naturalism remain.[35]

The difficulty of applying such methods to Scripture is of course widely recognised, since the first generations of critical scholars were conscious above all that the Gospel accounts would crumple under such treatment and the Jesus they present be readily conformed to another image than his own. In fact it is hard not to conclude that their inconsequence in this matter—drawing back from the logic of their own historiography—had the double effect of preserving New Testament criticism in a generally conservative cocoon,[36] while encouraging conservatives to hazard historical criteria for the interpretation of the Old Testament.

V. Some Conclusions

1. One of the curiosities of the post-War conservative evangelical resurgence, particularly in biblical studies and the development of allied scholarly resources, has been a general disinclination to methodological reflection upon the exercise. That is, only minimal attention has been focused on the question of the rationale of evangelical distinctives in the study of Scripture, and this is particularly the case in the United Kingdom. One reason for this state of affairs is the degree to which the

---

[35]In her energetic rebuttal of the historical-critical approach, Eta Linnemann notes one of its pre-requisites as the acceptance of 'atheistic historiography': *Historical Criticism of the Bible* (ET; Grand Rapids: Baker, 1990) 31.

[36]So, especially, the 'Cambridge Trio' of Lightfoot, Westcott and Hort, who were highly successful in using non-dogmatic argument to defend conservative New Testament positions. Willis B. Glover writes: 'In accepting the Cambridge defence against Strauss and Baur, the evangelicals accepted higher criticism in principle, without being fully aware of what they had done. They were also encouraged by the success of conservative New Testament criticism and disposed to believe that a thorough critical study of the Old Testament would likewise substantiate the main outlines of the traditional view of the Bible' (*Evangelical Nonconformists and Higher Criticism in the Nineteenth Century*, 284).

scholarly direction of the movement has been in the hands of Bible scholars and historians rather than theologians and philosophers. Indeed, perhaps most curious of all, there has been a parallel tendency to downplay the significance of both these disciplines—partly the fruit of those same influences which led our forebears of the nineteenth century to disengage from serious dogmatic reflection and argumentation in the matter of the authority of Holy Scripture and its implications for 'criticism'. This is of course doubly ironic, since it not only replicates the failed strategy of a century before, it does so in the context of a movement which has been established on the assumption that there are indeed theological warrants for a distinctive view of the historical interpretation of the Bible.[37] The general failure to generate scholarly discussion of the relations of Scripture and criticism has gone hand in hand with spoken and unspoken assumptions about the fruit of that relationship in, for example, the publishing policy of conservative evangelical houses such as the Inter-Varsity Press, whose commentaries, dictionaries, and, most notably, introductions,[38] have been handbooks of conservatism on particular critical and historical questions.

2. There is of course no need to deny the validity of historical-critical approaches to the interpretation of historical texts. The awakening historical consciousness of the eighteenth and nineteenth centuries, while less revolutionary than is sometimes suggested, undoubtedly led to a recovery of understanding of the ancient world. Our argument is not with historical criticism as such (though its own practice has varied and its canons have been argued), but with its application to the Holy Scriptures. Does our belief that the Bible is an historical human product require us to apply to its text the canons of general historical interpretation? Or does our belief that it is inspired by God require the development and employment of special principles of interpretation?

---

[37]The present writer presumed to argue such a case within the precincts of Tyndale House, Cambridge, in the 1983 Tyndale Historical Theology Lecture, subsequently published in *Tyndale Bulletin*; see note 18 above.
[38]Donald Guthrie, *New Testament Introduction* (London: Tyndale, 3 vols., 1961-5; 1 vol.,1970); R.K. Harrison, *Introduction to the Old Testament* (London: Tyndale, 1970). Tyndale Press was the academic imprint of the Inter-Varsity Press. In *Between Faith and Criticism* (San Francisco: Harper and Row, 1986) Mark A. Noll tabulates evangelical scholarly involvement in institutions and publishing projects, noting among other things the preponderant significance of British conservative scholarship in the post-War evangelical resurgence in the United States.

3. The legacy of the past century and a half is complicated by the Cheshire-cat survival of earlier generations of critical work. The most enduring example is, of course, the Graf-Wellhausen hypothesis, which has been systematically undermined and, in particulars, widely disowned within mainstream scholarship. The same could also be said, for example, of much of the earlier case for the disunity of Isaiah. Yet the idea of 'assured results', as the early consensus conclusions were called by their nineteenth-century proponents, lives on. The naive expectation of early conservatives that their engagement in historical-critical argument would lead to the reinstatement of traditional views on historical and literary questions proved sadly unfounded, not least because their old doctrine of inspiration had been replaced by new doctrines whose common assumption (indeed, whose single common feature) was that the old idea was no longer tenable. This same principle has worked its way through each individual discussion of critical questions, and ensures that much of the debate is focused no longer on the text itself but on and within the tradition of interpretation which is self-consciously that of the scholarly community. This makes it peculiarly difficult for conservatives to gain a foothold in debate; indeed, it makes it difficult for them to remain methodologically 'conservative' at all if they would also play a part in the larger debate. Their general commitment to the truthfulness and reliability of Scripture itself will tend to undermine the credibility of their case for particular conservative positions, even though the same arguments might credibly be offered by mainline scholars. This set of problems is of course a consequence of the paradigmatic character of the change which has come upon biblical scholarship, and the systemic marginalisation which that implies for those who *ex animo* are still working within the old paradigm.[39] It is at this point that the nineteenth-century conservatives made their big mistake, and that we must take most care.

---

[39]Kuhnian categories need to be used with considerable care, but can be illuminating in our quest to understand fundamental intellectual shifts. For an application to the nineteenth-century Scripture discussions, see the present writer's *Biblical Higher Criticism and the Defense of Infallibilism in Nineteenth-Century Britain*, 319-24. Hans Küng and David Tracy's symposium *Paradigm Change in Theology* (ET; New York: Crossroad, 1991) has curious features, including some basic inconsistencies and disagreements about method between contributors, but offers a stimulating series of discussions of ways of making sense of old and new in biblical-theological method.

4. Central to the conservative evangelical project has been the conviction that the liberal historical-critical agenda is subversive of the *theological* use of Scripture. It is for this reason that we reject the several middle-ground positions with which so much of the theology of the past century has been concerned—Barth and the 'Biblical Theology Movement', Childs' canonical approach, the literary focus, and those like Robertson Smith who sought to champion orthodoxy and yet claimed compatibility for such a position with the results of conventional historical-critical analysis. Our judgement as a community has been, in sum, that the indemnity is too high: historical criticism renders the biblical material unusable for the role in which it has served the church, as authorising our theological proposals and grounding our theological commitments.

Moreover, orthodoxy has itself been shaped, grounded, and reasoned out of Scripture—Scripture conceived as the infallible, inerrant Word of God. It is therefore impossible to appeal to the tradition of the church, or its credal and confessional sources, without implicitly affirming the conservative construction and use of Scripture. For they have been worked out on the assumptions which flow from the conservative position; the major premise of each one of their assertions is Holy Scripture construed as in the tradition. While it could reasonably be argued that Scripture is not to be trusted and that this discredits their witness, so that the radical deconstruction of Christian orthodoxy must follow, it cannot properly be maintained that the disintegration of the traditional understanding of Holy Scripture can be completed and leave the structure of orthodoxy intact. The alternative is of course theological development divorced from a realistic, historical reading of Holy Scripture, which must necessarily abandon confidence in authorial intent as central to canonical interpretation, the hinge of the divine and the human which marks the revelatory character of God's Word written and thereby gives it its divine authority.

5. Finally, we have to ask after our alternative, if alternative we have, to the historical-critical method.[40] Part of the problem we face is that a naturalistic historiography seems an altogether more coherent methodological tool than one which is open to supernatural causes and anticipates their influence at every point. It is no surprise that critics maintain that in no other way than their way can history be done. His-

---

[40]Gerhard Maier has sketched the outlines of an 'Historical Biblical Method' in his programmatic *End of the Historical-Critical Method*, especially 80-88.

toriography is conceived as the recovery of the truth from and through layers of potentially misleading and obscuring text; on naturalistic principles. So, it will not unreasonably be said, to approach the task of writing the histories of Greece and Rome with an open mind toward the activity of pagan divinities would make historical reconstruction impossible.[41]

In the case of Holy Scripture is it different? Alongside openness to the supernatural we have an equal conviction of the truth of the story. The need is not for reconstruction, it is for interpretation which will answer our questions according to the witness of the text. It is evident that such an approach will little commend itself outside the believing community. Moreover, it is not a method which will necessarily answer all our questions. There may be important areas in which we are left in suspense, since we are denied the naturalistic history machine which will always provide the most probable answer; there will be questions to which we simply have none, since we cannot apply the analogy of experience to accounts of experience with which ours has only an incomplete analogy. For the conservative theologian, Scripture must remain—as Gerhard Ebeling has characterised the tradition—'a special historia sacra or scriptura sacra in the ontological sense as a self-evident intellectual presupposition influencing his method of research'.[42]

---

[41]Which is of course the point, as becomes clear if we ask the question: how would we engage in classical historiography if, per impossibile, the Roman pantheon were believed to be an ontological fact? Does the deus ex machina mark the end of historiographic possibility?

[42]Gerhard Ebeling, Word and Faith (ET Philadelphia: Fortress, 1963) 47.

CHAPTER 11

Scripture and Evangelical Diversity with Special Reference to the Baptismal Divide

David F. Wright

Summary

Since Evangelicals affirm that Scripture as a whole is God-given, we refuse to acquiesce in current exaggerations of the diversity of biblical teachings. We must avoid devaluing subjects on which we continue to disagree, such as ecclesiology and baptism. As a dominical observance, baptism is a first-order issue, as 'one baptism' in Ephesians 4:4-6 shows. Its oneness should be sought in a single theology of baptism rather than a single form of administration. The constitutive oneness asserted in Ephesians 4 commits us to an unending quest to discern or recover our unity behind and through our differences.

I. The Challenge

The issue is this: is the credibility of our evangelical confession of Scripture as God's Word undermined or dissolved by our diversity—understood in a strong sense as our disagreements about the teaching of Scripture? The relationship between our common conviction of the God-given authority of Scripture and our divergent interpretations and applications of it could be examined from many angles. The social and cultural historian, for example, would highlight the currents of thought and life that have fostered or fathered different readings of the Bible in successive eras and in disparate contexts. But our concern in this paper is fundamentally a theological or doctrinal one. It will take seriously both the shared commitment to follow where Scripture leads that characterises the evangelical community and the integrity of our doctrinal diversity as constituted by sincere but discrepant appropriations of Scripture.

We could of course profitably focus largely on what supposedly unites us: are we really of one mind about the nature and status of Scripture? Can our protestations of concordant minds survive the deafening clamour of our discordant voices? Since I believe that in good measure they have so survived within the Tyndale Fellowship for half a century, I want to direct our attention elsewhere, although it will be impossible to avoid noticing some of the shafts of light that our transparent differences cast on our variant perspectives on the Bible.

Without an agreed starting-point, our conflicting evangelical conclusions would be much less of a problem. No one is disconcerted when travellers taking their bearings from different lodestars reach different destinations. Within the Tyndale Fellowship the common ground is expressed in the Doctrinal Basis of the wider Fellowship (I.V.F./U.C.C.F.) of which we are part, wherein we commit ourselves to believing in

> The divine inspiration and infallibility of Holy Scripture, as originally given, and its supreme authority in all matters of faith and conduct.

But for the purposes of this present discussion it would not greatly matter if our unifying platform were a much older statement, such as the Thirty-nine Articles or the Westminster Confession, or a more recent one, like the Lausanne Covenant. Given our united stance on this umbilical point, why the scandal of our grievous dissensions?

Let us spell out more closely the challenges that our disagreements pose to our professed agreement about Scripture. In a word, they place in the dock the adequacy of 'Scripture alone', that is, its ability to lead God's people by the Spirit to a right understanding without the help of a *magisterium*, an authoritative teaching office, whether this be ecclesial (papacy, council, body of tradition) or confessional (Calvin's *Institutes* or the *Roman Book of Concord*) or professional (the guild of biblical scholars). Do not our failures to agree the teaching of Scripture expose as fanciful our cherished devotion to the vernacular accessibility of the Bible to all who would read, in the conviction that it will infallibly lead them into all truth? What price the perspicuity of Scripture if we cannot reach accord on the subjects of baptism? or on one of the variety of ecclesiologies on offer in the ecumenical supermarket? or on the destiny of unbelievers, heretics and apostates? or on the role of God's electing love in determining the population of the eternal kingdom? or on the ordination of women to whatever we ordain men?

II. Perspicuity

Such questions range over a broad spectrum of underlying issues, a number of which we need not address in this paper. But let us not make our task unnecessarily intractable, in a kind of theological masochism. We hold no brief for an untrammelled privatisation of the Bible. I doubt if the Reformers' conviction of its perspicuity ever implied its normal spiritual capacity to teach the solitary reader, working unaided from scratch, the doctrines of, say, the Apostles Creed. The clarity and certainty (or definiteness) of Scripture, as Zwingli termed it, was thought to function more in a responsive mode. It denoted the verifiability of the Reformation gospel in the pages of the Bible by literate citizens at last able, thanks to translation and printing, to check for themselves. (The Bereans of Acts 17:11 were indeed a noble model.) The doctrine of perspicuity was part of early Protestantism's appeal to the Christian populace of Europe over the heads of the representatives of the Old Church, who demanded that discussion of such controverted themes be left in the theologically safe hands of the curia and the universities. The Bible's transparency came into its own in the public disputations—town-wide Bible studies, in effect—which so often issued in a community's quasi-democratic vote henceforth to live by the Reformation gospel. Teaching and preaching almost invariably preceded adjudication by popular resort to the open Bible. And basic to the whole enterprise was the Reformers' recovery of the plain or 'literal' sense of the Scriptures, over against the spiritualising or allegorising of much of the earlier tradition.

Thus William Tyndale's *Pathway into the Holy Scripture* sets forth the heads of evangelical doctrine before concluding in the following terms:

> These things, I say, to know, is to have all the scripture unlocked and opened before thee; so that if thou wilt go in, and read, thou canst not but understand. And in these things to be ignorant, is to have all the scripture locked up; so that the more thou readest it, the blinder thou art, and the more tangled art thou therein, and canst nowhere through... And therefore, because we be never taught the profession of our baptism, we remain always unlearned... And now, because the lay and unlearned people are taught these first principles of our profession, therefore they read the scripture, and understand and delight therein.[1]

Even in the Westminster Confession's very different affirmation, the qualifications are significant:

> All things in scripture are not alike plain in themselves, nor alike clear unto all; yet those things which are necessary to be known, believed, and observed, for salvation, are so clearly propounded and opened in some place of scripture or other, that not only the learned, but the unlearned, in a due use of the ordinary means, may attain unto a sufficient understanding of them (I:7).

The limitation here set for the scope of perspicuity—'those things...necessary to be known, believed, and observed, for salvation'—may be worth pondering in the context of diversity.

---

[1] *Doctrinal Treatises and Introductions to Different Portions of the Holy Scriptures* (ed. H. Walter; Parker Society; Cambridge: CUP, 1848) 27-8; also in *The Work of William Tyndale* (ed. G.E. Duffield; Courtenay Library of Reformation Classics 1; Appleford: Sutton Courtenay Press, 1964) 23-4. *Cf.* similarly his Prologue to the Exposition of 1 John: 'If our hearts were taught the appointment made between God and us in Christ's blood, when we were baptized, we had the key to open the scripture, and light to see and perceive the true meaning of it, and the scripture should be easy to understand', (*Expositions and Notes on Sundry Portions of the Holy Scriptures* [ed. Walter; Parker Society; Cambridge: CUP, 1849] 141; *The Work of William Tyndale* [ed. Duffield] 175).

III. Diversity Regnant

First, however, we must move back from the problem of evangelical diversity to the givenness of diversity in the Christian revelation. The point scarcely needs labouring. If the Bible in some sense has a single divine author, in an inescapably obvious sense it is the work of many varied human authors. An earlier age may have tended to assume that the unity prevailed over the diversity. The Westminster Confession, for example, bypasses the human authors when it affirms that

> it pleased the Lord, at sundry times, and in divers manners, to reveal himself, and to declare...his will unto his church; and afterwards,...to commit the same wholly unto writing (I:1).

Yet some appreciation of the distinctive characteristics of, say, the Old Testament prophetic books and the four Gospels has rarely been wholly absent in the church's life, even if both Augustine and Calvin expended energy on harmonies of the Synoptics and Calvin also on a harmony of Exodus-Deuteronomy. Although the plurality, as much as the diversity, of the four Gospels was felt to be theologically difficult in the earliest centuries,[2] from Irenaeus' time onwards the four creatures of Revelation 4:7 (*cf.* Ezk. 1:10, 10:14) were recruited to identify, and justify, the Gospels' fourfold witness. Even if much popular Christian piety, not solely in the evangelical mould, deploys the Bible in an undifferentiated fashion and harmonises instinctively, there can be no excuse for this collapsing of the pluriformity of Scripture when it ascends to the pulpit.

Today, however, diversity rules. Its superiority to unity and uniformity runs deep in the assumptions of our culture. Theologically, it is increasingly warranted by a more Eastern than Western doctrine of the Trinity, with differentiation enjoying primacy over oneness. In the study of the Bible the results are only too familiar. Not only is 'Biblical Theology' long dead and buried, and 'the theology of the Old Testament' a discipline in danger of demise, but one may not be on safe ground in talking even of 'the theology of Paul'—for why should Paul have been more successful than other writers in maintaining consistency (if indeed this mattered to him) over several years addressing

---

[2]O. Cullmann, 'The Plurality of the Gospels as a Theological Problem in Antiquity', in his *The Early Church* (ed. A.J.B. Higgins; London: SCM, 1956) 37-54; H. Merkel, *Die Pluralität der Evangelien als theologisches und exegetisches Problem in der Alten Kirche* (Traditio Christiana III; Berne: Peter Lang, 1978).

varied situations and readerships? Those who deplore these atomistic drives should not be blind to the floods of new light that a precise focus on topics such as the theology of Luke (the Evangelist, not the Gospel) continues to pour on Holy Scripture.

Evangelical diversity of the late twentieth century owes not a little to the magnification of diversity in recent academic theology. The radical Sojourners-type Evangelicalism of Mennonite and similar inspiration leans heavily on the Jesus of the Synoptic Gospels, while charismatic Evangelicalism majors on Acts and traditionally neglected areas of the Paulines. Both may be contrasted with the older mainstream for whom Paul is the purest gospel, and within Paul, Romans. The polarisation between kingdom ethics and creation ethics pits modern against ancient.

So even though conservative biblical scholarship remains resistant to contemporary pressures to fragment the Bible for purposes of critical study (and in this Fellowship we have set ourselves the goal of re-invigorating Biblical Theology[3]), nevertheless the high profile enjoyed by the diversity of Scripture has interacted in some interesting ways with inherited patterns of pre-critical diversity—for example, between paedobaptism and credobaptism, or between different ecclesiastical polities.

IV. Diversity and Devaluation

One outcome has been a relativising of differences. Not only would very few now concur either with Calvin in identifying four orders of ministry as given by the Lord to his church, or with the Anglican Ordinal to which it was 'evident unto all men diligently reading holy Scripture and ancient Authors' that the orders of bishop, priest and deacon existed from the apostles' time, but most would acknowledge that Scripture prescribes no one pattern of ministerial leadership. No more does it lay down a single framework for acts of worship—and certainly not one that forgets 1 Corinthians 14:26. Without surrendering the conviction that our own church's doctrinal distinctives and ways of ordering its corporate life are agreeable to Scripture, we now have ampler warrant for granting the same recognition to others also. Ecumenism has become both easier and more difficult: easier, because

---

[3]*Cf.* Dan Beeby, 'Scripture: From Rumour to Recovery', in *Gospel and Culture* Newsletter 17 (Summer 1993) 1-6.

churches have grown less inclined to advance exclusive claims, *e.g.*, for episcopacy or for infant baptism, but more difficult, because the issue rests increasingly on pragmatic considerations or the lightweight appeal of the pooling of insights, even when they are biblical ones.[4]

So there are dangers in a greater readiness to let the diversity of the biblical testimony provide a covering, as it were, for the divergences of church beliefs and practices. It may make us more vulnerable, or more captive, to tradition rather than Scripture. If our way of doing things is at best only partly biblical, the same is true of everyone else's way also. More seriously, the relativism bred by increasing acquiescence in diversity may foster indifferentism, or at least the devaluation of subjects on which agreement eludes us. One reason for the neglect, and hence weakness, of ecclesiology among Evangelicals, at least in a movement like I.V.F./U.C.C.F., is an understandable reluctance to tackle an issue that cannot fail to prove divisive in an interdenominational context. We cannot afford to give it a high profile, and perhaps it does not deserve a high profile. If we cannot reach a common mind on it, it cannot be too important. Such, I suggest, has been the fate of the doctrine of the church among Evangelicals.

More damagingly still, a compliant condoning of diversity, with the supposed blessing of Scripture's diverse presentations, may insidiously make common cause with a subjectivism or individualism that are destructive of the objective truthfulness of Scripture. It ceases to be public truth, accessible and ascertainable by agreed canons and criteria, and is instead privatised. When the unity of the biblical witness recedes behind its pluralism, it becomes that much easier to argue that my private reading of it, *coram Deo* of course, has validity. As Roy Clements has put it in an unpublished paper, 'Thus the Bible becomes a kind of Zen text, from which everybody gets their own spiritual buzz without being concerned to know whether it is the same buzz as anybody else.'[5]

It is time to move from general considerations to the particular case of baptism. The baptismal divide is not new; indeed, the sixteenth

---

[4]*Cf.* Ernst Käsemann's conclusion in his celebrated essay 'The Canon of the New Testament and the Unity of the Church' (*Essays on New Testament Themes* [London: SCM, 1964] 95-107 at 103): 'the New Testament canon does not, as such, constitute the foundation of the unity of the Church. On the contrary, as such (that is, in its accessibility to the historian) it provides the basis for the multiplicity of the confessions.'

[5]Roy Clements, 'An Overview of Evangelicalism Today', delivered at the UCCF Triennial Consultation, Swanwick, on 7th May, 1994.

century viewed it in altogether starker colours than we moderns are used to. The moderating of passions owes something to the greater modesty shown by both sides in appealing to Scripture, but it remains irreducibly a disagreement about the teaching of Scripture, even if that disagreement pivots not so much on proof-texts as on the proper relation between the two Testaments.

It is surely also a classic instance of apparently intractable division nurturing indifferentism. I well remember, during conversations between the Church of Scotland and the Baptist Union of Scotland, a senior representative of the Kirk, a cleric of impeccable ecumenical credentials, concluding that, if the Lord had allowed his church to be so divided for so long about baptism, he could not have meant it to be too important. (A consistent application of this criterion might dissolve the ecumenical movement altogether—or resolve all its problems at a stroke!) Evangelicals, whose defining characteristics, according to David Bebbington, include conversionism, have instinctively viewed their paedobaptism as something less than full New Testament baptism (a minimising tendency welcomed by credobaptists), while evangelical Baptists have too often operated with a diluted or desiccated baptismal theology. For the purposes of this discussion I will assume the commonly held differentiation between the two forms of baptismal administration, without considering more penetrating questions, such as how far either of them corresponds to the so-called converts' baptism of much of the New Testament.

It is my conviction that the New Testament does not allow us to regard baptism as a second-order issue, let alone an *adiaphoron*. Whether we call it a sacrament or an ordinance, we agree that it belongs to that very small category of acts that Jesus explicitly instructed his followers to perpetuate. Most ecclesiologies in the Reformation tradition make its proper administration essential to the being of the church. (Baptists who have been conscientiously unable to recognise paedobaptism as Christian baptism should have had great difficulty in discerning the church in paedobaptist communions, as their sixteenth-century forebears certainly did.) Our embarrassing disagreement about baptism has undoubtedly contributed to our widespread failure to make our baptismal experience and character the ground of exhortation, admonition and instruction as frequently as the New Testament does. Credobaptists may justifiably claim that paedobaptism renders this impossible, but I wonder if their own performance is much more creditable. Faced with confusion surrounding the ritual reality, we take refuge in spiritualising—even with passages like Romans 6:1-4, with a banal tautology as the outcome.[6]

Ecumenical progress in recent decades in both the Old World and the New has produced united churches in which both baptismal practices have equal status. The United Reformed Church in Britain and the Church of North India, to name two examples, offer both, strictly as alternatives. Hence there can be no question of allowing re-baptism of those baptised as babies, or of pressurising parents who choose not to have their infants baptised. This kind of way forward is hinted at in the influential Faith and Order document *Baptism, Eucharist and Ministry*.[7] What many will be tempted to sniff at as merely another brand of ecumenical fudge has recently received cautious endorsement from George Beasley-Murray, announcing his conversion to the recognition of the legitimacy of infant baptism on the part of credobaptists.[8] It is not too difficult to envisage other possible perspectives on this route round, or perhaps through, the impasse over baptism. When larger challenges, such as the balance of continuity and discontinuity between old and new covenants, remain unresolved, provisional action of this kind may be all that is feasible—and may be justified not despite their remaining unresolved but because of it.

Let us approach the question from another angle: are we right to assume that Christ the King and Head of the church intended it to observe only one baptismal practice? Adherents of both positions have traditionally answered in the affirmative. The occasional administration of baptism to adult converts on their own profession of faith by paedobaptist churches does not conflict with this answer, and in no sense makes them dual-practice churches in terms of the ecumenical accommodation noted above—for it does not concede the propriety of not baptising children born within the church community.[9] But it reminds us that the two baptismal stances are not neatly balanced alternatives, wholly exclusive each of the other. While Baptists have

---

[6]See my Laing Lecture, 'One Baptism or Two? Reflections on the History of Christian Baptism', *Vox Evangelica* 18 (1988) 7-23 at 7-8.

[7]Faith and Order Paper 111 (Geneva: World Council of Churches, 1982) 4-5 ('Baptism' 12, with Commentary): 'The differences between infant and believers' baptism become less sharp when it is recognized that both forms of baptism embody God's own initiative in Christ and express a response of faith made within the believing community.'

[8]'The Problem of Infant Baptism: An Exercise in Possibilities', in *Festschrift Günter Wagner*, ed. Faculty of Baptist Theological Seminary, Rüschlikon (International Theological Studies: Contributions of Baptist Scholars 1; Berne: Peter Lang, 1994) 1-14.

hitherto refused to recognise paedobaptism as baptism, and hence
have baptised all candidates *de novo*, paedobaptist churches have usually accepted believers' baptism as authentic Christian baptism.

V. 'One Baptism'

The nub of the issue is this: how should we understand our baptismal
diversity in the light of the Pauline affirmation of 'one baptism'?

> There is one body and one Spirit, just as you were called to the one
> hope that belongs to your call, one Lord, one faith, one baptism, one
> God and Father of us all, who is above all and through all and in all
> (Eph. 4:4-6, RSV).

These verses merit considered attention. Of this list of unifying realities, which constitute the basis on which Paul may exhort the
Ephesians to maintain unity in practice, baptism is the most visible and
concrete.[10] 'One body' in the context probably has a reference wider
than the single community of the Christians at Ephesus. One might
speculate on some other occasion about the implications of the non-
inclusion of 'one supper of the Lord'.

---

[9]Some paedobaptist theologians, such as T.F. Torrance, would deny that such cases
represent 'believers' baptism'. Such an attitude is sustained by the biblically
wholly unwarrantable assumption that infant baptism is the theologically normative baptism. This was the implicit, and sometimes almost explicit, assumption of
the Church of Scotland's Special Commission on Baptism of 1953-62, whose volu-
minous reports are distilled in *The Biblical Doctrine of Baptism* (Edinburgh: St.
Andrew Press, 1958), and *The Doctrine of Baptism* (Edinburgh: St. Andrew Press,
1966); T.F. Torrance was convenor of the Commission. In the early church, the reality is almost the reverse. In the first extant text which comes near to depicting
infant baptism as a routine (rather than, say, clinically emergency) practice, Hip-
polytus' *Apostolic Tradition* early in the third century, the inclusion of very young
children is discernible solely in the instruction that parents or someone else from
the family should speak for those little ones who cannot answer for themselves.
The whole of the rest of the complex ceremony envisages responsibly participant
candidates.

[10]For a conclusive refutation of the hypothesis that 'one baptism' means Christ's
one baptism on behalf of all in his atoning incarnation, crucifixion and exaltation
(argued by, for example, J.A.T. Robinson, 'The One Baptism as a Category of New
Testament Soteriology', *SJT* 6 [1953] 257-74, reprinted in his *Twelve New Testament
Studies* [Studies in Biblical Theology 34; London: SCM, 1962] 158-75), see W.E.
Moore, 'One Baptism', *NTS* 10 (1963-4) 504-16. See also my study, 'The Meaning
and Reference of "One Baptism for the Remission of Sins" in the Niceno-Constan-
tinopolitan Creed', *Studia Patristica* XIX (1989) 281-5.

Notice what exalted company 'one baptism' keeps—the Trinity and the constitutive spiritual qualities of faith and hope. ('One love' is also absent!) Although the definition of 'one body' has not escaped entanglement with the Babel of divided churches, or perhaps better, an internally divided church, 'one baptism' remains the most contentious of these given unities. According to credobaptists, the common baptism to be shared in and acknowledged by all does not encompass paedobaptism. As we noted earlier, champions of a baptism for believers only have perhaps rarely faced up to the implication of their position, namely, that most Christians for most of church history have been unbaptised. One suspects that living with this conclusion has been made tolerable only by devaluing baptism altogether.

VI. A Single Theology of Baptism

Does this mean, then, that modern ecumenical rapprochement entails the recognition of two baptisms, since no church union appears to have involved the abandonment of one of the two versions of baptism? Not if each of the two patterns can be understood in terms of a single theology, the obvious elements of which would include: baptism's dominical status, its grounding in the once-for-all saving work of Christ, its incorporation of the baptised in the body of Christ through the Spirit, and its expression of a response of faith to the gospel of Christ's redemption as it is appropriated for the baptised. I hope that such a summary embodies sufficient common ground for this present discussion to continue. I commend to you Beasley-Murray's similar listing of those 'elements of faith...cherished alike by churches which practice infant baptism and those which practice believer's baptism only'.[11]

It is also worth noting at this point the more general considerations behind his re-thinking exercise.[12] Since there is no single theology of baptism accepted by all Baptists, Baptists cannot insist on a Baptist interpretation of believers' baptism before recognising its authenticity when administered in non-Baptist denominations. One thing this means, I take it (Beasley-Murray does not spell it out), is that the validity of baptism on profession of faith cannot be made conditional on the acceptance, by candidate, minister or congregation, that such profes-

---

[11]Op. cit., 8.
[12]Ibid., 6-7.

sion is essential for every administration of baptism. Similarly, he argues, the currency of obnoxious interpretations of paedobaptism does not exclude the possibility of another interpretation of it being found acceptable to credobaptists. He proceeds to find this, to his own measured satisfaction, along two lines of thought—a view of infant baptism which sees it as attesting the beginnings of the work of grace in the baptised, and a reconsideration of the relation of believers' children to Christ's salvation which appeals to 1 Corinthians 7:14.[13]

We need not become preoccupied with the specifics of this argument, since we are reflecting on baptism for the sake of illustration rather than definition. I will, however, add one point of substance. Since all paedobaptist churches also baptise some non-infants, who seek baptism on their own initiative and answer for themselves (*i.e.*, responsibly, in a literal sense), these churches cannot afford to incorporate in their theology of baptism any elements that are applicable only to babies. So the helpless and unresponsive passivity of babies should not be made theologically integral to baptism; still less should traces of Adamic perversity be discerned in a frightened baby's squawking and squealing at the font. Baptism administered to tiny babies may be an admirable testimony to 'the priority of grace over faith' (a quasi-liturgical phrase in some Church of Scotland usage), but if true of the baptismal experience at all, it is surely no less true of a believer's baptism. Of ourselves we do not believe, nor do we baptise ourselves, but that does not require that none comes to baptism unless carried in another's arms. An obvious point, perhaps, but a telling illustration of the tendency for infant baptism to become the theological, as well as the practical, norm.

What makes baptism so helpful an example in considering evangelical (and wider) diversity is its inescapably visible expression of our differences. Often the situation is the very reverse: we use the same words, we perform the same or closely similar actions, but freight them with a varying weight of meaning. In the case of the Lord's supper, we may well feel that the different nuances of the three Synoptic accounts of the Last Supper, together with 1 Corinthians 11 and perhaps John 6 also, justify some diversity in interpretations of the observance. But not all readings of the supper pass muster, nor can divergences from the

---

[13]*Ibid.*, 9. My paper on '1 Corinthians 7:14 in Fathers and Reformers' will be published by the Herzog August Bibliothek, Wolfenbüttel, in the papers of its March 1994 Arbeitsgespräch on 'Die Patristik in der Bibelexegese des 16. Jahrhunderts'.

common core of actions, such as the continued withholding of the cup from communicants in many Catholic churches.

Even when we confess 'one Spirit,...one Lord,...one God and Father of us all', the common formula will undoubtedly conceal significant variations of belief. Is he the 'one Spirit' of charismatic immediacy, bestowing gifts, inspiring prophetic utterance and empowering all God's people, or is the 'one Spirit' thirled more to the authoritative exposition of the written Word and the faithful's reverent attendance thereupon and obedience thereto? Although in this instance the differences soon become evident, the intercessory prayer and evangelistic preaching of the Westminster Calvinist and the Wesleyan Arminian may not be recognisably discordant, especially if they owe vastly more to Scripture than to Westminster or Wesley. Words are elusive quantities, as the fathers of Nicaea discovered when they resorted to *homoousios*, and as twentieth-century drafters or refiners of doctrinal bases have perhaps been too slow to acknowledge. Has a written confession ever kept a church from falling into heterodoxy?

The attractiveness of recent attempts to bridge 'the waters that divide' is that they penetrate behind divergent practice and dare to claim that both administrations of baptism can be embraced within one theological framework with little remainder. The one baptises believers' babies and nurtures them within the community of faith until they profess the faith responsibly for themselves. The other dedicates or gives thank for believers' babies and nurtures them within the community of faith until in baptism they respond to the gospel in their own profession. For both categories of baptismal subjects the prospective perspective is critical, both from the early acknowledgement of a child as God's gift to be reared in and to faith, and from the later time of responsible decision, which is not so much an arrival as a fresh point of departure.

In this example of evangelical diversity, then, can we continue to do different things while believing, not precisely the same, at least broadly compatible things about them, within a bipolar framework of Christian nurture that binds together two significant moments in spiritual development? This proposal is arguably not a whit inferior to the dominant mode in which we do or say the same thing while believing different things as we do so.

VII. Dangerous Diversity

Some will judge that the diversity of our baptismal observances is well toward the soft end on a scale of intractability. I would demur (but not fervently) if only because of my conviction that our apparently irreconcilable disagreement has ministered to a general depreciation of baptism, as explained earlier. The deepening paganisation of society may assist the recovery of the New Testament's weighting of baptism. I would not for a moment deny that immensely graver challenges threaten to open up such deep chasms of diversity that institutional unity will experience insupportable strains. Is Jesus Christ the only Saviour of sinful humanity, or is it conceivable that the 'one God and Father of us all' of Ephesians 4 will be sundered from the 'one Lord', 'one Spirit, one faith, one hope' of Ephesians 4, let alone from its 'one body, one baptism'? Is the homosexual life-style as acceptable to God as the heterosexual, within precisely the same norms? Recent argumentation in favour of this enormous paradigm shift has sought to justify it in terms of the Trinity's differentiation-in-unity, and to base the rejection of discrimination against homosexuality on acceptance of diversity, not on our common humanity, in Adam and in Christ.[14]

These two pressure points, so vastly disparate in themselves, are nevertheless alike reinforced by the powerful all-inclusiveness abroad in the secular liberal establishment, which magnifies diversity, whether religious, cultural or sexual. Christian liberalism, it seems, lacks the courageous clarity to resist joining the celebration, and Evangelicalism is not immune to the temptations that afflict a minority perceived as intolerant, exclusive and mean-minded. We will need to be alert to the forces of the contemporary intellectual glorification of diversity combining with the thrust of current hermeneutics to shatter Scripture into a thousand pieces. In this context, our evangelical diversities are reduced to their proper proportions, although we dare not suppose that they are invulnerable to the distortions and exaggerations of the spirit of the age. Freedom of self-expression, individuality and non-conformity are unquestioned virtues; adherence to external norms, regard for the traditional and uniformity enjoy little esteem.

It behoves us, therefore, to be respectful of biblical limits to diversity. The sequence of magnificent unities set forth in Ephesians 4 could

---

[14]*Cf.* P.B. Jung and R.F. Smith, *Heterosexism. An Ethical Challenge* (Albany, NY: State University of New York Press, 1993) 187-8; M. Williams, 'Quest for an Evangelical Ethics', *Anvil* 11 (1994) 27-8.

bear extended reflection, not least in the light of Paul's response to the intolerable diversity of the Christians at Corinth. Their allegiance to human leaders, or even in a partisan sense to Christ himself, was incompatible with their 'one baptism' (whether in the name of Christ or of the Trinity), itself grounded in the 'one crucifixion' of Christ for all (1 Cor. 1:12-13). This approach to managing, and curbing, diversity is not altogether different from a Reformation perspective that insists on *solus Christus* and *sola fide* and *sola gratia*, as well as *sola Scriptura*. But instead of highlighting the 'sole' which excludes all others, so that, for example, salvation can be received solely by faith trusting in God's gratuitous mercy, and not by meritorious performance or heredity or nationality, Ephesians 4 directs us to the unifying realities in which our diversities may find common ground, as I have sought to do with baptism.

VIII. Discerning Our Unity

At stake in the phenomenon of evangelical diversity in the face of the perspicuity of the one Scripture is not so much the need to discriminate between the acceptable and the unacceptable (where, in Reformation terms, the fourfold *solus/a* comes into play), as the ability to discern our unity, rooted in commitment to the one Word of God written, behind and through our differences. A certain obligation weighs with me to take seriously the divergent view of a brother or sister who shares my professed fidelity to the scriptural revelation. Such an attitude is mandated by several considerations, ranging from our common fallibility 'in Adam', the virtue of docility, the diversity of the mode of the biblical witness, our lack (in God's wise providence) of an authoritative inspired interpretation of Scripture, the ecclesial setting of the unfolding of its meaning for God's people, and the hermeneutical significance of the entirely trustworthy truthfulness of Scripture. James Packer has somewhere drawn helpful attention to this last point. Just as the conviction that marriage is ordained of God for lifelong permanence fires the tenacity to work through, and even live with, discord and distress in one's marriage, so a belief in Scripture's infallibility never lets us off the hook of grappling not only with the problematic phenomenon of the text but also with our puzzling failures to agree on what it teaches. The dynamic sense of 'infallible'—incapable of failing us, sure not to deceive, bound to lead us aright—commits us to an unceasing endeavour to reach a common mind on Scripture's teaching.

An interesting comparison may be drawn between the opening verses of Hebrews and the first chapter of the Westminster Confession, partly quoted above. Hebrews contrasts the many and various ways of God's earlier speech through the prophets with his having now spoken by his Son. The exalted presentation of this one Son that follows in the first two chapters shows the sovereign character of this revelation 'in the last days'. The Confession, on the other hand, applies part of Hebrews 1:1 ('at sundry times, and in divers manners') to the whole span of God's pre-scriptural revelation (making no distinction between the prophets and the divine Son), and goes on to declare 'those former ways of God's revealing his will unto his people being now ceased', not since Christ the Son has come but since God has committed his whole revelation to writing. An intriguing instance of diversity of theological framework! What the Confession misses, by its creative use of Hebrews, is the central finality of Christ in God's revelation, but what neither of them tells us is that, though distributed diversity of divine utterance is a thing of the past (as both in different ways affirm), we have no unitary access to God's definitive Word, whether the focus is on his Son or his Scripture.

If we may be allowed to combine apostolic Scripture and latter-day confession, together they remind us of what our specialised concentrations on separate parts or strands or layers of the Bible frequently forget. ('I am a Paul man; don't ask me about Hebrews'; 'my field is Acts; ask someone else about John'; 'I'm for Q; let others rally round Mark.') Well, Christ is not divided, though we have many presentations of Christ. But though they be many, they together constitute one Word of God, like the many members of the one body of Christ. It is our insistent task ever to be striving to apprehend the one Christ in the one Scripture. This will mean not only, in terms of Article 20 of the Church of England, that the Church (nota bene!) may not 'so expound one place of Scripture that it be repugnant to another', but that we perpetually ask ourselves and our fellow-labourers whether our subtly differentiated expositions are true to the unities of Ephesians 4. Are our varying ecclesiologies recognisably expressive of 'one body', our Christologies of 'one Lord', our pneumatologies and charismatologies of 'one Spirit'? Criteria of consistency, complementarity, compatibility and the like will be important, but it will also be necessary to give further thought to the nature of the unity of faith that is intended to bind us together.

I assume that this unity is not to be conceived of in mathematical terms, as though different evangelical convictions about, say, women's ministry, were fractions of the truth which when added together made up a complete whole. Is the unity found along developmental lines, with one interpretation to some measure subsuming or capping another, and to that extent superseding it? Or is it best regarded as the unity of different perspectives on a single reality? None will be perfect or comprehensive, but their partiality will not be such that they can be fitted together like the discrete segments of a pie-chart. They will be complementary to each other not because there is no overlapping between them but because they all merit recognition as valid (but never impeccable or exhaustive) apprehensions of the 'one body' or the 'one baptism', *etc.*

My own experience, and perhaps yours also, would bear out the point at issue here. I operate with a certain body of functional theology which has (so I dare to believe) a leading influence on my routine thoughts and decisions. It has its strengths and weaknesses, its one-sided pre-occupations and its surprising silences and lacunae (*e.g.*, its blissful innocence of the millennial varieties of Evangelicalism—which might otherwise have served as a searching test-bed for this consideration of evangelical diversity). But when I hear or read others expounding a theme or an emphasis that have no place in my working theology, more often than not I instinctively recognise their truthfulness and importance. Yet rarely do such experiences lead to my rejigging my functional theology to incorporate what I have neglected or never known of. Some marginal adjustment may occur, but for the most part I am happy to let others be the guardians of, say, the eucharistic dimension of the church's being or the significance of the inclusion or exclusion of *Filioque*.

Not even the pope, with all his advisers and consultants, can hold the whole corpus of theology in his mind. As individuals we are diverse, and the communities and communions we comprise are diverse. Important ingredients of our diversity are our limitations as human beings—of time and space, of economic status, of intellect and industry, *etc.*—and as fallen creatures. A certain modesty is appropriate on these and other counts, especially when those with whom we do not see eye-to-eye share the same allegiance to Scripture.

IX. Charismatic and Reformed: some Concluding Reflections

Let me finally attempt to apply some of these general reflections to an influential divide in recent British Evangelicalism which is often located between Reformed and charismatic (where 'Reformed' has, I think, a broader reference than the tradition issuing from the Swiss-Genevan Reformation). It is in reality not so easily mapped. It is surely in good part cultural: classical and pop, or trad and mod, or broadsheet and tabloid. But then again it parallels in important respects the magisterial-radical breach in the sixteenth-century Reformation. In some cases it may embody different psychologies: cerebral and emotional, rational and affective, even spiritual and embodied—for it is one of the paradoxes of this divide that those who make most of the Holy Spirit insist most on visible, even physical evidences of his working.

How does this manifestation of diversity stand up to the scrutiny of Ephesians 4:4-6 or the Reformation's fourfold *solus/a*? Early critiques like that of F.D. Bruner[15] discerned in the stress laid on Spirit-baptism a Galatian-type threat to *sola gratia*, and we might add to 'one baptism'. More recently, claims for revelations and prophecies can appear to infringe on *sola Scriptura*. But it is difficult to conclude that responsible charismatic varieties of the Christian faith fall foul of Ephesians 4. The restriction of supernatural phenomena to the apostolic era alone itself seems a post-biblical or extra-biblical straitjacket.

The last paragraphs have scarcely scratched the surface, but it is no part of my purpose to enter into the substance of this debate. While I do not minimise the detrimental effects of this manifestation of diversity, and would myself regard the charismatic metamorphosis of considerable tracts of English Evangelicalism as more bane than blessing, the divide contains within itself, on my reading, significant intrusions of culture, tradition, temperament and taste. As an instance of evangelical diversity I do not view it as anywhere near as threatening to our common confession of Scripture as the baptismal breach. It will need to survive, as the baptismal split has done, centuries of biblical and theological scrutiny before its challenge looms equally large. Long before then it will surely in part have proved amenable to the

---

[15] *A Theology of the Holy Spirit. The Pentecostal Experience and the New Testament Witness* (Grand Rapids: Eerdmans, 1970).

wisdom we may now be learning as we seek to bridge 'the waters that divide'.[16]

---

[16]A useful starter is R.S. Fyall's booklet *Charismatic and Reformed* (Edinburgh: Rutherford House, 1992).

CHAPTER 12

Scripture and Experience

Thomas A. Noble

Summary

Twentieth-century Evangelicals have rightly emphasised the authority of Scripture, but the evangelical tradition equally affirms the validity and necessity of Christian experience. This affirmation may be traced back through the eighteenth-century Evangelical Revival and the Puritans to the Reformers. This experiential knowledge of God which 'takes root in the heart' (Calvin) is fully rational. The Evangelical via media *therefore embraces both objective and subjective aspects of experiential knowledge of God. God is objectively revealed in His Word, but known by the human subject only through the presence and work of His Spirit.*

I. Introduction

The twentieth-century evangelical emphasis on the authority of Scripture has sometimes been accompanied by a somewhat negative stance towards 'experience'. Evangelical Christians held the conviction that Scripture was the final authority as God's revelation, and there was an accompanying tendency to associate any emphasis on 'experience' with theological liberalism.

Perhaps one of the most widely influential books prompting this negative stance was J.I. Packer's evangelical manifesto, published by IVF (as it then was) in 1958: *'Fundamentalism' and the Word of God*. James Packer wrote the book in reply to widespread criticism of 'fundamentalism' provoked by Billy Graham's evangelistic crusades, the growth of evangelical groups in schools and universities and the increase of evangelical candidates for the ministry. The most sustained criticism had appeared the previous year in Gabriel Hebert's book, *Fundamentalism and the Church of God*.[1]

It frequently goes unnoticed that Packer's title, unlike Hebert's, places 'fundamentalism' in inverted commas. He had no love for the word (which was in any case of American coinage!) and laid no claim to it, but he recognised that what was often being attacked under that label was the evangelical tradition.

The core of Packer's argument was that the problem of authority, 'the most important question the Church ever faces', was that of finding the right criterion of truth. There were three claimants, Holy Scripture, church tradition and Christian reason, and these were adopted respectively by Evangelicals, traditionalists and 'subjectivists'. The subjectivist position, however, was something of a chameleon, appearing sometimes as rationalism (building on 'Christian reason') but sometimes as mysticism. Liberalism was a form of subjectivism combining both, taking its rationalism from Ritschl and its mysticism from Schleiermacher, but the essence of the liberal or subjectivist position was that the final authority for faith and life was the reason, conscience or 'religious sentiment' of the individual.[2] Liberals 'accepted the viewpoint of the Romantic philosophy of religion set out by Schleiermacher—namely that the real subject-matter of theology is not divinely revealed truths, but human religious experience'.[3]

---

[1]London: SCM, 1957.
[2]Packer, *Fundamentalism*, 50.
[3]*Ibid.*, 148.

Rupert Davies, writing ten years later, rose to the defence of what he identified as Schleiermacher's position, that the basis of faith lay in 'experience'. Davies' analysis was remarkably similar:

> Granted that many, or most, or perhaps all of the alleged truths of religion are not demonstrable by reason… is there any person or group of persons, any institution or document, or what-you-will, on whose word we may legitimately accept them and legitimately expect others to do the same?[4]

This was the problem which Schleiermacher had identified. The main contenders to authority (reason having been ruled out) were Scripture, tradition and experience,[5] and Schleiermacher had propounded a solution: that authority lay in 'inward feeling', which Davies interpreted as experience. Davies concurred in the judgement of David Jenkins that Schleiermacher as an apologist was the direct precursor of 'the existentialist theologians, such as Tillich and Bultmann, who put more stress on a man's awareness of God and its results for him than on the God of whom man is aware'.[6]

It was no doubt the reaction against existentialism in the 1950s and 1960s which strengthened this evangelical tendency to react against 'experience'. In his article on 'The Authority of Scripture' in *The New Bible Commentary*, G.W. Bromiley wrote:

> The challenge of liberal humanism consists again in individualistic subjectivism which it opposes to the objectivism of the orthodox doctrine of the Word of God. Outward authority is cast off, and it is replaced by the inward authority of the individual thought or experience.[7]

Francis Schaeffer too in his popular apologetics attacked 'upper storey experiences'.[8] 'Experience' was associated with Liberalism, existentialism and subjectivism.

Perhaps the earliest of these mid-century evangelical attacks on subjectivism was an unpublished one made by Dr. D. Martyn Lloyd-Jones at the private conference arranged by the IVF at Kingham Hill School in Oxfordshire in July, 1941, a conference which led to the founding of Tyndale House and the Tyndale Fellowship. There Lloyd-

---

[4]*Religious Authority in an Age of Doubt* (London: Epworth, 1968) 15.
[5]*Ibid.*, 36 and 19.
[6]*Ibid.*, 54.
[7]*The New Bible Commentary* (London: IVF, 1953) 21.
[8]Escape from Reason (London: IVF, 1968) 53.

Jones apparently ruffled some feathers by attacking what he identified as subjectivism in Evangelicalism during the preceding fifty years. According to his analysis, the current weakness in biblical theology among Evangelicals was that 'experience and subjectivity (in various forms) had been substituted in the pulpit for truly effective exposition of Scripture'.[9]

This analysis of Martyn Lloyd-Jones should alert us, however, to ask just exactly what the character of the evangelical tradition had been. Was an emphasis on experience a recent aberration in Evangelicalism, evident only in the late nineteenth and early twentieth centuries? And was an emphasis on experience a sign of subjectivism?

II. The Evangelical Revival: *Herzensreligion*

David Bebbington, in his most helpful history, *Evangelicalism in Britain*, covering the years from the 1730s to the 1980s, identifies four characteristics of evangelical religion:

> Conversionism, the belief that lives need to be changed; activism, the expression of the gospel in effort; biblicism, a particular regard for the Bible; and what may be called crucicentrism, a stress on the sacrifice of Christ on the cross.[10]

These he identifies as the most constant characteristics of Evangelicalism in Britain over these two hundred and fifty years. The third of these traditional evangelical emphases, that on biblical authority, has been particularly to the fore in the twentieth century in the wake of the rise of biblical criticism and the popularity of so-called scientific humanism. But the first, conversionism, has at times in the past been more prominent, and it is in fact wider than Bebbington's rather clumsy term suggests. For Evangelicals have traditionally emphasized not only the initial moment of conversion, but the whole life of faith, the whole of Christian experience.

The centrality of this emphasis is evident if we trace the heritage back to the leading figures of the eighteenth-century Evangelical revival. What is immediately apparent, and what has sometimes been

---

[9]Douglas Johnson, 'The Origin and History of Tyndale House', unpublished paper. On the conference see Geraint Fielder, *Lord of The Years* (Leicester: IVP, 1988) 83ff.
[10](London: Unwin Hyman, 1989) 3.

almost forgotten in more recent times, is their tremendous debt to German Pietism and its emphasis on *Herzensreligion*, the religion of the heart. In August Hermann Francke we find this emphasis not on a datable conversion so much as on Christian experience in the wider sense:

> We do not ask, 'Are you converted? When were you converted?' But we ask, 'What does Christ mean to you? What have you experienced personally with God? Is Christ necessary to you and your daily life?'[11]

Here what is sometimes forgotten by Evangelicals today is that Pietism and the eighteenth-century Evangelical revival in Britain and her American colonies was not so much a reaction against 'liberalism' (if the deism of that day may be anachronistically described as such) as it was a reaction against dead orthodoxy. It is in that context that we must understand John Wesley's comment:

> A man may be orthodox in every point... He may be almost as orthodox as the devil... and may all the while be as great a stranger as he to the religion of the heart.[12]

Faith therefore was not mere *assensus* but *fiducia*.

> It is not barely a speculative, rational thing, a cold lifeless assent, a train of ideas in the head; but also a disposition of the heart.[13]

Genuine Christianity was *Herzensreligion*. It was a matter of 'the heart strangely warmed,' of assurance ('an assurance was given me that he had taken away my sins, even mine...').[14] It was a matter of the witness of the Spirit, in short, of Christian experience.

Thus to the standard Anglican triad of Scripture, tradition and reason,[15] Wesley added experience. Albert Outler described this as 'the Wesleyan Quadrilateral', a term he was later to regret, since it seemed to convey to some the idea of four equal factors in the shaping of doctrine. He went so far as to claim:

---

[11]*Cf.* Donald W. Dayton and Robert K. Johnston, *The Variety of American Evangelicalism* (Knoxville: University of Tennessee Press, 1991) 178.

[12]John Wesley, *Works*, Vol. I (ed. Albert C. Outler; Nashville: Abingdon, 1984) 220: Sermon 7, 'The Way to the Kingdom', I, 6.

[13]*Ibid.*, 120: Sermon 1, 'Salvation by Faith', I, 4.

[14]John Wesley, *Works*, Vol. XVIII (ed. W. Reginald Ward and Richard P. Heitzenrater; Nashville: Abingdon, 1988) 250.

[15]*Cf.* R. Bauckham and B. Drewery (eds.), *Scripture, Tradition and Reason* (Edinburgh: T.&T. Clark, 1988).

Thus we can see in Wesley a distinctive theological method, with Scripture as its pre-eminent norm but interfaced with tradition, reason and Christian experience as dynamic and interactive aids in the interpretation of the Word of God in Scripture.[16]

Whether Wesley's theological method was distinctive in the interplay of these four factors may be debated, but it is evident that his emphasis on *Herzensreligion* or Christian experience was not unique to him, nor to the Arminian wing of Evangelicalism, but was equally shared by his Calvinist brethren. Whitefield, preaching on 'Walking with God,' could say that when we sit daily with Mary at Jesus' feet, by faith hearing his words,

We shall then *by happy experience* find that they are spirit and life, meat indeed and drink indeed, to our souls.[17]

In his account of his own conversion he wrote:

I now resolved to read only such as entered into the heart of religion and which led me directly into *an experimental knowledge* of Jesus Christ and him crucified.[18]

Most notably of course, Jonathan Edwards wrote in his *Treatise Concerning Religious Affections* in 1746:

If we be not in good earnest in religion, and our wills and inclinations be not strongly exercised, we are nothing. The things of religion are so great, that there can be no suitableness in the exercises of our hearts, to their nature and importance, unless they be lively and powerful... True religion is evermore a powerful thing; and the power of it appears, in the first place, in its exercises in the heart, its principal and original seat.[19]

Here again is the same motif: true religion is *Herzensreligion*. It is Christian experience. Robert Boyle Smith, in a recent comparison of Wesley and Edwards, concluded this:

---

[16]Albert C. Outler, 'The Wesleyan Quadrilateral—in John Wesley', *WTJ* 20 (1985) 7-18. *Cf.* also Albert C. Outler, *John Wesley's Sermons: An Introduction* (Nashville: Abingdon, 1991) 64ff.
[17]*Select Sermons of George Whitefield* (Edinburgh: Banner of Truth Trust, 1958) 170 (italics added).
[18]Timothy L. Smith, *Whitefield and Wesley on the New Birth* (Grand Rapids: Francis Asbury Press, 1986) 44 (italics added).
[19]Jonathan Edwards, *Works*, Vol. I (Edinburgh: Banner of Truth Trust, 1974) 238.

While the technical theologies of the two men differ greatly, they share very similar understandings of religious experience, and each wants to lead his respective audience into that experience.[20]

III. Puritans and Reformers on Experience

This characteristic emphasis on experience was not an invention of the eighteenth century, however. David Bebbington contends that, despite much continuity with earlier Protestant traditions, Evangelicalism was a new phenomenon of the eighteenth century. But while the discontinuities he cites as the basis for this judgement may be of some significance to the historian, they are not of theological significance.[21] The evangelical revival could not have been a *revival* at all unless it revived something which had previously existed. While Evangelicalism in every age no doubt has new features, the continuities are in fact much more significant. In the seventeenth century, it is undoubtedly the Puritans who were the Evangelicals of the day (although the label may not be commonly applied to them), simply because their origins as a movement lay in the attempt to reform and purify the church according to the best Reformed models. It was the Reformation which was their model, and it was for the Reformers themselves with their emphasis on the evangel that the word 'Evangelical' was first coined.

It is relevant to note briefly therefore how insistent the seventeenth-century Puritans were on religious experience. J.I. Packer in his recent study of the Puritans emphasizes that Puritanism was a movement of revival.[22] 'Personal revival was the central theme of Puritan devotional literature.' He quotes John Downame's *A Guide to Godliness*, where in the introduction to this homiletic treatise, Downame writes that the sermons are that 'part of Divinity... which consisteth more in experience and practice than in theory and application'.[23] Sinclair Ferguson attributes to John Owen the axiom that the Christian life is one of 'spiritual sense and experience'.[24]

---

[20]R.B. Smith, 'John Wesley and Jonathan Edwards on Religious Experience: A Comparative Analysis', *WTJ* 25 (1990) 130-46.
[21]*Evangelicalism*, 1, 35ff.
[22]J.I. Packer, *Among God's Giants* (Eastbourne: Kingsway, 1991) 41ff.
[23]*Ibid.*, 47.
[24]Sinclair B. Ferguson, *John Owen on the Christian Life* (Edinburgh: Banner of Truth Trust, 1987) 78, referring to Owen's *Works*, Vol. II, 36.

But for a definitive presentation of evangelical faith, we go further back to the Reformers themselves. James Atkinson maintains in
his Didsbury Lectures that the beginnings of the Reformation were
experiential, not doctrinal:[25]

> To apprehend Luther's experience of faith, to understand Luther's
> religious experience, is to know in essence the theology of the
> Reformation.[26]

He quotes the Reformer:

> When I had realised this I felt myself absolutely born again. The gates
> of paradise had been flung open and I had entered. There and then the
> whole of Scripture took on another look to me.[27]

Similarly the English Reformer, William Tyndale, writes of Christian
experience. Having written in his *Pathway into the Holy Scripture* of the
faith that justifies, he adds:

> Of which things the belief of our popish (or of their) father, whom they
> so magnify for his strong faith, hath none experience at all.[28]

Not only Luther and Tyndale but Calvin also writes of Christian experience. In reference to God's revelation of his attributes in Exodus 34:
6f., Calvin writes:

> Thereupon his powers are mentioned, by which he is shown to us not
> as he is in himself, but as he is toward us; so that this recognition of
> him consists more in living experience than in vain and high-flown
> speculation.[29]

Clearly too this is for Calvin a matter of the affections and disposition
of the heart.

> Whoever is moderately well versed in Scripture will understand by
> himself, without the admonition of another, that when we have to
> deal with God nothing is achieved unless we begin from the inner dis-
> position of the heart.[30]

---

[25]*Martin Luther: Prophet to the Church Catholic* (Exeter/Grand Rapids: Paternoster/
Eerdmans, 1983) 84.
[26]*Ibid.*, 88.
[27]*Ibid.*, 83.
[28]William Tyndale, *Doctrinal Treatises* (Parker Society; Cambridge: CUP, 1848) 13.
[29]*Institutes*, 1:10: 2.
[30]3:3:16.

He takes it for granted in writing about prayer, that

> no one can well perceive the power of faith unless he feels it by experience in his heart.[31]

Judith Rossall, in her recent Durham thesis, sees the Augustinian anthropology affecting Calvin's doctrine here in addition to the faculty psychology of the Scholastics.[32] For Augustine, 'will', 'love', 'soul' and 'heart' could be used virtually as synonyms, and the fundamental disposition of the heart or will, its ultimate orientation, either towards God in love, or away from him in love of the creature or self-love, determined the individual's status before God. Therefore, despite Calvin's use of scholastic intellectualism (the view that the intellect controlled the will) to describe humanity before the Fall, and despite his consequent view that, because the Fall had radically vitiated the whole human nature, the mind also needed to be converted, he nevertheless saw the focus of conversion in the affections of the heart.

He expresses this in his sermon on Ephesians 3:14-19:

> It is not enough then to have some vague knowledge of Christ, or to engage in airy speculations, as they say, and to be able to talk a lot about him, but he must have his seat in our hearts within, so that we are unfeignedly joined to him, and with true affection. That is the way for us to be made partakers of God's Spirit.[33]

But Rossall's study makes clear why this emphasis on the heart and the affections and on experience in Calvin does not topple over into subjectivism. Here is the key which explains why experience is an integral part of evangelical faith, but in a way quite different to the later tradition of subjectivism stemming from Schleiermacher.

---

[31] 3:20:12.

[32] 'God's Activity and the Believer's Experience in the Theology of John Calvin' (Ph.D., Durham, 1991), cited by permission of the Author. The next section of this chapter, 'Calvin on Experience as Fully Rational', is largely dependent on this significant thesis.

[33] John Calvin, *Sermons on Ephesians* (Edinburgh: Banner, 1973) 291f. *Cf.* also *Comm. I John* on 1 Jn. 2:3 and *Comm. Harmony of the Gospels* on Mt. 13:19.

IV. Calvin on Experience as Fully Rational

According to Rossall, when the Renaissance humanist concern with experience in the world as opposed to the abstract knowledge of the scholastics is seen as the background to Calvin's epistemology, it may be readily understood why experience is more central to Calvin's theology than might at first appear. For while, since Kant, experience has been treated as private and subjective, Calvin was a realist whose focus of interest lay not in the subjective appropriation of experience, but in the objective reality of that which was experienced. The background to Calvin's realism is to be seen, according to Rossall, in the thought of William of Occam, and particularly in his distinction between *notitia intuitiva*, direct knowledge of an object which is actually present, and *notitia abstractiva* in which the knowledge is not apprehended directly, but is known only in abstraction from its existence in a second-hand knowledge conveyed through language and concepts. This distinction between *intuitive* first-hand knowledge of direct acquaintance and *abstractive* second-hand knowledge by repute can be traced further back to Duns Scotus.[34]

Calvin's teaching can be distinguished from Occam's however in that he believes that we have direct intuitive knowledge of God as a result of encountering him in his self-revelation. We are not to 'rack our brains about God' with long and toilsome proofs of his existence. Rather:

> We are called to a knowledge of God; not that knowledge which content with empty speculation, merely flits in the brain, but that which will be sound and fruitful if we duly perceive it, and if it takes root in the heart. For the Lord manifests himself by his powers, the force of which we feel within ourselves and the benefits of which we enjoy. We must therefore be much more profoundly affected by this knowledge than if we were to imagine a God of whom no perception came through to us. Consequently, we know the most perfect way of seeking God, and the most suitable order, is not for us to attempt with bold curiosity to penetrate to the investigation of his essence... but for us to contemplate him in his works whereby he renders himself near and familiar to us, and in some manner communicates himself.[35]

---

[34]*Cf.* T.F. Torrance, 'Intuitive and Abstractive Knowledge from Duns Scotus to John Calvin', *De doctrina Ioannis Duns Scoti. Acta tertii Congressus Scotistici Internationalis. Studia Scholastico-Scotistica*, 5 (Rome: Societas Internationalis Scotistica, 1968), 291-305.

[35]1:5:9.

This passage quoted at length well illustrates the contention that for Calvin, 'experience' does not refer to isolated, subjective, more-or-less emotional events internal to the subject, but holistically to 'the arena of human life in which events occur which properly interpreted show that man deals with God in everything'.[36] God acts within the world in such a providential way in all the circumstances of our lives, accommodating himself to us, so that we may perceive his actions and encounter him in direct intuitive knowledge. So the believer recognizes the Creator from the 'marks of his glory' engraved upon all his works. The appropriate response is thanksgiving, piety and love for God.[37]

But the one God reveals himself not only as Creator but also as Redeemer, and each aspect of this *duplex cognitio* complements and presupposes the other.[38] This knowledge of God in creation only has a secondary role since in Christ, the believer encounters not simply the powers of God but his very presence.

> Hence all thinking of God without Christ is a vast abyss which immediately swallows up all our thoughts... We cannot believe in God except through Christ in whom God in a manner makes himself little in order to accommodate himself to our comprehension, and it is Christ alone who can make our consciences at peace so that we may dare to come with confidence to God.[39]

But if we experience God in Christ, that can only be an experience of God in his Word. Calvin integrates 'Word of God' as applied to Christ and 'Word of God' as applied to Scripture as fully as possible. Thus 'Scripture is vital to the experience of Christ, for only by a right understanding of Christ, perceived from the Scriptures, is it possible to find communion with him.'[40]

> This then is the true knowledge of Christ, if we receive him as he is offered by the Father, namely clothed with his gospel.[41]

---

[36]Charles Partee, 'Calvin and Experience', *SJT* 26 (1973) 169-81. *Cf.* also Charles Partee, *Calvin and Classical Philosophy* (Leiden: Brill, 1977).
[37]*Cf. Institutes*, 1:2:1; 1:5:9; 1:10:2.
[38]See the discussion of this in T.A. Noble, 'Our Knowledge of God according to John Calvin', *EQ* 54 (1982) 2-13, reprinted in *Articles on Calvin and Calvinism*, Vol. VII (ed. Richard C. Gamble; Hamden, CT: Garland, 1993).
[39]2:6:4.
[40]Rossall, 'God's Activity', 97.
[41]3:2:6.

To reject the gospel embodied in Scripture is to reject Christ himself, for Christ has no commerce with us, nor we with him, apart from Scripture.[42]

It is therefore evident, that since *a priori* the Word of God which is Scripture and the Word of God which is Christ cannot be separated, we cannot know Christ apart from Scripture. Consequently, our experience of God in Christ is rational through and through. It is rational first in that it is direct first-hand *notitia intuitiva*, and that intuitive knowledge of all real objects of experience is not only rational but the basis of all rational knowledge. It is not merely second-hand conceptual knowledge about Christ we gain—doctrines, truths, statements, propositions—but direct experiential knowledge of the living Christ himself present to us in the power of his Spirit. This intuitive knowledge is as fully rational as abstract conceptual knowledge.

But secondly and equally, this knowledge is fully rational in that it is conceptual from the beginning. It is not that the intuitive direct knowledge of Christ comes to us in a wordless, non-verbal, raw experience which may then be put into an arbitrary form of words either of our own choosing or that of the apostle or prophet. But it is rather that the incarnate and risen Word only comes to us clothed in the verbal Word of gospel and Scripture. As the self-revelation of the Incarnate Word to the apostles is inseparable from his spoken words, so his self-revelation to us in the Spirit is inseparable not only from his own spoken words but from the words of the apostles and prophets. For Calvin therefore, reason does not have a secondary role in experience, that of subsequent interpretation and explanation.[43] The experience itself is inherently verbal and conceptual, for Christ only comes to us 'clothed in his gospel'. The conceptual Word of Scripture is inseparable from the living Word, Christ, and the living Word is inseparable from God.

> Therefore, as all revelations from heaven are duly designated by the title of the Word of God, so the highest place must be assigned to that substantial Word, the source of all inspiration, which, as being liable to no variation, remains for ever one and the same with God, and is God.[44]

---

[42]*Comm. Gospel of John* on Jn. 12:48; *Comm. Harmony of the Gospels* on Lk. 11:27.
[43]See Rossall, 'God's Activity', 122.
[44]1:13:7 (Beveridge's translation).

In summary, in Calvin's thought the emphasis on experience is not subjectivist, because the accent falls not on our experience of God, but on the God whom we experience. There is no scholastic divorce between faith and experience on the one hand and knowledge and reason on the other. There is no divorce between irrational experience and rational knowledge, for rational knowledge is not only knowledge of the abstract, the conceptual, the doctrinal, the propositional. Intuitive direct knowledge of the real (and God is supremely real!) is equally rational. Such knowledge is therefore inherently experiential. But equally, this experiential, relational knowledge of the real God, a knowledge which not only 'flits in the brain' but 'takes root in the heart', is conceptual through and through. It comes to us through the irreducibly verbal witness of the apostles and prophets embodied for us in Holy Scripture.

V. The Evangelical *Via Media*

A return journey must be undertaken from the teaching of the evangelical fathers of the Reformation back to the twentieth century. This allows us to look more analytically at the Anglo-Saxon evangelical tradition in the light of Calvin. H.D. McDonald in his comprehensive and thorough study, *Theories of Revelation*,[45] opines that two broadly opposing doctrines of revelation appeared in England between 1700 and 1860: the subjectivist and the objectivist. Evangelicals are to be identified with neither.

McDonald traces the subjectivist tradition in England from the influence of Schleiermacher through Coleridge and F.D. Maurice, but also back before Schleiermacher to the early Quakers, Barclay, Fox and Penn, with their view of revelation as the indwelling light. Broadly, this wing stressed the immanence of God, had a tendency towards pantheism and spoke of revelation primarily in terms of the Spirit. But McDonald distinguishes the Evangelicals not only from this subjectivist tendency, but also, unlike Packer in *'Fundamentalism' and the Word of God*, from those he identifies as the 'objectivists.' On this wing he places the 'orthodox', quoting Bishop Butler, Samuel Clarke, William

---

[45]Published in two parts as *Ideas of Revelation* (London: Macmillan, 1959), covering 1700 to 1860, and *Theories of Revelation* (London: Allen & Unwin, 1963), covering 1860 to 1960, and in a one-volume edition, *Theories of Revelation* (Grand Rapids: Baker, 1979).

Law and others. These gave exclusive stress to the objective aspect of revelation. Revealed religion was conceived of as merely informational and conceptual, either adding a few ideas to natural religion, or as a body of disclosed truths to which assent had to be given. Broadly, this wing stressed the transcendence of God, had a tendency towards deism (sharing its rationalism although opposing it), and saw revelation primarily in terms of the Word.

By seeing the Evangelicals as distinct from both subjectivists and objectivists, McDonald has given us a fuller and more accurate analysis than Packer was able to do in his much briefer and more popular manifesto. The evangelical tradition of the eighteenth century achieved a balance by doing justice to both the objective and subjective aspects of revelation, seeing revelation in terms of both Word and Spirit. The Wesleyan wing leaned slightly more towards the subjective and McDonald characterises Wesley's doctrine of revelation as 'revelation by the Spirit through the Word'. The mildly Calvinist tradition of Charles Simeon leaned more towards the objective, a position characterised by McDonald as 'revelation in the Word through the Spirit'. But both saw Scripture as objectively the Word of God, and both saw that faith and knowledge of God was not simply a matter of accepting information. It was a living faith in the God of Scripture (and thus necessarily in Scripture too) made possible by subjective enlightenment by the Spirit.

The Evangelicals of the eighteenth century may therefore be regarded as truly the heirs of Calvin and the other evangelical fathers of the Reformation. Their view of revelation as simultaneously objective and subjective agrees with a description of the knowledge of God as relational or bi-polar. As a result of God's revelation in his Word by his Spirit, it is given to the human subject in grace to know God personally and experientially as the divine object. This experiential knowledge has therefore (like all genuine knowledge of the real or objective) both a subjective and an objective pole. The two are not mutually exclusive, but necessarily complementary in the relationship. Objective revelation in Scripture and in the presence of the living God in his Spirit, and subjective experience of the living God through his Word in Scripture by the Spirit are therefore, in the evangelical view, not contradictory but complementary.

It is fully in accord with the evangelical tradition right back to the Reformation therefore that Evangelicals today, after a period of about fifty years in which the objective aspect of knowledge of God has been emphasized, should now integrate with that emphasis a new appreciation of the subjective. Alister McGrath has recently written of the deficiency in the Anglican and Lutheran traditions in the seventeenth century until the emotional aridity and sterility and the experiential deficit were corrected by the emphasis on experience in Pietism and Methodism respectively. He writes:

> Unless theology is seen to address, interpret and transform human experience, it will be seen as an irrelevance to life.[46]

Roy Clements, in an unpublished recent paper, also recognizes the need:

> We need to acknowledge that, for a very long time, the Conservative Evangelical strand within Christianity has been wedded to rationalistic modes of thought. Sometimes that has led to a degree of academic aridity in the pulpit and an over-cerebral emphasis in our evangelistic techniques; a failure to recognise the importance of subjective and intuitive elements in faith, a failure even to recognise the importance of the Holy Spirit in authentic Christian spirituality. That the charismatic movement was in many respects a reaction against that over-emphasis on rationalism is obvious.[47]

But if a new appreciation of Christian experience is to be welcomed as restoring the balance of the evangelical tradition, nevertheless some caveats and clarifications should be borne in mind.

VI. Experience and Scripture in Evangelical Theology

Four theses may be presented therefore as an attempt to safeguard a balanced and authentically evangelical understanding of experience and its relationship to Scripture.

First, a distinction needs to be made between 'religious experience' and the Christian experience of God. The study of religion and of the religious experience of mankind is valid in its own right, but as a

---

[46] Alister McGrath, *The Renewal of Anglicanism* (London: SPCK, 1993) 78f. *Cf.* also the abbreviated form of this chapter in *Christian Theology: an Introduction* (Oxford: Blackwell, 1994) 192ff.

[47] Roy Clements, 'An Overview of Evangelicalism Today', delivered at the UCCF Triennial Consultation, Swanwick, on 7th May, 1994. *Cf.* also I. Howard Marshall (ed.), *Christian Experience in Theology and Life* (Edinburgh: Rutherford House, 1988), papers read at the 1984 Conference of the Fellowship of European Evangelical Theologians.

phenomenological, anthropological, psychological and sociological study, it can tell us little or nothing about the validity or objective reference of these experiences. Study of religion is essentially a study of the human subject, not of the divine object, however that divine object may be conceived. The validity of an experience is determined not by the effect produced on or in the subject, but by the reality and truth of the object which is experienced. Idolatry, as Calvin so profoundly analyses it, is the worship of the figments of our imagination, the worship of illusion and empty vanities.[48] That is not to say that such false gods may not take on a parasitic kind of existence and exercise a destructive sway over their worshippers. But the validity and truth of all experience is determined by the truth and reality of the object experienced. Hence the idea (from Schleiermacher) that there is a common core to all religious experience and that Christian experience is merely the particular form which religious experience takes in the Christian tradition is as absurd as the idea that a service of worship may be partly (or even chiefly!) Christian.

Secondly, within Christian theology, the individual's experience of God cannot be regarded as the final authority. Each may have the right of private judgement and the duty indeed to be true to conviction and conscience, but that does not mean that each is equally right! Neither can we regard the corporate experience of the church formulated in tradition as the final authority. Packer struck exactly the right note here in 'Fundamentalism' and the Word of God. There cannot be some combination of Scripture, tradition, reason and experience as the final authority. The final authority lies in Scripture alone (sola Scriptura), for in Scripture alone we have the Word of God.[49] And yet tradition, reason and experience each has a role.

Positively, the relationship of Scripture, tradition, reason and experience may be characterised like this. Scripture alone represents the objective pole in the relationship. The final authority in any area of study is not the 'expert', the one who has 'experienced' the object and verbalizes about it, for experts may be wrong, and no expert ever has exhaustive, final, unrevisable knowledge of anything! The final authority can only lie in the object itself. That is surely the point of the scientific experimental method. In this case we have to do not with a dumb object (as in many other areas of knowledge) but with the God

---

[48]1:2:8.
[49]Cf. the chapter in this volume by A.N.S. Lane, 'Sola Scriptura? Making Sense of a Reformation Slogan'.

who has spoken, the one who is originally and ultimately the divine subject and who has given himself to be known and has revealed himself in grace, making himself accessible and available as the divine object of our knowledge. That is why it is important to see that the witness of the apostles and prophets is not only their human witness as they directly and intuitively came to know the living God in his revelation in Christ for themselves. It is not merely the word of human experts or religious geniuses. Rather their truly and fully human witness as formulated in the Holy Scriptures is the result of the *prior* inspiration of the breath of God and so is to be understood as assumed into the divine revelation, as our humanity was assumed by the Word made flesh. Scripture is therefore the very Word of God to us. In this way our doctrine of Scripture (to continue the Christological analogy) is neither adoptionist nor Nestorian, but fully Chalcedonian.

Reason and *tradition* represent the subjective pole. 'Reason' is a short-hand way of referring to the activity of formulating and expressing this knowledge of the living God, gained through his Word and by his Spirit, in the mind of the Christian believer. 'Tradition' refers to the accumulated formulation of the church, the corporate subject, in creeds and confessions over the centuries. *Experience* is the intuitive experiential cognitive relationship between the two, human subject and divine object of knowledge, as expressed by the subjects. The respective role of the four is therefore well expressed in Outler's analysis, already quoted above, of Wesley's hermeneutical method: Scripture as the norm, but 'interfaced with tradition, reason, and Christian experience as dynamic and interactive aids in the interpretation of the Word of God in Scripture'.[50]

Thirdly, the concept of experience within Christian theology must be re-cast to lose the focus on the subjective. Martyn Lloyd-Jones put his finger on a persistent evangelical weakness when in 1944 he diagnosed the problem of Evangelicalism as subjectivism. The danger of all talk of experience is that because of our sinful preoccupation with ourselves (the *cor incurvatum in se*) we topple over into subjectivism and become fascinated with the state of our own souls. We become preoccupied too easily with the episodes of our own spiritual pilgrimage, our 'blessed experiences'. It is as if the bride were so entranced with the emotions and feelings of the wedding day and so wrapped up in her own reactions that she neglects to pay any attention to the bridegroom. There cannot be any true human knowledge of God without the true

---

[50]See note 16 above.

God giving himself in grace to be known, and equally there cannot be such knowledge without real human subjects to know him as they experience him. There is no knowledge without a 'knower', and it is therefore no more possible to eliminate the subjective pole than to eliminate the objective pole if we are to have true and genuine knowledge. But for such truly objective knowledge, the focus must be not on the subjective but on the objective pole, not on our experience of God, but on the God whom we experience.

This also implies that Christian tradition, our corporate, rational formulation of this experience of God in Christian doctrine, must therefore be always provisional and revisable in the light of our study of Scripture. Scripture must not be held captive to a dogmatic system. There is no final formulation of Christian theology (not even the creeds or the great confessions of the sixteenth and seventeenth centuries!) which is not relativised and in principle revisable in the light of our fresh grappling with the Word of God in Scripture and the new questions which each age brings to it. 'The Lord hath yet more light and truth to shed forth from his Word.'[51] Theology thus remains a living and developing science, subject to the authority of the Word of God.

Finally, in thinking of this objective pole of revelation, there are two dangers to be avoided. On the right of the evangelical *via media*, there is the scholastic idea that revelation is purely abstract and that revelation is to be equated with the Bible alone in the sense that revelation is purely verbal or conceptual or propositional. That is the position which McDonald characterised as 'objectivist' (as distinct from 'objective') and it is not true to the evangelical tradition. At times, evangelical apologetics in recent decades has sounded rather like this. The focus has been on the written rather than on the incarnate, crucified and risen Word, on the conceptual rather than the real. To this the words of Jesus in John's Gospel come as a warning: 'You search the Scriptures because you think that in them you have eternal life, but you will not come to me...'[52] On the left of the evangelical *via media* is the idea that there is some mystical or charismatic experience of God to be had apart from the rational, conceptual revelation in Scripture, or by falsely separating the incarnate Word from the written Word, or by regarding the Scriptures as anything less than the Word of God *in toto*.

True Christian experience is rational, experiential, converting, sanctifying and life-changing knowledge of God in and through the

---

[51] Attributed to John Robinson, pastor to the Pilgrim Fathers.
[52] Jn. 5:39.

incarnate Word by the Spirit. But as the evangelical tradition has insisted from the Reformation until today, that experience of God in Christ is only to be found through the evangel, the gospel, the Word of God embodied in the witness of the apostles and prophets in Holy Scripture.

CHAPTER 13

Sola Scriptura? Making Sense of a Post-Reformation Slogan

Anthony N.S. Lane

Summary

What is the meaning of sola Scriptura? The relation between Scripture and possible rivals (tradition and the teaching office of the church; Christian experience and prophecy; general revelation, human reason, human disciplines and culture) is considered. Scripture, although supreme, is neither the sole resource nor the sole source of theology. While the material sufficiency of Scripture is a part of what is meant by sola Scriptura, it is not the whole. Scripture is not the sole authority for theology. But the essence of the sola Scriptura principle is that Scripture is the final authority or norm for Christian belief.

I. Introduction

Sola Scriptura is often described as the formal principle of the Reformation, as opposed to *sola fide* and *sola gratia* which are the material principles. This must be qualified, on two grounds. First, the distinction between formal and material principles dates from as recently as the nineteenth century.[1] Secondly, although there are passages from Reformation times in which the words *sola* and *Scriptura* appear in close proximity,[2] *sola Scriptura* as a formula or a slogan post-dates the Reformation. But whenever the slogan was coined, its purpose was to encapsulate the teaching of the Reformers and it is as such that it will be interpreted in this chapter.

Like the other two slogans, *sola Scriptura* needs careful unpacking and clarification. The purpose of this chapter is to move beyond the rhetoric and to discern what the term meant and the extent to which it can still be held today. The following quote from a well-known evangelical writer, which out of *pietas* will remain unattributed, illustrates the extent to which the rhetoric can go:

> The Reformers' whole understanding of Christianity, then, depended on the principle of *sola Scriptura*: that is, the view that Scripture, as the *only* Word of God in this world, is the *only* guide for conscience and the church, the *only* source of true knowledge of God and grace, and the *only qualified judge of the church's testimony and teaching, past and present.*

While there may be a sense in which each of these claims can be sustained, it is also true that each one needs heavy qualification. The aim of this chapter is to supply just that qualification.

To talk of Scripture *alone* implies the exclusion of rivals. What might these rivals be? What other resources are available to the theologian? A number may be considered, which will be grouped into three major categories.[3] First, there are what may be called ecclesiastical resources. These divide into two: the Christian tradition and the teach-

---

[1]*Cf.* T. George, *Theology of the Reformers* (Leicester: Apollos, 1987) 82; G. Zweynert, 'Der Sinn der Formel sola scriptura' in *Verantwortung. Untersuchungen über Fragen aus der Theologie und Geschichte. Zum 60e Geburtstag Gottfried Noth* (Evangelisch-Lutherischen Landeskirchenamt Sachsens; Berlin: Evangelische Verlagsanstalt, 1964) 293; G. Ebeling, *The Word of God and Tradition* (London: Collins, 1968) 117-9.

[2]*E.g.*, Calvin, *Institutes*, 1:7:1, 1:18:3; 3:17:8; 4:8:12. Quotations from the *Institutes* (hereafter, *Inst.*) are taken from the edition of J.T. McNeill and F.L. Battles (LCC 20f; London: SCM, 1960).

ing authority of the church.[4] Secondly, there are less institutional Christian resources. Christian experience has been seen as a key to the correct interpretation of Scripture. More controversial is the phenomenon of prophecy in the church today. All of the resources so far named raise the question of whether Christian revelation ceased with the apostles. The third category consists of resources which are not specifically Christian. These include general revelation, the revelation of God through creation as opposed to specifically Judaeo-Christian revelation. Related to this, but distinct, is the appeal to human reason. What role should this have in the formulation of theology? Human reason as a tool has given birth to a great variety of human disciplines. Until the time of the Reformation the discipline which above all posed a challenge to theology was philosophy. Today's theologians need to consider many other disciplines, such as science, psychology, sociology and politics. Also relevant is the use of extra-biblical material (archaeology, ancient history and the like) in the interpretation of the Bible. Finally, the sum total of such human endeavour is subsumed under the general heading of culture.

Some may be surprised at the failure to mention God or Christ or the Holy Spirit. Of course, God is the one who reveals himself, Christ is the supreme revelation of God and the Holy Spirit leads the church into truth. But the point here at issue is *how* do we come to know God and Christ, through what means does the Spirit lead the church into truth?

All of these resources have played and continue to play a significant role in theology. In what sense, therefore, can one talk of Scripture *alone*? Various senses can be distinguished. It could be claimed that Scripture is the sole *resource* for the theologian. Or it could

[3]J. Macquarrie, *Principles of Christian Theology* (London: SCM, 1966) 4-17, gives a shorter list of 'formative factors in theology'. He includes revelation, but acknowledges that this poses the question 'how can we have access to it today?' (p. 8). This is why revelation is not here included. General revelation, through creation, *is* (if it exists!) accessible today, so is included. The three categories that I have listed correspond broadly to tradition, experience and reason in Outler's 'Methodist Quadrilateral', described in the chapter in this volume by T.A. Noble. Liberation theology has introduced a further dimension, the role of praxis. This has been excluded from explicit consideration, though many of the issues that it raises are covered under experience and human disciplines (economics and politics especially).

[4]*Cf.* A.N.S. Lane, 'Scripture, Tradition and Church: An Historical Survey', *Vox Evangelica* 9 (1975) 37-55, which in many ways complements the present chapter. As is there argued, the picture has often been distorted by considering Scripture and tradition alone, in isolation from the teaching of the contemporary church.

be claimed, more modestly, that Scripture is the sole *source* of Christian truth (however that term be understood). That raises the issue of the *sufficiency* of Scripture. Finally, moving in a different direction, it could be claimed that Scripture is the sole *authority* or *norm* for Christian belief. These different possibilities will be explored in turn.

II. Scripture the Sole Resource or the Sole Source?

Does *sola Scriptura* mean that Scripture is the sole (legitimate) resource of the theologian? There is a legend that the Muslim general 'Amr ibn-al-'As in the 640s destroyed the ancient library of Alexandria. This was supposedly on the instructions of the caliph, who stated: 'If these writings of the Greeks agree with the book of God [the Koran], they are useless and need not to be preserved; if they disagree, they are pernicious and ought to be destroyed.'[5] Does *sola Scriptura* imply a similar attitude towards the Bible? Such an attitude is impossible to sustain with any consistency and is not what was meant by *sola Scriptura*.

But suppose we decide that Scripture is not our sole theological resource. Maybe it should nonetheless be the sole source of Christian theology? But can one distinguish between a resource and a source? There is a real, but precarious distinction. A concordance, for example, is a valuable resource for biblical theology, but could hardly be called a source, except inasmuch as it actually contains the text of Scripture. A Greek lexicon, likewise, is a valuable resource, though it could become a source in its own right were it to introduce ideas which were not in fact there in the original.

Beyond the theological realm, the U.S. Supreme Court is a legal resource in that its purpose is to interpret American law and the U.S. Constitution. It is not itself a legislative body. That is the role of Congress. But to interpret the law results in 'making law' in a different, but highly significant sense. This illustrates two points. It is often hard for resources not to go on to become sources—in that sense the distinction can be hard. Yet the fact that we can talk of a resource becoming a source indicates that there is a conceptual distinction, even if there may be a practical problem in preventing the one from becoming the other.

---

[5]For the legend that 'Amr destroyed the Alexandrian library, *cf.* P.K. Hitti, *History of the Arabs* (10th ed; London: Macmillan, 1970) 166. For the alleged words of the caliph, *cf.* E. Gibbon, *The Decline and Fall of the Roman Empire* (London: Ball, Arnold & Co., 1840) ch. 51, p. 956.

The three categories of (potential) theological resources will each be examined in turn, to see whether *sola Scriptura* precludes their role either as a resource or as a source. The aim is not to resolve the issue of *what* role they should have in theology, which would require a number of lengthy tomes, simply to establish *whether* they have any legitimate role. To argue that they are legitimate resources or sources is not to be confused with putting them on the same level as Scripture.

It is not possible even to read the Bible, let alone to proclaim its message, without some use of reason. While the use of specific human disciplines, such as philosophy, biology or psychology, can and sometimes does lead to abuse, it is hard consistently to repudiate such use. Tertullian is well known for his negative comments about reason: 'It is credible, because it is absurd... it is certain because it is impossible.'[6] But such rhetoric should not be mistaken for a serious description of Tertullian's theological method.[7] Tertullian also spoke very negatively about the use of philosophy, especially in the following well-known passage:

> What has Jerusalem to do with Athens, the Church with the Academy, the Christian with the heretic? Our principles come from the Porch of Solomon, who had himself taught that the Lord is to be sought in simplicity of heart. I have no use for a Stoic or Platonic or dialectic Christianity.[8]

But Tertullian's rhetorical rejection of philosophy did not preclude him from appealing to it in his apologetic works[9]. It also did not protect him from being misled by Stoic philosophy into thinking of God as being composed of 'an impalpable corporeal substance which in some sense occupies space'.[10] Polemical rhetoric against reason and/or philosophy does not remove the need to come to terms with their role in

---

[6]*The Flesh of Christ* 5 (my translation). *Credibile est, quia ineptum est ... certum est, quia impossibile.* (PL 2:761).
[7]For an analysis of the passages cited at the previous and the following footnote, *cf.* J.L. González, 'Athens and Jerusalem Revisited: Reason and Authority in Tertullian', *Church History* 43 (1974) 17-25. Also on Tertullian's attitude to philosophy, *cf.* J. Daniélou, *The Origins of Latin Christianity* (London: Darton, Longman & Todd, 1977) 209-31.
[8]Tertullian, *The Prescriptions against the Heretics* ch. 7, in S.L. Greenslade (ed.), *Early Latin Theology* (LCC 5; London: SCM, 1956) 36.
[9]*E.g., Apology*, 21.
[10]R.A. Norris, *God and World in Early Christian Theology* (London: A.&C. Black, 1966) 92f.

theology. Augustine was more in line with the attitude of the early
Fathers as a whole when he stated that

> if those who are called philosophers... have said things which are
> indeed true and are well accommodated to our faith, they should not
> be feared; rather, what they have said should be taken from them as
> from unjust possessors and converted to our use.[11]

Related to philosophy is the issue of general revelation. Is this a legitimate resource for theology? The most notorious opponent of such a
claim is of course Karl Barth, especially in his controversy with Emil
Brunner.[12] But this polemical stance was not one that Barth could
maintain. In due course he acknowledged that while Jesus Christ is the
one Word of God, the one Light of Life, there are other 'true words' and
'lesser lights', including the physical creation and the non-Christian
world.[13] Whatever this may or may not imply, it certainly involves an
acknowledgement that what is understood by general revelation[14] is a
legitimate resource. For the denial of this one would need to move
beyond Barth to the theologian who took the principle of Christological concentration with full seriousness: Marcion.

If *sola Scriptura* does not preclude human reason as a theological
resource, does it preclude it from also being a source? To deny the
status of source to the area of general revelation and 'natural' human
knowledge leads to some odd conclusions. Is there nothing for the biblical scholar to gain from the study of the Greek language or ancient
history? Is it conceivable that the study of science and nature can contribute nothing to a doctrine of creation that is not already taught in
Scripture? How useful would be a contemporary Christian doctrine of
humanity that studiously refused to learn anything from modern
anthropology, psychology, sociology, biology, *etc.* unless it was
already found in the Bible? This does not imply an uncritical absorp-
tion of such disciplines, only that the denial that they have anything
distinctive to contribute is not realistic.

But what of natural theology? Today, for a variety of reasons that
need not detain us now, some more worthy than others, natural theol-

---

[11]*On Christian Doctrine* 2:40:60 (New York: Macmillan, 1958), where he compares
this with the children of Israel 'spoiling' the Egyptians (Ex. 12:35f.).

[12]E. Brunner and K. Barth, *Natural Theology* (London: G. Bless, 1946).

[13]K. Barth, *Church Dogmatics* IV.3(1) (Edinburgh: T.&T. Clark, 1961) 103-65.

[14]Whether we refer to general revelation, to 'natural' human knowledge or whatever, is not the point at issue. Whatever it is called, is it a legitimate theological
source?

ogy is somewhat out of fashion. Few would wish to encourage the formation of a full-blown natural theology, such as that of Thomas Aquinas. But what of natural theology in the sense of the attempt to learn about God through the medium of philosophical theology, independently of revelation? Is there nothing that such an approach can contribute to theology? Consider two traditional attributes of God: his impassibility and his incorporeality.

From around the turn of the third century A.D. to the middle of the nineteenth century, the belief that God is impassible was not seriously questioned by theologians. Now such a belief is all but universally regarded as a non-Christian aberration introduced by natural theology (in the sense of philosophical theology independent of revelation).[15] But this assessment needs some qualification. The early Fathers did not see this as an issue of natural theology. They were simply using their minds in interpreting the Bible. But does not the Bible present to us the picture of a passible God? Yes, but the fathers did not take such language literally, any more than they imagined that God has literal eyes that 'run to and fro throughout the whole earth' (2 Ch. 16:9). Talk of God as passible they interpreted as anthropomorphic (anthropopathic, for the pedant).[16] Most theologians today wish to take the language of God's feelings more literally, but are no more inclined than the fathers to ascribe a human body to God the Father.

The difference between us and the Fathers is not so much that we are more sceptical about natural theology, rather that natural theology today favours a passible rather than an impassible God. By contrast, natural theology is no more hospitable today than it then was to regarding God as having literal eyes and arms. Those who wish to revise the traditional doctrine of divine impassibility should not feel that it entitles them to adopt a morally superior stance towards the Fathers regarding the issue of natural theology.

How about the role of culture? Church history supplies warnings about the dangers of 'culture Christianity', a Christianity that succeeds in doing little more than provide a religious veneer to contemporary culture.[17] This might be seen in those in the past for whom the church was little more than 'the Tory Party at prayer' or today in those whose Christianity simply provides a religious cloak for the values of left-of-

---

[15]E.g., J. Moltmann, The Crucified God (London: SCM, 1974) 227f., where the doctrine is blamed upon 'the philosophical concept of God', and The Trinity and the Kingdom of God (London: SCM, 1981) 21f.
[16]Cf. H.M. Kuitert, Gott in Menschengestalt (Munich: Chr. Kaiser, 1967) 56-81.
[17]Cf. H.R. Niebuhr; Christ and Culture (London: Faber & Faber, 1952) 93-122.

centre liberal humanism. But while we may wish to disown such trun-
cated forms of Christianity, can we deny that culture is a source for the
theologian? To admit the validity of contextualisation in any sense is to
acknowledge culture as a source for theology. To deny this would be
to condemn theology to be totally abstract and non-contextual—if
indeed it were possible to produce such a culture-free theology.

Thus far I have argued why I do not consider *sola Scriptura* to preclude these areas of human knowledge from being legitimate
theological resources or sources, why such a stance is invalid today.
But what did the Reformers think about the role of reason and philosophy? Luther's hostility to reason, 'the devil's whore', is well-known.
He also protested vigorously against the intrusion of Aristotelian philosophy into theology.[18] In their conflict over the Lord's supper he
criticised Zwingli and Oecolampadius both for their use of reason and
for their acceptance of a philosophical dualism between spirit and matter.[19] Yet despite all this, Luther's own position towards reason was
not unequivocally negative and he was not himself innocent of all
philosophy.[20]

Again, there are those who have seen a sharp dichotomy
between Calvin, who rejected philosophical categories, and a later Calvinist scholasticism which reintroduced Aristotle.[21] It is certainly true
that Calvin makes relatively little use of philosophy, but he had no
principled objection to it and was as able as the next person to use Aristotelian distinctions when it suited him.[22] Thus, while the Reformers
were cautious in their use of reason and philosophy as a theological
resource, they did not deny them a legitimate role. *Sola Scriptura* in its
original sense was not intended to exclude reason and philosophy as
theological resources.

But what about human knowledge as a theological source?
Calvin was certainly open in principle to learn from 'secular' knowledge. 'Natural reason' is capable of great achievements when applied
to earthly as opposed to heavenly matters. Calvin discerns the admira-

---

[18]B.A. Gerrish, *Grace and Reason* (Oxford: Clarendon, 1962) 1f.

[19]H. Sasse, *This is my Body* (rev. ed; Adelaide: Lutheran Publishing House, 1977)
187-197.

[20]*Cf.* Gerrish, *Grace and Reason*; R.H. Fischer, 'A Reasonable Luther' in F.H. Littell
(ed.), *Reformation Studies* (Richmond, VA: John Knox, 1962) 30-45.

[21]*E.g.*, B.G. Armstrong, *Calvinism and the Amyraut Heresy* (Madison/Milwaukee/
London: University of Wisconsin Press, 1969) 31-42.

[22]*E.g.*, *Inst.* 1:16:9 (two types of necessity); 3:14:17 (four kinds of causes). *Cf.* V.L.
Nuovo, 'Calvin's Theology: A Study of its Sources in Classical Antiquity' (Ph.D.,
Columbia University, New York, 1964) esp. ch. 5.

ble light of truth in secular writers. To despise this is to dishonour the Spirit of God, who is its source.[23] It is not surprising, then, that Calvin can regard Plato's account of the five senses as 'true, or at least... probable'.[24] Again, in the ethical realm, Aristotle's distinction between incontinence and intemperance is 'very shrewd'.[25] It is not surprising, therefore, that Calvin accepted the 'modern scientific' picture of the universe.[26] In his *Warning Against Judiciary Astrology* Calvin makes considerable use of the findings of science, in this case astronomy.[27]

What of natural theology? Barth, in his opposition to Brunner, sought to enlist Calvin to his cause.[28] Clearly Calvin does not develop a full-blown natural theology in the manner of a Thomas Aquinas. But at the same time the opening chapters of the *Institutes* speak of knowledge of God that comes from a natural awareness of him and that can be derived from his creation. True, this is of little value to the unregenerate sinner, but the believer wearing the spectacles of Scripture can learn from it.[29]

The self-conscious discussion of culture is a modern phenomenon. The Reformers did not discuss its role in theology. But given that they did not regard *sola Scriptura* as denying philosophy any role in theology, they may be said to have had the same attitude to culture. Certainly, when it came to questions of the relation between the church and the state, they took great care to contextualise their theology in the culture of their time, to use modern jargon.

General revelation and 'natural' human knowledge (whether or not we choose to use to use these particular words to describe them) are legitimate theological sources. But one important qualification needs to be made. They are sources for the Christian theologian; they are not sources of Christian revelation. *Sola Scriptura* does not exclude

---

[23]*Inst.*, 2:2:12-17, esp. 15.

[24]*Inst.*, 1:15:6.

[25]*Inst.*, 2:2:23.

[26]*Cf.* W.S. Reid, 'Calvin's View of Natural Science' in E.F. Furcha (ed.), *In Honor of John Calvin, 1509-64* (Montreal: Faculty of Religious Studies, McGill University, 1987) 237. For our present purposes it is irrelevant whether for Calvin 'modern science' meant the Ptolemaic or Copernican system.

[27]M. Potter (tr.), 'A Warning Against Judiciary Astrology and Other Prevalent Curiosities', *Calvin Theological Journal* 18 (1983) 157-89.

[28]Brunner and Barth, *Natural Theology*, 94-109.

[29]*Inst.*, 1:1-6. *Cf.* G.J. Postema, 'Calvin's Alleged Rejection of Natural Theology', *SJT* 24 (1971) 423-34. The Belgic Confession of 1561, art. 2, says that God is known both by his creation and, more clearly, by his Word; see A.C. Cochrane (ed.), *Reformed Confessions of the 16th Century* (London: SCM, 1966) 189f.

their status as sources of *truth* (needing to be correlated with Scripture), but maybe it does exclude all but Scripture as a source of *Christian revelation*. This possibility needs to be considered as we turn to the specifically Christian resources.

What of Christian experience? Is this a legitimate theological resource, whether in the form of the theologian's own personal experience or, as with Schleiermacher, in the form of an appeal to collective Christian experience?[30] To say no would be to deny that the believer has any advantage over the unbeliever when he comes to do theology, a position that would command little support within the evangelical tradition. Experience as a source is more controversial, especially because of the way in which it can be misused. It must be remembered, though, that our aim is simply to ascertain whether it has any legitimate role as a source, not to claim that it cannot be abused as a source. An example of how the use of experience can become controversial would be the interpretation of the *charismata* today. To what extent should the New Testament records be read in the light of modern-day experience? But this controversy concerns not so much the validity of the appeal to experience as the question of the priority of sources, the proper relation between the appeal to experience and the appeal to Scripture.

The Reformers gave a high profile to the role of experience in theology. Luther's theology was forged on the anvil of *Anfechtung*.[31] He was particularly emphatic about the importance of experience for the theologian. Luther's whole theology bears the marks of his *Turmerlebnis*. It can be argued that the different emphases of Luther's and Calvin's doctrines of the law reflect their different experiential backgrounds.

Calvin's is very much a theology of experience.[32] He repeatedly appeals to experience, often using traditional refrains such as *experientia docet*.[33] God teaches us both through his Word and by experience.[34]

---

[30]Of the two forms of experience, the theologian's own experience is liable to be the stronger influence, while the appeal to collective Christian experience will have far greater weight. For this reason, the former is more likely to be a significant but unacknowledged influence, the latter more likely actually to receive mention.

[31]Cf. A.E. McGrath, *Luther's Theology of the Cross* (Oxford: Blackwell, 1985) 169-75, on *Anfechtung* and P. Althaus, *The Theology of Martin Luther* (Philadelphia: Fortress, 1966) 55-63, 173-8, on experience.

[32]Cf. W. Balke, 'The Word of God and Experientia according to Calvin' in W.H. Neuser (ed.), *Calvinus Ecclesiae Doctor* (Kampen: Kok, 1979) 19-31.

[33]*Ibid.*, 20.

[34]*Comm. Ps.*, 71:17.

'With experience as our teacher we find God just as he declares himself in his Word.'[35] When considering the mode of our communion with Christ in the Lord's supper, he confesses: 'I rather experience than understand it'.[36] When expounding his doctrine of the inner witness of the Spirit, Calvin claims that he speaks 'of nothing other than what each believer experiences within himself'.[37] This emphasis is not surprising given that the gospel is

> a doctrine not of the tongue but of life. It is not apprehended by the understanding and memory alone, as other disciplines are, but it is received only when it possesses the whole soul, and finds a seat and resting place in the inmost affection of the heart.[38]

The Reformation *sola Scriptura* was certainly not understood to be denying the role of Christian experience in theology.

But what of the more controversial question of prophecy, of ongoing communication from the Holy Spirit? This issue was raised acutely in the second century by the Montanists. They claimed that the Holy Spirit was now issuing fresh instructions which abrogated some of the teaching of the New Testament,[39] an approach which was rejected by the church. From that time on, Catholic teaching was defended on the grounds that it was apostolic, tradition being one of the means by which this was claimed

The same issue as was raised by the Montanists is also raised in a more acute form by the *Book of Mormon* and by all other claims to further revelation. But does one wish to maintain that God has said nothing since the completion of the New Testament? There is a careful balance to be held here. The dogmatic constitution *De divina revelatione* of the Second Vatican Council maintained that:

> The Christian dispensation, therefore, as the new and definitive covenant, will never pass away, and we now await no further new public revelation before the glorious manifestation of our Lord Jesus Christ.[40]

---

[35]*Inst.*, 1:10:2.
[36]*Inst.*, 4:17:32
[37]*Inst.*, 1:7:5.
[38]*Inst.*, 3:6:4.
[39]On Montanism, *cf.* J. Pelikan, *The Emergence of the Catholic Tradition (100-600)* (Chicago/London: University of Chicago Press, 1971) 97-108; D.F. Wright, 'Why were the Montanists Condemned?', *Themelios* 2 (1976-77) 15-22.
[40]*De divina revelatione* 1:4 in W.M. Abbott (ed.), *The Documents of Vatican II* (London: Geoffrey Chapman, 1967) 113.

This is a carefully crafted statement. What is excluded is 'further new public' revelation. Private revelation, such as individual guidance, is not excluded.[41] Again, what is denied is not that God still reveals himself (such as through the gospel), but only that he now expands the definitive revelation through Christ given in apostolic times. Similarly, pope Pius X in his decree *Lamentabili* rejected the view that revelation constituting the object of catholic faith was not completed with the apostles.[42] This position is one with which Evangelicals should have no quarrel.

Where does that leave the status of prophecy today?[43] If it is given the status of public revelation, this conflicts not just with evangelical teaching but even with the traditional Roman Catholic position. The statement by a well-known charismatic leader that if a prophecy is approved by those appointed to test it it should be received on the same footing as Scripture is therefore excluded. Leaving aside the claim to continuing revelation, this is a claim to infallibility that makes the Vatican I definition of papal infallibility appear timid in the extreme. If, on the other hand, prophecy is seen as a word to a specific situation, not claiming wider authority and not adding to the Scriptural revelation, then it need not be seen as contrary to the *sola Scriptura* principle.]

Experience and prophecy represent, in many ways, the two extremes of the spectrum of what we have called less institutional Christian resources. In between them would come a category such as guidance, which would embrace a variety of phenomena, such as a

---

[41] The Council of Trent, for instance, allowed the possibility that God might reveal to a Christian, by special revelation, that he will persevere to the end; see Canon 16 concerning justification in J.H. Leith (ed.), *Creeds of the Churches* (3rd ed; Atlanta: John Knox, 1982) 422). For Roman Catholic theologians in the sixteenth century who held to ongoing *public* revelation, *cf.* G.H. Tavard, *Holy Writ or Holy Church* (London: Burns & Oates, 1959) 151-71.

[42] *Lamentabili*, ch. 21; see H. Denzinger and A. Schönmetzer (eds.), *Enchiridion Symbolorum* (34th ed; Freiburg/Basel/Vienna: Herder, 1967) no. 3421. N. Lash, *Change in Focus* (London: Sheed & Ward, 1973) 16, cites and expounds the decree as if it had stated without qualification that revelation ceased with the apostles. *Cf.* further on this subject, R.J. Bauckham, 'Tradition in Relation to Scripture and Reason' in R.J. Bauckham and B. Drewery (eds.), *Scripture, Tradition and Reason* (Edinburgh: T.&T. Clark, 1988) 128.

[43] The issue is not whether or not the genuine gift of prophecy is being exercised today, nor whether this is happening in 99% of the alleged occasions or only 1%, but only whether or not it is not *in principle* inconsistent with *sola Scriptura*. On *sola Scriptura* and prophecy, *cf.* G. Cole, 'Sola Scriptura: Some Historical and Contemporary Perspectives', *Churchman* 104 (1990) 27.

sense of call to the ministry or the claim that 'God told me' where I should go to live. Since these fall between the categories of experience and prophecy, they may be considered to be covered in principle by the discussion of those two issues.

Another related issue is that of the 'Inner Light'. This is a term that covers a multitude of sins—some literally sins![44] Again, most of the issues are the same as those raised by experience, prophecy and guidance. There is, however, the further element that some have turned and still turn to the Inner Light as an alternative to Scripture. Such an approach is clearly contrary to the *sola Scriptura* principle.

What of the Reformers' attitude to prophecy? Luther faced those who set Spirit against Word, appealing to the Inner Light. His opposition to such a position was unequivocal:[45]

> The enthusiasts of our day condemn the external Word, yet they do not remain silent but fill the world with their chattering and scribbling, as if the Spirit could not come through the Scriptures or the spoken word of the apostles but must come through their own writings and words.[46]

Calvin handled the same issue, confronting in a chapter of the *Institutes* those who, 'with great haughtiness exalting the teaching office of the Spirit, despise all reading and laugh at the simplicity of those who, as they express it, still follow the dead and killing letter'.[47] It is noteworthy how Calvin responds. The Holy Spirit, the author of Scripture, does not contradict himself. He neither teaches people to despise the Scriptures nor teaches contrary to those Scriptures:

> Therefore the Spirit, promised to us, has not the task of inventing new and unheard-of revelations, or of forging a new kind of doctrine, to lead us away from the received doctrine of the gospel, but of sealing our minds with that very doctrine which is commended by the gospel.[48]

---

[44]In the words of J.S. Whale, 'belief in the inner light may be the shortest road to the outer darkness' (quoted by S. Neill, *Christian Holiness* [London: Lutterworth, 1960] 29).

[45]*Cf.* G.H. Williams, The Radical Reformation (SCES 15; 3rd ed; Kirksville, MO: Sixteenth Century Journal Publishers, 1992) 1247-50.

[46]*Smalcald Articles*, Pt. 3, art. 8; see T.G. Tappert (ed.), *The Book of Concord* (Philadelphia: Fortress, 1959) 312.

[47]*Inst.*, 1:9:1. *Cf.* J. Calvin, *Treatises Against the Anabaptists and Against the Libertines* (Grand Rapids: Baker, 1982) 221-9.

[48]*Inst.*, 1:9:1.

The emphasis lies on the Spirit's consistency and therefore the appro-
priateness of testing alleged manifestations of the Spirit by the
Scriptures which he inspired. What Calvin is objecting to is prophecies
which are contrary to Scripture or which claim priority over it. Prophecy which was tested by Scripture would not infringe the principles of
this chapter. Regarding the office of prophet, he states that this was
raised up at the beginning of the Lord's kingdom and is now and then
revived 'as the need of the times demands'. The class of prophets
'either does not exist today or is less commonly seen'.[49] The gift (as
opposed to office) of prophecy Calvin tended to assimilate to preaching.[50]

Finally, the category of ecclesiastical resources—the Christian
tradition and the teaching authority of the church. Are these excluded
by *sola Scriptura*? There are those who have taken a very negative attitude to the use of tradition.[51] Both some of the Anabaptists and some
of the early Brethren felt that they did not need tradition. There are at
least two problems with such an attitude. The first is that those who
despise tradition often end up re-inventing the earliest heresies of
church history. Both the Anabaptists and the Brethren returned to the
second-century heresy that Mary was merely the host mother of
Jesus.[52] As has been said, those who are ignorant of history are condemned to repeat it.

Secondly, it is simply not possible to jump back to the Bible as if
nothing has happened in the intervening millennia. Suppose one
opens one's Bible at the beginning and reads 'In the beginning God'.
What is meant by the word 'God'? One brings to the text a prior understanding of the word. This prior understanding is certainly open to
correction, but what is not possible is to approach the Bible with a mind

---

[49]*Inst.*, 4:3:4.
[50]*Cf.* P. Elbert, 'Calvin and the Spiritual Gifts' in P. Elbert (ed.), *Essays on Apostolic
Themes* (Peabody: Hendrickson, 1985) 127f.
[51]Tradition in this chapter is used in the broad sense of the sum total of the Christian heritage handed down from previous ages, Scripture alone excluded. *Cf.* Y.M.-
J. Congar, *Tradition and Traditions* (London: Burns & Oates, 1966) 287f. and the
W.C.C. Report *Scripture, Tradition and Traditions*, in P.C. Rodger and L. Vischer
(eds.), *The Fourth World Conference on Faith and Order. Montreal 1963* (London: SCM,
1964) 50-61.
[52]Melchior Hofmann was an Anabaptist who held this view (Williams, *Radical Reformation*, 490-95). For the early Brethren, *cf.* F.F. Bruce, 'The Humanity of Jesus
Christ', *Journal of the Christian Brethren Research Fellowship* 24 (1973) 5-10. For
Menno Simons' hostile attitude to tradition, *cf.* George, *Theology of the Reformers*,
274-6.

empty of all Christian tradition. The nearest that one gets to this is the extremely rare case of someone with absolutely no contact with Christianity who picks up a portion of Scripture and is converted through reading it. While this situation is not quite impossible it is hardly the ideal pattern to be followed by the Christian theologian! Thus Alexander Campbell's advice to 'Open the New Testament as if mortal man had never seen it before'[53] is scarcely possible and certainly not desirable.

Thus, apart from the arrogance and folly of despising all that the Holy Spirit has taught the church over two millennia,[54] the rejection of tradition as a resource and a source[55] is simply not viable. The most that can be achieved is a combination of the rhetoric of the rejection of tradition and an exclusion from consideration of all but a very narrow band of Christian tradition

What of the teaching authority of the church? Again, some have waxed lyrical about their rejection of it, but it cannot be avoided except by those who advocate a purely individual Christianity. An example of such an individualistic approach to *sola Scriptura* is seen in Abraham Lincoln, who defended the Bible as absolutely true, yet rejected all 'man-made creeds and dogmas.' As he himself put it, 'I am not a member of any Christian church, but I have never denied the truth of the Scriptures.'[56] Such an individualistic Christianity based on the Bible to the exclusion of creeds, clergy and even church represents one possible understanding of *sola Scriptura*, but not the historic understanding.

Any church that has preachers is by so doing putting them in a position of teaching authority. Francis Newman said of J.N. Darby that 'he only wanted men "to submit their understanding *to God*," that is, to the Bible, that is, to his interpretation!'[57] The same applies to those who take their adherence to *sola Scriptura* to the point of rejecting all creeds. The formal rejection of creeds is in practice combined with a tight con-

---

[53]Cited in N.O. Hatch, 'Sola Scriptura and Novus Ordo Seclorum' in N.O. Hatch and M.A. Noll (eds.), *The Bible in America* (New York/Oxford: OUP, 1982) 72.
[54]*Cf.* R.E. Webber, *Common Roots* (Grand Rapids: Zondervan, 1978) for a call to Evangelicals to take tradition more seriously.
[55]For an example of tradition as a source, it is only through later tradition that we are able to identify the 'Lord's Day' of Rev. 1:10 as Sunday.
[56]N.O. Hatch, 'Sola Scriptura and Novus Ordo Seclorum', 59.
[57]Cited in F.F. Bruce, *Tradition Old and New* (Exeter: Paternoster, 1970) 14 (his emphasis).

trol of doctrine by those in authority using the yardstick of an unwritten and unacknowledged tradition.[58]

But what of the Reformers? Did their understanding of *sola Scriptura* exclude tradition or the teaching authority of the church? Far from it. Calvin's writings are liberally sprinkled with citations of the Fathers as authorities.[59] Luther was less enthusiastic than Calvin about appealing to the Fathers, but also made extensive use of them.[60] Neither of them, nor any of the other magisterial Reformers, wished to do away with tradition as a theological resource or a source. The conclusions of the early ecumenical councils were accepted.[61]

There *is* one type of tradition that the Reformation rejects. This is described by Heppe as 'the dogmatic tradition, which prescribes *credenda* and *agenda* not contained in Scripture'.[62] Chemnitz lists eight different types of tradition, of which it is only the eighth (traditions which pertain both to faith and morals and which cannot be proved with any testimony of Scripture) that he rejects.[63]

But if the Reformers continued to appeal to tradition, surely they had no time for the teaching authority of the church? It is true that they rejected the teaching authority of the contemporary Roman church. But they did not wish to replace the authority of the pope with private judgement and anarchy. One has only to consider the history of Calvin's ministry in Geneva to realise that he had a very high concept of the teaching authority of the church and the need for the church to define doctrine. This attitude was shared by the early Reformers as a whole, to the extent that they were prepared to put people to death for false teaching. However they understood *sola Scriptura*, it was not in such a way as to exclude the teaching authority of the church. Since they drew up confessions of faith to which people were required to

---

[58]*Ibid.*, 13-15; *cf.* J. McIntyre, *The Shape of Christology* (London: SCM, 1966) 26f.: 'In the Reformed church, we somewhat pride ourselves on cutting away the tangle of tradition, forgetting both that tradition may be a genuine medium of interpretative insight and that by now we have created our own rather rigid traditions which have a greater rigidity for all our pretending that they do not exist.'

[59]*Cf.* A.N.S. Lane, 'Calvin's Use of the Fathers and the Medievals', *Calvin Theological Journal* 16 (1981) 149-205.

[60]*Cf.* J. Pelikan, *Obedient Rebels* (London: SCM, 1964) 27-104 on Luther's 'critical reverence towards tradition'.

[61]*Cf.* Lane, 'Calvin's Use', 173f.; Calvin, *Inst.*, 4:9; Pelikan, *Obedient Rebels*, 54-76. *Cf.* Scots Confession of Faith (1560), ch. 20 in Cochrane (ed.), *Reformed Confessions of the 16th Century*, 178f.

[62]H. Heppe, *Reformed Dogmatics* (Grand Rapids: Baker, 1978) 30f.

[63]M. Chemnitz, *Examination of the Council of Trent*, Part 1 (St. Louis: Concordia, 1971) 217-307.

assent, they did not object to the idea that the teaching authority of the church may act as a source. The Reformers were also, unlike the author quoted at the beginning of this chapter, happy to call preaching itself the Word of God.[64]

We have examined all of the potential resources outlined in the introduction. The conclusion is that the Reformation *sola Scriptura* slogan was not understood as a denial that any of these was a legitimate theological resource or source.[65] In fact there is positive warrant for their use, with the one exception of prophecy. With prophecy, there is more ambiguity since Calvin at least understood it differently from modern-day charismatics, but the Reformers did not (to my knowledge) use the *sola Scriptura* argument as an objection *in principle* to contemporary prophecy. But while the Reformers permitted and used all these resources, it does not follow that they are all on the same footing. Scripture is *the* theological resource, the others are very definitely subsidiary resources.

III. The Sufficiency of Scripture?

Perhaps to ask about resources and sources is the wrong approach. Perhaps the true meaning of sola Scriptura lies in the sufficiency of Scripture? At first sight this seems to be supported by the sixth of the Thirty-nine Articles of the Church of England:

> Holy Scripture containeth all things necessary to salvation: so that whatsoever is not read therein, nor may be proved thereby, is not to be required of any man, that it should be believed as an article of the Faith, or be thought requisite or necessary to salvation.

But as the title indicates, the issue is 'the sufficiency of the holy Scriptures *for salvation*.' The same qualification is found in the twentieth article, on the authority of the church, and the twenty-first article, on the authority of general councils. Neither is to enforce any doctrine as necessary for salvation which does not come from the Bible. Similar qualifications are found in other Reformed confessions.[66]

---

[64] Second Helvetic Confession, ch. 1 in Cochrane (ed.), *Reformed Confessions of the 16th Century*, 225.

[65] The discerning reader may have noticed that almost all of the resources mentioned have in fact been used in this chapter, an evidence that the argument used is not purely theoretical! The (arguably precarious) distinction between a resource and a source has not proved to be important.

Is all Christian truth to be found in Scripture? Is the Bible materially sufficient? The trouble with such a claim is that it says both too little and too much. This can best be seen by a brief survey of the history of the debate. In the early centuries of the church there was appeal to tradition as a source of Christian doctrine, alongside Scripture. But the role of tradition was to convey the same apostolic teaching as Scripture, not to add to it. Irenaeus appealed to tradition against the Gnostics because they would not accept the church's scriptures. The point at issue was whether Catholic Christianity or Gnosticism represented authentic Christianity. Appeal to the New Testament was of limited value because the Gnostics had their rival scriptures. The most effective approach was to appeal to the continuous tradition of teaching found in the churches which the apostles had founded. These churches agreed with one another (unlike Gnosticism) and agreed that it was Catholic Christianity, not Gnosticism, that was the religion taught by Christ to the apostles. The tradition to which Irenaeus was appealing was summarised in a 'rule of faith' which contained a basic summary of Christian doctrine much like the later Apostles' Creed. This tradition was not a supplement to Scripture but rather a basic summary of its key teaching.[67]

In due course the church faced a number of issues which led it to qualify the early belief in the sufficiency of Scripture. Three examples will suffice to illustrate this. First, there was the issue of those who accepted the Scriptures but whose interpretation of them was different to the established orthodox position. The Arians, for example, insisted on denying that the Bible taught the deity of Christ. Secondly, as time went on important theological questions were raised to which the Bible gave a less than clear answer. The most noteworthy example in the early church was the deity of the Holy Spirit. The deity of Christ was, at least in the view of the orthodox, taught abundantly clearly by the New Testament. But evidence for the deity of the Spirit was less clear. Finally, in the course of the Middle Ages the church faced the issue that some of its doctrines did not seem to have a biblical basis and were being challenged. This happened, for example, with John Wyclif.

How did the church react to these challenges? Three different types of response may be found. Vincent of Lérins, in the fifth century, accepted that 'the canon of the Scriptures is complete, and is abun-

---

[66]*E.g.*, Belgic Confession, art. 2,7; Second Helvetic Confession, ch. 1 in Cochrane (ed.), *Reformed Confessions of the 16th Century*, 190, 192, 224); Westminster Confession, 1:6.

[67]*Cf.* Lane, 'Scripture, Tradition and Church', 39f.

dantly sufficient for every purpose,' but went on to observe that 'we can find almost as many interpretations as there are men', listing many of the heretics of the early church period.[68] Thus while Scripture is materially sufficient, it is formally insufficient in that it needs an authoritative interpreter. So those who would unmask heresy should do so 'first, of course, by the authority of divine law [Scripture], and, second, by the start tradition of the catholic church'.[69] Vincent proposed a simple test to spot the true interpretation. We need to take care to hold that which has been believed everywhere, always and by everyone.[70] In fact very few doctrines pass Vincent's test, but the basic point is the need for tradition as an interpreter of Scripture.

A second response was to appeal to tradition as a supplement to Scripture. An important step in this direction was taken by Basil of Caesarea in his defence of the deity of the Holy Spirit. One of his arguments was drawn from the wording of the doxology. He defends the use of this argument on the grounds that some of the beliefs and practices of the church are found in written teaching, others in a mystery by the tradition of the apostles. Both have the same force. This was an important precedent for the appeal to tradition to make up the *lacunae* of Scripture and was treated as such a precedent by western medieval canonists.[71]

A third response is also found in medieval Catholicism. This was to continue to affirm the material sufficiency of Scripture and to use allegory to derive from it the desired results. Given the ingenuity of medieval allegorists, this posed no serious problem. It was such an approach that caused Scripture to be described as a nose of wax. As an ancient ditty put it: *Hic liber est in quo sua quaerit dogmata quisque; invenit et pariter dogmata quisque sua.*[72] Thus medieval Catholicism repeatedly affirmed the material sufficiency of Scripture.[73] But such affirmations should not be taken as indicating that the medieval Catholic Church was willing to affirm only that which could be supported from Scrip-

---

[68]Vincent, *Commonitory*, 2:2 in G.E. McCracken and A. Cabaniss (eds.), *Early Medieval Theology* (LCC 9; London: SCM, 1957) 38.

[69]*Commonitory*, 2:1 in *Ibid.*, 37.

[70]*Commonitory*, 2:3.

[71]Basil, *The Holy Spirit*, 27:66f.; 29:71. *Cf.* Lane, 'Scripture, Tradition and Church', 41.

[72]'This is the book in which everyone looks for his own convictions—and everyone likewise finds his own convictions.' See Y.M.-J. Congar, *Tradition and Traditions*, 385

ture—rather that it was confident that whatever it affirmed could be supported somewhere in Scripture!

The issue of the sufficiency of Scripture surfaced again at the Council of Trent, this time in a highly charged polemical context. The Roman Catholic Church faced a sustained onslaught against some of its teaching on the grounds that it was not Scriptural. How did the Council respond? For centuries it was generally assumed that Trent, in its *Decree Concerning the Canonical Scriptures* (8 April, 1546), appealed to tradition as a supplement to Scripture. This interpretation was first questioned in the nineteenth century and then more seriously from 1956 onward.[74] The publication of the Acts of the Council debates at the beginning of this century cast a new light on the significance of Trent. The first draft of the decree on Scripture and tradition stated that the gospel is 'the rule of all saving truth and moral discipline' and that this truth is contained 'partly in written books, partly in unwritten traditions'. After some debate, the final version stated that gospel is 'the *source* of all saving truth and moral discipline' and that this truth *and discipline* are contained 'in written books *and unwritten* traditions'. Both versions state that God is the author of the traditions, but the final draft limits these to traditions 'pertaining both to faith and to morals'.[75]

---

[73]*Ibid.*, 111-18. For Thomas Aquinas and *sola Scriptura, cf.* B. Decker, 'Sola Scriptura bei Thomas von Aquin' in L. Lenhart (ed.), *Universitas*, Vol. I (Mainz: Matthias Grünewald, 1960) 117-29; S.H. Pfürtner, 'Das reformatorische "Sola Scriptura"— theologischer Auslegungsgrund des Thomas von Aquin' in *Sola Scriptura? Ringvorlesungen der theologischen Fakultät der Philipps-Universität* (Marburg: Elwert, 1977) 48-80. For later medieval discussions, *cf.* H.A. Oberman, *The Harvest of Medieval Theology* (rev. ed; Grand Rapids: Eerdmans, 1967) 361-93.

[74]The debate was initiated by J.R. Geiselmann, 'Das Mißverständnis über das Verhältnis von Schrift und Tradition und seine Überwindung in der katholischen Theologie', *Una Sancta* 11 (1956) 131-50.

[75]The originals are found in *Concilium Tridentinum. Diariorum, Actorum, Epistularum, Tractatuum Nova Collectio* (Freiburg: Herder, 1901ff.) 5:31, 91. For an English translation of the final version, *cf.* Leith, *Creeds of the Churches*, 402. The alterations in the final version have been shown in italics. M. Bévenot argues, in two important articles, that *mores* at Trent has a meaning broader than 'morals' and includes the issue of discipline ('"Faith and Morals" in the Councils of Trent and Vatican I', *Heythrop Journal* 3 [1962] 15-30); and that *traditiones* meant 'observances' rather than conceptual additions to Scripture ('Traditiones in the Council of Trent', *Heythrop Journal* 4 [1963] 333-47). If he is right, the decree has little, but *not* nothing, to say concerning the material doctrinal sufficiency of Scripture. In fact his view is questioned by J. Ratzinger, 'On the Interpretation of the Tridentine Decree on Tradition' in K. Rahner and J. Ratzinger, *Revelation and Tradition* (London: Burns & Oates, 1966) 50-68.

The awareness that the draft had been changed gave birth to vigorous debate concerning its significance. The statement that the truth of the gospel is found in Scripture and tradition leaves open, in a way that the 'partly... partly' formula does not, the possibility that the entire truth of the gospel is found in Scripture—*i.e.* that Scripture is materially sufficient. This claim was vigorously contested, but it can hardly be denied that the wording of the decree is compatible with a belief in the material sufficiency of Scripture—though whether that was intended by the Council fathers is another matter.

The interpretation of the Tridentine decree was the subject of vigorous debate in the decade following Geiselmann's article (1956). But why then? It was of more than academic interest because this was the time of the Second Vatican Council, when the dogmatic constitution *De divina revelatione* was being written. This document was revised no less that four times before reaching its final form. The first draft had spoken of the sources (plural) of revelation and had clearly regarded tradition as supplementing Scripture.[76] After much controversy, the final version remained neutral on the question of the material sufficiency of Scripture, an implicit recognition that Trent had not settled the issue.[77]

There are those, then, who argue for a Catholic *sola Scriptura*.[78] But at the last stage Pope Paul insisted on the insertion of a sentence that negates the *sola Scriptura* formula, without, however, denying the material sufficiency of Scripture: 'It is not from sacred Scripture alone that the Church draws her certainty about everything which has been revealed.'[79] If this sentence is considered dispassionately, it is clear that it is not contrary to the approach being taken in this chapter. To deny that tradition, reason or Christian experience can in any way strengthen our certainty about the gospel would be an odd position to take.

If Trent and Vatican II both permit belief in the material sufficiency of Scripture, does this mean that Rome has returned to the position of the Early Church? No. Take a dogma like the Assumption of the Virgin Mary. It is not that Catholic exegetes' confidence of being

---

[76]For the history of the document, *cf.* H. Vorgrimler (ed.), *Commentary on the Documents of Vatican II*, Vol. III (London: Burns & Oates, 1969) 155-66.

[77]*Cf.* esp. *De divina revelatione*, ch. 2 and, for commentary on it, Vorgrimler (ed.), *ibid.*, 181-98.

[78]*E.g.*, K. Rahner, *Theological Investigations* Vol. VI (London: Darton, Longman & Todd, 1974) 107-12.

[79]*De divina revelatione*, 2:9 in Abbott (ed.), *The Documents of Vatican II*, 117. *Cf.* Vorgrimler (ed.), *Commentary*, 194f.

able to prove such a doctrine from Scripture has suddenly increased. It is more the case that historical studies have shown that the earliest tradition offers no more support for the doctrine than does Scripture. If the doctrine is to seen as part of the apostolic deposit of faith, neither Scripture nor tradition suffices. The supplementary view of tradition has lost its appeal because tradition fails to 'supplement' where it is needed.[80] Thus the emphasis moves to the development of doctrine. The Marian doctrines, for example, are 'implicit' in Scripture and early tradition, becoming explicit only after centuries of development. Thus affirmation of the material sufficiency of Scripture is compatible with Roman Catholicism in general and the Marian doctrines in particular. Clearly this is not the meaning of the Reformation *sola Scriptura* since it proves to be compatible with that which it was designed to exclude.

If the material sufficiency of Scripture is not the meaning of *sola Scriptura* because it claims too little, it also fails the test for precisely the opposite reason—because it claims too much! While *sola Scriptura* was a universal Protestant stance, the material sufficiency of Scripture was the subject of controversy, between Lutheran and Reformed, between the establishment and the Puritans in the Church of England. Is the church free to devise new ceremonies? Lutherans claimed that she is, so long as nothing is contrary to Scripture.[81] The same point is made in the Thirty-nine Articles.[82] Puritans claimed, by contrast, that the church is limited to what is positively commanded by Scripture. This 'regulative principle', as it came to be called, was opposed by Richard Hooker.[83]

As can be seen, the 'regulative principle' is not accepted by Lutheranism, nor by the Church of England which in the time of Hooker was clearly a Reformed church. It can not therefore be seen as the Reformation meaning of *sola Scriptura*. Furthermore, it is a stance which would preclude the establishment of a body like the Tyndale Fellowship, for which there is no biblical warrant. But does this have anything to do with theology? Is this not just a dispute about ceremo-

---

[80]This is frankly acknowledged by Rahner, *Theological Investigations*, Vol. VI, 91-3, 105f., 109f. Also in *Theological Investigations*, Vol. IV (London: Darton Longman & Todd, 1966) 143-7.

[81]While many statements of Luther unequivocally assert the material sufficiency of Scripture (*cf.* Althaus, *The Theology of Martin Luther*, 3-8), elsewhere he demands only that tradition not be contrary to Scripture. This is how he defends infant baptism (*cf.*, 334f., 359-63).

[82]Articles 20, 34.

[83] R. Hooker, *The Laws of Ecclesiastical Polity*, Book 2.

nies? Not quite. For Luther, the practices which are justified on the grounds that they are not contrary to Scripture include infant baptism, Sunday worship and the retention of images in churches.[84]

Mention of infant baptism raises the question of whether Scripture is not intended to contain ambiguities and silences. The New Testament is abundantly clear about the pattern of converts' baptism, but says little or nothing about the situation of those brought up in a Christian home. Whatever happens for them, it will be different from the pattern of converts' baptism seen in Acts. Perhaps the silence of the New Testament was intended in order to leave the church the flexibility to adapt its practice to changing situations?

There is a further reason why the Protestant *sola Scriptura* principle does not mean the material sufficiency of Scripture. Protestants do not accept Roman Catholic claims that their Marian doctrines are 'implicit' in Scripture. But they would be unwise to base this on the requirement that all doctrine must be explicit in Scripture. The history of Christian doctrine is not just the story of the repetition of Scriptural statements. With our modern historical perspective we are able to see the way in which all doctrines develop. At the very least there is a process of arrangement of biblical teaching into a coherent whole. In most cases there is also further development as questions are faced to which no direct answer is given in the Bible itself. There are different ways in which this process can be understood,[85] but for the present it suffices to acknowledge that it exists. The Bible contains the raw materials for a doctrine of the Trinity, it cannot faithfully be interpreted other than in a Trinitarian manner, but it does not contain a developed doctrine of the Trinity.

Finally, there is one crucial doctrine that is definitely not contained in the Bible. As has been said, the one page of the Bible that is not inspired is the contents page! The canon of Scripture is crucial for *sola Scriptura*, but is itself not found in Scripture.

Sola Scriptura does not simply mean the material sufficiency of Scripture. But it would be wrong to suggest that the two have nothing to do with one another. The material sufficiency of Scripture is at least a part of what is meant by *sola Scriptura*,[86] even though it needs to be qualified in a number of ways. Protestants object to doctrines like the

---

[84]*Cf.* n. 81, above.

[85]For a more recent guide to thought in this area, *cf.* P. Toon, *The Development of Doctrine in the Church* (Grand Rapids: Eerdmans, 1979). *Cf.* also A.E. McGrath, *The Genesis of Doctrine* (Oxford: Blackwell, 1990).

[86]*Cf.* Calvin, *Inst.* 1:7:1, 1:18:3; 4:18:12

Assumption of the Virgin Mary not least because they see no evidence for them in Scripture.

IV. Scripture the Sole Authority?

If Scripture is not the sole theological resource or source, if the sufficiency of Scripture does not exhaust what is meant by *sola Scriptura*, perhaps it means instead that Scripture is our sole authority? This would appear to be the position of the 1536 Confession of Faith of the Genevan Church: 'We affirm that we desire to follow Scripture alone as rule of faith and religion, without mixing with it any other thing which might be devised by the opinion of men apart from the Word of God.'[87] The Formula of Concord likewise affirms that the Bible is 'the only rule and norm according to which all doctrines and teachers alike must be appraised and judged'. Indeed, 'Holy Scripture remains the only judge, rule, and norm according to which as the only touchstone all doctrines should and must be understood and judged as good or evil, right or wrong.'[88]

These statements appear to be unequivocal. Yet, as we shall see shortly, the word 'only', in this context, is not meant to be taken too strictly. The claim that Scripture is our sole authority is in fact no more viable than the claim that Scripture is our sole resource or source. Indeed, the two are not unconnected in that each of the resources may be said to be authoritative insofar as they contain truth. This section need, therefore, not be so long as the others.

Reason has an authority which cannot be denied. This is acknowledged by the Westminster Confession, which states that the whole counsel of God 'is either expressly set down in scripture, or by good and necessary consequence may be deduced from scripture'.[89] To give a somewhat facetious example, when Matthew tells us that Jesus sat down (Mt. 5:1) it is reason that tells us that he was not at that moment standing up.

What of the area of 'natural human knowledge'? What this has to offer us has authority not as Christian revelation but only so far as, and on the grounds that, it is true. It is authoritative because it is true, not vice versa. For example, what biology or archaeology might have to tell

---

[87]Art. 1 in Cochrane (ed.), *Reformed Confessions of the 16th Century*, 120. *Cf.* Calvin, *Inst.* 3:17:8.
[88]Tappert, *The Book of Concord*, 464f., *cf.* 503-6.
[89]Westminster Confession 1:6.

us is authoritative for theology only so far as and on the grounds that it is true. The argument 'biology says' or 'archaeology says' (or 'archaeologists say') has no inherent weight beyond the truth or otherwise of the claim. This approach is similar to that which Aquinas had towards Aristotle. He treated Aristotle as a weighty authority, but only so far as he felt that Aristotle had truth on his side.[90] Where he felt that Aristotle was wrong, he felt bound by no authority to follow him. Similarly with culture. Theologians are bound to be influenced by the culture in which they live and it will have a certain authority for them. But the views of culture, whether towards adultery, homosexuality, the status of women or democracy are to be accepted or otherwise only on the grounds of their truth, not simply because that is what our culture says.

What of Christian experience and prophecy? If reason and human disciplines have authority by virtue of being true, we cannot say less for Christian experience. There are doctrines which can be rejected on the grounds that they simply do not accord with Christian experience. Claims that believers should never fall sick would fall into this category. Prophecy, for those who accept that it exists today, will have some authority in the specific context. To claim for it authority as new public revelation is contrary to the position that has been argued above.

Tradition also has authority. Certainly for the Reformers the early fathers were 'authorities' to be cited in theological debate. The creeds and the decisions of the early councils, likewise, had an authority. The Formula of Concord, quoted above, appears to deny this. But in the same section the authors pledge themselves to the Apostles', Nicene and Athanasian Creeds. They insist that 'all doctrines should conform to the standards set forth above,' which include these three creeds.[91] While they make clear that these standards are subordinate to Scripture, it is nonetheless clear that they are accorded a real authority. Or, to put it differently, they may be subordinate standards, but to call them standards means, by definition, to accord them authority.

Finally, the Reformers all held to the teaching authority of the church. This is clearly seen by the manner in which they produced confessions of faith and required subscription to them. Indeed the same Formula of Concord that proclaims Scripture as the 'only judge, rule,

---

[90]The example of Aquinas will serve to make another point. Aquinas thought he was following Aristotle only so far as reason led him, but his process of reasoning was moulded by Aristotle to a greater extent than perhaps he realised.
[91]Tappert, *The Book of Concord*, 465; *cf.* 502-4.

and norm' also intends that the *Book of Concord* (containing the ancient creeds, the Formula of Concord and earlier Lutheran documents) should become

> a single, universally accepted, certain, and common form of doctrine which all our Evangelical churches subscribe and from which and according to which, because it is drawn from the Word of God, all other writings are to be approved and accepted, judged and regulated.[92]

No mean authority! The Reformers did not deny the authority of the church.[93]

The truth of the above analysis is, perhaps, best seen by considering those who have taken *sola Scriptura* to the point of claiming to reject all other authorities. Lincoln's individualistic approach did not spring out of the blue. It came in a culture which increasingly emphasised 'private judgement', partly in accord with the Enlightenment rejection of traditional authorities. This approach initially was used against Protestant orthodoxy, to challenge doctrines like the Trinity. In time it was successfully appropriated by Evangelicals, giving birth to a populist hermeneutic of 'every man his own interpreter'.[94]

Such an approach in one sense finds its warrant in Luther, who stood alone against the full force of medieval Catholicism. Yet such a democratisation of theology was the intention neither of Luther nor of the other Reformers. Protestants from Luther on 'found [*sola Scriptura*] an effective banner to unfurl when attacking Catholics on the right, but always a bit troublesome when common people began to take the teaching seriously'.[95] Yet it has to be acknowledged that private judgement is an abuse to which Protestantism is particularly vulnerable, as Newman shrewdly observed.[96]

---

[92]*Ibid.*, 506; *cf.* 465: 'All doctrines should conform to the standards set forth above.'
[93]*Cf.*, *e.g.*, First Helvetic Confession, ch. 16, 'Concerning the Authority of the Church' in Cochrane (ed.), *Reformed Confessions of the 16th Century*, 105.
[94]Hatch, 'Sola Scriptura and Novus Ordo Seclorum', 59-78.
[95]*Ibid.*, 61.
[96]J.H. Newman, *An Essay on the Development of Christian Doctrine* (London: 1845; repr. Harmondsworth: Penguin, 1974) 430f.

V. Scripture the Final Authority?

Finally we come to the point that definitively separated the Reformers from the Roman Catholic Church, that is the essence of the *sola Scriptura* principle. It is not that Scripture is the sole resource, the sole source or the sole authority. It was not for the Reformers, it is not for us and it cannot be. Nor is it the material sufficiency of Scripture. This was held by the Reformers—but with qualifications. It has also been held at least by some within the Roman Catholic Church over the centuries. Nor is it that Scripture is the sole authority. It was not for the Reformers, it is not for us and it cannot be.

What then is the essence of the *sola Scriptura* principle? It is that Scripture is the final authority or norm for Christian belief. This point is aptly stated in the Westminster Confession:

> The supreme Judge, by which all controversies of religion are to be determined, and all decrees of councils, opinions of ancient writers, doctrines of men, and private spirits, are to be examined, and in whose sentence we are to rest, can be no other but the Holy Spirit speaking in the scripture.[97]

Nearly a century earlier the 1559 Gallican Confession of Faith made the same point, that 'no authority, whether of antiquity, or custom, or numbers, or human wisdom, or judgements, or proclamations, or edicts, or decrees, or councils, or visions, or miracles' should be set against the Scriptures. On the contrary, 'all things should be examined, regulated and reformed according to them'.[98] Shortly after, the Belgic Confession said much the same.[99] The Formula of Concord, likewise, despite its rhetoric of 'only judge, rule and norm', in effect acknowledges Scripture as instead the final or supreme norm. The authority of tradition, creeds and the contemporary church is acknowledged, but these should be subordinated to Scripture.[100] They are 'not judges like Holy Scripture, but merely witnesses and expositions of the faith, set-

---

[97]Westminster Confession, 1:10.

[98]Art. 5 in Cochrane (ed.), *Reformed Confessions of the 16th Century*, 145f. It proceeds to acknowledge the three ancient creeds, on the grounds that they are in conformity with the Word of God. *Cf.* Scots Confession of Faith, ch. 20 in Cochrane (ed.), *Reformed Confessions of the 16th Century*, 178f.

[99]Art. 7 in Cochrane (ed.), *Reformed Confessions of the 16th Century*, 192. Similarly, Second Helvetic Confession, ch. 2 in Cochrane (ed.), *Reformed Confessions of the 16th Century*, 226f.

[100]Tappert, *The Book of Concord*, 464f; *cf.* 502-6.

ting forth how at various times the Holy Scriptures were understood by contemporaries in the church of God'.[101]

Against what is Scripture asserted to be the final authority? All three documents name tradition and church authority. They also each refer to what we have called 'less institutional resources': 'private spirits' (Westminster Confession); 'visions' and 'miracles' (Gallican Confession); alleged revelation from angels (Belgic Confession, Formula of Concord; cf. Gal. 1:8). Thus all three documents state that Scripture is the final norm over against the other 'Christian' resources or authorities.

Stated differently, *sola Scriptura* is the statement that the church can err.[102] Tradition and the teaching office of the church are unavoidable and invaluable resources. They have a real authority—but not a final authority. Karl Barth expressed it well when he affirmed the authority of both church and tradition, seeing them both in the light of the Fifth Commandment, to honour our father and mother. This authority is real but limited, in that both are subject to the Word and therefore to Scripture. They are open to be reformed and corrected, while Scripture is not.[103] In the words of the traditional formula, Scripture is the *norma normans non normata*, the norm or rule that rules but is not itself ruled

Where does this leave creeds, whether the ancient creeds or Reformation confessions? These have a value as representing the wisdom of the church and presenting the teaching of Scripture. But they have no independent authority and are not to be accepted if contrary to Scripture at any point. Congar accuses Protestants of hypocrisy here, claiming that in practice 'these confessions have no more been revised than the conciliar dogmas, and their normative value is just as absolute'.[104] This is not altogether fair. It is true that the text of the confessions has not been revised, but conservative Protestants have not been unwilling to be critical of, for example, the Chalcedonian Definition or Reformation confessions like the Westminster Confession.

---

[101]Tappert, *The Book of Concord*, 465.
[102] Thus the crucial stages in the emergence of the Reformation doctrine are at Leipzig in 1519, when Eck drove Luther to assert that tradition and church can err, and at Worms in 1521, when Luther refused to bow before the tradition and authority of medieval Catholicism. *Cf.* B.A. Gerrish, *The Old Protestantism and the New* (Edinburgh: T.&T. Clark, 1982) 54.
[103]K. Barth, *Church Dogmatics*, I.2 (Edinburgh: T.&T. Clark, 1956) 585f.; *The Humanity of God* (London: Collins, 1967) 10.
[104]*Tradition and Traditions*, 422.

Here is where the difference with Rome lay and still lies. This
was the issue that divided the confessions at the time of the Reformation, which explains why they were unable to reach agreement on
other issues. It remains the supremely dividing issue today. Geiselmann, who argues that Trent does not exclude the material sufficiency
of Scripture, rejects the Protestant *sola Scriptura*. He sees it as implying
three things: the material sufficiency of Scripture, Scripture as its own
interpreter and Scripture as the *norma normans et iudex controversiarum*.
Of these he acknowledges only the first, and even this he later quali-
fies.[105] Yves Congar likewise affirms the material sufficiency of
Scripture, but denies its formal sufficiency.[106]

The issue is slightly complicated by the fact that Catholic writers
can speak of the normative role of Scripture. For Rahner it is the normative *norma non normata*.[107] For Congar Scripture governs tradition
and the church and is not governed by them.[108] Geiselmann refers to
Scripture as the *norma normans*.[109] However, none of these means by
this the same as is meant by Protestant writers. Geiselmann goes on to
deny that Scripture is our source and norm epistemologically (*Der Erk-
enntnis nach*) in that it needs an authoritative interpreter,[110] and the
others argue similarly.[111] The tension is seen equally clearly in Vatican
II. It is affirmed that the teaching office of the church 'is not above the
word of God, but serves it'. But this is undermined by the earlier statement that

> the task of authentically interpreting the word of God, whether writ-
> ten or handed on [*i.e.* tradition], has been entrusted exclusively to the
> living teaching office of the Church, whose authority is exercised in
> the name of Jesus Christ.[112]

At the end the day, if there is an infallible interpreter of a text, who has
the final word as to its interpretation, it is the interpreter that is the final

---

[105]J.R. Geiselmann, *Die Heilige Schrift und die Tradition* (Freiburg/Basel/Vienna:
Herder, 1962) 95f., 271, 282; *idem*, 'Das Konzil von Trient über das Verhältnis der
Heiligen Schrift und der nicht geschriebenen Traditionen' in M. Schmaus (ed.), *Die
mündliche Überlieferung* (Munich: Hueber, 1957) 204f.
[106]Congar, *Tradition and Traditions*, 379-86, 409-24.
[107]Rahner, *Theological Investigations*, Vol. VI, 89-95.
[108]Congar, *Tradition and Traditions*, 422.
[109]Geiselmann, *Die Heilige Schrift und die Tradition*, 272.
[110]*Ibid.*
[111]Rahner, *Theological Investigations*, Vol. VI, 93; Congar, *Tradition and Traditions*,
421f.
[112]*De divina revelatione*, 2:10 in Abbott (ed.), *The Documents of Vatican II*, 117f.

norm. Against this, *sola Scriptura* asserts the supremacy of the text over its interpreter. Of course, Scripture needs to be interpreted, but it does not need a normative interpretation.[113]

This raises the issues of Scripture as its own interpreter and of the perspicuity of Scripture. These are major issues relevant to *sola Scriptura*, but for the discussion of which there is no space here. Suffice it to say, with a recent ecumenical document, that

> even though modern historical study and the cultural relativity of all language complicate the process of interpretation, the Word of God as it is communicated to us in the Scriptures remains the final judge of all teaching in the Church.[114]

This is a (arguably the) fundamental principle of the Reformation. But Protestants need to acknowledge honestly the price to be paid. Vincent of Lérins was exaggerating somewhat when he claimed that without the authority of the church's interpretation we can find almost as many different interpretations as there are people.[115] Luther was told at the Diet of Worms that the *sola Scriptura* principle would give birth to a thousand different interpretations of the Bible and a thousand different churches.[116] This rhetorical exaggeration has turned out to be an understatement. The price is high. But is it higher than having doctrines such as the recent Marian definitions accepted uncritically by all Christians?

What of the position of Scripture with reference to reason and 'natural human knowledge'? It is not in fact in this context that the *sola Scriptura* principle is invoked. Scripture is seen as the final norm of Christian revelation. But what sense does it make to call Scripture the final norm of 'natural human knowledge'? Is the Bible (presumably 1 Ki. 7:23) to be the final norm for the value of π? The relation between Scripture and human reason or natural human knowledge raises questions about the authority and reliability of Scripture. But these debates are not the context of the Reformation *sola Scriptura* principle and they are not especially forwarded by it.

---

[113]*Cf.* Bauckham, 'Tradition in Relation to Scripture and Reason', 123.

[114]P. Empie *et al.* (eds.), *Lutherans and Catholics in Dialogue VI: Teaching Authority and Infallibility in the Church* (Minneapolis: Augsburg, 1980) 29.

[115]*Commonitory*, 2:2.

[116]R. Lints, *The Fabric of Theology* (Grand Rapids: Eerdmans, 1993) 292.

VI. Conclusion

'The Bible, I say, the Bible only, is the religion of Protestants.' This, perhaps the most famous affirmation of *sola Scriptura*, in context means that for Protestants it is not the doctrine of Luther or Calvin, not this or that Reformation creed that is the 'perfect rule of their faith and actions', but the Bible. Traditions, popes and councils contradict one another. 'In a word, there is no sufficient certainty but of Scripture only for any considering man to build upon.'[117] But, as has been argued, this rhetoric is not to be taken too far. 'Despite their protestations of "sola Scriptura," the Reformers showed that the "Scriptura" has never been "sola".'[118] Again, *sola Scriptura* did not for the Reformers mean *nuda Scriptura*.[119] It has been shown that neither for the Reformers, nor for Protestant theology does *sola Scriptura* imply that Scripture is either the sole source or the sole resource, although it is undoubtedly the supreme source. The material sufficiency of Scripture is a part of what is meant by *sola Scriptura*, but on the one hand there is Catholic sense to the affirmation and on the other hand it is not intended to be taken too rigidly. Despite rhetoric about Scripture as the sole authority, this again is not to be taken literally, save by those who wish to substitute the authority of their own private judgement in the place of other authorities. But for the Reformation and for evangelical theology Scripture remains the final authority, to which one can appeal against all ecclesiastical authority. This was and remains the heart of the meaning of *sola Scriptura*.

---

[117]W. Chillingworth, *The Religion of Protestants a Safe Way of Salvation* (1687; repr. London: Thomas Tegg, 1845) 460ff.

[118]J. Pelikan, *Reformation of Church and Dogma (1300-1700)* (Chicago/London: University of Chicago Press, 1983) vii.

[119]George, *Theology of the Reformers*, 81, 315.

Biblical References

329

Old Testament Apocrypha

Modern Authors

Subjects